ALICE MILLIGAN AND THE IRISH CULTURAL REVIVAL

For my daughter, Jessica Morris

Comhairle Contae
Átha Cliath Theas
South Dublin County Council

South Dublin Library
Self Service Return

Friday, May 04, 2012 - 10:44
Borrower number: *********51.00**

Title	Due	Fee
Story of Irish museums 1790-2000 culture, identi	28/05/12	None
Alice Milligan and the Irish Cultural Revival	28/05/12	None

You have no other items on loan

Amount owing: NONE

Please note: This does not include any charges for overdue items which have not yet been returned

Thank you for using this service

Alice Milligan
and the
Irish Cultural Revival

Catherine Morris

FOUR COURTS PRESS

Typeset in 10.5pt on 13.5pt AGaramondPro by
Carrigboy Typesetting Services for
FOUR COURTS PRESS LTD
7 Malpas Street, Dublin 8, Ireland
www.fourcourtspress.ie
and in North America for
FOUR COURTS PRESS
c/o ISBS, 920 NE 58th Avenue, Suite 300, Portland, OR 97213.

A catalogue record for this title is available
from the British Library.

ISBN 978–1–84682–313–8

Printed in England
by Antony Rowe Ltd, Chippenham, Wilts.

Contents

LIST OF ILLUSTRATIONS   7

ACKNOWLEDGMENTS   11

INTRODUCTION   15

1   Alice Milligan: a life   22

2   Revival   84

3   Identity   140

4   Memory and commemoration: 1798 in 1898   185

5   Drama   221

6   Republican tableaux and the Revival   252

CONCLUSION 'The scattering of the company'   278

NOTES   295

BIBLIOGRAPHY   310

INDEX   325

Illustrations

FIGURES

1	Alice Milligan and Anna Johnston, Belfast 1895	23
2	Methodist College, Belfast	25
3	Headed notepaper showing the Bank Buildings, Belfast's first department store	28
4	Cover page of second issue of the *Shan Van Vocht*, February 1896	35
5	Roger Casement	41
6	Front cover of *Four Irish songs* by Alice Milligan and her sisters Edith Wheeler and Charlotte Milligan Fox, 1910	46
7	Woodcut illustration of sheet music by Seaghan MacCathmhaiol in *Four Irish songs*, 1910	46
8	'Mayo Love Song': words by Alice Milligan, music by Charlotte Milligan Fox in *Four Irish songs*, 1910	47
9	Statement by Alice Milligan, June 1916 to Sinéad de Valera	52
10	'Antigone at the Abbey Theatre': poem by Alice Milligan, from *New Ireland*, 16 March 1918	57
11	Alice Milligan at Draperstwon Feis, County Tyrone, c.1946	81
12	Milligan's reflections on Carey ballad sung in Donegal	96
13	Woodcut illustration of Alice Milligan and her father traveling through Donegal, from *Glimpses of Erin*, 1888	98
14	Frontispiece of *Glimpses of Erin*	101
15	Extract from three surviving pages of Alice Milligan's unpublished novel *The Cromwellians*	122
16	O'Connell Bridge	129
17	Sketch of Parnell by Alice Milligan in her diary, June 1891	131
18	Parnell's funeral procession through Dublin, October 1891	135
19	The National Library of Ireland	136
19a	Magic lantern projection, from *La Nature*, 391 (1880)	139
20	Belfast in the 1890s	141
21	'For the Old Land', column, *Shan Van Vocht*, 1897	142
22	Henry Joy McCracken Society advert, from the *Northern Patriot*, 1895	160
23	The first issue of the *Northern Patriot*, 1895	163
24	Advert showing subscription rates of the *Northern Patriot*	165
25	First issue of *Shan Van Vocht*, January 1896	171

26 Accounts of the *Shan Van Vocht* submitted to Alice Milligan
from J.W. Boyd, publisher — 175

27 Photograph of Alice Milligan and Anna Johnston, *c.*1896 — 177

28 Cave Hill, Belfast — 186

29 Grafton Street with union jacks waving *c.*1898 — 199

30 1898 Centenary Commemoration march through Dame Street
to St Stephen's Green — 201

31 Dedication page of *The life of Wolfe Tone* — 210

32 Adverts in *Shan Van Vocht* — 211

33 The front page of Milligan's lost melodrama *The French are on the sea* — 218

34 The final tableau of *The French are on the Sea* — 219

35 Community theatre and audience benches being created in
County Antrim, *c.*1904 — 222

36 List of costume wigs for tableau and drama show by Milligan,
Dublin, 1901 — 225

37 *The green upon the cape*, Milligan's first scripted play published
in *Shan Van Vocht*, April 1898 — 232

38 Illustration of English prison guard from Milligan's play *The
deliverance of Red Hugh*, *Weekly Freeman*, March 1902 — 235

39 Front of postcard advertising 1907 Theatre of Ireland production
of *The last feast of the Fianna* — 238

40 Reverse side of postcard addressed to Joseph Holloway — 239

41 Milligan's sketch of John O'Leary in her 1900 production of
The last feast of the Fianna — 243

42 Members of the Derry and Belfast Gaelic League performing the
first Irish language play in Derry, 1898 — 245

43 Sketch by Milligan showing inner and outer regions of stage. In the
distance would be performed tableaux often behind a gauze curtain — 248

44 Sketch of Oisín leaving Tír na nÓg, *c.*1900 — 249

45 Sketch of two women on their way from Mass in Donegal — 253

46 'The lament for the dead'; woodcut by Seaghan MacCathmhaoil
from *Four Irish songs* by the Milligan sisters, 1910 — 254

47 Patrick Pearse's magic lantern and glass slides, St Enda's,
Rathfarnham — 258

48 Front cover of Feis Ceoil programme, Belfast, May 1898 — 261

49 Only surviving script of a tableaux show — 263

50 Gaelic tableaux in Belfast: sketches and description by Milligan of
show performed in 1898 by the Belfast Gaelic League and the
Belfast Arts Society — 266

51 Maud Gonne's list of tableaux that she asked Alice Milligan to design
for a show with the Fay Brothers and Inghindhe na hEireann
(Daughters of Ireland) in 1901   268

52 Irish tableau staged by the Gaelic League during the Irish Cultural
Revival period. Anna Johnston as Princess Grania's waiting maid   270

53 Queen Maeve tableaux staged in Belfast in 1898   272

54 Photograph of tableaux staged in Cushendal, *c*.1906   275

55 Sketch of Roger Casement by Milligan in the court room during
his trial in 1916   283

56 Dedication page of Milligan's 1908 collection of poems *Hero Lays*,
edited by Æ   289

PLATES

appear between pages 192 and 193

1 Front cover of *Hero Lays*, poems by Alice Milligan, 1908

2 Front cover of *Sons of the Sea Kings*, children's novel by Alice Milligan and her
brother Seaton Milligan, 1914

3 Front cover of *Poems of Alice Milligan*, Educational Series of Ireland, *c*.1923

4 'Carsonia: the Great Betrayal', supplement to *The Republic*, 26 February 1921

5 'At the Castle' poem by Milligan, June 1936

6 Front cover of *Glimpses of Erin* by Alice Milligan and Seaton Milligan, 1888

7 Front cover of only surviving membership card of the Irish Women's
Association founded by Alice Milligan in 1894

8 Back cover of Irish Women's Association membership card

9 Alice Milligan's list of the pen names used by writers throughout the *Shan Van
Vocht*

10 Front cover of the *Northern Patriot*, 1896

11 The membership card of the 1798 association, 1898

12 Front cover of Alice Milligan's *The life of Wolfe Tone*, Belfast 1898

13 Grave decoration image from *Weekly Freeman*, 26 June 1897

14 Front cover of *Daughter of Donagh*

15 Front cover of *The last feast of the Fianna*, February 1900

16 A hand typed, hand sewn manuscript play by Milligan

17 'Stand to the guns! Henry Joy McCracken leading the rally at the Battle of
Aughrim', *Irish Weekly Independent*, December 1895

18 'Rejoice Oh Greatly', *Weekly Freeman*, 4 June 1887

19 'At their mercy', *Weekly Freeman* supplement, 8 April 1882

20 'The Land Bill mirage', 19 March 1881, *Weekly Freeman*

21 Sketch for costume design of Queen Meave by Milligan *c.*1898–1901

22 Milligan's sketches for costumed tableaux

23 Jack B. Yeats, 'Communicating with Prisoners', *c.*1924

24 Elizabeth Young as Deirdre in play of the same name by Æ (George Russell)

25 Alice Milligan and the Irish Cultural Revival exhibition

26 Gaelic League teacher in Connemara using Froebel spheres to teach mathematics

27 Ronan McCrea, *Projective technique* (1994). An installation at the Pearse Museum, St Enda's Rathfarnham, Dublin

28 Postcard created by National Women's Council to celebrate the Alice Milligan exhibition on International Women's Day, 2011

29 Woman carrying turf in Donegal *c.*1898

ILLUSTRATION CREDITS

Alice Milligan Papers, Allen Library, O'Connell Schools, Dublin 3, 4, 6–8, 12–15, 21–5, 27, 32–4, 36, 41, 43–6, 49–51, 55, 56, *plates* 1, 2, 7, 8, 9, 12, 14, 15, 21, 22; Anna Johnston Papers, Donegal, 26; Eric Milligan Papers, Bangor, County Down 1; Francis Joseph Bigger Papers, Belfast Public Library 35; Moyra Cannon, 11; National Library of Ireland 2, 5, 9, 10, 16–20, 28–31, 37, 38, 39, 40, 42, 48, 52, 53, *plates* 3–6, 10, 11, 13, 16, 17–20, 24–6, 28–9.

Acknowledgments

Writing this book has been a real privilege and a pleasure. Over years of research I have received generous support from friends, fellow researchers, artists, librarians, and many individuals in the outstanding academic and cultural institutions of Ireland, Britain, Europe and America. I have encountered remarkable people who have led me to make so many research discoveries and to develop new lines of argument. But from the outset I would like to acknowledge that this work would not have been possible without the immense creative solidarity, generosity and support of my daughter Jessica Morris, and my dear friends Joan Melia, Frances Catherine Wilde and Lawrence Wilde.

I am thankful to my extensive family in Liverpool and I express my deep gratitude to my mother and father for their kindness and commitment. I would also like to acknowledge some of the inspired individuals who opened up multiple intellectual spaces for me in Liverpool and Cambridge: Joan Melia, Ada Melia, Margaret Quinn, Mike Mangan, Sister Mary Agnes, Sister Mary Columba of the Sisters of Mercy, Anne Sullivan, Corinna Russell, Gillian Beer, Penny Wilson, Vaughn Pilikian, Heather Glenn and Tim Marlow. Over the years I have received nothing but enthusiastic generosity from all of Alice Milligan's descendents who have taken the time to share with me their memories and archives. I thank Marion and Eric Milligan, Mr and Mrs Milligan-Turner, Rosemary and John Wilson, Polly and Michael Stone and Philip Williams in particular for the care they have taken with the manuscripts in their possession and for the access they allowed me many years ago. I am forever in the debt of Seán MacRéamoinn for all of his conversation and introductions. I thank Ben Kiely, Sheila MacAleer, Moya Cannon, Breandan O'Flanagan, Danny Donnelly, the Ben Kiely Summer School and everyone in County Tyrone and across Ireland who invited me to talk about my research at summer schools, local community centers or who contacted me to share their memories and insights into Alice Milligan's life and work. I don't think we would have much trace of Alice Milligan's creative practice or its radical implications without the writings and archives kept by some of her contemporaries: I therefore thank Thomas MacDonagh, George Russell (Æ), Ernest Milligan, Henry Mangan, Brother Allen (of O'Connell Schools), Mary and Padraic Colum, Susan Mitchell, Áine Ceannt, Seamus MacManus, Lilly Brennan, Douglas Hyde, Roger Casement, Francis Joseph Bigger, Bulmer Hobson, Sinead de Valera, Kate Maxwell, and all those others who knew Alice Milligan personally and who took the time to reflect on the significance of her cultural practice in publications, memoirs and letters. We should all be grateful to them not least for the care they took to preserve Milligan's letters and manuscripts but for their generosity in gifting these documents to public libraries.

Educational, research and publication grants and fellowship awards were not just important for the production of this book: they were essential. I would therefore like to thank the institutions that endowed me with undergraduate, postgraduate and postdoctoral scholarships and fellowships: New Hall College and the University of Cambridge, the University of Aberdeen, Trinity College Dublin, St John's College, Oxford, the Institute of Irish Studies at Queen's University Belfast, the University of Sussex, the John Hume Global Irish Institute and the School of English at University College Dublin, the National Library of Ireland and the Irish Writer's Centre in Dublin. I am thankful for the awards I received from the Irish Research Council for the Social Sciences, the Irish-Scottish Academic Initiative awards council, the British Academy, the Director and Board of the National Library of Ireland, the Senate and the Publications committee of the National University of Ireland and the Tyrone Association of Dublin. The enthusiastic support for this book project by the Lord Mayor of Liverpool, Neil Peterson and Liverpool City Council has pleased me greatly. I am delighted to publish with Four Courts Press who have worked so hard to bring this book to press.

There are some key figures in history, film, visual culture, politics, literature and drama that have had a huge impact on my work. The intellectual rigor, the unflinching practical wisdom and the generous friendship of Jane Ohlmeyer over a period of almost two decades has done much to shape the development and the completion of this book. Similarly, my research work into the Irish Cultural Revival was transformed and enriched over the long haul by Luke Gibbons's academic generosity, his conversation, by his many public talks, publications and by his interdisciplinary approaches to Irish cultural history. I would not have come near to understanding the networks and nuances of Irish historical and visual culture, politics, drama and the act of writing without the intellectual engagement of figures like Luke and Jane, Lawrence Wilde, Seamus Deane, Maeve Connolly, Stephen Rea, Dennis McNulty, Joe Cleary, Val Connor, P.J. Matthews, Emer Nolan, Thomas Kilroy, John Kelly, Diane Negra, Gerry Smyth and Richard Ford. In particular, I thank Frank Krutnik for his inimitable support and belief in this project and for his immense friendship during so many of the years the book was in process of becoming. Declan Kiberd's generosity in reading every chapter as I wrote it while at University College Dublin from 2008 to 2010 was one of the greatest pleasures and privileges of my time there.

The National Library of Ireland has encouraged and facilitated my research work into Alice Milligan so greatly that I want to place the library alongside the institutions and individuals that have structurally made the work possible. I thank all the staff at the library for making the long hours in the reading rooms so rewarding. I was very honored to be invited by the National Library of Ireland in 2009 to communicate the findings of my research in an exhibition and to make a short film. Curating 'Alice Milligan and the Irish Cultural Revival' had a fantastic impact on my writing of the book. It also proved to be an extraordinarily unique introduction of Alice Milligan's work to a national and international public. I am grateful to Tom Desmond, Catherine Fahy, Honora Faul, Elizabeth Kirwin, Orla Sweeney, Brenda O'Hanlon, all our colleagues at Martello Media, and to Ros Kanavagh for sharing with me their time, skills and insights. I am very privileged indeed to have worked with Katherine McSharry whose input into the creation of the Milligan exhibition had a hugely positive impact on my completion of this book. Fiona Ross as director of the National Library of Ireland stands in a league of her own for dynamic intellectual engagement and support of the Irish archives. I will be forever grateful to her for the incredibly generous support she has given to the progression of my research and to the public dissemination of Alice Milligan's archives and work. The collaboration between Trinity College Dublin and the National Library is tremendously positive and gave me a new set of colleagues that have assisted me at every stage of the way in bringing this book project to completion. I thank in particular John O'Hagan, Simon Williams, Robin Adams, Linda Doyle, Mary Apied and Brian McGing for being such tremendous colleagues and friends. Thanks also to John Hegarty, Paddy Prendergast, and to all my fellow colleagues at Trinity's Long Room Hub, Trinity library and across the university.

I would like to acknowledge the following people who have inspired me while I have been writing this book. So many of them have given their time to this project – many have read draft chapters, or engaged with me after public talks: their insights and comments undoubtedly helped me to develop my arguments in this book. So many have advised me on sourcing images and opened up new areas of research to me through their suggestions for new archive materials and reading lists. In short, my research for this book would have been much the poorer without the generous support I have received from: Dolores Gibbons, Oonagh Young, Patrick Murphy, David Lloyd, Tessa Giblin, Margaret MacCurtain, Jonathan Cummins, Terry Eagleton, Kevin O'Neill, Siobhan Byrne, Angus Mitchell, Caoimhín Mac Giolla Léith, Richard Kirkland, Brian Keenan, Tom Paulin, Thomas Kador, Brian Crowley, Aoibhín de Búrca, Susan McKay, Eamonn Ó Ciardha, Bea MacMahon, Ivana Bacik, Joe Lee, Brian Jackson, Lynne Parker, Willa Murphy, Helen Carey, George Watson, Vincent Woods, Angela Bourke, Micheál Ó Siochrú, Ciaron Deane, Declan McGonagle, Kevin Kavanagh, Lionel Pilkington, Joe Westmoreland, Jerome Ó Drisceoil, Charles Atlas, Ivy Wilson, Anthony Glavin, Elaine Byrne, Lia Mills, Dermot Bolger, Trish Lamb, Loretta Glucksman, Phil Kilroy, John Waters at NYU, Mary Cullen, Vaari Claffe, Robert

Young, Jesse Jones, Alice Maher, Clare Hutton, Mark Garry, Liam Donnelly, Margaret Kelleher, Tim O'Connor, Dorothy Cross, Ruarí Ó'Cuív, Anne Fogarty, Aurélien Froment, Niamh O'Malley, Brian Friel, Peter Sheridan, Hannah Shepard, Sinead McCoole, Mick O'Dea, Karl Haselden, Margaret O'Callaghan, Joe McBrinn, Ian McBride, Lisa Farrelly, Robert Tracy, Kathleen Williams, Joe Lee, Mary Quinn, Patricia Scott, Walter Benjamin, Andy Pollak, Fiach Mac Conghail, Peter Collins, Peter MacDonagh, Mary Burgess, Ríona Nic Congail, Ben Levitas, Sheena Barrett, Niamh O'Sullivan, Mary McAuliffe, Mary Cremin, Padriac E. Moore, Ita Daly, and Clare Wills.

Dublin has been an inspired place to write this book – indeed, I don't think I could have understood the generosity and sociability of creative networks that made the Irish Cultural Revival possible without having experienced it all first-hand. I am thankful to everyone who has supported this project. I would especially like to express my gratitude to the following people for their encouragement, kindnesses, enthusiasm and assistance: Shirley Ohlmeyer, Jamie and Richard Parker Ohlmeyer, James Flannery, Laurie Uprichard, Iseult Deane, Christina Kennedy, Willie White, Alice Rekab, Nelly Rousseau, Yvonne Scott, Laura Gibbons, Louisa Carroll, Rachel Dowling, Barry Gibbons, Adrienne Flemming, Richard Boyd Barret, Nessa Cronin, Louis de Paor, Frank Allen, Michael Colgan, Geraldine Mitchell, Neil Middleton, Mick Foley, Christine Kelly, Seamus Heaney, Mary O'Malley, Peter Maybury, Declan Long, Orla McBride, Ciaran Murphy, Joanna Banks, Attracta Halpin, Conor O'Malley, Eleanor Methven, Jack Benny, Tom Bartlett, Lori E. Said, Anne Carney, Margaret Ward, Lois MacKinnon, Catriona Crowe, Eugene Downes, Anthea McTiernan, Peadar MacManus, Catriona Curtis, Ruth Barton, Pauric Dempsey, Jacqueline Davis, Sarah Glennie, Ita Daly, Mike Scott, Orla McBride, Pauline Turley, Marie Burke, Dorin and Oisin Ó Siochrú, Kirsi Hanifin, Jean Brennan, Linda Doyle, Johanna Archbold, Oonagh Desire, Michael Hill, Mary Cullen, Éimear O'Connor, Michael Farrell, Hadrian Larouche, Sunniva O'Flynn, Margery Oberlander, Sean Kissane, Oonagh Walshe, Pat Clerkin, David Dickson, Anne Carney, Tadhg Foley, Rosita Boland, Mary Daly, Glenn Hooper, Tom Morgan, Paul Rowley, Maire Mac Conghail, Tom McGurk, Nikki Gogan, Larry Flynn, Barbara Dawson, Eileen Cooney, Peter Fallon, John Hutchinson, and Caroline Hancock. My under-standing of Milligan's work and indeed the international contexts of the Irish Cultural Revival was transformed and enriched by the conversations I was privileged to have with Gabriel Byrne while writing this book. I would like to thank Gabriel for reading a much earlier draft of the manuscript and for all his insightful comments and thoughts that he brought to this work.

Introduction

> Freedom is as yet to all appearances a far off thing; yet must we who desire it work for it as ardently and as joyously as if we had good hope that our own eyes should behold it.
>
> Alice Milligan, the *Shan Van Vocht*, 7 February 1896.

In April 1953 the recipient of the Nobel Peace Prize and founder member of Amnesty International, Sean McBride, put out a call for Alice Milligan's papers to be collected. McBride was concerned that Milligan's story should be remembered not least because her cultural and political work was so in tune with the human rights principles of Amnesty. Throughout her life Milligan protested against the disempowerment of Irish people under occupation. She raised public awareness of Irish political prisoners held in English prisons and raised funds for prisoners' families and for the widows of executed insurgents. She wrote petitions to the British home office on behalf of Roger Casement, staged plays, published poems and researched articles to highlight the plight of those incarcerated during the Irish War of Independence. The imprisoned speechless body became the abiding visual metaphor for so many of the issues addressed in Milligan's work. In writing about and by staging personal, political and cultural states of imprisonment, Milligan explored what it was to be 'othered' and to have empathy with 'the other'.

In her 2009 collection of essays *Listening to grasshoppers: field notes on democracy*, the Indian writer and human rights activist Arundhati Roy begins by asking a series of non-rhetorical questions that demand an urgent answer:

> What have we done to democracy? What have we turned it into? What happens once democracy has been used up? When it has been hollowed out and emptied of meaning? … What happens now that democracy and the Free Market have fused into a single predatory organism with a thin, constricted imagination that revolves almost entirely around the idea of maximising profit? Is it still possible to reverse this process? Can something that has mutated go back to being what it used to be?[1]

In her eighty-seven years, Alice Milligan never experienced the kind of national democracy that she worked towards. Yet she never gave up resistance and protest because she believed in a better future for Ireland. Freedom existed as a radical ideal that related to multiple parts of her life from 1866 to 1953.

The freedom Milligan was writing about in Belfast in 1896 was less a tangible reality than a state of mind. A belief that things could be different and that individuals and communities could unite together to make that difference. While this book is about the radical cultural practice of Alice Milligan it is also about the extensive networks of people that she connected with throughout her life. Milligan and many of her contemporaries imagined a national drama and a national literature and a national theatre and a national language that were international in scope. Their ambition required communities of activism, generosity of time and collectivism of thought. Milligan and the people she worked with from the 1890s through to the 1940s assumed democratic freedom in order to prove its existence was possible even at the most local level. Community, like freedom, took on a textured presence in Milligan's life because she looked for the origins of Ireland's possible future in its historical cultural past.

From the 1890s, Milligan began to think of herself as a citizen of the Republic she wanted to live in, rather than as a colonized subject of the empire in which she actually lived. She recognized Irish people from all walks of life and from multiple backgrounds as the sole agents of political change; and these changes did not need to be led by legislative or legal interventions made by the colonial elite. She urged people to make changes in their daily lives to alter the Irish economy at local level and to alter their consumer patterns in favour of Irish products that were not made exclusively for imperial export. In her own lifetime Milligan sourced the materials – woodblocks, paper, printing presses, costumes – and labour for her publications and theatre productions within Ireland. She encouraged local co-operatives in the face of an emergent modern capitalism. The development of a confident, articulate national Irish culture in Irish communities at home and abroad was undoubtedly one of the most revolutionary interventions of modern history. The Irish Cultural Revival was Ireland's velvet revolution. Unknown workers and political activists and cultural practitioners acted both together and alone in challenging the legacy of occupation. Much of their work has been forgotten as so much was divided and lost in the years immediately following 1916. Serious consideration of Milligan's place in history was stimulated by the Northern Ireland Peace Agreement which opened up new possibilities for Irish scholarship. But was there anything that Alice Milligan did in her lifetime that speaks to us now?[2]

This book is about the praxis of community remembrancing that I have identified as existing during the revival period in a range of commemorative events, nationalist iconographies, performances and publications. The critical intervention of Alice Milligan provides a unique lens through which the traditional narrative of the revival can be refocused to take account of forgotten modes of cultural practice. Like Francis Ledwidge in Seamus Heaney's poem, Milligan was indeed a figure 'in whom all the strains criss-cross'.[3] The paradoxical set of identities that she embodied found expression in the unique textual and non-textual forms of cultural production she was drawn to (such as newspapers, popular journals, street theatre, drama festivals, local feiseanna, tableaux, pageantry, public commemorations and magic lantern shows).

At the height of the Irish War of Independence, poet Susan Mitchell wrote a series of articles devoted to 'the hero tale of Irishwomen'.[4] For Mitchell this was a tale that needed telling not only because it had been excluded from the annals of history but also because this moment of crisis and division required more than ever the involvement of Irish women. Mitchell dedicated the first of her profiles to a woman she saw as vitally important to the shaping of new possibilities for modern Ireland. For Mitchell, Alice Milligan had almost single-handedly 'taken up the torch' from the United Irishmen and the Fenians and had 'carried it bravely forward' into a new era in which the promise of a unified and independent nation finally seemed on the verge of realization.[5] In her article Mitchell located Milligan as a key figure of continuity who linked current debates on Irish nationhood to signature moments, movements and figures of the past. But Mitchell also saw Milligan as more than a mere torchbearer. Milligan qualified as a 'heroic Irishwoman' because her prolific and multifaceted work had, across several decades, shed new light upon the republican struggle and its relevance. Moreover, Milligan's work and life illustrated how the cultural revival was itself a complexly overdetermined phenomenon that drew its energy and its identity from multiple sources and constituencies.

Five years earlier Milligan had also been chosen by Thomas MacDonagh for the first in a series of profiles on Irish poets. MacDonagh's article in the *Irish Review* provides a fascinating perspective on Milligan's contemporaneous significance as a figure who – as a northerner, as a woman, and as a protestant – challenged the sectarian divides that impeded a fully inclusive nationalism:

> It is meet [appropriate] that this Irish National poet should be a woman. It is meet that she, like so many of the Irish Volunteers, should be of North East Ulster. Alice Milligan, Ulster Protestant, Gaelic Leaguer, Fenian, friend of all Ireland, lover of Gaelic Catholic as of her own kith … Alice Milligan is the most Irish of living poets and therefore the best.[6]

Mitchell and MacDonagh were by no means alone in celebrating Alice Milligan. For example, in 1926 George Russell looked back on her as 'a girl of genius' who was the first architect of Ireland's national theatre movement.[7] W.B. Yeats told in *Autobiographies* how he left one of Milligan's Irish theatrical productions 'with my head on fire' inspired to hear his own plays spoken by Irish actors.[8]

Given such ecstatic praise from her peers, how is it, then, that within more recent studies of the Irish Revival, Alice Milligan appears, if at all, as a minor player in this pivotal era of transition and cultural achievement? Most often she can be found within the footnotes of the official histories, meriting brief mention because one of her plays was staged by the Irish Literary Theatre or because she was a friend of Yeats, Maud Gonne, James Connolly and Roger Casement. It is indeed curious that Milligan's status has been so dramatically eclipsed. For Mitchell, MacDonagh and Russell – as well as for such other luminaries as Éamon de Valera and Sean McBride – Milligan was clearly an energizing force within the Revival.[9] For contemporary scholars, however, Milligan is little more than a bit player on the historical stage. The 'Alice Milligan and the Irish Cultural Revival' exhibition that I curated with the National Library of Ireland and this book both aim to set the record straight by relocating Milligan within the contexts of her time.[10]

The turbulent period in Irish history from the death of Parnell in 1891 to the founding of the Free State in 1921 is most famously conceptualized as an 'Irish Revival'. A golden age in Irish national literature, theatre and language, the Irish Revival established new parameters for Irish cultural identity as the country prepared itself for modernity as a post-colonial nation state. Most scholarly accounts conceive of the Revival as a predominantly textual movement that was spearheaded by a small yet distinguished cohort of now canonical Dublin-based litterateurs. Such accounts tend to overlook the vital role played by more ephemeral, less 'legitimate' forms of culture that were equally significant in shaping the character and consciousness of the Revival. As my book will suggest, to understand fully the cultural and political climate of this period, it is essential to examine a more wide ranging set of cultural outlets such as newspapers, novels and community shows of tableaux as well as the dramatic splendour of the Abbey Theatre. Such forms of cultural production were seen and read by far greater numbers than could access the 'literary' texts of the Revival. It is essential, too, to consider how other forms of popular cultural expression such as street parades, public commemoration and visual iconographies helped to define and energize the emerging national culture. More importantly, perhaps, is the thorny issue of the north – its relationship to the classic years of the Revival and, even more crucially, to the divisive territorializing of the post-partition era.

This book offers a fresh and vital recontextualization of this Revival period by examining the career of Alice Milligan. Besides her prodigious literary output (four novels, eleven plays, a political travelogue, a biography, numerous articles, short stories and poetical works), Milligan was a tireless political activist and journalist, who remained so across six decades. Drawing upon extensive archival research I will explore Milligan's unexamined work in drama, short stories, poetry, *tableaux vivants* and newspapers, as well as her prolific involvement with political and cultural organizations. As a figure working on the boundary of conventional ideas of literature and politics, Milligan placed herself literally at both the centre and the periphery of the Revival: it is my contention that she has remained radically unrepresented in the histories of both. There are three principal difficulties in charting a coherent map of Milligan's work and career: first, her books remain long out of print and sometimes only appeared in unindexed publications such as Irish educational pamphlets. Second, her manuscripts are scattered across a broad range of public and private archives, many of which only came to light during the course of my research, public talks and interviews. Third, Milligan published the vast bulk of her literary and political writing in newspapers and journals in order to connect with local, national and international audiences.

In 1903 George Russell wrote in a letter to an American publisher: 'There is a girl named Alice Milligan who has written better verses I think than any of our women writers but who is too lazy to publish them anywhere except in local papers where she forgets all about them.'[11] Milligan's private letters prove that she never forgot about her poems as Russell claimed: even as late as the 1930s, Milligan was still trying to collect her works in order to republish them in the new context of anti-Partition newspapers. Yeats too liked to reach wider audiences for poems specifically of a political or patriotic type via newspapers. Milligan published in newspapers to reach specific audiences directly. Even in her first novel published in 1890, a shipwrecked character stumbles into a cottage in Donegal only to find the walls covered in illustrations from the weekly press. This was a rural people and an international diaspora with a highly literate oral, visual and textual sensibility: it was precisely this radical constituency of readers that Milligan hoped to connect with in publishing her plays, stories, poems, songs, travelogues, political and cultural ideas in a broad range of newspapers. For Milligan and for many other women, publishing in newspapers also supplied an immediate income and a public platform for their ideas and writing. As we shall see, newspaper publication enabled Milligan to disseminate literary scripts quickly and cheaply, a particular bonus for rural Gaelic League branches that wished to access and produce Irish plays. Much of my research activity has thus understandably taken the form of extensive literary archaeology.

Since I began my research I have unearthed many previously unknown archival traces of Milligan and the broad range of contemporaries she worked with. In the 1990s I managed to gain access to all the private Milligan family archives (including diaries, photographs, letters and obscure publications). I was also granted interviews with Milligan's surviving relatives as well as with many other people – such as the writer Benedict Kiely who used to visit Milligan in Omagh in the 1930s and early 1940s. I traced Milligan's extensive literary, cultural and political writings published in over sixty Irish journals and newspapers. I have collected every historical interview and radio transcript featuring Milligan and examined the records about her cultural and political activities in the pre-Civil War secret police files, post-Partition state files, home office papers, Irish newspaper reviews and journal articles. In addition, I sourced all the private and public manuscript collections with significant Milligan holdings across Ireland, Northern Ireland, Scotland, Britain and the US. My research has been further energized by contact with local community groups: at the numerous talks I have delivered across Ireland since 1995 volunteers have frequently come forward with new reminiscences, manuscripts, biographical information, and rare photographic or literary materials.

In the first chapter of this book I draw on all this material to provide the first ever complete biographical overview of Milligan's life story as it unfolded across almost a century of Irish political history. In the following five chapters I assess Milligan's literary and cultural output during Ireland's anti-colonial struggle which later became the backbone to an anti-Partition protest movement. The second chapter charts Milligan's transformation from a northern Protestant unionist writer to a nationalist cultural activist. Chapter three examines the extent to which identity politics impacted upon the conflicts Milligan faced in the 1890s when she worked to put Belfast on the map of the Irish Cultural Revival. Taking the 1898 Centenary as a case study, chapter four examines the politics of commemoration in Milligan's cultural practice and assesses how the events of the Centenary impacted on the broader Revival project. Milligan's active role in the formation of an Irish National Theatre movement that began to take shape in Belfast from 1897 is the subject of chapter five. I discuss her manifesto for 'national theatre in rural districts' in Chapter 6 and consider her development of the tableaux form as part of the National Theatre and national language movements. Finally, in the conclusion I discuss Milligan's political and cultural activism in the years following Partition and assess her contemporary resonance as a political icon whose cultural legacy forms a key part of the unacknowledged history of Irish women.

Milligan's career exists because of the Irish Revival – her writings and activities were a response and a contribution to the cultural movements initiated in Ireland. From 1891, she energetically engaged with the various strands of this cultural renaissance and was herself a critical innovator in shaping its goals. The Irish Cultural Revival was defined by the multiple organizations that celebrated Ireland's history, industry, music, literature, culture and language. As such it re-envisioned an Irish national identity separate from England. Declan Kiberd's

Inventing Ireland firmly acknowledges the profound accomplishments of the revival and its architects:

> That enterprise achieved nothing less than a renovation of Irish politics and a new understanding of politics, economics, sport, language and culture in its widest sense. It was the grand destiny of Yeats's generation to make Ireland once again interesting to the Irish, after centuries of enforced provincialism following the collapse of the Gaelic order in 1601. No generation before or since lived with such conscious national intensity or left such an inspiring (and, in some ways, intimidating) legacy. Though they could be fractious, its members set themselves the highest standards of imaginative integrity and personal generosity. Imbued with republican and democratic ideals they committed themselves in no spirit of chauvinism, but in the conviction that the Irish *risorgimento* might expand the expressive freedoms of all individuals.[12]

Alice Milligan made a profound intervention into the Irish Revival in a period in which the meaning of Irish culture was radicalized into an active force to generate dialogue and inspire social and political change. I hope that this book will help to revive Milligan's reputation as a major cultural and political activist and will stimulate further interest in the turbulent period of Irish history through which she lived. In undertaking this research my aim has been not simply to reclaim Alice Milligan as an unjustly forgotten writer and activist during this foundational moment of modern Ireland, but also to provide new ways of interpreting the Cultural Revival itself.

CHAPTER ONE

Alice Milligan: a life

> If the political history of the past twenty-five years in Ireland ever comes to be written by someone who studies other authorities than the newspapers, someone who has really an intimate knowledge of the personalities who were at the root of the biggest Irish political movement of today, they would discover, we believe, that the infant nurse who looked after it while it was yet inarticulate and who expressed its wants was Alice Milligan.
>
> Susan Mitchell, *Irish Homestead*, 1920.[1]

Alice Milligan's commitment to literature was inextricably bound up with her political concerns. Because Milligan expressed her politics through poetry, journalism, short stories, dramas and novels more than through any other medium, her place as a writer and activist requires careful definition within a political and organizational context. But it is also important to understand Milligan's familial, religious and educational background so as to highlight the dimensions of Irish life of which she was, and was not, part. While the poet Susan Mitchell derided newspapers as a legitimate archival source in establishing Milligan's centrality to the Irish Cultural Revival, it is largely through the daily press that we can trace much of her life history. Milligan's story simultaneously unfolds articulately in private diaries, unpublished memoirs, radio broadcasts and through her voluminous correspondence with close friends. The personal and the political, the public and the private were not separated by Milligan: her life story was completely determined by her own interventions into the Irish independence movement over a period of six decades. Thomas MacDonagh observed in 1914 that Milligan was 'without thought of herself, and with thought always of Ireland's cause'.[2] While Milligan's cultural output has been little documented, even less is known about the chronology of her life and the private contexts in which her work was produced.

The three sections of this chapter will provide a biographical overview of Milligan's career in order to contextualize the themes that will emerge throughout this book. The first section will cover the early years of Milligan's life, her 'official' Anglo-centric education in the north and her first publications. I will argue that Milligan's own self re-education developed within the publishing and organizational structures of the emerging cultural Revival movement. The second

1 Alice Milligan and Anna Johnston, Belfast, *c.*1896.

section focuses specifically on events that took place in Milligan's personal life in the years immediately following the Easter Rising of 1916: Milligan's struggle to achieve economic and social independence as a writer was completely bound up with the national fight for political independence. By the time the Irish Free State was founded in 1922 Milligan was already living in the newly founded state of Northern Ireland. The final section of this chapter will explore the challenging familial and political contexts that informed Milligan's cultural production in the decades that followed the Civil War.

1866–1915

Alice Milligan was born in a village on the outskirts of Omagh in September 1866. She was the third of thirteen children born to Methodist parents, Seaton Milligan (1837–1916) and Charlotte Burns (1842–1916). In 1910 their son Ernest Milligan (a medical doctor resident in England) wrote the following description of his family to his fiancée:

> Now sweetest for a few sketches out of my family cupboard. My people have nothing to boast of, my father was a poor boy who made his own way in the world, his people were poor and any education he got was while he worked as an apprentice in a shop in Omagh & after he became a commercial traveller. My mother's people had a small drapery shop in Omagh, and her mother was a small farmer's daughter; any money that was left after her father & mother died went to educate her & apprentice her brother … my brothers & sisters got good education.[3]

The Irish linen trade was the connection that brought Alice Milligan's parents together. While Charlotte Burns worked in a linen shop in Omagh, Seaton Milligan actually started out as a commercial traveller for the drapery partnership Robertson, Hawkins and Ledlie. In 1879 Seaton Milligan was promoted to an executive position when the drapery firm established its business centre in the Bank Buildings, Royal Avenue, Belfast. The family immediately moved from Gortmore and took up residence at Royal Terrace (on the Lisburn Road) where they lived until 1893; from there they moved to the Antrim Road near Cave Hill. All nine surviving Milligan children were enrolled at Methodist College, Belfast.

Methodism offered Irish girls of wealthy parents educational opportunities unrivalled by any other religious organization in the nineteenth century. Alice Milligan (and her four sisters and four brothers) were provided with an exceptionally privileged and enlightened education at Methodist College, Belfast, a school that set a precedent when it welcomed female pupils from its foundation

2 Methodist College, Belfast, where Milligan went to school after the family moved from Omagh to Belfast in 1870s.

in 1868: 'within a few weeks of opening, the College added to its scheme and issued a new challenge to convention and habitual usage. It was thought more than an achievement'.[4] As a pupil at the school from 1879 to 1886 Milligan demonstrated an amazing and versatile range of abilities by winning scholarships in mathematics, science, scripture, natural philosophy and music.[5] It was here that she first began to publish poetry in the school magazine *Eos*. At the age of seventy-five Milligan dismissed this impressive early part of her formal education. Instead, she believed that the informal 'Irish' education she received in childhood from listening to Irish-speaking farm labourers offered greater insight into her life story:

> I was in fact tired out by examinations, having gone in for the junior intermediate at an early age, in the year 1879 – and winning a junior exhibition in 1881, had to go on retaining it. I don't think I would include this examination business as part of my education.[6]

From 1886 to 1887 Milligan studied English literature and history as a pupil of King's College, London.[7] King's established a series of 'Lectures for Ladies' in

1878 but it was not until 1885 that these classes became recognized as an official women's college of the university.[8] It is worth noting the courses that Milligan studied in London not least because she drew heavily upon this syllabus for the content and language of her second novel *The Cromwellians*, a historical romance written in Elizabethan English and set in the seventeenth-century plantations of Ireland. The history syllabus for 1887 was taught by the Irish historian J.R. Gardener who offered a colonial view of Irish history over several periods and topics included: 'The Irish Rebellion'; 'Irish and Scottish Wars'; 'The Protectorate'; 'Cromwell's Parliaments'; 'War in Scotland and Ireland'; and 'Views of Edmund Burke'. Professor Hales taught Milligan the English literature and language courses she sat in the same year which similarly included a celebration of Empire: 'Some general characteristics of the Elizabethan age – its ardent patriotism – its maritime enterprise – its intellectual keenness'. Edmund Spenser's *The Faerie Queene* Books I and II were among the texts recommended on the reading list. In London Milligan immediately joined the Shelley Society whose members also included George Bernard Shaw and Gabriel Rossetti. Milligan recalled how as a student in London in September 1886 she first heard of Yeats from Annie Horniman (later patron to the Abbey Theatre) whom she sat next to at a party:

> 'You have a poet of your own coming up in Ireland,' she said, 'whom the world will be talking about before long – Billy Yeats, son of an artist living out near Kew.' It was the first time I had heard the name.[9]

As soon as she returned to Belfast in 1887 Milligan co-wrote a travel book of Ireland with her father. *Glimpses of Erin* was published in 1888 and very much reflected the constructive unionist values of her familial upbringing. Seaton Milligan's self-educated eager intellectual cultural pursuits had a major influence on Alice Milligan's early career, and indeed, on her later cultural activism. In 1884 he was made a member of the Royal Antiquarian Society and in 1887 he was voted onto the board of the Royal Irish Academy. Both he and Alice Milligan were members of the Belfast Naturalist Field Club where they attended regular meetings, lectures and field trips. The regionalism of this particular group has been interpreted as a reflection of the anxiety felt by northern unionists about the growing success of the Home Rule movement throughout Ireland. Certainly, the contents of *Glimpses of Erin* grew out of the authors' involvement with the Belfast Naturalist Field Club: the 'Erin' of the title constituted the north-east corners of Ulster and the book directly addressed an English readership both in marketing and in content.

Alice Milligan further developed the central themes of *Glimpses of Erin* when she created her version of the perfect English tourist in her first novel *A Royal*

Democrat (1890). Set in the 1940s, the novel relates the exploits of an English king who is shipwrecked off the west coast of Ireland. Cormac King does not declare his identity until the end of the novel when he is able to use his monarchical connections to barter a form of self-governance for Ireland. Ironically and somewhat prophetically, an Irish republic is declared in the novel at the end of 1949 after a secret deal is made between the British establishment and the monarchy. In both works, Ireland is a place outside of time and on the periphery of modernity: in *Glimpses of Erin* one resident in Rathmullen describes his life as a pre-colonial pastoral idyll: 'We have no times up here; we have no call to know the clock, risin' when we're rested, and lyin' when we're tired, and atin' our meat when we think fit'.[10] After the shipwreck in *A Royal Democrat* the English monarch immediately notices: 'his watch had stopped'.[11] In a way, Milligan herself was out of time in the years preceding 1891: she later said that she 'learned nothing of Ireland' from her formal education.[12] These early publications were marketed to an audience in England and in her view the future of Ireland (like the past) did not belong to the Irish.

Milligan's first two books were written while she was training to be a teacher in Derry and Belfast. She eventually sat her teaching exams in Liverpool in 1891. From 1888 to 1890 she taught Latin at the MacKillip's Ladies Collegiate School in Derry. While there Milligan first began to learn spoken Irish (and in her recollections about this she revealed that she was also using the same Irish text books as Synge):

> In Derry I think I was nearer to something on the lines of the Gaelic League Branch ... I advertised in a local paper for an Irish teacher, and in response to an advert went to an address which I found to be a neat little tobacconist's shop kept by a Donegal man. He offered, as well as I remember, without any fee to give me as much Irish as I wanted, if I could come on Sunday afternoons to the sitting room of his house, where they had a weekly assembly of Irish speakers, singing and talk and any amount of fun. They had no books and he could not read a line of Irish. I had gone through the first two primers of The Irish Preservation Society, and was armed with Joyce's Grammar, O'Curry's MSS. Materials, O'Reilly's Dictionary, and Irish copybooks. I said that if I could teach him spelling and writing and his party taught me conversation and pronunciation, we would have an excellent class.[13]

Between 1890 and 1891 when her sisters Charlotte and Edith travelled to complete their educations at the music conservatories in Europe, Alice Milligan went instead to Dublin where she worked for a short time as a teacher. One interviewer later reflected on the limited opportunities that existed for Milligan to

3 Headed notepaper showing the Bank Buildings, Belfast's first department store where
Alice Milligan's father Seaton was executive director in the 1890s.

learn Irish before the Gaelic League was established in 1893: 'At that time there
were few facilities for learning Irish in the capital – particularly for young
Protestant ladies. However, her father was a member of the Royal Irish Academy,
and he arranged that a copyist employed in the Academy should give her private
lessons.'[14] Milligan's time in Dublin proved to be a foundational experience in
which she began to reinvent herself in tandem with the rapidly shifting Irish
political landscape. In 1937 she wrote a biographical sketch of her life to be
presented on radio. In this extract she recalled that her education only really began
when she moved to Dublin:

> Alice Milligan had been at school at the Methodist College Belfast, at
> Queen's College Belfast and at King's College department for women in
> London. But her really important studies were pursued, when residing in
> lodgings she read daily in the Royal Irish Academy and the National Library
> Dublin. She had lessons in Irish twice weekly, from a teacher recommended
> by Mr MacSweeny, the affable secretary of the Academy … Miss Milligan
> had learned some Irish from her relatives [who were] native TírEoin speakers
> from earliest childhood. But residence in Belfast interrupted this and she
> plodded along with Neilson's Grammar, The Irish Preservation booklets till
> her intermediate and RVI career over, she came up to read in the Dublin
> libraries & took private lessons in the language till Connradh na G [the
> Gaelic League] was founded.[15]

Milligan explained her time at the Royal Irish Academy in more detail in another
memoir: 'I had my first Irish lessons in the reading room of the Academy in

Dawson St, by kind permission of the Assistant Librarian Mr McSwiney who kindly pointed out to me the various famous scholars who passed in and out.'[16]

Her time in Dublin proved to be politically as well as culturally transformative. In May 1891 she described in her diary how she had experienced a political epiphany: 'While in the tram going up O'Connell St I turned into a Parnellite. The conversion was sudden and almost unaccountable – perhaps it won't last'.[17] But it did last, and when Parnell died in October of the same year she was back in Belfast lamenting how this 'day of national mourning' was not being fully respected in the north (especially by her relatives who insisted on attending a musical). It was around this time that poet James Cousins noticed that Milligan was beginning to gain a reputation as a nationalist. As a postboy working in Belfast, he later recalled how Milligan was viewed by the unionist business community in the city:

> Messages had a special attraction for me, as the delivery of finished jobs to various shops made pleasant acquaintances. One of these was a high-up man in the Bank Buildings, which was what later was known as a departmental store; a Mr Milligan who had what I privately regarded in my almost fifteen year old mind as a distinction, but others regarded as a black mark on his alleged Protestantism – a red-haired daughter who was reputed to be a red-headed Nationalist, Alice by name.[18]

In her diary entry for the night of Parnell's funeral Milligan articulated a separateness from her immediate surroundings and, by implication, her upbringing: 'I am in the enemy's camp, if I had but the money I would go to Dublin to be with people who feel as I feel.'[19] We see from her diary entries how Milligan began to consider how Ireland might achieve independence through a collectively organized movement rather than by the actions of one individual (male) leader: 'The last vestry of independence is gone, except some new man come to the front, or the spirit of the people – becomes strong enough to take the stand that Parnell took.'[20]

At the end of 1891 Milligan took her teaching exams in Liverpool and then returned to take up a post in Belfast where she wrote of her exceptional boredom at having to endure conversations about 'trivial subjects as women's dress, feather boas etc'.[21] Despite the fact that as a woman she was banned from voting, Milligan was fired up by constitutional politics of the Irish National Party. On Sunday 17 July 1892 she wrote:

> I have spent the past week breathlessly waiting for the election results. Since the Monday before West Belfast election, I have been a staunch Nationalist

& longed for the return of Sexton. I went with papa to the meeting in the Ulster hall, Mr Davitt, but was not near enough to have a chance of recognising him … Priests kept to the back ground & Sexton pitched into Belfast Town council in fine style.

Arnold Foster was brought home in fine style.

Majority now only 24 – almost useless, anyhow Tories haven't even got that 24 – so they can't sneer at it.[22]

On her twenty-sixth birthday on 14 September 1892 Milligan was busy on her self re-education programme. She continued to construct historical ballads from the prose texts she read and she found herself completely overwhelmed by the poetry of Thomas Davis:

I did a good day's work analysing half the Irish history & writing the ballad of Aileach – yesterday I wrote 'Cahir O'Doherty' – Then in reading Fontenoy by Thomas Davis I experienced that sudden thrill – of pain almost – creeping sensation all over … Walt Whitman's Old Ireland, The West's Awake (Davis) thrilled me in the same way – strange that one should be so physically affected by a poem.[23]

The first anniversary of Parnell's death in October 1892 was eclipsed by the death of Tennyson: an event that seemed to signify to Milligan a sense of an emptiness in the English cultural templates that had defined so much of her thinking to date:

1st Anniversary of the death of Parnell – Tennyson is dead. I have not seen the papers. 'The old order changeth'. He was Wordsworth's contemporary – his successor and who is to come next? Browning is dead & Matthew Arnold, the only undisputedly great poets … – our great men are rapidly disappearing … The new century will bring new men, new hopes – but there is a lonely feeling about this century end as one by one the acknowledged great pass away.[24]

Tennyson's death signifies an 'ending' for the English reference points Milligan had so far relied upon. In contrast, the 1890s in Ireland were full of new beginnings, new cultural organizations, new voices, and a new literature which she herself would contribute so much to establishing. The 'loneliness' and loss of 'all the great men' that Milligan felt at the end of 1892 was soon replaced by a year of fervent activity. 1893 was a landmark year for Milligan in which she began to contribute to the emerging cultural revival movement. Milligan herself defined 1893 as significant in shaping her own political and cultural Irish consciousness. Áine Ceannt wrote of this period after interviewing Milligan in the late 1930s:

> It was after the Parnell split with the resurrection of Fenianism in the air, that she found inspiration & 'The Return of Lugh Lamh Fada' appeared May 12th 1893 in *United Ireland* under Edward Leamy's editorship. Her next poem was 'Brian of Banba'.[25]

Milligan self consciously wrote about and reflected upon the period 1891 to 1893 as a series of personal, political and cultural epiphanies: arriving in Dublin to study Irish, reading in the National Library and becoming a Parnellite on a tram along O'Connell Street. When she joined a newly founded Irish language class in Belfast in May 1893 it represented the moment of her 'entrance into the living Gaelic movement'.[26] This was the year she also met Yeats for the first time: an encounter that she later recalled as another vital moment in her self-becoming. In a 1942 radio broadcast entitled 'Yeats, Martyn, Moore and the Irish Literary Drama: A retrospect' Milligan recalled: 'My first memories of Yeats marks a turning point in my own literary development for I had been educated without any reference to Irish History or Culture.'[27] Meeting Yeats was a defining moment not least because he provided her with a counterpoint against which she would develop her own cultural ideas.

Milligan also viewed the completion of her unpublished Cromwellian manuscript novel at the end of 1893 as another significant landmark because in this novel she had started a life-long process of rethinking the colonial role of Protestants in Irish history:

> It was written at the time that the breach occurred between Irish Nationalism and English Democratic Puritanism. In the long period devoted to working on it, my own political opinions became clearly and firmly defined, and the bulky Ms has ever since been preserved as a memorial to my own political development.[28]

Twice in this period Milligan articulated her anxieties about Belfast: after Parnell died in October 1891 she referred to it as 'the enemy's camp'. Then in June 1893 she urged Lady Aberdeen and T.W. Rolleston (the two founding members of the Irish Industries Association) to avoid the political factions of Belfast and set up their first northern branch in Derry. In the wake of Parnell's death Milligan privately lamented that she longed to 'go to Dublin to be with people who feel as I feel'. Yet from 1893 Milligan sought out and found both imagined and real communities in Belfast. In 1941, she explained how the early nationalist press in

Dublin had provided her with a vital alternative to the 'strictly Tory and Protestant'[29] formal education of her upbringing in which she claimed to have 'learned nothing of Ireland'.[30]

Her diary from 1891 to 1893 is bursting with almost daily references to the act of newspaper reading, as though it was a main event that connected her with a live debate and real community beyond the confines of her own social world: 'read *Weekly Independent* all day and posted sonnets'; 'spent last night reading back numbers of *United Ireland*'; 'Bought papers'; 'went to the library to read papers'.[31] Newspapers connected Milligan with the community of voices she fervently began to engage with; they also provided her with an income and a regular space for publication. As she recognized in later life, the Irish nationalist presses with their publication of poems and literary debates introduced her to a popular knowledge of Irish national history and contemporary Irish literature: 'I received my education in Irish History and Literature first of all from cheap paper back books and articles in *United Ireland* and *The Freeman*.'[32]

Milligan had so far been happy to contribute to organizations and publications that had already been established (such as the Dublin nationalist newspapers, the Irish Industries Association in Derry and the Irish language classes that had been set up by Francis Joseph Bigger under the auspices of the Belfast Naturalist Field Club). But by the end of 1894, she began to form her own cultural groupings that were both feminist and nationalist in outlook. In November Milligan founded three branches of the Irish Women's Association in Belfast, Moneyrea and Portadown. Four months later, in February 1895, she became vice-president of the Henry Joy McCracken Literary Society. She reported about both organizations in her weekly column 'Notes from the North' that had been commissioned by the Dublin-based, *Irish Weekly Independent*. By September 1895, however, so much cultural activity was happening in Belfast that Milligan struggled to contain and convey the information in this single column.

By October 1895, the McCracken Society found a solution to this problem by launching its own journal, the *Northern Patriot*. Again Milligan was at the helm as editor and she was joined in this role by her associate Anna Johnston. The Johnston–Milligan alliance turned out to be a vital partnership that would have a profound impact on the direction of Milligan's life and on Belfast's cultural scene. Anna Johnston (1866–1902) was a poet publishing Irish national verses in Dublin's newspapers under her pen name 'Ethna Carbery'. Together, Milligan and Johnston represented the only two female members of the McCracken Society and they wrote the bulk of the journal as well as commissioning all contributions. The *Northern Patriot* ran for three monthly editions during which time it absorbed not only Milligan's 'Notes from the north' column but also all of her literary publications (poems and short stories) that she had continued to produce on a weekly basis for Ireland's nationalist presses. While the journal was a major publishing outlet for both women, they also took the opportunity to commission work from new writers. Each edition consisted of editorials, short stories, poetry, and reports about the McCracken Society and other Irish nationalist cultural events taking place across the north.

But things began to fall apart at the end of 1895 when the sponsors of the McCracken Society discovered that 'Ethna Carbery' was in fact Anna Johnston, daughter of Fenian activist, Robert Johnston, who was a key figure in the secret organization, the Irish Republican Brotherhood (the IRB). Anna Johnston was sacked after refusing to resign and even this followed a fractious period in which she (and Milligan) were denied keys to their own offices. Milligan resigned in solidarity with her co-editor after a resolution could not be agreed and in spite of the offer of full editorial control. Infuriated by the undemocratic way she and Johnston had been treated by the McCracken Society, Milligan went on to make her protest public. In a contentious battle fought out daily in the letters pages of *United Ireland*, Milligan described the sexist injustices that had been in operation during their editorship of the Society's journal. The women's greatest revenge came just four weeks after they left the *Northern Patriot*: Milligan and Johnston launched their own monthly cultural journal the *Shan Van Vocht* ('poor old woman') on 15 January 1896. In 1941 Milligan explained the circumstances under which she and Johnston founded their new journal. This story was revealed during Milligan's response to a query in the *Irish Press* regarding northern Protestant descendents of the United Irishmen who had fought in the rebellion of 1798:

> Roddy is anxious to know how the descendents of '98 Presbyterians who rallied at Ballynahinch stand today. I cannot speak up to date but when a little paper which Anna Johnston and I were editing called 'The Northern Patriot,' after three issues was captured by opponents of advanced nationalism, Anna was in despair as she had drawn on her Dublin friends for subscriptions and with her father's absence in America, we were in a financial dilemma. At this juncture a Presbyterian Unitarian Minister from Moneyrea walked in with a sum of money from subscribers in Down, and with this we risked printing the first number of the 'Shan Van Vocht'.[33]

The minister was in all likelihood Protestant Home Ruler the Revd J.B. Armour whose wife, Jenny Armour (1864–1930), was a member of Milligan's Irish Women's Association.

Milligan was named sole proprietor of the *Shan Van Vocht* but the women acted as joint editors. The *Northern Patriot* had given the women great training in accounts, negotiating with publishers and printers, commissioning works, researching and writing to deadlines. While the *Northern Patriot*, the McCracken Society and the Irish Women's Association were saturated in an anguished northern regionalism, the *Shan Van Vocht* took advantage of modern transport networks to actively connect with readers across Ireland, England, Scotland, America and even Argentina. The women's global vision for the journal was reflected in a strong national and international subscription list. The journal also fostered an equally impressive array of new writing that the women commissioned from emerging voices of the Revival that included James Connolly, Nora Hopper, and Seamus MacManus. Part of the journal's success derived from the links that the editors forged with other cultural and political activists, emerging organizations and new initiatives. This broader outlook was further reflected in the advisory board that the editors immediately established in Belfast and Dublin that included members of the Gaelic League, the Irish Literary Society and the Amnesty Association.

One of the defining events of the 1890s was the centenary commemoration of the insurrection against British rule in Ireland led by the United Irishmen in 1798. The Centenary was organized in an intensely structured way: with a central Executive, local branches and representatives. By 1897, a detailed plan of events was already mapped out and underway. Milligan's public role as a journal editor and founder of several cultural organizations, meant that she was elected to the Executive as well as to several Ulster branches of the Committee. From her perspective, the 1790s represented the first time that Protestants had united with Catholics (and the 'native Irish') against British colonial rule of Ireland. Milligan's project to reimagine and reconfigure the role of Protestants in contemporary Irish society was in large part informed by her understanding of the significant contribution made by northern Protestants to the culture and politics of the United Irish movement. In November 1895, Milligan had informed readers of the *Northern Patriot* that she believed the ideals of the United Irishmen had an intellectual and cultural resonance for contemporary Ireland: 'These anniversaries of ours are no empty celebrations. We mean not alone to honour the dead but their principles that live as well.'[34] Milligan viewed the commemoration as a major opportunity to make a political intervention. Throughout 1897 and 1898 she articulated her ideals through organizing street parades, exhibitions, collecting oral histories, publishing small biographies and pamphlets, travelling with lectures, theatre productions and magic lantern shows. Anna Johnston and Milligan gave over most of the *Shan Van Vocht* to planning and advertising the commemoration. They thematized short stories, poetry, published educational lectures and collected oral histories of the northern United Irish movement from readers. Annoyed at being constantly turned away from '98 Executive meetings because of her gender,

The Shan Van Vocht

Yes Ireland shall be free
From the centre to the sea,
And hurrah for liberty
Says the Shan Van Vocht.

VOL. I.—No. 2.   BELFAST, 7TH FEBRUARY, 1896.   PRICE TWOPENCE.

America.

America! America!!
Hearken! oh, mighty foster-land,
A harp-note peals across the sea
From the green hills whereon we stand
Waiting with hearts that shall be free.

When Ireland's sons upon your shores
Were famine-driven, and fever-flung,
You stretched, amid the tempests' roar,
The helping hand to which they clung.

And in your day of dire distress,
When all that loved you leapt to war
Against the red flag pitiless ——
You called the exiles near and far.

You did not call to them in vain
Who found a home upon your breast,
They rose to rend your galling chain,
And dying gave to you their best.

Over a hundred years have gone
Since, Queen triumphant of your fate,
You stood in the glow of Freedom's dawn,
And England crouched before your gate.

And records of your trials tell,
As North alert, met South awake,
How Irishmen poured shot and shell
Against each other for your sake.

Now, on the verge of war's alarm,
In our expectancy we crave
The strength of your indignant arm,
The counsel of your wise and brave.

In memory of old times, that were,
Of those who fought, and fell, and died,
Your rapture or your grief to share,
Let not our pleading be denied.
America! America!!

The Captain's Daughter.

"In comes the Captain's daughter, the Captain of the yeos,
Saying, 'brave United men we'll ne'er again be foes!'"

HER father was not captain of the yeos, but late of an infantry regiment in her present Majesty of England's service, retired and living on his Irish estate; they were mere moonlighters, not "brave United men" at all, not then at least, but they have learned better ways since, and the quotation strikes just the right note for my story, so in spite of petty inaccuracies you have it there to begin with. Here then is a true account of how she met them, I need not tell you who told me.

4 Cover page of second issue of the *Shan Van Vocht*, journal co-edited by Alice Milligan and Anna Johnston, February 1896.

Milligan set up two feminist organizations that ensured women a voice in the commemorations. Being an editor of a key journal gave Milligan a very vocal and public role in determining not only the commemorative events of 1898 but also in making sure that Belfast had a leading part.

In the early months of 1899, when all the frenetic activity associated with the Centenary was over, Milligan and Johnston took stock of their role within the Irish cultural scene. In April they concluded that their journal was operating in a very changed landscape: since launching the *Shan Van Vocht* in January 1896 the cultural Revival had started to take shape with an eclectic range of organizations, initiatives, journals and publishing outlets. Johnston and Milligan set up meetings with Arthur Griffith at which they transferred their subscription list to his new journal, the *United Irishman*. The *Shan Van Vocht* provided a microcosm of what Milligan hoped could be the Revival's highest aspirations and achievements: it was a collaborative project between a Protestant and a Catholic; its success depended upon a broad community of support; it gave unique space for Irish women writers and activists to communicate their ideas; it engendered a literature that was national in every way; and it placed the complexities of the Irish language and northern politics firmly within an international cultural movement.

Winding down her full-time work as editor enabled Milligan to devote more of her energies to both the emerging national theatre movement and the Gaelic League. From 1898 Milligan developed a form of storytelling in which narrative was conveyed through a combination of staged pictures, pageant, magic lantern slides, live music and off-stage (often bi-lingual) narration. Milligan's plays and tableaux shows were produced by a variety of theatre groups and cultural organizations that incorporated the spectrum of the Revival's broad interests. These included Gaelic League branches, the Belfast College of Art, village schools, the Irish Literary Theatre, and *Inghinidhe na hÉireann* (Daughters of Ireland). Milligan was thus able to make connections between the wide community of people involved in the Revival: such as William Butler Yeats, Augusta Gregory, the Fay brothers, and Maud Gonne, as well as with educationalists in rural Ireland.

Her work was popular also with schools and amateur theatre groups who wanted assistance in developing theatre and language projects within their local areas. In fact, Milligan's vast correspondence demonstrates how she tailored plays and tableaux scripts to meet the very practical demands of those who contacted her. In 1901 a teacher from Dundalk asked Milligan to write a play for pupils in the national school. The request is a good example of the extent to which Milligan was prepared to work within the restrictions amateur groups operated under: 'It is the girls of our national schools here who are going to act the play. We have them of all ages from sixteen down, with a couple of eighteen years of age.'[35] Her plays and drama shows were tremendously successful with the early Revivalists winning her great praise from both nationalist organizations and individuals: Yeats, for instance, remarked in his *Autobiographies* how the 'Abbey style' of acting had been influenced by the stillness of Milligan's tableaux shows and that her spoken plays performed by Irish actors had inspired him to use Irish dialect in his own plays. A direct line from Beckett's stilled characters who are fixed in dustbins, mounds of earth and funeral urns can be traced back through to the stillness of the 'Abbey style' and further back again to the frozen silent bodies produced as 'living pictures' by Milligan in the early years of the Revival.

As the Abbey Theatre opened its doors at the end of 1904, Milligan began to channel her energies into further integrating her democratic and localized vision for Irish national theatre within the Gaelic League movement. She believed that the success of the movement to save the Irish language from extinction did not depend entirely upon formal textbook and classroom learning. Instead, she argued that the Gaelic League and the national theatre movement could unite to create the cultural conditions that would give the Irish language meaning. Milligan applied for a full-time paid lectureship with the League as soon as posts were advertised in October 1904. By this time, the *modus operandi* of the language movement was firmly established:

> Full time Timirí or Organizers travelled round the countryside establishing new branches. These were served by the travelling teachers, who in addition to holding language classes, taught Irish dances, history, folklore, music, and organised feiseanna, céilithe and aeríochtaí. The next fifteen years saw the League at the height of its power. It is probably no exaggeration to state that in this period it did in fact fulfil the function of an Adult Education Movement ... The Gaelic League remained unchallenged for many years ... as a provider of entertainment, especially of Irish music and dancing, in those days when cinema, radio and television were as yet unknown.[36]

In applying to work for the League in a more formal capacity, Milligan stated that her main aim would be to raise funds through a mixture of tableaux, drama and magic lantern lectures. The job application is worth quoting in full as it gives a fascinating insight into how Milligan wanted to find a way to consolidate her work with amateur drama groups within the Gaelic League. Money was a central concern to Milligan and she argued that a monthly salary would defeat the object of her fundraising. Whereas in the early 1890s Milligan had taken stories from Seaton Milligan's library and made them into plays and poems for the Revival movement, in 1904 she proposed to utilize the magic lantern slides from his collection within the national language movement:

I have lantern slides at my disposal in my father's collection, to illustrate every conceivable sort of lecture, History, Scenery, Antiquities & Irish Industry & Country life – I could also organise plays and tableaux in districts where they would do better than lectures. I think I could make a real success of the business as I have very definite views & plans as to how to go about it which I think you would approve. We should get money from the general public who are not so far supporting the League at all, & at the same time we should arouse their interest & attract their sympathy. I have been for years giving help and support for Irish entertainment often to bazaars & charities which use the Gaelic movement as an extra attraction & in fact I am more or less imposed on having to lend costumes and go to a lot of terrible plumy tableaux & making sketches. I would be much more content if my efforts contributed to some definite end. I would not wish to be employed for a weekly salary, as I feel that with the main object of benefiting the League funds, it would not be every week possible to make oneself worth salary & expenses – that to keep constantly on the move would keep up expenses & I would do better to make headquarters in my own home, at no expense to myself or anyone else, whilst engaged in making arrangements and that payment would be by a percentage of the profits sent into the League Treasury after each lecture and entertainment.[37]

After she was hired as a travelling lecturer for the 'English speaking districts' of Ireland in October 1904, Milligan set out on an extensive programme of lectures, drama shows and meetings across the country. Her appointment was not without controversy: as late as 1946 (at the age of 80) she revealed in an interview that Patrick Pearse:

Never concealed from her his opinion that since she was not a fluent speaker of Irish she should not be employed as an organiser by the League. This objection she countered by remarking that her job was to raise money and not to teach the native language.[38]

Milligan felt strongly that her own position as a 'learner' could be viewed as an exemplary position rather than a disadvantage not least because she could encourage other learners by personal example. This was especially important in the north where Milligan met with Protestants who, like herself, had been raised to believe that Ireland was not their nation and that Irish was not their language. One Protestant Gaelic Leaguer described in 1929 how Ireland had been constructed in her formal education as a primitive land with: 'no history but a history of disgraceful tribal squabbles of half-naked people who had to be held down by a civilised conqueror'.[39] So despite Pearse's opposition, Milligan set about establishing new branches across Ireland. She generated funds through public events organized with those workers already involved with the League (such as Thomas MacDonagh with whom she organized Co. Cork). In May, for instance, she visited 17 districts in West Cork and reported that she had 'consulted the leading Gaelic workers as to the prospects of work in that district'.[40]

By linking disparate localities Milligan helped to unify an Irish consciousness; a process further energized by the efficient postal systems, the mass circulation of newspapers and Ireland's extensive railway networks. Her Gaelic League work in villages across Ireland had a lasting impact, particularly on those who were later involved with the Easter Rising. In 1917 one Irish Volunteer wrote to tell her that her Gaelic League visits to their area would not be forgotten: 'If we ever write the history of [the Gaelic League in Castlecomer] we can tell of how you came to the rescue in the days when everyman's hand was against us.'[41] The colonial hostility to the Gaelic League was indeed palpable at this time. Throughout October 1905, for instance, the newspapers were full of press reports regarding the arrest and imprisonment of carters in the west of Ireland (Galway and Mayo in particular) for writing their names in Irish on their carts. In August of the following year the National Bank in Ireland refused to accept Irish signatures while the National Bank in London simply closed down all Gaelic League accounts.

Shortly after she began as a travelling lecturer, political activist Terence MacSwiney engaged Milligan on 'the question of bringing the bulk of the northern protestants who are non-unionist into the national fold'. He wrote an extensive letter to her in March 1905 from his home in Cork:

> I know there are sterling protestant nationalists in the north but I would like to see Tone's Ideal realised and Ulster today as national as in '98 ... It depresses me to think of the difference today and the little attention it gets. I think national unity should be one of the first items on the national programme – and if properly striven for I believe it could be realised.[42]

Religious identity was not an easy issue to reconcile even among the Gaelic League workers themselves. Many feared that as Protestants they would be considered hostile to Irish nationalist history and culture. In an article published after the execution of Roger Casement in 1916, Milligan stressed the dilemma Protestants faced about whether to declare their religious allegiances to fellow Irish cultural activists. She recalled how in 1906 they had both been present at a Gaelic League event in the north:

I was at some trouble to put in an appearance at the nearest Protestant
church, saying, 'It is as well to let them see I am a Protestant Nationalist!'
Roger Casement, who was present, said very determinedly, 'Well, I don't
want them to see that I am a Protestant.'[43]

Although Casement did not actually convert to Catholicism until the night before
his execution, this extract suggests that he was perhaps 'wavering' in his faith as
early as 1906. It is more likely that Casement felt worried that other Gaelic
Leaguers would view his Protestantism as complicit with ascendancy rule in
Ireland. Unlike Maud Gonne and Constance Markievicz, Milligan never
converted to Catholicism. Markievicz and Gonne rejected their Protestant
identities as a means of establishing their opposition to colonial power. Elizabeth
Coxhead offers an analysis of Maud Gonne's conversion:

She had long felt drawn to the church of the people, while Protestantism
was associated with her own class, the oppressors. And if the Catholic
bishops were lukewarm or even hostile to the nationalist cause, she had
found a very different attitude among the ordinary priests, who had shown
themselves staunch allies in her battle against evictions and famines.[44]

Markievicz was formally accepted as a member of the Catholic Church in October
1917 following her imprisonment for her part in the 1916 insurrection. By
refusing the option of aligning herself with Irish Catholicism, Milligan was
effectively opposing a dualistic regime of national identity. Instead, she promoted
the idea that Irish culture did not belong to any one class or religious grouping
within Ireland. Culture, for Milligan, was not a static concept rooted in colonial
religious stereotypes; she viewed this emerging culture a dynamic force that could
be shaped by new generations within and outside of Ireland regardless of their
religious and class affiliations.

Even before she received MacSwiney's letter, Milligan had resolved to make the
north a central location within her League remit. The projects she helped initiate
demonstrate her commitment to unite the north within the broader national
movement through the Gaelic League. Milligan was involved in fundraising for
the establishment of intensive training courses for the Irish teachers such as in
Cloughaneely in Co. Donegal (1906). In 1907 Milligan was a driving force in an
organization called the Ulster Delegates of the Gaelic League. Other members
included Ada MacNeill, Roger Casement, Stephen Gwynn, Francis Joseph Bigger
and Seamus MacManus. Milligan worked closely with Casement in organizing
and fundraising for the Gaelic League (particularly in Antrim). She recalled how
in the winter of 1906 Casement organized a series of five 'lecture entertainments'

5 Photograph of Roger Casement.

for Milligan along the Antrim Coast. They travelled together for these, staying with League friends along the way: 'we had talk, till late in the nights, about how the cause of Ireland might best be served and the old tongue revived'.[45] Together with other Gaelic Leaguers, they worked to amalgamate the cultural and language activists in the north and to set up an Ulster Training College to further promote 'the cultivation of the Irish tongue and literature in Ulster'.[46]

In November 1907, Milligan attended the Congress of Celtic Union in Edinburgh as the delegate representative of the Gaelic League. On her return to Ireland she immediately called for a protectionist policy for Irish-made goods. In an article to the press she argued that the other 'Celtic' peoples present at the conference had the luxury to discuss cultural unity above economic solidarity because the areas they represented were not impoverished by colonialism. Attendance at the pan-Celtic conference led Milligan to a unique economic analysis of the failure of the Union to generate industry:

Every section of the Celtic revival was considered, except just this one of industry. The archaeology, languages, music, art, and folklore of the Highland and the Gael, of Wales, Manxland, Cornwall, and Brittany were exhaustively treated. Nothing was said as to the practicability of an inter-Celtic treaty for the protection of our produce, and looking around me at the prosperous Scotland and self-contained Wales (as there represented), I considered that the industrial question wasn't worth mentioning, and that it was only in downcast, decaying Ireland that the stimulus of patriotism of protection needed to be applied.[47]

At the same time (late 1907) Milligan involved the League in the campaign to establish inclusive and unashamedly 'Irish' technical institutes in the heart of the industrial north: 'Belfast is very decidedly in Ireland, and in what the Gaelic League calls Irish Ireland, and in time its technical committees and its colleges and schools and libraries will be worthy of our city's old reputation.'[48]

Milligan was engaged with multiple and overlapping forums of cultural activity and publication throughout the years leading up to 1916. While working full time for the Gaelic League she also continued to publish short stories, poems and plays in a broad range of newspapers and journals. In 1908, her friend George Russell (Æ) believing that Milligan had produced 'the best patriotic poetry written in Ireland in my time',[49] brought out the first volume of her poetry. *Hero Lays* was funded by the same Irish community in Argentina that Milligan had supported through the *Shan Van Vocht* in the 1890s [Plate 1]. Pádraic Colum reflected on the volume's lasting significance after he met Milligan in Omagh in 1929:

> I realized what a lucky thing it is that we have a volume of Alice Milligan's 'Hero Lays'. But for Æ's insistence we should not have it. For this poet is more disinterested than any poet I have ever known: she has only written out of some affection for a comrade or out of some mood of exaltation that she wanted some comrades to share in; never for fame, and certainly never for money. And she, with another woman, Emily Lawless, has written the most heroic poetry that has been written in Ireland in our day.[50]

Russell worked closely with Milligan throughout 1908 in selecting the poems for the volume. Yet he found her anxiety about offending Catholic priests totally unrealistic and comical. Milligan had urged Russell not to include the autobiographical poem 'When I was a little girl' in the collection because it explored a Protestant unionist child's secret longing to join the militant republican Fenian movement in the 1860s. Russell wrote the following playful response to her:

I am not going to yield to you about that child poem. Not unless you make a death or glory business out of it … Seriously I don't think that poem would irritate anybody not even a Unionist. The hostility to the Unionist movement is dead and the movement has become part of history and the record of a child's enthusiasm is not going to whip up any antagonism now. Please, please leave it in. It will be recited at Convent schools and taught more than any other poem in the book. I cannot give it up to you and that's flat! Now what have you to say. It's your move. My cards are on the table. Are you going to fight? The story of your little night dressed Fenian has put fire into me and in the name of that child I confront you and defy you. Do your worst![51]

In the end Milligan did allow the poem to be published and Russell was proved right about the popularity of 'When I was a little girl': the poem was taught in many (convent) schools across Ireland and it won a place on the curriculum in the 1950s. A great many who I interviewed in Co. Tyrone and many who attended the Alice Milligan exhibition at the National Library of Ireland between November 2010 and March 2011 could recite the poem which they had learned at school.

A significant dimension of Milligan's career from 1909 was her collaborative work with her siblings. The *Ulster Herald* reflected in 1966 that Alice Milligan's upbringing in the north had been defined by extreme political differences within her own family:

The Milligan family afforded the not unusual example in the Ulster of the time of political divisions among its members. Alice was ardently nationalist. Others of the family were staunch Unionists, and some were prominent in the anti-Home Rule cause.[52]

It was precisely these familial political differences that make Alice Milligan's legacy so hard to interpret and define in contemporary Irish society. The Milligan family grave was desecrated by both 'sides' during the recent Troubles: loyalists objected to the presence of a British Army captain sharing burial space with a 'Republican' poet; republicans viewed that Alice Milligan's memory was degraded by the staunch unionist positions of her siblings. Ironically, one of Milligan's first publications revealed her objection to this type of dichotomous politics being imposed on Irish identity by colonial assumptions. In her 1888 poem 'Ode to political tourists' she is scathing about the simplistic labels placed on the Irish by English voters who visit the country to confirm ideas already formed elsewhere: 'They came, they saw, they criticized, they stayed about a week / And now with a familiar air of Ireland they speak … / What brought our lords and masters here to visit their dominions? / They came, be sure, to find new facts to back up old opinions.' In this poem, Milligan argues that it is only by engaging with the lives of those on the 'other side' that a more nuanced approach to Irish identity and politics can be achieved: 'If any one would know the truth about the Irish question, / He'd better see the other side & follow my suggestion.'[53]

In the lead up to the First World War, Milligan witnessed the increasing marginalization of the north's cultural history. Her own family's support for the Union mixed with their fervent engagement with Irish culture, offered Milligan a working example of a multifaceted and nuanced model of national identity. In response to the increasing anti-Irish discourse generated by the northern unionist opposition to the second Home Rule Bill of 1912, Milligan used her public voice to remind readers of Belfast's inclusive Irish cultural history. In an article published in the *Irish Independent*, for instance, she objected to the sectarian undertone of the new Protestant Covenant:

> The present day politicians who have chosen to associate their obstinate determination to remain separate people amid the native population of Ulster, have scarcely shown a sense of discrimination in usurping the historic title of the covenanters. The main object and policy of their agitation has been to unite Protestants of all denominations in bitter united opposition to the Catholic Irish.[54]

In part, the threat of sectarian separatism accounts for her continued commitment to work on cultural projects with family and colleagues who were not aligned in any way to her political outlook. Between 1910 and 1916 she collaborated with at least four members of her immediate family (all of whom were active supporters of the Union) on publications and Irish cultural events that related directly to the north.

In 1910 she worked again with her father in the Ferguson Centenary in Belfast and in doing so she took every opportunity to highlight the importance of the north for the poet's work:

> This centenary will be marked without any doubt in the capital of Ireland by cultivated men and women of all classes, without distinction of political or religious differences, amongst the literary Irish of London and of America. Is it not time that we in Belfast were making some move to centralise the movement in his native place and in the northern county which he writes of in his greatest poems?[55]

Milligan and her father set up a committee to help raise the profile of Ferguson in Belfast and offered 'a tribute to the poet from a Belfast point of view'.[56] The press reported the lecture Alice Milligan delivered in 1910: 'She gave a sketch of the northern capital as it was a hundred years ago, and concluded with a description of the poet's grave on the hill of Donegore, outside the city.'[57]

In 1909 and 1910 she undertook a series of tours of Antrim with her sisters Edith Wheeler and Charlotte Milligan Fox. The three sisters recorded and transcribed songs by Irish singers. They then published articles and musical scores about 'folk songs in County Tyrone' in the *Journal of Irish Folk Song* (a publication jointly founded by Charlotte Milligan Fox and Seaton Milligan in London in 1904). Like the Ferguson Centenary lecture, Milligan's promotion of the Irish songs drew attention to the fact that Irish culture was being excised from the history of the north:

> To a good many people it will be news to hear that there are Gaelic speaking areas in Tyrone. In spite of the plantations, the Irish language still survives in the territory of the O' Neill's.[58]

In 1911, Alice Milligan contributed research about eighteenth-century Irish historical and cultural life for Charlotte Milligan Fox's book *Annals of the Irish harpers*. In the preface the author acknowledged: 'From first to last I have relied much on the help of my sister, Miss Alice Milligan, who has had considerable experience and knowledge of Irish history.'[59] Between 1913 and 1914, Milligan co-authored a children's novel based in the Icelandic sagas with her brother William (just before he left to fight in the First World War). *Sons of the Sea Kings* was researched in the Linen Hall library and written in Bath where Alice Milligan was helping to look after her brother Ernest's three daughters [Plate 2]. Alice Milligan introduced her brother Ernest to James Connolly in 1896 and encouraged him to establish the first Belfast branch of the Irish Socialist Republican Party. As a medical doctor in England he renounced this radical Irish politics when he joined the British Labour Party. Yet over the years he remained broadly sympathetic to his sister's political outlook and continued to publish poems, newspaper articles and to write radio plays. Ernest's three daughters were taught by Alice Milligan at different stages of their childhood in England.

Two professors of the American Catholic University commissioned Milligan in 1914 to write an essay about the history of Irish women. In this project, Milligan was in the company of friends: *The glories of Ireland* included many of her associates from the Revival such as Roger Casement, Eleanor Hull, Douglas Hyde, Francis Joseph Bigger and Joseph Holloway. The editors set out their rationale in the introduction:

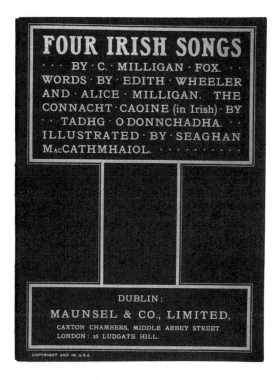

6 Front cover of *Four Irish songs* by Alice Milligan and her sisters Edith Wheeler and Charlotte Milligan Fox, 1910.

7 Woodcut illustration of sheet music by Seaghan MacCathmhaiol in *Four Irish songs*, 1910.

8 'Mayo Love Song': words by Alice Milligan, music by
Charlotte Milligan Fox in *Four Irish songs*, 1910.

The performance of the Irish race in many fields of endeavour are entirely
unknown to most people … Hence there came to us the thought of placing
in record, in an accessible, comprehensive, and permanent form, an outline of
the whole range of Irish achievement during the last two thousand years.[60]

Milligan was asked to examine the place of women in Irish history because it was
a subject she had already written extensively about believing that: 'The worth and
glory of a nation may well be measured and adjudged by the typical character of
its womanhood'.[61] In her conclusions she asked: 'And what of the women of
Ireland today? Shall they come short of the high ideal of the past, falter and fail, if
devotion and sacrifice are required of them?'[62] Educationalist, poet and playwright,

Thomas MacDonagh chose to answer this question in an essay of his own published in 1914.[63] He argued that Milligan herself provided a powerful example of the intervention made by contemporary Irish women in defining Irish cultural history. She was the most significant poet of his generation, he suggested, precisely because her life and work encompassed a radically inclusive Irishness. Hers was an identity and a politics that grew out of the marginal positions she inhabited as a northern, Protestant woman who had denounced the unionist Anglo-centric doctrine of her upbringing. Hers was a cultural practice that gave voice to those (like herself) who were so often consigned to the footnotes of colonial history.

While Milligan was clearly writing and publishing in the years leading up to 1916, she was also busy working as a full-time carer of her aging parents in Bangor. After she cancelled a lecture trip to Scotland, Milligan explained the situation to her fellow Gaelic Leaguer, Margaret Hutton. As the only remaining unmarried sibling Milligan clearly felt responsible for the immediate welfare of her parents: 'I cannot now leave home for more than a night at a time as one brother has married & gone, & Charlie is away from home too so except sisters come home on visits, there is no family except myself.'[64] When asked to contribute to a volume by Irish biographer and editor D.J. O'Donoghue, she replied apologetically: 'I cannot be sure that I am capable of turning out a good new poem just now – as a matter of fact I have only written one poem in a period of eighteen months & as at present I am residing in lodgings with my mother & an invalid brother. I have not an hour's seclusion'.[65] Her friend and fellow Revivalist, T.W. Rolleston wrote sympathetically: 'I am very sorry to hear of all your trouble about relatives' illnesses'.[66] In 1910 she asked Francis Joseph Bigger to send her some prints of the United Irishmen for a lecture that she had been forced to scale down: 'I had intended writing a carefully thought out semi-historical political address, but am now busy helping to nurse my mother who has been very ill & have neither time nor energy to make preparations ... am getting the loan of some views of historic places from my father.'[67] In the first four months of 1916 Milligan would bury both her parents and her younger sister, Charlotte Milligan Fox. The Easter Rising (which broke out two weeks after her father died) would propel Milligan into a period of distress that would be matched by a fervent cultural and political activism of solidarity and protest. All the heroic names from legend and history that Milligan had written into literature were suddenly replaced by the names of her contemporaries. Her brother Ernest later reflected: 'My sister had many griefs; one of her earliest was the death of a brother aged ten, a year older than herself (when in Belfast about 1875). Also in 1902 a younger sister drowned, then Ethna Carbery's death [also in 1902]; and there were others with whom she was deeply attached.'[68]

1916–30

From 1916 to 1923 while Ireland was consumed by violent conflict, Alice Milligan waged her own private war of independence. Between January and April 1916 she nursed both her parents and her sister Charlotte Milligan Fox through illnesses in Ireland and London: after her mother died in January, Milligan travelled to look after her sister in London; Charlotte died in March and then Milligan nursed her father through his final weeks of life. The death of her parents unexpectedly signalled a new beginning for Milligan because it marked the first time she was in a position to choose where to live. In late 1916 she moved to Dublin, rented an apartment at 23 Kildare Street and invested in 'The Irish Bookshop' at 45 Dawson Street. Her bid for economic autonomy was funded by book sales: between 1917 and 1919 Milligan sold off the library that she and her father had constructed. In 1938 she recalled in a letter to actress Máire Nic Shiubhlaigh: 'I kept myself in 1916 through selling books and rare pamphlets.'[69]

These book sales are critical to our understanding of Milligan's life because they tell us much about the source material that formed the intellectual backbone to her literary and political writings. After Milligan's own death in 1953, an obituary in the *Derry Journal* astutely picked up on just how vital Seaton Milligan's library had been to his daughter's cultural development and the direction her life took: 'it was in his extensive library that she first learned the story of Ireland'.[70] This library provided the bedrock and inspiration to Alice Milligan's early literature. The initial book sales give a unique insight into the contents of Seaton Milligan's library: an almost comprehensive listing of the original holdings can be reconstructed from Milligan's papers which contain auction lists, private orders, letters, and adverts carried by journals such as the *Irish Book Lover*.

While the books had once provided Alice Milligan with a new intellectual realm of freedom, she now hoped they would help her achieve economic liberation. At the end of 1917, she sent a list of Irish texts to one bookseller stating: 'I am urgently in need of funds as I have reached the last month of the first year in which I have had to look after my own affairs.'[71] The following year she was in an equally difficult situation when she contacted her friend Francis Joseph Bigger who was also involved in selling books on her behalf:

> I am this week living on credit & just waiting for supplies – going TWICE to Bath, in England … & subscribing to election funds, and making an investment in this shop was too much for one half year's expenditure – and I am just in the last weeks of my half year.[72]

Milligan's time away from acting as a family carer was short-lived: her brother William Milligan was demobilized as a captain in the British Army in 1917 and he returned from war ill and completely dependent on alcohol. While he initially went to stay with his brother Ernest who was a medical doctor in England, the unmarried sister was immediately given responsibility for her brother's welfare. From England she appealed to Bigger for assistance in selling off more books, believing that if she could get enough money together she would be able to determine her own future:

> I am quite without means of subsistence except in a dependant position with relatives better off than myself & bitterly opposed to my political views and activities. I am in fact and have been for some time practically interned – The sale of these documents would be helpful in an effort I am making towards independence.[73]

Her initial plan was to help William find work in the north of England so that he would be near Ernest Milligan and his family. This would then enable her to return to Dublin. She explained to Bulmer Hobson:

> Willie has settled down into domestic routine and is T.T. [teetotal] here … If he was on his own – working at Building and with Ernie's home within reach for weekends, I might look forward to returning to Ireland.[74]

This idea didn't work out after William failed to secure work in England. Milligan ended up returning to the Kildare Street apartment in Dublin with William Milligan where she began to help him develop his publishing career. In 1921, however, brother and sister fled the city under mysterious circumstances which forced Alice Milligan to literally leave all belongings behind. The explanation for this sudden departure was only made public in 1966 when Alice Milligan's younger brother Charles (then Lord Mayor of Bangor) revealed that his sister 'was living with my brother, Captain W.H. Milligan, in Dublin, and the IRA gave him 24 hours notice to get out or he would be shot. My sister packed up with him in England.'[75]

Milligan was struggling to establish a life for herself in Dublin at a time of immense political upheaval in which Ireland was consumed by insurrection, a War of Independence and a Civil War. By the time she moved out of Dublin, the country was on the brink of Partition: after 1922 the newly founded state of Northern Ireland (under predominantly Unionist governance) would exist separately from the twenty-six counties of the Irish Free State. While it was a time of upheaval and confusion for Milligan, it was also a period in which she was

incredibly productive both politically and culturally. In fact, her own feelings of
being 'interned' by family opposed to her views further developed her affinity with
the political prisoners whom she actively supported in the wake of 1916. The first
Irish prisoner she extended solidarity to was her old friend and fellow Gaelic
League worker, Roger Casement.

Casement was arrested off the south coast of Ireland just days before the
insurrection. He was transported and imprisoned in London where he was
executed in August after being found guilty of high treason for his plot to rally
anti-English support among German-held Irish prisoners of war. Milligan
petitioned on Casement's behalf and published several articles about his cultural
work in Ireland, particularly his involvement in the Irish language movement in
the north. An Irish Volunteer who had escaped arrest in 1916 congratulated
Milligan for providing a unique insight into Casement's work in Ireland:

> Read your very interesting contribution to the Catholic Bulletin re R.C. It
> was splendid and supplied something that had been lacking in all the
> accounts previously published – eg., a first-hand account from one who
> understood him and his aims. Others who knew him in this way were still
> under lock and key.[76]

The most curious feature of Milligan's relation to Casement was the central role
he played in her visionary works. In a 1917 private letter to George Russell,
Milligan confided that Roger Casement's trial and execution had been 'foreseen
and foretold' as early as 1894 in automatic writings, visions and dreams.[77] She
defined herself as, 'not so much a visionary as an interpreting intelligence' whose
role it was to publish this documentary evidence so that 'Roger Casement's
personal and political character will be cleared of all suspicions'.[78] A year later
Milligan submitted accounts of the visions to a leading Catholic theologian in
Dublin and to the writer Seamus MacManus for publication in America. T.W.
Rolleston, the co-founder of the Irish Industries Association, had apparently been
keeping the documents in a safe from as early as 1910. In 1921 Milligan disclosed
her supernatural revelations to her friend, actress and writer Sinéad de Valera (Ní
Fhlannagáin), arguing that: 'an explicit account with all names, dates and definite
proofs given would have an immense effect in restoring union and in uniting
Ulster'.[79]

The 'List of witnesses' Milligan drew up in defence of her psychical beliefs was
largely made up of unionist members of her own family: 'I have never on a single
occasion witnessed a spiritualist séance or sought consultation with a medium –
messages came to me generally from the very relatives who seek to restrain me and
detach me from the Irish movement.'[80] Milligan named her siblings as the central

List of Witnesses

Mr T. W. Rolleston. Imperialist. Great Censor. Formerly a republican. has been informed of the circumstances from first to last. (1894 — 1910) He pressed me to submit my evidence to psychical research investigation, but I awaited the fulfilment —

Other Witnesses are. Mr W. H Milligan. Home Rule Imperialist, anti Sinn Fein. Ex Military officer + my brother. He has exerted all his influence in the past few years to keep me out of politics —

Dr. Ernest Milligan (my brother) formerly a Nationalist + friend of James Connolly) now resident in England. Anti Sinn Fein.

Mrs G. H. Wheeler (my Sister). O.B.E. formerly Hon. Sec. of Carsonite Women's Organisation. Bitterly Orange + anti-Irish.

Mrs R. Fox, (my Sister) resident in London Imperialist — as a girl of 17. had a Vision. Feb 9. 10. 1894. foretelling recent events in Ireland —

Luke Rooney. brother of Wm Rooney. Dublin
Miss M. Johnson Lisnaveane - sister of Ethna Carbery —

Dr Jim Killen. Presbyterian Nationalist. Derry.
Seumas Mac Manus. New York.
Lily O Brennan. Dublin
? CK Wilson Herbert Place Dublin. Ulster Orange Principles

9 Statement written by Alice Milligan after 1916 to Sinéad de Valera regarding her dreams and visions relating to aspects of Irish republicanism, which includes this list of corroborators. Sinéad de Valera Papers, National Library of Ireland.

'hostile witnesses' who had supplied much of the psychical documentation. She describes the late Charlotte Milligan Fox, who had experienced the first vision in 1894, as 'a rabid Imperialist'. Her brother William Milligan was a 'Home Rule Imperialist, anti-Sinn Féin ex-military officer'; while her sister Edith Wheeler, secretary of the Carsonite women's organization was, according to Alice Milligan, 'bitterly orange and anti-Irish'.[81] Milligan seemed to have total conviction that the document in her possession had the power to undermine even the Ulster Unionist's anti-Home Rule doctrine contained in their 1912 Covenant. She informed George Russell of just how widespread and popular occultist practices were among women in the north:

> my sisters … are silly about psychical research – all the Unionist Headquarter ladies have been attending lectures in psychical research & their minds are ripe to be impressed. Given an impression & their Covenant etc dissolves into nothingness.[82]

Unsurprisingly, Milligan's attempts to publish this material as a booklet entitled, 'The vision splendid' were unsuccessful. In the early 1920s, Milligan was still trying to publish a formal book and set of articles which brought together the psychical research she had mentioned in private letters to Sinéad de Valera and George Russell following the execution of Roger Casement in 1916. Milligan described the book to her friend the political activist and publisher, Bulmer Hobson: 'It is psychic, but would be in a form which Irish Catholics would not object to – in fact I have a letter from an eminent Irish Catholic cleric commending it.'[83] Hobson rejected the manuscript of the book by tactfully suggesting that such work may find greater success in England. While waiting to see if the book would be accepted there, Milligan 'dashed off 7 or 8 of these psychic articles'[84] and sent them to the Dublin newspapers (where they were also rejected). Even as late as 1933, Milligan wrote to the Irish-American republican activist, Joseph McGarrity, on the subject: 'Don't show the little pamphlet to anyone till you hear from me – I'll send you some extraordinary convincing notes shortly … I never heard of Pope Benedict's blessing till last year – yet it was foreseen in my home on Cavehill in 1894. Also Casement's Trial.'[85]

Casement had asked Milligan to write a poem about the trial – a request she publicly fulfilled in four poems which were published in censored form in the Irish nationalist presses: 'The ash-tree of Uisneach', 'In the Wirral', 'Antigone' and 'The prison grave'. However, a very different commemoration of Casement emerges in Milligan's private psychical correspondence. Describing the process of revelation to George Russell she explained: 'Things came to me … told in sequence at intervals, sometimes spread over months, separate dreams or visions which fitted together like a puzzle to illustrate a poem.'[86] Milligan considered that the publication of her findings would represent her 'poetical and sublime' homage to Casement and prevent the Partition of Ireland. It is through these scribbled, strange, confused documents; these private letters to major public figures that Milligan would write her (co-authored) poem for Casement. In all their abstract contradiction and belief in the supernatural and the unexplainable, Milligan tried to mediate the conflicting voices of her time and make sense of what had happened to the phenomenon that was her friend and comrade, Roger Casement.

Immediately following Casement's trial, Milligan embarked on a series of prison visits to Irish political prisoners who had been deported to England following the insurrection. Her political work in this area formed part of a movement to help support the families and widows of Irish Republican soldiers. In January 1917, Irish books and manuscripts began to be auctioned in Dublin to raise funds for the Irish National Aid and Volunteer Dependants' Fund. While she sold books through her 'Irish Book Shop' in Dublin to raise money to aid prisoners' families, she also supplied Irish prisoners with Irish history books. Prisons in England after 1916 provided intensive training and education for Irish Republicans and Milligan subsequently received letters from ex-prisoners about the importance of the material she had supplied. Milligan not only knew all the leaders of the 1916 Rising who were executed, but she knew a great many of the men incarcerated in English prisons. The fact that so many of the prisoners had been involved in the national language movement was a point Milligan made in July 1939 when she opened the feis in Enniskillen. The *Ulster Herald* reported some of her speech in which she explained how the prisoners she had visited in the aftermath of the Easter Rising had been intellectually mobilized and culturally energized through Gaelic League cultural networks:

> In the songs of our land alone our language will live forever. It is strange that when in the course of her work for the Gaelic League, she toured through England and Ireland, she found in prisons many of those who in earlier years had been helping in her Gaelic League work. It appeared that through learning Gaelic, they had a strong feeling of nationality in their hearts and had been able to venture much for Ireland.[87]

Milligan conveyed her experiences of being a prison visitor in a series of autobiographical poems that she published in the republican Irish newspaper, *New Ireland* between 1916 and 1919. Milligan was not a daughter, mother or wife of any of the executed or imprisoned republicans. Yet she identified strongly with the plight of prisoners and their families. This was not surprising as so much of her Revival literature had focussed on prisoners, uprisings, Irish historical 'rebels' and the role of women in political conflict. As a single woman accustomed to extensive travel alone, Milligan could access prisons in England in a way that many family members and friends could not. In much the same way as she had received occultist messages in the lead up to 1916 ('messages came to me generally from the very relatives who seek to restrain me and detach me from the Irish movement'); Milligan constructed herself as a messenger who passed news and information between families and prisoners. Her own family tragedy adds a dimension of resonance to her mourning: her body in 1916 became a site through which the personal and the political were visually unified. In her poem 'Arbour Hill, May 1916' the soldiers mistake her mourning for republican solidarity with the executed leaders of the Rising. They refuse to speak to her until they realize that she seeks news about living prisoners, not dead comrades:

> For parents both, and sister dear,
> Mourning I wore from foot to head.
> They deemed I sought some kinsman's grave,
> Whom lately they had buried near,
> Among the martyred dead ...

Milligan's poems from 1916 to 1922 are multilayered forms of expression. They come out of direct experience within the contemporary political and emotional landscape of Ireland's anti-colonial and civil strife. They are often dedicated to a friend or a comrade (such as those with whom she attended the trial of Roger Casement including Antrim-based Gaelic League worker Ada MacNeill and the Irish historian Alice Stopford Green). Milligan uses a very personal mode of address to express her own subjective experience through the pronominal 'I' as a conversation with the dedicatee 'you'. The direct references to the self and to 'you' in the poem create an intimate discourse that is placed within a very public context: the poems were all published in newspapers yet Milligan writes these poems as though they are private messages written for personal viewing by friends. In the poems that she published between 1916 and 1923 Milligan addressed a national solidarity; an audience committed to the same united Irish objectives as herself.

For a short time after 1916, the career of Éamon de Valera signified for Milligan a political awakening for Ireland. When he escaped from Lincoln prison in February 1919 she wrote a poem entitled, 'Merely players. To S... A memory of tableaux and a play'. This poem was published in March 1919 in *New Ireland* and dedicated to Sinéad de Valera (Ní Fhlannagáin) with whom Milligan had worked in the Gaelic League and national theatre movement. The poem draws the comparison between Red Hugh escaping prison in her 1902 play and de Valera's

own audacious prison break. 'Red' Hugh O'Donnell (1572–1602) was lord of
Tyrconnell and led an uprising against the English in 1593 after his daring escape
from Dublin Castle the previous year. Ella Young recalled that at the turn of the
century when first performed in a 'little shabby room' in Dublin, Milligan's drama
was a 'prime favourite' among amateurs and audiences. Young suggests that
nationalists interpreted the work as an anti-colonial resistance play, reading Red
Hugh's liberation from captivity as 'the symbol of Ireland escaping'.[88] The 1919
poem directly addresses Sinéad de Valera who helped Milligan stage *Red Hugh*
in 1902 as part of a production put on by the women's feminist republican
organization *Inghinidhe na hÉireann* (Daughters of Ireland):

> Memory holds a garish picture of you
> Kneeling with a Celtic cross above you
> Under the saintly Brigid's cloak of blue.
> Innocent and fair to all beholders
> With your rippling hair about your shoulders,
> When we staged the drama of Red Hugh.
>
> So when came your hour of heaviest sorrow,
> Words of mine your prayerful lips could borrow;
> Prayer for such deliverance as he knew,
> Who from Dublin on a night of snowing
> Fled with his companions onward going
> Over hills and vales of Wicklow through.
> …
> Did you dream then, ere a day departed,
> You would smile exultant, happy hearted,
> And the whole sad land rejoice with you?

As with so many of her poems published in the immediate aftermath of 1916,
Milligan here addresses a very specific 'audience'. This poem communicates
directly with those who were part of a specific moment of Irish cultural (and
feminist) history. In referencing the 1902 production of *Red Hugh*, the poem
becomes another example of how Milligan conceived of the events of 1916 to
1922 as being somehow already 'visioned' or encoded within the Irish Cultural
Revival movement of the late nineteenth and early twentieth century. Although
Milligan disagreed with much of his politics after he took government office in the
Free State in 1932, she displayed political loyalty to Éamon de Valera on key
national issues: she supported him during the Civil War; agreed with his

> ## "ANTIGONE" AT THE ABBEY THEATRE.
> ### DUBLIN, 5th MARCH.
>
> Too-rarely,—rarely in heroic strain
>   The players stir us in these hurrying years,
> Too seldom thrill our hearts with noble pain,
>   Or ask for golden grief our gift of tears.
>
> Now thanks to these by whom at length is shown
>   Oh not unworthily or with light intent,
> The unyielding tyrant on the Theban throne,
>   All his outspoken pride and punishment.
>
> By the blind seer foretold,—the awful power
>   Of divine justice smites for deeds unjust:
> Low, low among the helots see, him cower
>   Like a poor maniac moaning in the dust.
>
> Stricken he lies, vain all that hoard of wrath
>   Furiously hurled to make the helpless fear,
> Since even Ismene the frail and trembling hath
>   Proved brave at last, for love of her sister dear.
>
> And who that saw thee sad Antigone
>   Bearing the burnished urn with stately tread,
> But thought of some among us, sad as she,
>   Who may not pay due rites unto their dead.
>
> For these the august, the antique voices plead
>   Vainly—in vain Tireisias warns of fate,
> One near speaks lightly—" Not half bad indeed
>   And nicely staged, but scarcely up to date."
>
>   ALICE L. MILLIGAN.

10 'Antigone at the Abbey Theatre': poem by Alice Milligan, from
New Ireland, 16 March 1918.

opposition to the Treaty; and in the late 1930s she voted in favour of his proposed amalgamation of his Anti-Partition League with the Northern Anti-Partition Council that she had helped found. De Valera, in turn, would recognize her contribution to the national cultural movement with an honorary doctorate in the 1940s. Indeed, after her death in 1953, Charles Milligan (Alice Milligan's youngest brother) recorded how de Valera wanted a volume of Milligan's poetry to be published: 'This morning I received a letter from the President Mr Éamon De Valera … suggesting that a collection should be made.'[89]

The poems that Milligan produced in the years immediately following 1916 are a dialogue and a reflection upon the contemporary changing landscape of Ireland. Milligan tells this story almost as a private conversation between friends who have suffered and those who continue to suffer. The poems explore the intimate private responses (by those free and by those still imprisoned) to the trauma of conflict. For instance, 'Girls from the pine forest' depicts how prisoners in solitary cells and strangers outside the prison walls simultaneously (and spontaneously) commemorate the death of republican hunger striker, Thomas Ashe.[90] During the period 1916 to 1922, Milligan was involved in several overlapping political and cultural events: she worked on behalf of the Irish Volunteers Dependants' Fund; campaigned for Sinn Féin on the Falls Road in Belfast during the 1918 elections; published political pamphlets, and edited and published the literary works of her friend the writer and mystic, Florence Wilson.

As her poems about the Abbey's 1918 production of *Antigone* and the references to Irish tableaux suggest, Milligan was still very preoccupied with the role of drama in Irish politics. In 1917 she assisted the director of the Ulster Literary Theatre, Fred Morrow, in his Belfast production of her Ossianic trilogy: Oisín's mythical journey through an unrecognisable homeland in search of lost comrades carried a particular resonance when performed in the context of war-torn Ireland. In the midst of Civil War and on the eve of Partition, Milligan republished her Cromwellian play, *The daughter of Donagh*: 'Insistent that our politicians should be ever mindful of the lessons of history and that our poets and dramatists should not be forgetful', she prefaced this historical drama about sectarian displacement with a reminder of its contemporary significance.

The last poem Milligan wrote in the 1920s was 'Till Ferdia came' published in December 1922. The Irish Civil War is placed against the mythic fatal conflict that erupts between Ferdia and his foster brother Cuchulainn. The story of the two warring brothers had first been produced by Milligan as a series of tableaux in the early years of the Revival. In 1898 the pictures of Ferdia fighting his brother were designed by Belfast Gaelic League members whose politics and religious affiliations were extremely diverse. As I have already noted, for Milligan the Gaelic League wasn't just about reinstating the Irish language, it was about creating the cultural conditions that would give the Irish language meaning. In this context tableaux became a symbol of the body awaiting speech. Later chapters in this book will show that the tableaux were vital for the inclusion of northern Protestants like Alice Milligan whose upbringing led them to believe that Irish was not their native language or their national culture. Silence represented a half-way house, a space, a means of crossing borders and transgressing the barriers erected by years of colonial occupation. The pictures produced in Belfast in the late 1890s were created by a unionists, nationalists and republicans. In this particular story, Milligan explained that the pictures:

> Showed the fight of Ferdia and Cuchulainn at the Ford … The combat was
> most difficult to pose, and the success of this ambition was largely due to Miss
> Praeger who, as a sculptor, was able to secure for us fine models, and Mr John
> Carey's effective posing of the athletes chosen to represent the epic heroes.[91]

In 1922 these frozen bodies were animated in Civil War. If the tableaux during the Revival were a symbol of the national body awaiting speech, the language that these images found in Irish history after 1916 stopped national dialogue for the best part of a century. The 'noble tale' of 'The glory of the Northern Gael' with which Milligan begins and ends her 1922 poem, is given a modern 'live' context when the names of Ireland's ancient legendary figures are replaced by those of her contemporaries. The poem pays homage to the Irish men killed during the Civil War including Michael Collins (1890–22 August 1922), Erskine Childers (1870–24 November 1922), Harry Boland (1887–31 July 1922) and Cathal Brugha (1874–7 July 1922). In particular, Milligan reflects how Dublin was brutally transformed by the murder of men who had once walked side by side along its streets. In this and other poems such as *Antigone*, Milligan suggests that the tragedies of ancient literature have found a new level of trauma in Ireland because 'fealty' had been transgressed. In 1933 Milligan explained the background of the poem to Joseph McGarrity: 'It is brief and embodies what was his [Casement's] last request. If you don't get it, I'll try to send it after you. It was written after seeing Ella Young's *Antigone*, in which the dishonouring of the body of a fallen foe, is the subject.'[92] In 'Till Ferdia came', Ireland is personified as a mother of two warring sons who themselves embody national division:

> 'Oh grief! Of griefs beyond all other,
> Two valiant sons of one fond mother;
> Two brothers, pledged to Ireland's righting,
> In severed ranks were sternly fighting
> In cause opposed.'[93]

Milligan worked hard to avoid rifts within her own family, whose members had been personally affected by multiple traumas within the space of four years: these included four private family deaths (a second sister of Milligan's died of cancer in 1920); the conflict and executions that followed the Easter Rising; and the violence encountered on the battlefields of the First World War. After Milligan and her demobilized brother fled Dublin under an IRA threat, they ended up living in Belfast and Antrim and then in Co. Tyrone: 'I am living in seclusion here in the north,' she immediately informed Mrs Erskine Childers.[94] William Milligan eventually found work with the Office of Public Works in Belfast and Alice Milligan moved with him to help set up home. Douglas Hyde wrote to her rather flippantly, 'Fancy you having turned domesticated!'[95] But she communicated the real nature of the situation to Francis Joseph Bigger:

My demobilised brother has been left to live with me. He has an appointment under the corporation, which has not come off on account of the
building strike … We are in a sort of bungalow, looking out on the old Feis
field and he is busy at a novel … – None of my relatives are inclined to give
me a helping hand, as they find that my political activities are restrained by
financial embarrassment.[96]

While William Milligan was for large parts of his life unable to keep down
formal employment, Alice Milligan attempted to establish an alternative source of
income for him. Throughout the 1920s she completely occupied herself with the
literary career of her brother who wrote mainly 'boy's own' adventure stories. She
not only co-wrote novels and stories with him; but she took on the full-time role
as his literary agent sending manuscripts to publishers, reviewers, and newspapers.
Drawing on all her connections in Irish publishing, Milligan secured book
publications for her brother with the Martin & Lester press in Dublin and made
sure his novels were serialized in journals such as *Banba* and the *Derry Journal*. She
even sought out encouraging information from the publishers to help boost her
brother's confidence: 'Do let me know of Dublin reviews of *The Drummer*
anything favourable would inspire Willie to finish the other story, which would
be important before he takes up building work again.'[97] Throughout the years she
also worked behind the scenes to reconstruct his broken family life. As one letter
to Bulmer Hobson makes clear, Alice Milligan viewed the publishing and private
life of her brother as intimately connected:

Don't send Willie any royalty money just at present – if you answer his letter
just say you are looking into the matter. We are expecting his wife over and
I don't want him to spend his resources before she arrives.[98]

Despite telling Hobson, 'I don't get much time for writing',[99] Milligan did
actually manage to engage in four publishing ventures of her own throughout the
decade. The first of these was a collection of verse that she described as, 'a small
group of poems, not historical or political'.[1] This was marketed by the Educational
Company of Ireland for the secondary schools curriculum [Plate 3].[2] The second
was a formal book and set of articles that brought together the psychical research
she had mentioned in private letters to Sinéad de Valera and George Russell
following the execution of Roger Casement in 1916. From 1923 to 1924, Milligan
republished poems from her *Hero Lays* collection on a monthly basis in the
nationalist journal, *The Gael*. Finally, in 1927, the Educational Company
commissioned and published a selection entitled *Stories of the Celtic nations* aimed
at children and intermediate exam students.[3] The last glimpse we get of Milligan

in this decade comes from Pádraic Colum who was inspired to write his first play after seeing Milligan's dramas staged in Dublin in 1900. He visited her in a village in Co. Tyrone in 1929 while collecting material for a travel memoir, *Cross roads in Ireland* that he published on his return to New York the following year. After talking with Milligan and hearing her recite some poems, Colum realized that hers was a literature and a politics deeply rooted in the history of Ulster Irish radicalism:

> The daughter of a Belfast business-man, Alice Milligan writes and speaks as if there were nothing between her and Gaelic Ulster – no plantation, no John Knox, no industrial Belfast. It was probably through Irish traditional music, which her family had a great deal of interest in, that she kept a link with the Tyrone clansmen who were amongst her forebears ... The older Ulster Presbyterian had a core of Republicanism which went to form leaders for the 1798 insurrection – very earnest, very devoted men. Alice Milligan is heir to this Republicanism.[4]

1930–53

Milligan hoped that William Milligan, his wife Maud and their son Edward would form an independent life together after they were reunited as a family. Yet she actually found herself living with them in a remote village in Co. Tyrone as a dependent and a full-time carer right through to 1941. Ernest Milligan later recalled: 'I don't think my sister wrote much after 1919 she was living with my brother Willie and his wife and son (now dead) and moving with them from place to place. Dublin, Belfast, Rathfriland, Cookstown, Ballymagorry, Lisburn, Mountfield ... The society she was in was not the kind to inspire her and she had to do a lot of domestic work and try to keep the home together.'[5] In 1936 Milligan reflected on her own circumstances: 'I'm sort of interned prisoner for 19 years'.[6] Throughout the 1930s, Milligan continued to look after her alcoholic brother who was laid off work for large periods. We learn from the bemused letters of his sister that William Milligan's greatest dilemma in 1935 was whether to leave her to look after his wife or: 'whether he should take me with him, to look after him building the police barrack!!!'[7] She actually ended up looking after both husband and wife after her brother suffered 'a stroke of the gravest sort.'[8] His illness had been preceded by a tragedy that beset the family in 1934 and which Milligan related in a letter to Joseph McGarrity in New York: 'The household here is in deep trouble – my nephew, the only son had a paralytic stroke on March 11 & can not speak or stand. We are nursing him night and day. He was very brilliant and clever but thoroughly Anti-Irish objecting to my working for even Dublin papers.'⁹ On the anniversary of Edward Milligan's death a year later in 1935, Alice Milligan found herself nursing Edward's mother:

> Maude has an acute bronchial cold and I've been up all night. It is the anniversary of Edward's death of pneumonia at Summer after we had pulled him through wild wintry weather. Since early March his speech had come back & he was reciting lines of Longfellow & Swinburne.¹⁰

At the end of 1936 William Milligan suffered another stroke: 'my brother has been seriously ill for 6 weeks & may not perhaps retain his job in consequence'.¹¹ Milligan nursed him for seven intense months until he died in June 1937. Her letters reveal how William Milligan's death precipitated new battles with other members of her family. On the day of the funeral she described how her future was being taken from her without consultation by family who she felt cared little about her welfare or her wishes: 'My brother died Friday night. Funeral to day – brothers from Belfast here & very officious & unpleasant, planning to anchor me in some quiet corner with Maud.'¹² Charles Milligan, like his brother William, had been in the British Army (fighting on the side of the British in Ireland during 1916). Like his sister Edith (for her services with the Ulster Women's Unionist council during the First World War), he too was awarded an OBE.¹³

Milligan's way of countering the wishes of her family (and the British military presence at William Milligan's funeral) was to write to all the nationalist papers explaining why she had pulled out of speaking at a series of anti-Partition meetings. She also named the prominent republicans who had written to her in sympathy: these names included Éamon de Valera, Áine Ceannt, ex-senator Joseph Connolly and ex-IRB chief Mark Ryan (who had gained her access to Casement's trial in 1916): 'I am writing through death & all to Donegal & Derry papers – to explain absence from meetings and have death notice in Derry Papers – to show my side distinctly to all whom my opinion would influence.'¹⁴ The headline in the *Irish Press* drew stark attention to the politics of the sister rather than saying anything at all about her brother: 'Alice Milligan bereaved. Well known Nationalist poet's loss.'¹⁵ The memorial notice placed the death and its impact on Milligan in the context of her work in the forthcoming General Elections: 'Already with her pen she was preparing to help the cause so dear to her heart.'¹⁶ Her Sinn Féin election work of 1917 and 1918 were also mentioned. Milligan's actions indicate that she felt greater solidarity with the community of strangers that she connected with through nationalist and republican Irish newspapers than she did at that time with her own private family. Her suspicions that they were trying to restrain her continued in the years following her brother's death. For example, she told friends that she resented how the money gifted to her by her brother Seaton was being controlled on her behalf:

> My youngest brother here is holding up 200 dollars cabled me from California on the excuse that I am in desperate need of clothes which he will see me provided with, whereas I count on it to secure my independence.[17]

From 1935 to 1941 Milligan spent considerable time caring for her English sister-in-law Maud with whom she had a very difficult relationship: 'My sister-in-law is an invalid', she told McGarritty in 1933.[18] She explained cancellations of lectures to her friend Lily O'Brennan in Dublin: 'Maude is my trouble ... what can I do – I can get no human being to look after Maude at night.'[19] By this time, the sister-in-law had stopped paying towards household expenses and accused Milligan and others of stealing from her: 'I am fairly worried horribly by my sister-in-law's mental sanity'.[20] In 1938 she told her friend, Abbey actress Máire Nic Shiubhlaigh:

> I have no cash at all for a couple of months ... of course I can get clothes and food on credit till then but not perhaps newspapers or washing done or any attendance that has to be paid for in cash. My sister-in-law ... has a small income but regards it merely as dress allowance and pocket money and thinks I should keep the house. I have hard work to do and little time to write.[21]

In other letters to friends in the Free State she revealed: 'Maude does not intend to pay for anything ... she has not quite control of her faculties.'[22] Her letters from 1937 contain the endless refrain of cancellations due to her domestic responsibilities: 'I can't arrange for anyone to stay nights with Maude'.[23] By the late 30s she wrote desperately: 'When I get some trusted person to look after my sister-in-law I'll dash off for a weekend, even if I have no broadcast.'[24] To pay for Maud's debts in the late 30s Milligan was forced to sell personal items including a watch made in Belfast that had been given to her at her birth in 1866; as such it had measured out her life and the sale was symbolic of the years Milligan felt were being taken from her. On hearing of the death of Anna Johnston's sister, Maggie, she was again full of regret for a life not lived:

> I feel broken – haunted about her & always thought she and I would end our days living together in Donegal. It makes me angry with those I am serving & helping when I think how little I ever did for dear Maggie who

needed help and care – & had done much for me – dear to me as any sister – I admired her so much, perhaps more than Ethna.[25]

All of her letters throughout the 1930s express fury at living in such a remote location: 'It is perfectly absurd for people to live 8 miles from the train with no connection.'[26] Not having access to transport also made it difficult for her to get supplies to and from the house: 'we have no car connection now with Omagh … I can't get to town on any business & it's hard to provide even.'[27] In July 1935 she thanked her friends, the artists Seamus and Estella O'Sullivan, for inviting her to visit them in Donegal but confessed that it was another journey she was unlikely to make: 'Here I am behind the mountains and no one passes … I have been nowhere for years.'[28] Milligan did not feel at home either in the house, the village or the state that she found herself committed to. After the death of her brother in 1937 she reflected: 'I am trying to make this house nice – my only comfort would be if I could have a room always for a friend.'[29] In 1938 things didn't seem any better: 'It is awful here. Hard even to post back.'[30] Her letters and manuscripts are often written on the back of whatever she can find such as William Milligan's old work documents or used Christmas cards: 'I have not got any proper paper,' she apologized, 'and can't get out to buy any.'[31] Then later the same year she informed friends:

> I don't believe I'll get to Dublin again for ages if ever – & motor cars are hard to hire for getting into Omagh, petrol being controlled as is proper – I seem to be actually interned – the censor & all makes the post really chancy.[32]

Her frustrations were intensified at this time with her feelings of growing old. In 1934 she asked her friend Cathal O'Byrne to stand in for her at a broadcast in Belfast because nursing her nephew had taken its toll: 'I have been feeling broken down.'[33] Later that she year she expressed dismay at having to pull out of an event in Dublin: 'I have been again and again disappointed about going up … but some one is constantly ill & now I am feeling stiff & old & tired & almost unable for any journey.'[34] Planning to record for radio in Dublin, Milligan was extremely cautious about any post-production social plans: 'I was ill in the winter with kidney trouble and don't want to go about or do anything but rest after the journey.'[35] In 1932 she described the difficulty of living in a place without running water: 'I was very unwell for a few days … I put it down to carrying & drawing from a barrel, buckets of water.' In 1934 she scribbled: 'I am not very well, sight somehow failing'.[36] (Despite these complaints of ill health, Milligan would actually remain physically active and mentally alert right through to the early 1950s.)

By the end of the 1930s, the defeated tone of Milligan's letters suggest that she had stopped fighting to attain an independence of living: 'I somehow don't feel as sad ... it must be simply resignation.'[37] She wrote of her regret that she and her sister-in-law had not taken the opportunity to move to a cottage built by one of her cousins on the land of her childhood: 'The house was built in the exact spot where as a child of 6 or 7 – I used to play in a pretty field with a lovely view of the mountains. I would have been like Goldsmith's "here to return and die at home at last".'[38] Yet despite her thoughts of approaching death, Milligan did not accept her circumstances passively, nor was she simply contented to await the end of life. Her letters reveal that in the midst of her struggles she was all the time figuring out a way to negotiate her role as a carer in the North with her desire for a more politically and socially fulfilled life. Following the death of William Milligan in 1937 she formed a plan to live part time in Dublin:

> I have almost decided that when I go up next to broadcast [to Dublin], I must look out for an unfurnished flat and flit up, even if we have paid rent in a loan here. I will not live long if I cannot be where I can get care and attention when needed.[39]

In a later (unsuccessful) bid to secure freedom she applied for a Dublin based post of 'gatekeeper' to the Board of Assistance that had been advertised in the *Irish Times*.[40]

The 1940s began with the kind of problems that Milligan was by now painfully familiar with: money was short; Maud was ill; and bad weather made isolation worse. Her problems were compounded in July 1940 when the Belfast Evacuation Scheme forced her to take in evacuees and move to a small house in the village. In one letter she confided how difficult she was finding the situation due to the high levels of drink the adults consumed. As a long-term carer for an alcoholic, Milligan would have found this situation particularly distressing:

> I am having a rather desperate time in the process of uprooting evacuees for whom I took a small house (by order of the local authorities) turn out rather undesirable mother and aunt (of small interesting boy and sister) not sober at nights – I resident in room of same house in Mountfield ... The evacuees spoke of returning to Belfast but on account of the children I persuaded them not to do in haste – but if they plan to do so, I won't detain them.[41]

Locals in Mountfield recalled in 1995 how Alice Milligan stayed away from her home as much as possible when this family were living with her; they would see her walking up and down the village lane waiting for the nights to pass.

The 1940s, like the previous decade, continued to be financially difficult. Milligan once again found herself selling off as many belongings as possible. She expressed her distress and financial vulnerability at not having any immediate help close to hand:

> I am grappling with problem of dispersing of furniture and books & pictures to meet expenses & deal with Maude's debts – a journey into town by motor costs 6/ – & with all this tangle I might be left very short ... It is the last month of my financial year ... Dr Ernie in England [Milligan's brother] would help me ... but a letter would take too long for some emergency – I went in to talk to bank cashier but was too late. I was really very much broken up, but am gradually rallying ...[42]

In October of the same year, she wrote that she would not make it up to Dublin for the oireachtas: 'I keep company in thoughts with those far away or departed & hope some good will come out of all the turmoil.'[43] She was clearly struggling to make ends meet and once again she began to sell off books and attempted to raise funds by writing newspaper articles:

> It is now rather urgent to raise money as we have to pay the rates by the end of the month or be prosecuted – and I'm selling some books – John O'Donovan edited – but won't sell any except to a seminary or library – Dealers send that sort of thing to the U.S.A. ... I have quite a lot of writing in prospect & would well go on with it even if newspapers are not hospitable.[44]

Alice Milligan was seventy-five when her familial duties in Mountfield eventually came to an end; she had another twelve years of life ahead of her. In January 1941 she wrote: 'We are snowed in and very isolated of late.'[45] In April 1941 she informed friends in the Free State: 'Maud died this morning after long period of somnolence'.[46]

From 1930 alternative family networks of friendship and political protest were interconnected for Milligan. She considered the Dublin home of three Irish republican feminist friends to be her 'political head quarters'.[47] Lily and Kitty O'Brennan and their sister Áine Ceannt (widow of the 1916 Irish Volunteer Éamonn Ceannt) were Milligan's closest comrades during the final two decades of her life. It is in her letters to these sisters (and Lily O'Brennan most of all) that we hear about Milligan's daily struggles to live in the North and her difficulties in caring for a family who opposed her political views. Alice Milligan first got to know the sisters during the campaign to raise funds and awareness for Irish political prisoners after 1916.

The feelings of internment and imprisonment that Milligan had started to feel in the years immediately following the Rising reached a peak in the 1930s. Her frustrations did not emanate solely from her duties as a carer for her staunch unionist relatives; nor was her anger simply a product of the isolationism of living in a remote village without transport. Milligan considered Partition an affront to all that she had worked to achieve in Ireland and she found the new state of Northern Ireland almost unbearable. In the pages of the *Irish Press* in 1936 she warned that the bigotry that she had witnessed in Belfast in the 1890s was becoming endemic across the whole of the Partitioned state: 'Under the Stormont Government this nasty sectarian bitterness has come to life in mid Ulster.'[48] After the death of Parnell in October 1891 Milligan privately described in the pages of her diary the feelings of estrangement she suddenly felt from the unionist community of Belfast: 'If I had but the money I would go to Dublin to be with people who feel as I feel.'[49] Almost fifty years later, Milligan still felt ill at ease in the sectarian colonial landscape of the North. In March 1938 she explained the different codes of civility she personally felt operated in the Free State and in Northern Ireland:

> I am not settled in heart in this place – & of the Northern people personally known through a long life – I have never felt or received the universal helpfulness & kindness there is down there [Dublin & the Free State] – even from strangers or slight acquaintances, kindness & courtesy – 'Everyman's hand against another' – seems the Northerners favourite motto.[50]

Practical transport arrangements were made very difficult with the post-Partition dismantling of the railway networks that had once made travel across Ireland so easy. The railway had united Ireland in much the same way as it did India. Where as during the Revival years Milligan had been able to reach even the remotest village in Ireland by regular rail; from mid-1930s she struggled to make it anywhere. She vented her frustration to friends in Donegal:

> A curse upon the Border & those that made it – only for that a Taxi from this village would take me right through in a hasty call and back – but a complex mixture of taxi – trains, buses & limited time baffles me.[51] [Plate 4]

In July 1938 another trip to the Free State had to be cancelled: 'there is a ban against return over Border & I wouldn't get up at all.'[52] The Second World War only made security controls across to the Free State more intense. In July 1940, for instance, she was prevented from travelling because she did not own a photograph of herself and had no way of obtaining one: 'I read that passport photos are needed ... I had been planning to get up to Dublin in a day or two but nothing seems possible to plan nowadays.'[53]

In the wake of 1916, Milligan's increasing feelings of disempowerment were articulated through her intensive solidarity for Irish political prisoners. In the 1930s her own sense of internment found its rhyme in the exile of six counties of Ulster from the rest of Ireland. She began a letter to the press entitled 'Ulster and exclusion' with a dramatic statement of self: 'I who live here in virtual exile and imprisonment'.[54] It is no coincidence that the Revival's most popular anti-colonial tableaux depicting a chained female personification of the nation, 'Erin fettered; Erin free', gained renewed popularity at anti-Partition protests across the North. When Milligan reviewed the shows for the newspapers, she stated that the nationalist community did not require explanations of the tableaux to understand the political symbolism of their code: 'everyone knows' what the pictures mean, she declared.[55] By 1938 Milligan's own private domestic and political incarceration would have added an extra resonance to her understanding of the frozen image of an imprisoned female body.

Milligan challenged the paralysis generated by her circumstances with a relentless campaign of political and cultural resistance. Everything she produced and wrote, all the lectures she gave and the contacts she forged were directly connected to the protests against Partition. In 1938 she wrote to Máire Nic Shiubhlaigh: 'I am a good deal in northern Anti-Partition politics now and friends who at first helped me may now shy off. I can write poetry through all and have done a lot of '98 ballads.'[56] Two years later she told Lily O'Brennan in Dublin: 'I am happier now that I am busy into all that's going on about the north – partition – .'[57] Throughout the decade she was constantly travelling (and trying to travel) to Belfast and Dublin for anti-Partition meetings. She confided mysteriously to O'Brennan on one occasion:

> I have to go up to Belfast – in an anti-partition meeting (very urgent) and I have to see some Dubliners on that subject. These friends can advise me about some of the controversial matters discussed at the Belfast Partition committee.[58]

As was the pattern of her career, Milligan's political work in the 1930s and 1940s was structured within the framework of formal organization. In 1931 she became a founding member of the Ulster Anti-Partition Council and the Northern Council for Unity. She contributed to the writing and publication of pamphlets produced by both organizations. In January 1938 she was one of sixteen signatories of 'Partition of Ireland: the roots of discontent, disorder and distress', a pamphlet published by the Northern Council for Unity. That same year, she agreed to the proposed merger between the Northern Council for Unity and de Valera's Anti-Partition League. Milligan used every possible means to convey the message of the anti-Partition campaign. In the North, for instance, the cultural festivals of the Gaelic League (which Milligan had helped to set-up in the early years of the Revival) became a key rallying point for the anti partition movement and a major platform for Milligan and her comrades to unite in solidarity. Some of the methods used by the Anti-Partition League replicated those first energized in the early years of the Revival period: community language festivals (such as the feis); grave decoration ceremonies; and the marking of public anniversary commemorations. Milligan drew attention to the anti-Partition movement at events such as her lecture at the opening of the Tyrone feis; her speech given when laying a wreath at the grave of Thomas Davis; and her public talk from the main platform at the Wexford 1798 Commemorations.[59]

Radio also offered Milligan a modern form of public address that had not been widely available during the years of the Revival. In the 1930s she used radio broadcasts as a way of reaching a new audience with memories about the activists of the past such as James Connolly, Roger Casement, and W.B. Yeats. But she also used her refusal to broadcast as a political protest. Her brother Charles Milligan recalled after her death in 1953 that his sister would have nothing to do with a British broadcast: 'Some few years before her death the BBC wished to use some of her poems in conjunction with others from Ulster. But she would have nothing to do with the BBC.'[60] On another occasion Milligan took the opportunity to stage a political protest when she was asked to represent Ulster in a programme called, 'The five provinces greet the nation' for St Patrick's Day 1938. Brendan Flanagen (he and his father smuggled Milligan's letters across the border in the 1930s) recalled in 2006 how he watched Milligan refusing to speak into the microphone until the Union Jack was lowered from the Omagh Court House.[61] The authorities eventually conceded to her request as the incident was in danger of holding up the live national broadcast event. Milligan understood the political power that flags represented in the public space of occupied territories. The title of her 1898 poem 'Under which flag?' had been used by James Connolly as the title for his 1916 play staged at Liberty Hall just three weeks before the Rising.[62] Actor and Irish Citizen Army soldier, Sean Connolly, raised the Irish Tricolour on the stage of Liberty Hall; three weeks later he was shot dead by the British army as he raised the same flag above Dublin Castle. The second verse of Milligan's

1938 poem 'At the Castle' warns of the often fatal consequences of displaying the Irish republican flag in the North [Plate 5]:

> 'Up where I come from, if flown were those colours
> Or wound among flowers for a grave in the grass
> Dearly you'd pay for the like of such boldness
> As did the good men beside Money glas.'[63]

Milligan's political activism came at great personal cost: from 1933 she was forced to engage in a convoluted process of subterfuge. One correspondent in answering a letter on her behalf described what was happening: 'Miss Milligan has instructed me to write to you and tell you that her letters were being seized.'[64] Pat Flanagen (Brendan's father and writer for the *Derry Journal*) explained the situation to Joseph McGarrity:

> Perhaps you are not aware that Miss Milligan holds different political views to other members of her family and in consequence it would be better to communicate with me at the above address and any particulars you may require I will communicate them to her. I am posting this letter in the Free State in order to ensure its safe delivery.[65]

That censorship was present in her private home is obvious in this and other letters. Milligan advises her friends in Dublin to 'mention no names' in letters posted to her home in Omagh.[66] Milligan observed that her mail had been 'suppressed' by the state as well as her family since she responded in 1933 to a request by a US biographer for information about Roger Casement: 'except I send a letter 40 miles from here to be posted, it doesn't get through'.[67] Milligan protested against this new censorship by reworking and republishing her poems that had been tampered with by the British censors in the years 1916 to 1919. In July 1933 she informed Lily O'Brennan: 'I have rewritten and improved a poem which was published in 1917, the censorship days & much had been taken out.'[68] This was actually 'The ash tree of Uisneach' which she published on the anniversary of Casement's execution on 3 August 1933 in the *Irish Press* under the new title, 'A ballad of Roger Casement'.[69] Yeats' Casement poem later in the 1930s also first appeared in the *Irish Press*. In 1917 Milligan signed her Casement poem with the initials of the Irish language version of her name: 'E. Ní. M'. In 1933 she signed the revised Casement poem 'I.O.': it was the first time since the early 1890s that she had used the initials of her pseudonym 'Iris Olkyrn'. The signature could have been a defensive reaction against further state interference of her mail and personal freedom: in the 1990s people in Mountfield village recalled how Milligan was regularly humiliated by being made to daily sign in to the Army Barracks across the road from where she lived.

Milligan not only tried to reclaim poems censored in the past but she also attempted to reintroduce literature published during the Revival to new audiences. Under the Irish version of her name Eilís Ni Maeleagáin, she republished poetry that she considered to be 'outstandingly National' by writers such as Douglas Hyde, Thomas Concannon and Michael Cavanagh who had been integral to the Gaelic League's early success. The poems were accompanied by footnotes in which Milligan gave detailed contextual information about the authors, the poems and the times in which these works had been originally produced. Milligan resituated this poetry in the new context of partitioned Ireland, as though the poetry that had been thrown away long ago with yesterday's news contained the seeds of something vital for the new struggle. Milligan reactivated this past literature and the anti-colonial context of its production within the new political and public context of the North. In a letter to Áine Ceannt, Milligan explained how she had managed to find the poems in the back pages of her own Belfast journal, the *Shan Van Vocht*. That Milligan was forced to borrow copies of her own work from other people is perhaps another instance of her dispossession:

> I didn't get poems finished but have three in hand – one Arbour Hill, one ballad of Wexford & another on Belfast, am also copying in Irish various poems about '98 by an Craoibhinn [Douglas Hyde], written in the *Shan* & am sending them to northern papers – 'The Marching Song of the Gaelic Athletes' is well known, but there are several others. My bank manager (formerly of the Irish National Literary Society Dublin Secretary under Dr Sigerson) is leaving Omagh. He had lent me a bound copy of the *Shan Van Vocht* & before returning the book I am copying these things in view of Wexford Centenary.[70]

In her public output throughout the 1930s, Milligan defined herself as the voice and arbiter of memory. Indeed, after Partition she was often cast by friends and journalists as a symbolic link between the Revival movement and anti-Partition struggle; as an embodiment of the cultural connection between the North and the Free State. A journalist who interviewed her during the Wexford commemorations in 1938 observed: 'Watching the march past, linking northern and southern tradition, was the famous poetess Alice Milligan who made the deeds of the Antrim '98 ring by many an Irish fireside.'[71] Joseph McGarrity visited Milligan twice in Omagh in the early to mid-1930s and asked her to forward work to him for publication in America. She wrote after his second visit in April 1934: 'your visit was an event in my life linking me back to the cause for which I live'.[72] Significantly Milligan does not use the past tense here to describe the Revival movement: for her it was a living struggle rooted in a past that was still being fought out in the new context of a partitioned Ireland. Poet Joseph Campbell had written a similar phrase to Milligan in January 1934 when he invited her to serve on the advisory board of his American *Irish Review*:

> It is like a breath out of the heroic past in Ireland to write down your name. I often mention you here in New York to my students, when I speak of the pioneer days of the Literary (and political) Revival. How are you? And how is the north, your calf-ground and mine? Uliad is still part of Eirine, and all the machinations and cowardices of the Britishers and pro-Britishers can never take it away.[73]

Campbell viewed Milligan as not simply a voice of the past but as a republican able to offer an insider's view of the North. He commissioned from her a series of articles called 'Ulster letters' to help raise awareness of the Irish political situation for the diaspora: 'We are trying to move the great ignorant, inert mass of Irish America – a Herculean job!'[74]

Milligan was asked by McGarrity and Campbell to contribute poems from her back catalogue to the New York *Irish Review*. In particular, they were interested in the political poems she wrote in the wake of 1916 and her autobiographical signature poem, 'When I was a little girl'. But during this time Milligan also wrote new poems and articles that were inspired by rare visits to the Free State to attend historical events: these included an excursion to Dublin for the signing of Ireland's new Constitution in December 1937 and a lecture tour of Wexford during the 1798 commemorations in 1938. The expedition to Enniscorthy raised Milligan's spirits: 'I feel braced up by the trip', she told Lily O'Brennan afterwards.[75] When interviewed by the press, Milligan commented that she had travelled from the North not only to speak at the commemorations but to 'get the "atmosphere" for another '98 poem this time one on Myles Byrne'.[76]

Byrne (1780–1862) fought in the 1798 insurrection with the United Irishmen in Wexford and then later joined forces with Robert Emmet's 1803 rebellion. In a letter of 1937 Milligan informed Áine Ceannt that she had been researching this topic for some time. The letter reveals how historical and contemporary personalities were intimately connected in Milligan's mind. Milligan sees traces of her friend Lily O'Brennan in Myles Byrne's sister; her comparison here substantiated Pádraic Colum's 1929 observation that 'Alice Milligan writes and speaks as if there were nothing between her and Gaelic Ulster': 'I'm reading Miles Byrne's memoirs [published in 1863] for months every night – his little sister is like Lily'.[77] On the trip to the commemoration she reflected: 'I wanted particularly to see where Myles Byrne came from as I have an unfinished poem – the scene pitched at his home'.[78] At first she was disappointed to find the building half destroyed, but was delighted when she was able to gain the information she needed through an ex-IRA prisoner: 'when he sat to talk & take tea, it came out that when he was on the run he had slept in Myles Byrnes home, now in ruins & described the whole scene and surroundings'.[79] In Walter Benjamin's 1938 essay, 'On the concept of history' he argues that writing about the past in times of conflict is always an act of reimaging the present: 'To articulate what is past does not mean to recognize "how it really was." It means to take control of a memory, as it flashes in a moment of danger.'[80] This is characteristic of how Milligan devised her poems, plays and short stories: she drew on oral histories (often given by political activists) to reinflect and enrich the historical moment in contemporary conflict.

In April 1938 the British state banned commemorations of 1916 across Northern Ireland. The newspapers carried the following statement issued by the British government outlawing all republican political gatherings during the Easter period:

> Under the Civic Authorities (Special Powers) Acts, the six county minister of Home Affairs (Sir Dawson Bates) has imposed a ban on any meeting in the six Counties to Commemorate the Insurrection of Easter Week 1916, 'or for the promotion of the objects of the Irish Republican Army or any other unlawful association'.[81]

Milligan's response to such censorship was to break her twenty-two-year silence on the subject of the Easter Rising. Milligan wrote regretfully that she had not written about the leaders of 1916 at the time of the insurrection. It was not until the new Irish constitution was ratified on 29 December 1937 that Milligan found a language and a voice through which to 'express' herself. She explained the background of her inspiration to Lily O'Brennan in several letters written as she drafted and researched the poem throughout 1938. The day the new constitution was ratified Alice Milligan stayed in the Ceannt-O'Brennan household in Dublin. While they were out of the house in the morning, Milligan read Éamonn Ceannt's last letter written to his wife, Áine, from his prison cell in Kilmainham just hours before his execution:

After breakfast in your downstairs room I read again and again the Kilmainham letter over the mantlepiece – it seemed better to me, than to hear the guns, & see the armed guard ride through Dublin – all my thoughts were of those who died – I wish I had wrote a little poem to express myself. Maybe I will soon. Your ever loving Alice[82]

This experience of reading Éamonn Ceannt's last letter resonated with Milligan as a foundational moment in her own life and she refers to it over and over across several letters:

I'm half way through a ballad of Myles Byrne & Wexford – When I came back in January [to Omagh] – everyone said you were there on Constitution day – What did you do? – and I said I sat alone at breakfast – you were at mass & I read from first to last the letter of Éamonn Ceannt to his wife – calm & noble & wise & giving counsel through her to all Ireland, against compromise or trust or surrender – .[83]

In this extract Milligan gets closer to describing what it is about Ceannt's last letter that she finds so resonant: although it is a personal letter to his wife and son it is also a communication 'to all Ireland'. This is very similar to the personal 'letter' type poems that Milligan published in the *Irish Press* after 1916: like Yeats' poem 'Easter 1916' Milligan addressed personal friends publicly in verse. In Áine Ceannt's living room Milligan placed herself in the physical and psychological space of the loyal wife and loyal widow.

This is just one instance in which Milligan reveals her intense identification with the women involved in 1916 (the widows of the executed leaders most of all). There are examples in her letters that demonstrate how she privately took it upon herself to uphold their legacy in contemporary Irish society. Her total boycott of the Irish writers' society, PEN, is a good example of this. Milligan refused to attend anything the society organized after its secretary, Sean O'Faoláin, critically reviewed the prison letters of Countess Markievicz in the *Irish Times*. 'I don't speak to Sean O'Faoláin', she explained to Kitty O'Brennan who was the co-secretary of PEN:

I wrote by return to the secretary & said that I had several communications from the P.E.N. Club & had never answered one of them as they came from a young man S. O'Faoláin who had written an outrageous attack on Constance Markievicz in the *Irish Times*, & that I had intended to propose his expulsion from the Academy of letters, & was only prevented from doing so by the illness of Mr Yeats, as I did not want to vex or worry him in any way – as the matter stands I won't go up! except I hear from this secretary (a new man) that O'Faoláin is no longer on the committee.[84]

On another occasion, she innocently shook the hand of nationalist politician Alfie Byrne at a commemorative function in Dublin Castle which Milligan attended with the 1916 widows Kathleen Clarke and Áine Ceannt. As soon as she discovered that Byrne had stood against Áine Ceannt for the position of Lord Mayor she wrote furiously to Lily O'Brennan: 'I wish I'd slapped him now'.[85] Milligan took a very negative stand against her old comrade of the Revival period Maud Gonne who was a more complex 1916 widow. Gonne had separated from her republican activist husband John McBride soon after their son was born. Milligan's loyalty to the memory of McBride caused her to question the validity of Gonne's claim to her status as an 'Easter Week Widow'. Milligan not only refused to align her anti-Partition work with Gonne but she also refused to attend any public event at which she was present. On several occasions Milligan questioned Gonne's Irish republican credentials by insinuating that she was too busy looking after the English soldiers in the First World War. She also took a harsh anti-feminist moral stand against Gonne for leaving her husband in the first place: a position that completely negated McBride's alleged alcoholism and domestic violence:

> Miss Gonne was I believe nursing for the allies in Paris in 1916. I'm not sure but I think so & her husband had been 'dismissed' for about 12 years before his death in 1916. As an Easter Week widow she is an absurdity & an insult to John Mac Bride's memory.[86]

As I noted in the introduction to this book, Sean McBride, founder of International Amnesty, paid homage to Milligan's loyalty to the memory of his father and to the committed solidarity she had shown throughout her life to Irish political prisoners: after her death in 1953 he, along with others, put out a public call for her papers to be collected and archived.

Like Yeats before her, Milligan felt the need to 'write' the names of the 1916 leaders out in prose and in verse: 'I have tried to have some intimate touch about each'. Asking her friend to copy out parts of Éamonn Ceannt's letter, she told Lily O'Brennan of her plan, 'to put some of the actual words into metre':

> I have divided my Arbour Hill poem in 2 ... I begin with Colbert & Houston – Mallins – generally & Mdme Markievicz in particular & John McBride, Thomas MacDonagh, Plunkett. James Connolly. This makes 7 of Arbour Hill – with 7 to follow. The Pearses. O'Hanrahan. Clarke. Ned Daly – Sean Mac Dermot. Éamon Ceannt – I have tried to have some intimate touch about each & I don't seem to know much of anything in particular about O'Hanrahan, though strangely his face stands out more vividly than any. I

saw him always at work in the League rooms – seemingly disturbed when addressed, not like Barret, O'Daly and Sean T, ready to chat. Pearse didn't chat either. Was O'Hanrahan book keeping or writing for *Claidheamh Soluis* – or what? Was he a native speaker & did he write a book?.. Was O'Hanrahan from West or South – Are the Miss O'Hanrahans still in a shop up in Phibsborough? … I finish with constitution day 1938 … – would you copy for me a few lines the essence of the letter the voice of the dead saying trust not – yield not. I'd like to put some of the actual words into metre – I recall perfectly the sense & trend of it all.[87]

Despite endless research and prose writing, Milligan didn't actually complete or publish the 1916 poems: somewhat like her 'vision' letters about Casement, Milligan's 1916 poem exists in the prose letters to close friends. As though for Milligan the act of privately remembering and sending out letters from her own isolation in the north was a political act of solidarity in and of itself. In June 1913, Patrick Pearse proclaimed to readers of *Irish Freedom* that Milligan's work gave Irish 'heroic names a place in history'.[88] Perhaps this 'place in history' was also a private place in which 'poems' in verse and prose were communicated directly to those who understood both their political intention and the painful conditions under which they were produced and read.

Áine Ceannt drew attention to the direct impact of Milligan's literary production for her contemporaries in a 1937 radio programme: 'It is only recently, the past year or two, she got comfort from an article in the *Press* describing how [Irish Volunteer] Seaghan MacDiarmuid had recited her poem "Brian of Banba" to cheer & uplift his fellow prisoners waiting the end in Kilmainham.'[89] Milligan's words entered into the physical space of another prison cell in 1981 when her poetry was again read by an Irish Republican prisoner close to death. Bobby Sands asked for Milligan's poetry to be smuggled into his cell in the Maze prison during the hunger strikes. For Sands, Milligan's poetry clearly symbolized the subterranean history of Northern political solidarity. She was a torch bearer who illuminated his time of darkness with her own engagement with an earlier moment in the republican struggle.[90] Her plays, *tableaux vivants*, poems and newspaper articles published in the 1930s reactivated Ireland's silenced histories and re-placed them in the public and private domains of republican comrades. When the novelist Benedict Kiely visited Milligan during his pre-university years between 1938 and 1941, he encountered a 75-year-old woman who believed it her duty to 'tell to the living' the stories of the past. In 1939 he wrote a poem about Milligan that included the following two verses:

How her lips could give life to the dead who had died,
To the dead men she loved when they laboured in life:
To that strange man of visions, poor Pearse. By his side
Was the laughing MacDonagh. Apart from the strife
In his wattled hut, laboured of music and song,
Was Yeats, the great poet, who half understood
What was meant by the conflict. And none in the throng
Was dearer than she who, with life to begin
Gave her white song to God by the shores of Loch Finn.

Great shadows. They passed, one by one, in my mind
While she talked in the half-light of that quiet room,
An old withered woman. And yet on the wind,
That was low in the limes, I could hear the dull boom
Of big guns in the city. Could hear the sharp rattle of rifles, the cries
Of the men. And over the vision, cut deep in the skies
Were lettered in gold, the undiminishing names.
She had known them and loved them, stood by them in life,
She had lived, when they perished in fighting and strife,
To tell to the living why those men had died.[91]

The death of her sister-in-law, Maud, in April 1941 marked a sea change in the domestic circumstances of Alice Milligan. In December 1941, she moved out of Mountfield to stay with her friend Eleanor Boyd at her home 'Maxwell's Walls' in Co. Antrim. A letter written by Boyd in 1953 (one month before Milligan died) reflected on the history of their long friendship. Milligan, she explained, had always taken her nationalist friends out to visit the house, particularly those activists considered too political by her own family:

> We have known Miss Milligan all my life. She used to bring all her nationalist friends – John O'Leary, O' D' Rossa, &c out to my fathers house 12 miles from Belfast … My father was a nationalist nephew of Joseph Bigger.[92]

The time living in Antrim marked an exceptionally happy period for Milligan. In January 1942 she wrote that although the farm she was living on was very isolated, just having access to a car and a telephone made the world of difference. (The telephone and her increased happiness almost certainly account for the fewer letters available to document Milligan's life in the 1940s.) She was also liberated from the feeling of constantly being politically maligned by those she is living with:

I am staying with old friends in Co Antrim … I had a great time at
Christmas driving around to see old friends around Belfast and Antrim. My
things are still stored in Mountfield … We are miles from any town but
cockmotor works and phone and so it doesn't matter.[93]

Throughout the decade she continued to be involved in organizations such as
the Irish writers' society PEN, the Anti-Partition League and the Indian Famine
relief movement initiated by de Valera. She wrote short stories, poems and articles
for the nationalist papers and submitted transcripts for radio shows. In 1944 she
sent a detailed historical narrative outlining the career of United Irishman, Napper
Tandy, as background material for Kitty O'Brennan's '98 play. In the letter she
enclosed with the manuscript was a question that symbolized her new found
freedom to travel and be present: 'when is the next oireachtas? I don't want to miss
it'.[94] Movement between home, Belfast and Dublin immediately became more
possible for Milligan and her letters indicate that she took every opportunity to
get involved in social events, political gatherings and election campaigning. But
even within this brave new world, Milligan (at a time when she was herself older
and physically less able) still acted in some way as a carer for her elderly friends:

> I can't leave at present as my friend's not well and has no sister relative, or even
> female servant with her. Seven miles from a town. I had a great day in Dublin
> – day of election. Went to many meetings and took invalid friends of mine to
> poll – so often saw Mrs Ceannt – I have been lame a while and unable to walk
> to the bus which connects with Belfast. Farming is great struggle and
> government inspectors interfering and ordering. I am near Slemish and often
> think of St Patrick as herds' boy. We have great herds of swine.[95]

In the final decade of her life Milligan's work was celebrated nationally and locally.
Queen's University, Belfast started the proceedings when the literary department
honoured Milligan's work as a poet. In an interview at the university she took the
opportunity to point out the Irishness of the Belfast she had grown up in:

> Miss Alice Milligan said that in her schooldays Belfast was definitely a more
> Irish city than Dublin. That had been changed by the resurgence of the
> Gaelic language and institutions in Dublin. For the last hundred years the
> Irish language and traditions were taught and studied in Belfast: one striking
> difference she noted – in the north one had to answer the arguments of
> living people: in the South the unanswerable argument was a quotation
> from Emmet or Davis.[96]

In July 1941, the National University of Ireland awarded her an Honorary Doctorate at Iveagh House in Dublin. The degree was conferred by Éamon de Valera and the president of University College Dublin, Denis Coffey, gave an address in which he reflected on Milligan's important intervention in the early Revival movement:

> She was a pioneer in many fields, tireless in energy, and absorbed in the love of Ireland. She worked for years, both in prose and verse in the widely read journals of Arthur Griffith. At the outset of the Irish dramatic revival, she wrote several plays including *The Last Feast of the Fianna*, which were staged by the National Literary Theatre, the forerunner of the Abbey Theatre. She gave exceptional work to the Gaelic League, lecturing under the auspices of the League throughout Ireland on Irish history, and her Lantern Talks and *Tableaux Vivants* are well remembered in aiding the movement for national culture ... While inspired by her ideals to associate with the political movements of the time in Ireland, it can be truly said her propagandist efforts were devoid of bitterness and the partisan spirit ... No future record of the relations of Irish literature with the history of Ireland in those fifty years can fail to commemorate the ... poetry of this distinguished Ulster lady.[97]

The portrait painter Seán Sullivan (1906–64) honoured his friend in a different way by sketching a picture of her (this remains one of the few images of Alice Milligan).

In May 1942, a group of Milligan's friends (including writer Helena Concannon) began to collect subscriptions for a fund they intended to present to her with a selection of poems they wanted to collect:

> While she is still alive we think something should be done to show appreciation of her work. We feel there is a more definite obligation on us of making to her some return however slight, for a lifetime's work that brought no income, no royalties, but left her much poorer in worldly goods.[98]

But by October the project was abandoned due to the time-consuming and difficult task of actually tracing Milligan's extensive output: Milligan's work was published over six decades in the unindexed pages of at least fifty different newspapers and journals:

> It was proposed to publish by subscription a collection of her poems. We much regret we do not find that feasible at present. There is the difficulty of collecting the poems. Miss Milligan has been writing for over fifty years and

has kept no copies of her work, not even records of the time and place of publication, so indifferent was she to self interest. There is now the added difficulty of paper shortage.[99]

The following year the subscriptions that were not returned were given to Milligan as a presentation at the Tyrone feis in Omagh. Milligan was privately embarrassed and annoyed by the event: she didn't like money being raised for her when she had spent so much of her life fundraising for others; nor did she like the idea of receiving charity from those people who she considered to be her political enemies. Milligan named the Fine Gael politician Richard Mulcahy as one of her opponents not least because he had supported the Treaty in the Irish Civil War. Milligan described to Lily O'Brennan how uneasy she felt at being presented with a cheque for £150 at the feis: 'In recognition of services in past – it is in a way upsetting and puzzling to me, as an enthusiastic cleric went round collecting this without my knowledge and from all and sundry including people ... I am most definitely opposed to.'[1] After the feis Milligan immediately donated the money to the election funds.

Towards the end of her life the commemorations continued. In 1949 her brother Ernest gave an illustrated lecture about his sister's career to the London Irish Literary Society. Seamus MacManus published *We sang for Ireland* in 1951, a volume of poetry by Milligan, Anna Johnston and himself. It was a homage to the women who had produced the *Shan Van Vocht* in 1890s Belfast. The gold and green bound copy of the complete journal gifted by Anna Johnston to Seamus MacManus on their wedding day in 1899 can be read in the National Library of Ireland. MacManus had played a vital role in promoting the journal in America. In 1950 Milligan moved out of Eleanor Boyd's farmhouse in Co. Antrim to a cottage in Tycur, Co. Tyrone where she lived with two elderly sisters. In her diary for January 1892 Milligan had ominously written: 'I made my will':[2] she probably could not envisage then that she would not need such a document until April 1953 when she died aged 87. (In fact, she would not need the document of a will at all: at the end of her life Alice Milligan had no personal belongings, savings, or property of her own.) The *Irish Times* reflected that despite the intense political and sectarian conflicts in Ireland, Milligan had managed to achieve 'an honourable synthesis' in her cultural work:

> Poetry and politics have little liking for each other's company. The politician who turns to verse, and the poet who turns to propaganda, frequently find that they are making the worst of both worlds. Alice Milligan showed that an honourable synthesis was possible. Her political idealism and literary achievement were interlocking expressions of a forthright and withal sensitive personality.[3]

11 Alice Milligan at Draperstown Feis, in County Tyrone, *c.*1946. Photograph in papers of Sheila MacAleer, a school teacher who visited Milligan in the 1930s and 40s.

Not long after Milligan died, a friend who had been storing some of Alice Milligan's papers since the IRA threat of the early 1920s, wrote to Ernest Milligan urging him to write a biography of his sister.[4] In her letter Molly Killeen told some of this story herself and in doing so provided a snapshot of the years from 1917 to the early 1950s. She writes about how Milligan often took away books from the house to raise funds for political prisoners and their families. She also noted that Milligan's support for de Valera was limited after he was elected to government in 1932. As a radical female activist and a full-time carer, Milligan would have struggled to accept the limited political space imagined for Irish women by de Valera and his administration. The letter makes clear that although Milligan herself did not support the Treaty, she could understand the position of those (like Killeen herself) who did. Finally, she puts to rest the assumption that Milligan would not talk to Irish publishers Gill & Co. about the publication of a selection of her poems because Richard Mulcahy had been involved in helping to raise funds for the project:

> Time after time she took away letters and books. Some she told me she sold
> to give money to the defence cuts of 1916 men, for extra, they had small

allowances. Your brother [Charles Milligan] spoke of her 'lame ducks' but I knew none. We accepted Treaty. A. M. [Alice Milligan] said Owen Roe and O'Neill would have done so, but she was a republican. She came and stayed, as usual, but there was not just the same freedom. She followed De Valera with enthusiasm, but after he went in to the Dail though she attended government functions, – (came to garden party in Park), she kept closely in touch with the remnant who stayed outside. Trouble there also, some in jail, and their dependents had no public funds. It all disturbed her, but she was in touch with these, she told me she had trouble at border with letters and books – at Mountfield there she meant to keep on room to house her belonging. She had some objectionable evacuees. She came directly to me when rid of them. I forget she was down again when she found friends wanted to make presentation … one lady friend had sent her direct cheque for £100. She went to return it. No truth in story that she refused poems to be published because Richard Mulcahy had subscribed – they were all really token subscriptions – but she knew his name was there before she saw Mr Gill.[5]

Without Killeen's letter we would not know that Milligan was aware that an Irish publisher was bringing out a collection of her poems. Indeed, it must have been rewarding for her to know that such an imaginative and comprehensive selection of her poetry was being conceived. The book was published the year after her death in 1954 and remains a most significant tribute to Alice Milligan's life's work: not only were poems collected from many newspapers but her old friend from the National Theatre movement, Henry Mangan, offered readers his invaluable biographical insight into Milligan's long and varied career. The book was in part financed by her brother Charles Milligan who supplied £50 for the publication costs and £20 towards clerical support. Ernest Milligan also supplied Mangan with biographical information and literary material for the volume. Both were genuinely delighted with the commemoration to their sister.[6] The publication of the poems in 1954 certainly meant that Milligan's story would not be completely forgotten. It even led to the recording of some of her poems by both Decca Records and Angel Records in New York in the late 1950s. Joseph McBride (John McBride's brother) wrote: 'Her great sense of duty to her country, her family and her friends was unique … she sang of great events as they happened.'[7]

Alice Milligan is rarely mentioned in histories of Ireland, except as a once-off playwright whose brief interlude of fame ended with the Irish Literary Theatre's 1900 production of *The last feast of the Fianna*. As a result of Milligan's relegation to the footnotes of history, the organizations to which she was closely associated went unrecorded for decades. Such non-canonical forms of expression as newspapers and *tableaux vivants*, which were so vital to Milligan's cultural nationalism, have also been ignored in conventional accounts of the renaissance. Whereas Maud Gonne would see herself elevated to the status of a nationalist icon, Milligan was denied such celebrity either in her own lifetime or posthumously. There are tangible reasons why she has proved resistant to cultural canonization, but it is worth stressing that, despite her drive and her accomplishments, Milligan was also remarkably self-effacing. Throughout her career, the concerns of self were consistently subordinated to the broader cause to which Milligan pacted herself. Milligan's public and private work was so committed to national issues as to indicate that she viewed the personal narrative of her own life as the story of Ireland itself. Indeed, she often wrote as though she were not in possession of her own voice – which was given over as an instrument to speak to, and on behalf of, others. To speak of Milligan is to address her unending search for a voice: it was in speaking for the dispossessed of history ('the remnant who stayed outside') that she spoke for herself.

CHAPTER TWO

Revival

This chapter will explore the themes of identity and national belonging in Alice Milligan's earliest publications from 1888 to 1893. Forgotten publications such as *Glimpses of Erin* (1888) and *A Royal Democrat* (1890), form part of a continuum of Milligan's ideas about the limitations of the Home Rule debates, the richness of pre-colonial Irish civilization, the potentials of co-national democratic alliances, and the place of women in Irish society. An unease about the political trajectory of these two books exists, not least because Milligan herself never once mentioned either book after she underwent a political epiphany in 1891. A transformational shift took place in the aftermath of Parnell's death that registered at the level of national consciousness and stimulated a new direction in Milligan's own self-conscious advancement as an Irish cultural practitioner. After the death of Parnell, Milligan began to explore the historical legacy of Protestantism in Ireland through historical fictions such as her unpublished novel, *The Cromwellians*. In so doing, she developed an autobiographical narrative voice (expressed further in poems such as 'When I was a little girl' and 'October ode') which in part sustained (and explained) her own cultural position within the emerging national movement.

This three-part exploration of Alice Milligan's early writings will provide unique insight into the personal journey of a northern Protestant woman as she moves from one community into another. The first section will examine the 1888 travel book that she published with her father; part two will offer a contextual reading of her first (and only) single-authored published novel; while the final section of the chapter will focus on Milligan's reflective re-examination of the legacy of Protestants in Irish history and contemporary culture. It is in these poems, travelogues, diary entries and fictions that we witness the moment Milligan stopped feeling like a non 'native' in the country in which she was born and in which she was living. By 1893, Alice Milligan stops attempting to imagine herself into the mindset of English tourists travelling adventurously around a colony: just as ideas about an 'Irish Renaissance' and national 'Cultural Revival' were starting to circulate, Alice Milligan decided that Ireland was in fact her nation.

Glimpses of Erin

Milligan's first writings appeared at a time when the 'Irish question' was hotly debated as 'the great set piece of Victorian politics'.[1] During the scramble to stake imperial claims all over the world Ireland, Britain's oldest colony, was re-negotiating the terms of her relationship within empire. While recognizing the weight of contrary opinion, the English Liberal Prime Minister, Gladstone, remained convinced that 'purely Irish matters should be dealt with by a purely Irish authority'.[2] Although one of the bill's central recommendations was the re-establishment of an Irish Parliament in Dublin, Gladstone nonetheless asserted that Home Rule 'had no necessary connection with separatism'.[3] Finding this argument difficult to accept, unionists considered Home Rule for Ireland a fatal threat to Britain's imperial solidarity. Gladstone reasoned in *Aspects of the Irish question*, however, that the bill 'aims, in the main, at restoring, not at altering, the Empire'.[4] The leader of the Tory party and Prime Minister from 1886 to 1892, Lord Salisbury, considered the Irish unfit for self-governance, reasoning: 'You would not confide free representative institutions to the Hottentots.'[5]

In *Glimpses of Erin*, Alice Milligan and her father Seaton set out to dispel such comparisons between the Irish and other colonial subjects. *Glimpses of Erin* appeared midway between the defeat of the first Home Rule bill in 1886 and the Parnell split of 1890 that irrevocably fractured the Irish Parliamentary Party. The publication also marked a transitional period for Milligan herself: the book was written on her return to Belfast from studying English history and literature at King's College, London and just before she embarked on her momentous trip to Dublin in 1891 (via a year teaching in Derry). The timing of the book in relation to the Home Rule debates is significant because of the extreme political views that had become current and that were in part provoked by the bill. In a sectarian discourse that would be later reanimated in the lead-up to Partition in the early 1920s, the Irish National League attempted to disprove the assumption that 'the Protestants of Ulster are all opposed to Home Rule'.[6] They argued that Ulster 'is not a Protestant province, but a province containing Protestant majorities in its north-eastern corner and Catholic majorities almost everywhere else'.[7] In 1886 the Irish Loyal and Patriotic Union emphasized a comparable religious and political division. In one of their pamphlets *Irish public opinion on Home Rule*, the Irish public was exclusively defined as the various sections of the Protestant church.[8]

The community of 51,000 Methodists in Ireland (of which the Milligans were a part) offered a united opposition to Home Rule throughout the 1880s:

> We would deplore any steps which might be taken, either by the government or by legislature, which would weaken the bonds which unite this country

with Great Britain, and which would tend to the legislative independence of Ireland – a measure which, in our judgement, would be fraught with evil to the best interest of the United Kingdom.[9]

To counter the view that all Protestants opposed the bill, the Quaker Fabian activist, Alfred Webb, published a pamphlet entitled, *The opinions of some Protestants regarding their Irish Catholic fellow-countrymen.*[10] Those included in his survey insisted that they were not afraid of a parliament that would give Catholics pre-eminence. In the same pamphlet the Protestant nationalist and writer Charlotte Grace O'Brien noted that the Catholics she encountered were always very tolerant of their Protestant counterparts, and claimed that: 'I have never known any authenticated instances of religious intolerance' expressed on behalf of Catholics against Protestants in Ireland.[11] Alice Milligan and her father never renounced their Protestantism, but they did offer a more nuanced political radicalism which challenged the historical loyalism of Methodists in Irish history.

In *Glimpses of Erin* they argued that Ireland was differentiated from other colonized peoples and spaces by its geographical propinquity to England but also by the longevity of the colonial relationship. As such, they suggest that Ireland's geographical proximity to England should qualify it for preferential treatment.[12] Invoking Dickens' novel *Bleak House* (1853), they compare Ireland to Mrs Jellaby's neglected and unruly children. Preoccupied with the children of the empire, Mrs Jellaby ignores the needs of her own offspring. This analogy enables the authors to characterize the 'great English Empire' as an actual 'home':

> England would be as neglected as the home of Mrs Jellaby if Englishmen took an interest in 'all sorts of men and conditions of men', and forget to take a special interest in the sort of men and women that are nearest to them.[13]

The authors do not extend the ideological metaphor of the Irish as children or the empire as 'home' beyond their introductory remarks. Instead, they develop a visual metaphor for the individual character and history of the Irish that makes them deserving of such 'special interest'. A New York magazine in the early months of 1888 published a photograph depicting 'the face of America'. In Ireland, the Milligans suggest, such a technological experiment would have no meaning because the Irish cannot be so easily unified in one national identity: 'The features of some sixty or seventy persons were blended into one face which had in it something of them all … It would be impossible on this principle to give a picture of the average Irishman.'[14]

The ideas expressed by the Milligans formed part of a very contemporary debate about how individual nations might realize their separate identities within the colonial structures of empire. Conceiving of Ireland as merely one of numerous colonies within an 'enormous political fabric', Gladstone envisaged the empire as comprising 'a multitude of subalternate integers'.[15] He maintained that the permanence and solidity of the empire would be strengthened if the Irish were charged with the governance of their own 'subaltern structure'.[16] In defining the Irish as a country made up of individuals whose faces cannot be sublimated into one international body, the Milligans suggest that the Irish should not be considered by Gladstone as merely another 'subalternate integer'.

Glimpses of Erin came out of Seaton and Alice Milligan's joint membership of the Belfast Naturalist Field Club, an organization that promoted interdisciplinary research into the natural landscapes of Ireland (and of the north, in particular). Sean Lysaght comments on the northern rootedness of the organization whose members 'had been enthusiastically engaged in exploring the wildlife, plants, and antiques of the north-east since the foundation of the club in 1863, and there were still many virgin fields for botanical exploration in the 1880s'.[17] Clive Hutchinson claims that the northern regional focus of the group on the corner of Ireland most inhabited by Protestant unionists intensified in the late nineteenth century in revolt against the growing independence movement: 'as the demand for Home Rule grew throughout the country, the middle classes centred their scientific interests more and more on Ulster and looked less to the remainder of the island of Ireland'.[18]

Alice Milligan, like John Millington Synge, was an active participant and prominent member of the Naturalist Field Club from the mid-1880s. Her diary entry for August 1892 gives some insight into how members on a trip from Belfast to Carrickfergus were encouraged to examine and scrutinize everything from archaeological finds, library holdings, to railway scales. The group first visit the new free library (opened in 1888) where 'we inspected the collection'. When they reached the train station 'we inspected the weighing machine'.[19] The north (including counties Sligo and Donegal) is the focal point of the tours outlined in *Glimpses of Erin*, however, this is less an attempt to regionally shut off the north from the rest of Ireland than an opportunity to recontextualize these areas within Irish national history and culture. The authors use travel to connect the north with the rest of Ireland, forging links between the local and the national.

The pronouns denoting authorship throughout the book are very flexible: the collective 'we' is occasionally replaced with 'the writer' when Seaton Milligan speaks from private experience as a commercial traveller or when he makes reference to his own private archaeological finds. Similarly, the poetry by Alice Milligan that appears throughout the book is attributed specifically to her and signed 'A. L. M' (Alice Leticia Milligan). But on the whole, the book reflects the involvement of both father and daughter with the Belfast Naturalist Field Club; it articulates their interest in developing Irish commerce, and announces their mutual wish to make a thoughtful intervention into the future prospects and status of Ireland. Five years after the publication of *Glimpses of Erin*, Alice Milligan and Seaton Milligan would again work together when they gave their active support to Lady Aberdeen's Irish Industries committee. After 1895 Alice Milligan developed a radical nationalism at which point she became less involved in the Belfast Naturalist Field Club (although she continued to review the cultural activities of the group for various newspapers throughout the 1890s). Her politics by the mid-1890s were very different from her father's constructive unionism and she would later denounce Lady Aberdeen in the pages of *Sinn Féin* as a colonial philanthropist. In contrast, Seaton Milligan's position changed little and he continued to publish on archaeology and landscape conservation through to his death in 1916.

While their paths certainly divided along political lines, father and daughter were always culturally aligned.[20] They shared a mutual interest in Irish history; they collected manuscripts and books and created photographs and magic lantern slides for the Belfast archaeology societies. These images were often used by Seaton Milligan for his public lectures (to the Royal Irish Academy, for instance); the same slides were then reinterpreted by Alice Milligan in her theatre and Gaelic League work. It is significant that the same images could be rendered for very different audiences in very different locations: in a way, this is precisely the radical space that Milligan activated through visual culture (photographs or tableaux). Images were open to interpretation by multiple audiences from different linguistic, ethnic, religious, gender and political backgrounds. They could therefore connect simultaneously with the individual as well as the broader community.

Glimpses of Erin is a work that is hard to classify in terms of genre: it is presented as a travel book aimed at an English market, yet the three tours they detail are confined to the 'appendix' that is published after a lengthy educational tour through eleven chapters on Irish national cultural history. The book contains an introduction, nine chapters on the history of Ireland from 'Ancient civilisation' to 'Ireland under the Stuarts'. The nineteenth century, Irish education and cultural life are dealt with in the final two chapters of the book under the headings 'Sketches of country life' and 'Learning and culture'. The extensive appendix, 'Tours off the beaten track', is divided into three sections: 'Sligo and the West', 'The Antrim Coast and the wilds of Donegal' and 'The Gap of Mamore,

Innishowen'. Thirty-two pages of advertisements which book-end the text assure readers that they can buy anything in Ireland, stay anywhere, travel comfortably, swiftly and safely ('No feeling of fear need deter even the most nervous from visiting scenery as beautiful as any in Europe')[21] across large areas of terrain. The book is richly illustrated with maps and drawings of places, artefacts, and people.

Poetry is given a unique status in the Milligans' reconstruction of Ireland's history and culture: quotations from Irish poetry preface chapters. Irish poems are printed in full at the end of chapters where they further texture the histories that precede them. The works by Irish writers are also used as archival evidence to support historical and archaeological finds discussed by the authors. John O'Donovan's poetic translations from ancient manuscripts, for instance, are included as evidence that pre-colonial Ireland was not a land of savages or barbarous 'half-naked people':[22]

> This poem is of extreme interest, as it shows the country 1,200 years ago was Christian and well governed; that historians existed who recorded the truth; that people were brave and warlike, and had all the necessaries of life in abundance.[23]

The Milligans' only reproduce and quote from poetry by Irish poets such as Oliver Goldsmith (1730–74), Samuel Ferguson (1810–86), Thomas Moore (1779–1852), John Savage (1828–88) and Aubrey De Vere (1814–1902). In her next book, Alice Milligan quotes Irish, English and American poets at the start of each chapter to demonstrate the three places most central to the Irish political struggle.

In *Glimpses of Erin* Alice Milligan's own poetry is set amidst lavish drawings and woodcuts, the works of other Irish poets, stories from Irish history, maps of national transport networks, and pages of illustrated advertisements. Such rich and varied contexts would be replicated for the literature that Milligan published in the busy pages of Irish newspapers for the next six decades of her life. Her seven ballads and poems published in *Glimpses of Erin* deliver an alternative (and often specifically female) version of events. Poems from the 1888 edition are: 'The vision of St Granuaille', 'The Lord of Dunluce', 'Mary Bannan. A night scene of '98', 'Wexford Bridge. A story of '98', 'Doonie Rock', 'Lord Edward's wife', 'The lament of Niamh' and 'A valley in Innishowen'. As we shall see, her poem 'Ode to political tourists' was in direct dialogue with specific passages in the section entitled 'Off the beaten track' in which the authors denigrate this limited mode of touristic engagement.

When the prose narrative in *Glimpses of Erin* does not provide enough information to introduce the poems, Alice Milligan explains the historical or legendary contexts in short prefaces. Explanatory prefaces and detailed footnotes were a characteristic of Milligan's democratic approach to the publication of poetry from the late 1880 through to the 1940s, especially when it appeared in newspapers. Explaining the historical, political or mythological background to her poems was an educational courtesy to the reader. As Gavan Duffy pointed out in 1892, a key aim of the Revival was to make available (cheaply) the Irish history, legend and literature that remained 'out of print, or locked up in costly editions'.[24] *Glimpses of Erin*'s celebration of Irish writers offers an early contribution to this project. But as an educationalist and a trainee teacher, Milligan did not assume knowledge from her readers and she aimed to involve the public as much as possible in the process of learning and understanding.

'The lament of Niamh' is introduced in *Glimpses of Erin* by a short preface in which Milligan explains the story that has inspired her poem:

> A beautiful Irish legend tells how Ossian, warrior and poet of the Fenian band, went, after the death of his son Oscar, to live in the land of Youth Tir na nÓg with Niamh, a fairy lady. At length he was seized with a longing to return to his native land, and Niamh bade him farewell, warning him not to dismount from his fairy steed, else he could never return. Ossian found that all his old companions were dead, and everything changed in Erin. In a moment of forgetfulness, he dismounted from his steed, which plunged into the sea, and swam away, leaving the warrior poet.[25]

Milligan's 1888 poem about Ossian and Niamh significantly predates the publication of Yeats' *The wanderings of Oisín* (1889) and reveals how both writers were preoccupied with the same material in the late 1880s. The Ossianic tales would have been of particular interest to both Yeats and Milligan because of the pre-Christian setting of the legend. The story of Oisín was absolutely vital to Milligan's cultural work and it was a narrative that she returned to again and again throughout her career. After 1898, she viewed Oisín's renewed commitment to Irish political consciousness as an essential metaphor for cultural Revival. The dialogic exchanges between St Patrick and Oisín were, in Milligan's opinion, the earliest example of drama in Ireland; a theory she developed in both textual argument and in practice. Her Ossianic trilogy of plays was published in newspapers and staged by Yeats as part of the Irish Literary Theatre's repertoire, as well as by Gaelic League groups as choreographed tableaux shows. In the latter, the three plays of the trilogy merge into one play about memory and national belonging: as Oisín tells St Patrick the story of his life, his memories of the past were visualized through live still 'pictures' performed on an inner stage behind a gauze curtain.

Just as Alice and Seaton Milligan drew upon the work of Irish poets to illustrate their arguments in *Glimpses of Erin*, so the history they narrate is similarly taken from publications by Irish scholars, historians and translators: these include John Patrick Prendergast, John O'Donovan, Eugene O'Curry, George Stokes' lectures at Trinity College Dublin, Charles Wright, Margaret Stokes, Thomas Caulfield Irwin, William Carleton, and Geoffrey Keating. They source further material in Irish journals such as the *Dublin Penny Journal* and the *Ulster Journal of Archaeology*. In using the work of Irish intellectuals (many of whom were their near contemporaries) and by citing the most up-to-date lectures and journal articles produced in Ireland, the Milligans demonstrate that Irish learning is not just a thing of the past but a living dynamic of the country: 'when other nations in Europe … were in a state of barbarism, Ireland had a system of education which deserves the admiration of modern days'.[26] Their project in enlightening an English readership about Irish scholarship and writings is reminiscent of Charlotte Brooke's preface to *Reliques of Irish poetry* published in 1789 in which she argued that the English administration and settlers in Ireland had much to learn from ancient Irish literature and poetry: 'The British muse is not yet informed that she has an elder sister in this isle; let us then introduce them to each other.'[27]

Similarly, the economic deprivation of late nineteenth-century Ireland is located within the historical legacy of colonial legislation that, the authors suggest: 'destroyed the rising industries'.[28] In fact, many of the views that Alice Milligan would later express about the economic failures of the Union in promoting trade in Ireland, have their foundation in this early work. In *Glimpses of Erin* the Milligans argue that 'commercial prosperity in Ireland would go towards solving the vexed land question'.[29] Another dimension of the land problem is the endless waves of emigration:

> There is a continual selection of the fittest going on in the country, and the best of our strength and intelligence and commercial enterprise goes to enrich the colonies or foreign countries … wealth is lost to this country in the person of emigrants.[30]

The destructive rigidity of an imposed class system is considered to be a key impediment to economic prosperity in Ireland because it divided society into three classes: the gentry, the middle class (made up of farmers and business people), and the working classes. The gentry are 'like Royalty' represented in Ireland 'by deputy' and are known only as 'collectors of rent'.[31]

The authors offer interpretations about why 'this wide distinction between classes' has become so extreme: 'one is the absence of wealth among business people. Wealth is a leveller of the difference of birth, more so than education or personal worth.'[32] In Alice Milligan's first novel, published in 1890, the class system is one of the first things a newly arrived visitor to Ireland notices: 'Cormac was astonished to see class distinction so rigidly observed.'[33] Arguing that this class system is detrimental to the development of Irish industries, the authors of *Glimpses of Erin* propose that the construction of manufacturing towns across Ireland would generate wealth as well as stem the tide of emigration. Irish cities such as Belfast and Cork, they complain: 'are lacking in many of the advantages found in English towns of smaller size'.[34] They envisaged that the manufacturing towns in Ireland could generate a national market for Irish goods and increase local economies:

> Commercial prosperity in Ireland would go far towards solving the vexed land question, by decreasing the competition for farms, and giving some occupation in their own country to those who, failing to get land, go to Australia or America. A market would be created for agricultural produce at home among commercial and manufacturing classes, and the endless agrarian disputes and outrages would cease with the struggle for a bit of ground … So while appreciating the good points in agricultural life, we should desire to see in this country more manufacturing towns.[35]

Tourism on the surface is the key economic idea in Ireland's regeneration endorsed in *Glimpses of Erin*. But the tourism which the Milligans promote is not the kind in which the Irish 'perform' national stereotypes for 'their lords and masters'.[36] Their ideal is a tourism which is historically and culturally informed and which is not destructive or exploitative of either the landscape or the people. While tourism is vital to Ireland, the Milligans are determined to identify the kinds of tourists that they do not want. These include those who cannot respect the land they visit:

> An English tourist, we are sorry to state, was recently found by the resident clergyman [of St Columbcille, Drumcliffe] trying to hammer a piece off the cross to put with his geological specimens.[37]

This example is also a coded reference to the colonial attitude of the English who collect indigenous artefacts from the colonies for their museums and private collections at home.

The other kind of tourists that the Milligans wish to discourage are 'political tourists'. On their final excursion the authors are accompanied by two English women who are made to exemplify an especially limited mode of tourist engagement. The women – one nationalist, the other unionist – are described as 'political tourists' whose 'sympathies were with different political parties and the object of each was to convert the other'.[38] The authors scorn such overtly political discourse and its foregrounding of the terminology of land war and conflict: 'such words as "rent", "arrears", "eviction", "outrages", "coercion"'. On their visit the 'political tourists' read scenery through its political connotations. Lough Swilly, site of the 'Flight of the Earls' in 1607 and the place where Theobald Wolfe Tone was arrested after a naval battle in 1798, becomes a divided referent which signifies opposing ideological and historical meanings for the women:

> Then the Nationalist lady, looking back to Lough Swilly, would wax eloquent in historical allusions, whilst her companion, pointing to the ships of the British fleet then in the Lough, would talk about the Spanish Armada, and calculate how far the guns of the *Devastation* could carry. The presence of these ships seemed to exercise a disturbing influence on the mind of the Nationalist, and it was noticed that she was more cheerful when at length they were hidden from sight.[39]

The unionist celebrates the arrest of Tone, while the location evokes the political memory of defeat for the Nationalist.

Alice Milligan directly continues this theme in her 1888 poem 'Ode to political tourists'[40] in which she mocks those who visit Ireland simply to reaffirm previously formed opinions. In tight rhyming couplets, Milligan analyzes the limited possibilities allowed by the dichotomous politics of the unionist–nationalist debate. This group of visitors to Ireland are treated far more harshly than in *Glimpses of Erin*, partly because in prose they are depicted as two slightly comical women. The authors find a suitably trivial and inoffensive means to end the political rift between the two female travellers. While taking tea in a cottage the women are served from a pot decorated by a picture of the leader of the Irish Parliamentary Party:

> Peace was declared between the politicians as they enjoyed the comfortable meal, although we felt nervous for a moment when pretty Mary Doherty put on the table a cream jug, ornamented by a not too flattering likeness of Mr Parnell. Our Nationalist, smiling gently, asked the Unionist if she would take both sugar and cream. 'Both', the latter replied curtly, and the subject dropped.[41]

In contrast, Alice Milligan renders the 'political tourists' in her poem as generalized voices of English party politics. As an antidote to fixed or partisan perspectives, Milligan suggests that unionists should take the role of the Liberals while the nationalists perform as Tories. Milligan envisages that Home Rule would eventually be won by the Tories and opposed by the Liberals as Gladstone urges his supporters to 'vote *against* a Home Rule bill'. The poem highlights the simplistic divisions which mark alliances in British politics and fix the limits of the Irish question:

> If any one would know the truth about the Irish question,
> He'd better see the other side & follow my suggestion:
> Let Tories to the tenants go, and listen to their story,
> And Liberals from landlords learn tales of outrage gory.
> Then what a change will come across the spirit of the scene,
> And in the House of Commons naught will be as it hath been.
>
> (lines 17–22)

There is a self-conscious and sophisticated duality at the centre of *Glimpses of Erin*: it is written by two authors of two different genders and generations; it is written in two different genres (poetry and prose); it is marketed to the English yet it speaks directly to the Irish; it is published in both England and Ireland.[42] It is speaking to two audiences from different perspectives at the very same time: it at once seems to be an attempt to honour the English with a 'Patriotism that has gone out of fashion', yet at the same time the narratives empower the Irish. There is also a doubleness in the stories told by the authors in which they imply things without actually saying them. For instance, the Milligans are careful to show that the extensive presence of local constabulary at Orange processions in the north is 'of course' simply part of their official duties to police such parades:

> Troops of the Irish constabulary often swell the ranks of the party procession. They are there, of course, on duty; but they improve the appearance of the turnout as they march along guns on shoulder.[43]

In other parts of the book, the authors ventiloquize ideas that they could not overtly claim as their own through the opinions expressed by others. They quote the words of an unidentified curate to voice a radical view about the elimination of sectarian marches across the north: 'An Ulster curate … urged toleration' and suggested that 'the destruction of all orange flags and drums in the waters of the historic stream'[44] would be a fitting way to mark the two hundredth anniversary of the Battle of the Boyne.

The authors claim to be able to 'talk calmly' about key moments of colonial occupation that predate the Act of Union in 1800 when the Irish Parliament was dissolved by England. Yet they nevertheless take the opportunity to dispute dominant Anglo-centric interpretations of earlier periods. While the large-scale massacre of Protestants in 1641 is controversially dismissed by the Milligans as propaganda, the atrocities perpetrated against the Irish by Cromwell are not disputed but highlighted: 'The English soldiers sent against the rebels were unpardonably cruel.'[45] Rejecting Thomas Carlyle's heroic portrayal of Cromwell, they note: 'Such was the work performed in Ireland by Cromwell whom some regard as the apostle of liberty.'[46] The authors grant English policy makers 'the benefit of the doubt' but only after the injustices ('wars, rebellions, ill feeling on the part of the governed') have been articulated. These injustices, they state, were 'brought about by government officials, who perhaps meant all for the best'.[47] The 'perhaps' in this sentence gives enough room for doubt on the part of the Irish and for the authors to simultaneously introduce the idea of reconciliation. They suggest that the colonial experience (once acknowledged) opens up a space for more progressive relations:

> Many of the causes of Ireland's misfortunes have disappeared; others are disappearing. She may hope to live in friendship with England, and share in the welfare of that great country.[48]

As Methodists the authors view this desired 'friendship' with England in distinctly religious terms: 'She may hope to realise the words of Scripture, addressing to another nation unfortunate as she: – "lift up thine eyes round about and see: all they gather themselves together, they come to thee."'[49]

Most revealing, perhaps, is the limited subject position that the authors assign to the English who are relegated from rulers to 'tourists'. Ireland is not presented as a tourist resort for English visitors but as a country with a distinct history, culture and possible economically prosperous future. The position of the English in Ireland is dictated to them by the authors: 'We feel … they wish'. In reducing the English to mere 'tourists', the authors indirectly point out how absurd it is for an ill-informed, non-present electorate to hold a major stake in Irish affairs:

> The greater number of those who, at elections, take some share in deciding Ireland's fate, have not time or means to spend in travelling even to such a short distance.[50]

While the book at first seems to be marketed to the English, it is also a book that is speaking directly to an Irish audience. This duality is expressed almost through code.

> ^ 'I well remember meeting a woman of the
> type I have described, Singing a lament for
> the Death of Charles Stewart Parnell.
> And at the time of the Phoenix park
> tragedies, when Vengeance had been done on
> the informer I heard a ballad Singer
> come up the street ~~with triumphant~~
> ~~cl—~~ of Bundoran in Co Donegal
> with triumphant shout, announcing
> to the whole world
>   Now Carey's flat in his cocked hat
> He's in a warm corner.
> I hope no harm will come to the arm
> That Slew the base informer
>
> O Donnell brave he shot the knave
> He done his work right well Sir,
> And let us ~~all~~ now, rejoice for him
> He sent him off to Hell Sir

12 Extract from lecture notes recalling Carey ballad sung in Donegal in 1882.

A consciousness about secrecy runs through the book: the authors intend to show only 'glimpses of Erin' to the English, not the whole place. The character of the Irish cannot be viewed in a single photographic image, nor can a country be understood by a single visit or within a single book. Although it is introduced as a travel guide to promote a greater sense of political responsibility in the English, the book often speaks more directly to the Irish themselves. The Milligans are careful about who they are speaking to and mindful about what they say. Their allusion to the Irish spy, James Carey, is significant in establishing the necessity of code in Irish speech and public space. Carey was a republican activist who helped organize the assassinations of English government officials in 1883. He turned Queen's evidence during the trial at which he revealed the identity of 'the Invincibles' who had

carried out the Phoenix Park murders. Carey emigrated to set up a new life in
Australia where he was murdered by an Irish immigrant labourer, Patrick
O'Donnell, who had tracked him down. In *Glimpses of Erin* the authors reflect how
quickly the story was re-animated through popular street ballads:

> But politics are dangerous, as the minstrel sometimes finds to his cost.
> Once, shortly after the death of the informer Carey, when Patrick
> O'Donnell's trial was going on, we saw a crowd round a woman who was
> singing a ballad on the subject. It began in the usual way –
>
> 'Good people all, give ear to me,'
>
> And so on. The last verse ran thus: –
>
> 'O'Donnell brave, he shot the knave,
> And done his work right well;
> I hope no harrum will come to the arum
> That sent the knave to – ,'
>
> well, to use Carey's own euphemism, 'removed' him to another place. As the
> sale of the ballad was commencing, a censor of the press appeared on the
> scene in the shape of a stalwart policeman, who scattered the crowd right
> and left, and 'removed' the singer.[51]

This exact incident was recalled over ten years later in a lecture to the London
Irish Folk Song Society by Alice Milligan's sister, the musician Charlotte Milligan
Fox who also must have been present with the family in Donegal in 1882:

> At the time of the Pheonix Park tragedies, when vengeance had been done
> on the informer I heard a ballad singer come up the street of Bundoran in
> County Donegal with triumphant shout, announcing to the whole town:
>
> 'No Carey's flat in his cocked hat
> He's in a warm corner
> I hope no harm will come to the one
> That slew the base informer
> O'Donnell brave he shot the knave
> He done his work right well sir
> And let us now, rejoice for how
> He sent him off to hell, Sir.'

But this was a case calling for the interference of the public censor in the
shape of a stalwart policeman who promptly seized the sheaf of printed
ballads – they were scattered to the wind.[52]

13 Woodcut illustration of Alice Milligan and her father traveling through Donegal, from *Glimpses of Erin*, 1888.

That Patrick O'Donnell was immediately hailed as a hero in song is not surprising. Under the banner 'Events from the Old World' the *New York Times* reported the response of the leader of the Irish National Party to the murder of Carey: 'Mr Parnell … said that the Irish should rejoice that the justice denied by the government had at last been accomplished.'[53] Carey also features as a reference point in Alice Milligan's next book in which an Irish character warns the disguised English King that his spying (however well intentioned) will never be acknowledged by the nationalist community in Ireland: 'They wouldn't of course allow a monument to your memory into Glasnevin; for amongst the people for whom you are going to die you will be considered another Carey.'[54] The events of the early 1880s formed part of the popular cultural memory that James Joyce later activated in the consciousness of his fictional characters.[55] As Luke Gibbons has pointed out James Carey springs to Bloom's mind in *Ulysses* (1921) when he suspects that another character in the book, Corny Kelleher, is actually a secret agent working for the British colonial administration in Dublin Castle. Gibbons suggests that even in thinking about Carey, Bloom is careful not to give him just one name: 'Never know who you're talking to. Corney Kelleher he has the Harvey Duff in his eye. Like that Peter or Denis or James Carey that blew the gaff on the Invincibles.'[56]

This doubleness in *Glimpses of Erin* is represented as part of the Irish character. On the one hand the authors insist that English 'tourists should lose no opportunity of speaking to the people or of seeing their houses'.[57] Yet there is no guarantee that the linguistic and ideologically bilingual exchanges witnessed by English visitors will fully translate. The Irish people depicted in the book are capable of 'mourning and merrymaking', 'laughter and "keaning"' at one and the same time.[58] The two codes exist also in language: 'As she chatted, now in Irish, now in English'.[59] The introductory remarks in *Glimpses of Erin* may lead the reader to think that the book is part of an auto-ethnographic project in which the authors will explain the 'manners and customs' of the Irish for the benefit of English voters. Re-evaluating the colonial relationship between the two nations, the Milligans' book seems to restore the bond that the Home Rule debates have weakened. Their representation of Ireland explicitly courts the attention of potential English travellers, inviting them to take a political role in the shaping of a new relationship with Ireland:

> The presence of so many English tourists and visitors in our country is extremely encouraging. We feel that they are interested and sympathetic, and that they wish to understand us honestly, and take their share of government as a responsibility.[60]

But the book is in no way a straightforward travelogue and in taking the English literally 'off the beaten track', the authors steer the reader away from national stereotypes. The central modes of transport used to move their visitors from the main centres of tourism are trains. Alice Milligan was brought up in a family whose livelihood depended upon the railways: Seaton Milligan was a commercial traveller from the early 1860s until 1878 when he was promoted to an executive position in Belfast's first department store.

The tours of the Belfast Naturalist Field Club also made full use of the rail links across Ireland (and Ulster in particular). Alice Milligan herself utilized the railways from the 1890s to develop and strengthen national consciousness: she travelled by train to stage theatre and magic lantern shows within rural communities; she distributed play scripts nationally in the pages of newspapers;

she corresponded with a vast number of cultural and political activists through Ireland's remarkable postal system. Sometimes eight posts a day were delivered across Ireland by trains (and ferries) which meant that Milligan and her generation could write and receive letters almost like we write and receive digital communication. In short, the sophisticated and affordable railway network system in Ireland (replicated in India) made the Irish Cultural Revival a local, national and global movement. As we saw in the last chapter, it was this ease of national travel and communication that Milligan mourned so intensely during the post-Partition years when her mail was censored and the railways dismantled. Citing Ruskin's recent objections to the destruction of English landscapes in broadening the railways across England, the authors of *Glimpses of Erin* point out the democratic value of railways not least because they empowered industrial workers with fast and cheap access to the clean air and pleasures found in rural landscapes:

> Without this convenient and rapid mode of travelling, most dwellers in cities and large manufacturing towns would be quite ignorant of country life and natural beauty. Does it not make the many toilers more happy to be carried quite away from the mill or counting house to the sea, or the lakes, or the hillside in the short space of a Saturday half holiday? Are they not more healthy from breathing the country air, and more content that all the delights are within reach? Be assured that any steam engine which travels between London and some beautiful place by the sea has made more lovers of nature than all Mr Ruskin's grand writing about mists and clouds and sea foam. Nor is the 'iron horse' itself an unlovely object in a landscape.[61]

Workers in *Glimpses of Erin* are mainly women. 'Erin' is of course a feminized landscape but the women depicted in the book are not 'Kate of Kilarney' characters who perform national gendered stereotypes for colonial touristic display. The women who inhabit the cottages Alice and Seaton Milligan visit, are bi-lingual workers whose homes encompass the multiplicity of their Irish identities: they are at once domestic residences and work spaces in which they produce material for the Derry factories. The other two sets of women present in *Glimpses of Erin* are the English unionist and nationalist 'political tourists', and the female personifications that visually represent Erin and Britannia. Doubleness of identity exists even in the visual representations that form part of the book. *Glimpses of Erin* promises the English tourist a voyage into unseen, untrodden and, by implication, uncolonized landscapes. A unique selling point of the book is that the Milligans offer to show their English visitors locations in Sligo, Donegal and Co. Antrim that are not mentioned in any of Thomas Cook's tours or in the

14 Frontispiece of *Glimpses of Erin.*

contemporary travel guides produced by the *Irish Times.*[62] As the book's coy title intimates, the writers are reluctant to reveal the whole body of Erin, exposing only certain seductive areas to the gaze of their English readership. The title itself casts Ireland as an ancient and unfamiliar realm. The introduction is preceded by a graphic frontispiece that appears to serve as a symbolic map of the ensuing discussion. It provides a striking condensation of the idealized relations between England and Ireland seemingly propounded by the Milligans, depicting the female figures of Britannia and Erin amiably shaking hands.

The illustration displays a painstakingly symmetrical ordering: Erin has a harp while Britannia carries a shield and sword; the Irish wolfhound is mirrored by the lion; Britannia's ship finds its counterpart in an ancient round tower and a monastic ruin covered with ivy. Erin is associated with signifiers of history, culture, music and religion, but Britannia has the power of exploration and conquest – defined by motifs that show her to be a voyager, discoverer, conqueror. Britannia's ship is secured to the shores of Ireland by a rope – she can arrive and leave at will, she is a visitor to Ireland and she finds safe harbour there. In turn, Ireland can offer her guest both sanctuary and cultural edification. This image supports the introductory remarks in which the Milligans apparently render Ireland as a gift to its imperial partner, presenting it as a pastoral playground where Britannia's sons and daughters can escape the harsh commercial realities of modernization and urban life: 'all can find some congenial soil in Ireland'.[63] Yet the front of the book offers a very different version of events in which Britannia is completely absent. The decorative cover is dominated by one figure only: Erin standing alone, emblazoned in gold against a deep green background. Again she has her wolfhound and harp but in this image Erin looks as though she might have just waved a friendly (but firm) goodbye to her visitor. On the front cover of *Glimpses of Erin*, the female body is looking out, waving, signalling, gesturing, looking forward, projecting her body out towards an audience, waiting for her glance to be caught by the eyes of those who can read between the lines [Plate 6]. Alice Milligan is another daughter about to strike out: she too is looking forward towards a national future that she will play a significant part in constructing.

A Royal Democrat

Milligan's first novel, *A Royal Democrat* (1890) develops the discussion of the Home Rule issue mobilized through *Glimpses of Erin*. The novel literally begins in the exact location *Glimpses of Erin* ends: the hero of the story, Cormac King, is washed up on Inishowen – the location of the final tour explored by the Milligans in 'Off the beaten track'. Set fifty years in the future, the novel depicts an Ireland that is still firmly bonded to English governance. Milligan is able to side-step the complex and contending discourses of late nineteenth-century Irish politics by placing her characters in a context freed from present constraints. Rather than engaging with the problematic issues of the land wars and Home Rule debates, Milligan constructs an apologia for English monarchical rule in the form of a heroic romance of cultural unification. *A Royal Democrat* centres upon Arthur Cormac, the prince of Wales, who is both heir to the English throne and the product of a complex cultural mix: his father is English, but his mother is of Irish extraction. Combining the blood of Gaelic and English, the prince is able to straddle the cultural divides he discovers in Ireland. Although most at ease among the southern Protestant bourgeoisie, he can also mix with the Irish peasants of the west. Prince Arthur, presented as an exemplary figure of cultural bonding, nonetheless confirms rather than challenges the status quo.

A Royal Democrat explores Prince Arthur's personal crisis when he faces the prospect of inheriting his father's throne, a conflict connected to a broader debate on Ireland's struggle for self-determination. On his return from a tour of the colonies, Arthur is shipwrecked off the west coast of Ireland where he becomes an early Joycean adventurer of Ireland: 'He had been comparing himself with the shipwrecked Ulysses as he sat drying himself under the rock.'[64] Prince Arthur arrives in the west and immediately sheds his identity and becomes the person he wishes to be. The emotional and intellectual journey made by the prince in many ways articulates the new sense of national becoming that Milligan perceives growing in Ireland. In addition, her own personal life is in some ways paralleled by her lead character. Like Milligan, Prince Arthur's formal education has also just come to an end; in the year after this novel was published, Milligan would start on her own political adventures. Dublin in 1891 presented Milligan with a sense of freedom in which she could forge a new identity for herself that was historically rooted but not historically determined. Similarly, Cormac King awakes from his near drowning off Ireland's west coast with a renewed sense of hope: 'He would have a chance of making a way for himself in the world, instead of merely dropping into one ready for him.'[65]

Both *Glimpses of Erin* and *A Royal Democrat* pre-empt how the west will be celebrated by her contemporaries (such as Yeats, Synge and Gregory) as a site of authentic Irishness during the Revival period: a place where the past lives through the modern and where journeys of self-reinvention begin. On arrival in Ireland Prince Arthur discovers not only that his father, the king, has expired but that he himself is presumed to have died at sea. Declaring himself to the world, however, the prince capitalizes upon the misapprehension so that he can free himself from his regal responsibilities and live as an independent man. Echoing the name of the ancient Irish high king Cormac Mac Airt, he poses as Cormac King, a visitor recently arrived from America. Previously fascinated by the role of the Irish Parliamentary Party, Arthur willingly involves himself in the Irish political scene. A series of circumstances leads to his association with a violent land revolt in Derry, after which he is rounded up with other Irish political prisoners and dispatched to London. The prince's life is saved when Nola Shane, his Irish Protestant friend, forwards his private locket to the queen of England. The queen, Cormac's cousin, recognizes the miniature photographs contained within the locket and grants a royal pardon for the prisoners and at the same time concedes Home Rule to Ireland. Cormac chooses not to accept his place as an English king but remains in Ireland with Nola as his wife. At the end of the novel relations between Ireland and England are strengthened on all fronts as prefigured by this national marriage.

Echoing the introductory remarks expressed in *Glimpses of Erin*, the English prince conceives of Ireland as occupying a distinctive place in the British empire by comparison with the other colonies. The aim of his imperial voyage, as Cormac's tutor puts it, is 'to strengthen the attachment to England and to the crown'.[66] Visiting India, Canada, Australia and New Zealand, the Prince plays the role of the pampered and frivolous tourist:

> Our hero was displaying himself to the delighted multitude of the colonies. He attended a ball in an ice palace in Canada, shot tigers in India, and received gorgeous presents from enthusiastic Rajahs. He saw the gold-fields of Australia and the beauties of New Zealand – no colony was forgotten.[67]

Ireland becomes the site of the unconscious or even the preconscious in this novel: rather than being an endorsed part of his official itinerary, the visit to Ireland is an involuntary event. When Cormac arrives there, he is stripped of the signifiers of his colonial authority – his ship, *The Indian Emperor*, is smashed to pieces when it makes contact with Irish soil. After the shipwreck the prince wakes up in the west of Ireland to discover 'His watch had stopped'.[68] History, in this book, cannot be escaped even in a futuristic fiction.

In *Glimpses of Erin* Milligan and her father refrain from overtly charting the 'history' of the period following the 1800 Act of Union. They explain that this part of Ireland's story cannot so readily be consigned to the realm of 'safe' and distant history:

> We promised to abstain from talking politics, and so must not enter into any discussion on the event which followed the '98 rebellion – namely, the Union. On both sides we can talk calmly now about the Plantation of Ulster or the Cromwellian settlement; but it would be impossible in the present day to speak of the union without becoming a politician.[69]

In contrast, Alice Milligan finds a licence to voice her political interpretation of English governance of Ireland from 1829 to 1888 in the fictional context of her prose novel. She begins with an overtly political overview of events that her father would undoubtedly have shied clear of:

> Early in the 19th century, the Roman Catholics of Ireland were freed from the disabilities that up till then had left them at the mercy of a tyrannical Protestant minority. The suppression of trade and manufactures at an earlier period had impoverished the country, and constantly recurring famines thinned the population.[70]

The rise of the Irish Parliamentary Party under Parnell is described as a 'bright ray of hope … cast upon the darkness'; a constitutional politics that has a simultaneous counterpart in the self-defence mechanisms undertaken by the tenants under Michael Davitt's Land League. The non-fictional part of Ireland's 'ancient history' is concluded with an assessment of how nationalist hopes for Home Rule were dashed by the election of 1886 which 'resulted in the return of a Unionist majority'. Under which 'The Coercion Bill was passed, and the struggle between the people of Ireland and the law was commenced ... The struggle went on with unabated fury until 1892.'[71]

Nineteenth-century Irish nationalist politics is fictionalized in the period 1886 to 1894 and relegated as a nightmare of history. The political leaders of Milligan's own time are swiftly erased to make way for an English prince who travels Ireland in disguise, offering political guidance to those he encounters. The second chapter, 'In which we deal with ancient history', describes how the leaders of the Land League and Parliamentary Party were killed, exiled or imprisoned during several waves of revolution after 1892:

> John Dillon fell, shot by an English bullet whilst leading a patriotic band from the mountains of Tipperary to attack the hostile camp. Michael Davitt and William O'Brien were executed, the former being taken off Galway in a ship which had come from America, under his command, with fresh supplies of men and arms. The latter was captured after a gallant campaign in Ulster ... Dr Kane also fell a victim ... The war was suppressed in the other provinces, the last place to yield being Galway, which held out in hope of reinforcements from America. When Michael Davitt was taken on board the ship destined for that city, all hope was lost, and the capital of Connaught surrendered.[72]

This violent intersection between fact and fiction caused consternation in the Irish nationalist press. The brutal treatment of her contemporaries met with unfavourable comment in Belfast's *Irish News*: 'Miss Milligan assumes that the present Irish movement will fail. We hope that the assumption is altogether fiction.'[73] A reviewer in *United Ireland* was affronted by Milligan's dismissive treatment of the Irish Parliamentary Party:

> She has taken the bold step of anticipating, by way of prelude, that an insurrection has broken out in Ireland, and that some leaders of the Irish Parliamentary Party, including the editor of this newspaper [William O'Brien], have been disposed of by the very comfortable process of hanging or shooting – an assumption against which we beg to offer our respectful dissent either as a piece of prophecy or a matter of good taste.[74]

Though members of the Irish Parliamentary Party are eliminated, Milligan's novel is a thinly-veiled critique of the contemporary political scene. Milligan's prose demonstrates how her own political unconscious is already in rebellion. For example, MacNamara takes the role of the constitutional politician Parnell, while Davoren is a surrogate of the more militant figure of Michael Davitt. The Land League is translated into the Liberation League, which similarly offers evicted tenants money for re-housing schemes. The Sunburst Band, led by the American O'Doherty – alias Sir Cahir, is a thinly disguised version of the Fenians – whose flag featured a sun burst. Sir Cahir O'Doherty (1587–1608) was a historically resonant figure who, as the last Gaelic lord of Inishowen, led a rebellion in 1608.

The prince of Wales may consider himself an enlightened democrat, but the futurist Ireland he inhabits is stunted by colonial impediments. For instance, in the novel the period 1894 to 1939 witnesses a repeat of the seventeenth-century plantations and Ireland is devastated by famine. While the appearance of the English monarch is transformed, he continues to promote a conservative agenda to strengthen the bond between England and Ireland. By assuming the role of a paternalistic teacher, Cormac attempts to suppress the influence of the Sunburst Band. In Dublin he is formally employed as a mentor to the son of Mr Shane – a nationalist MP – until a Protestant Home Ruler urges Cormac to become his teacher:

> Come and be my political instructor. I'm awfully ignorant on some points that you seem to know a lot about. You know all about the different socialist theories and you seem to understand the muddle of foreign politics as well as anyone.[75]

As this extract suggests, the novel portrays the Irish as dependent upon instruction and guidance from their enlightened visitor. When Home Rule is eventually bestowed upon them by the benevolent English monarchy, Molly Shane says: 'What if they go on fighting among themselves, just for the fun of it!'[76] – implying that the Irish are constitutionally incapable of ruling their own country.

Cormac not only despises militant activism but also insists that the Irish need not act at all. Whenever the Irish characters protest that violent revolt is the only solution to the continuing eviction and genocide of their race, Cormac attacks their position. Acting as an apologist for colonial policy (and articulating the words suggested for the English in *Glimpses of Erin*), he insists 'English people are ashamed of the wrong they have done you'.[77] In his opinion, Ireland's freedom can only arise from social changes in England: 'There may be a revolution in England soon, there is certain to be at least great agitation. Then Ireland's claims will not be forgotten, for your Irish members are helping England's cause, and through it their own.'[78] Cormac informs his friend Kildare, that the two countries share common enemies against whom they should unite in order to combat: 'England's foes are still those of Ireland, and in my opinion the freedom of the two countries can only be gained by a united effort on the part of both.'[79] The long-term colonial bond between the two countries is utilized by Cormac to highlight their mutuality:

> They have been so long together that the terms of their welfare are now identical, and when the democracies of both countries come to see this, England and Ireland will become friendly, and work together for freedom.[80]

Cormac argues on several occasions that Ireland's fight will be won on the back of English democratic victory 'at home'. Several times unity between 'the English democracy and their Irish allies'[81] is foregrounded in dialogue. But where did Milligan's ideas about such co-national allegiances and shared democracies come from?

As Milligan looked at Ireland fifty years into her future, she looked back fifty years to the Ireland her parents were born into: in *A Royal Democrat*, Ireland in the 1940s is firmly rooted in the language and ideas advocated in the 1840s. The Chartist reform movement, though based in England, was headed by an Irish leadership and boasted a huge Irish membership due to the large numbers of Irish immigrants resident in Britain. The Chartists aimed to further connect the 'English democratic cause and the discontents of Ireland'[82] by inserting a call for the Repeal of the Union into their political manifesto. Terms like 'an alliance of the common peoples of Great Britain and Ireland'[83] that are articulated by characters in *A Royal Democrat* were in frequent use in the 1840s. Furthermore, Cormac's ideas are reminiscent of those propounded by the Irish leader of the Chartists. Feargus O'Connor was the son of an Irish Protestant landlord, who fought with the United Irishmen in 1798 and entered British parliament as an Irish MP in 1833. In Milligan's novel, Cormac suggests that further hardship and suffering by the Irish will direct them to unite with their sympathetic English counterparts. In 1841, O'Connor had argued that only a period of 'Tory rule and coercion' would drive the Irish to solidarity with the English working classes.[84] But whereas O'Connor hoped that further pain would energize a new anger among the Irish that would connect with those similarly oppressed across the water, Cormac King proposes that endurance of hardship (not rebellion) will inspire sympathy from the democrats in England. The novel's conclusion proves Cormac's strategy to be successful.

In the 1840s, pamphlets were produced in Dublin urging the Irish to support the Chartist movement: 'The poor man's cause is the same everywhere'.[85] The Irish secret society known as the Ribbonmen also offered a precedent for the joint democratic alliances evoked by Milligan in *A Royal Democrat*: the secret society in her novel, the Sunburst Band, is in fact an amalgamation of the Fenians and the Ribbonmen. Rachel O'Higgins, the first historian to document the extensive Irish involvement in Chartism, argues that: 'Ribbonism helped strengthen radical and chartist organizations in northern England.'[86] The Irish formed a radical part of the English workforce not least because of the leading roles they took organizing their fellow workers in the English towns and cities that they emigrated to. In giving evidence to a Parliamentary Committee in London, one employer complained how the Irish were always at the forefront of industrial disputes, lockouts and wage negotiations: 'where there is discontent, or a disposition to combine, or turn outs among the work people, the Irish are the leaders, they are the most difficult to reason with and convince on the subject of wages and regulation in factories.'[87]

The Irish in Ireland sought to unify and strengthen their own insurrectionary ideals when radical political upheavals took place across the water. In circumstances similar to those imagined in Milligan's novel, the Ribbonmen, under the leadership of Dublin coal porter Michael Keenan: 'envisaged a countrywide rising against the government and hoped to enlist the cooperation of a section of English Radicals, who were believed to be on the point of revolt should Queen Caroline be convicted of treason.'[88] A magistrate giving evidence to a parliamentary select committee in 1835 also mentioned that the Ribbonmen had plans to set up a monarchy independent of England's, if their national (and inter-national) insurrection was successful:

> Hill Wilson Rowan, a stipendiary magistrate, declared that he had been informed by witnesses that its principle object was 'to overturn the British government in Ireland, to subvert the Protestant religion, to recover the forfeited estates, and, when strong enough, to establish an independent Monarchy in Ireland under Roman Catholic King.'[89]

Ideas about dual monarchy and democratic alliances were historically present for Milligan (particularly in a novel so obsessed with political history and transformation). At a time when there were at least one million Irish immigrants living in England, William Smith O'Brien attempted to align the Young Ireland movement with the Chartists: 'if England has a garrison in Ireland, we too, have a garrison in England'.[90] Cormac King's lead role in Milligan's fiction results in a reverse of this statement. The English garrison in Ireland is fortified by the secret presence of an English monarch who reconstitutes his own relationship with Ireland while striking a bargain on behalf of the English establishment. But just as Feargus O'Connor's move from Ireland to England became a symbol of Irish revolutionary interventionism striking from within the heart of Empire; so in Milligan's novel, Cormac's move from England to Ireland transfers that engine of change from the centre of empire to the peripheries of the colonial outpost.

As soon as he leaves the west and arrives in Dublin, Cormac immediately aligns himself with a conservative constitutional politics. He departs from Inishowen because he 'could no longer hope to restrain the people by his influence'.[91] This section of the novel establishes Cormac's opposition to nationalist radicalism and he begins to spy on the activities of the Sunburst Band. He overhears the owner of the 'Western World' Hotel in Dublin talking proudly about the activities of a Lord Edward Fitzgerald – which he assumes is a code name for one of the members of the Sunburst Band. Fitzgerald is a multiple signifier in the novel: the name at once is code for the leader of the Irish rural discontent, it is the name of the Protestant United Irishman of the 1790s and the name that gives Cormac an Irish lineage. Like the Ribbonmen, the Sunburst Band operates through 'an elaborate system of signs and passwords, which usually took the form of simple questions and answers, accompanied by gestures'.[92] Cormac becomes an agent of the Irish MP MacNamara who comments: 'You have served me well, Mr. King … I hope something will come of your detective work'.[93] After learning about the secret society by spying, Cormac rather hypocritically urges them to forsake 'the old way of secret conspiracy, which is sure to fail'.[94] Cormac argues that physical violence against the new plantations and the continuing evictions is fruitless; like Charles Stewart Parnell's 1887 Westport speech in which he endorsed the Land League, Cormac advocates stoical forbearance: 'hold on without crime, but with pluck and determination, to your homes and fields'.[95]

The novel identifies Cormac repeatedly as 'our hero' – a term that denotes not just his central role in the story but also his status as a figurehead of social and political transformation. When news reaches the Shane household that most of the evicted Irish in the west are supporters of the Sunburst Band, Mike Magennis tells Cormac: 'I wish sir, you had stayed on, for they are all joined to Sir Cahir now.'[96] Nola echoes this sentiment when she asserts that Cormac's presence there could forestall militancy:

> 'I wish you had stayed with them,' said Nola, quietly; 'you would surely have helped them with wiser advice than they are likely to get from that American O'Doherty … How terrible it will be if there are crimes committed that might have been prevented. I wish you had stayed.'[97]

The Protestant Home Rulers with whom King associates regard any form of violent agrarian resistance to the colonial settlers as retrogressive. To quell the uprising, Cormac and Kildare bond together to infiltrate the Irish-American led Sunburst Band and destroy it from within. In fact, the Irish-American O'Doherty (alias 'Sir Cahir'), only gains legitimacy and is allowed his own version of national marriage after he decommissions his weapons and returns to Ireland as a rich and successful businessman. American militant intervention in the Irish conflict is simply not allowed to succeed in this novel: resolution is only achieved by the discreet negotiations among the highest echelons of the English establishment. Cormac considers it his duty to return to his 'peasant friends' and 'save them from shame and the black shadow of foolish crime'.[98] He repeatedly encourages the evicted peasants to move into the mountains, where the presence of so many dispossessed people will elicit the sympathy of the English settlers. As Cormac sees it, social progress is best achieved through emotional and passive protest. The novel records the success of this policy:

> The plan which grew out of their anxiety to prevent murder has been adopted on eviction estates in many parts of Ireland, and has everywhere acted as a safety-valve. The Government is puzzled to know why landlords and planters are so rarely shot now.[99]

The Sunburst Band is so in awe of Cormac's leadership skills that their main organizer, O'Doherty, proclaims: 'With a decent army he might be a new Napoleon, and conquer empires'.[1] O'Doherty and Nola both consider Cormac to be the appropriate leader of the Irish under Home Rule: '"If England rejects him," she thought, "we will have him for our King, and be at last a free and great nation".'[2] For Milligan's Irish characters, a simple exchange between the rulers of the colony and the colonized power is sufficient to secure Ireland a 'place among the nations' of the world.[3] Cormac's unlikely scheme eventually results in the political reforms he envisaged:

> The determined stand made by the Irish tenantry checked the great plantation scheme, and won for them the sympathy of the English democracy ... In the spring of 1948, the Queen consented to open the first Irish Parliament and the gracious Royal pardon was extended to most of the political prisoners.[4]

In the novel, the Irish people are not allowed to achieve Home Rule themselves through constitutional debate or militant activism, but are awarded restricted independence as the result of a secret pact made by the English establishment. The new Irish parliament fortifies the connections between England and its colony – the queen reaffirms an overt monarchical presence and inaugurates regular confidence-building trips to the colony.

Milligan's futurist vision of Ireland is not one in which new technologies magically transform the landscape or the problems encountered by the people who inhabit the land. There are no modernist technologies in Milligan's futurist projections: Ireland in the 1940s is a place where people still move about on carts and trains; warfare is still conducted by 'musketry'; the Irish still fight 'red coats'; and cottages are still burned to the ground as endless sites of brutal evictions. The first cottage that Cormac enters after his shipwreck looks like one of the rural dwellings from *Glimpses of Erin*. The interior walls are decorated with cuttings from newspapers:

> His eye was attracted by some gaudy pictures fastened to the wall … They were not very flattering likenesses of public men – caricatures of the leaders of the Liberals and Tories … Peggy produced some well thumbed back numbers of a weekly national journal, and some more cartoons. 'They're very good, some of them, and they brighten up the place.'[5]

In an 1815 preface to one her novels Lady Morgan claimed that literary fiction has always 'exhibited a mirror of the times in which it was composed; reflecting morals, customs, manners, peculiarity of character, and prevalence of opinion. Thus perhaps, after all, it forms the best history of nations'.[6] Images from newspapers adorn the cottage walls in *A Royal Democrat* while the rest of the paper is kept for re-reading ('back numbers' are 'well thumbed'): this fictional account is also a window through which we as readers are invited to witness the profoundly nuanced literacy in political culture that existed in the remotest and poorest areas of Europe at the end of the nineteenth century.

It is exactly this advanced visual and textual culture in Ireland that Milligan would later engage with more fully in the community tableaux shows she devised as part of the national theatre and language movement. The nationalist papers in Ireland included colour 'pull out' supplements that depicted politics through personified images of Ireland as 'Erin'. Often political conflicts (particularly between England and Ireland) were conveyed through human characters (or what Cormac calls 'caricatures'). These early political posters were meant to be detached from the newspaper and hung on walls. Milligan after 1896 transfers these pictures onto the stage, and in doing so she created a mode of drama that tapped into an already present national visual and popular consciousness. As we will see, in a further attempt to reach this broad and culturally sophisticated constituency of rural readers, after 1891 Milligan also began to publish all of her own writings in newspapers.

Newspapers provide more than visual entertainment in the novel: they are essential as a plot device for moving events on: readers are quickly given 'a brief statement of facts' from a newspaper before the next stage of the novel unfolds. They are also used to convey information between characters who are separated by large geographical distances – Cormac finds out about his father's death (and his own) through the newspapers collected in Peggy's cottage. Similarly, characters in Dublin only learn about the insurrection in Derry through the press reports. In fact, characters sometimes rely on the newspapers for information about events that are actually unfolding around them. Nola Shane interprets the conflict in Derry through a newspaper even though the riots are literally taking place 'in front of her eyes'.[7] Nola's aunty in her house named 'Gortmore' (the actual name of the place in Co. Tyrone Alice Milligan was born) relates the backstory of the Derry riots to a friend who has been away by reading aloud extracts from her newspaper scrapbook. We know that Milligan herself kept newspaper scrapbooks of her own poems and articles in the 1890s which are now in the Francis Joseph Bigger papers in Belfast's public library.

Although *A Royal Democrat* is set sixty years ahead of the time it was actually written, the book's futurism resides less in technological advances than in Milligan's inadvertent political forecast of the ideas and situations that would come to pass in her lifetime. First, Parnell's death occurs in the novel in 1894: 'Mr Parnell died in America shortly after the opening of the revolt; and though his loss was deeply deplored, his followers lived to be thankful that he had been spared the agony of seeing his life-work undone.'[8] Mention of Parnell's untimely death to some extent explains the continual wrong dating of the work as being published in 1892 rather than 1890. Second, at the end of the novel an independent Irish parliament based in Dublin is won in 1948: the Republic of Ireland Act which dissolved the Free State was actually passed when Milligan was 82 years old in December 1948, legislation that transferred absolute executive power to the Irish government over 26 of the 32 counties of Ireland. Third, Milligan pre-empts how the Irish Parliamentary Party under John Redmond's leadership in 1914 would support the English in fighting World War I in the misguided belief that Ireland's loyalty would be rewarded with Home Rule legislation. A scenario is recounted early on in *A Royal Democrat* in which Home Rule is wiped off the agenda at the end of the nineteenth century when England is consumed by a world war that:

> Rendered immediate legislation on the Irish question impossible … The safety of the British Empire was threatened, and the Irish Party proved

themselves loyal supporters of the government, exerting their influence to make the rule of Ireland as easy as task as possible ... under the war terror the country [England] had undergone a reaction in favour of Conservatism ... when peace was restored the Home Rule party in England was insignificant.[9]

Finally, the dual monarchy that is established at the end of the novel is an idea of Irish governance that would be hotly debated by Milligan and her contemporaries during the Revival. This was a model of co-equal governance based on Austria–Hungary whereby two separate self-ruled kingdoms shared the same monarch from the 1860s through to 1918. By the time the founder of Sinn Féin, Arthur Griffith, suggested dual monarchy as a possible solution for Ireland in 1904, Milligan (in conjunction with Terence McSwiney) was completely opposed to the idea.[10] However, as *Glimpses of Erin* and *A Royal Democrat* demonstrate, in 1890 Alice Milligan was still very much influenced by the discourse of British Liberal democracy and the dual monarch idea of co-equal governance that had been propounded in the 1870s by Gladstone and the prince of Wales (late king Edward VII). Indeed, Milligan's own fictional democratic king of England may have been based loosely on the Prince of Wales who was considered somewhat of a maverick outsider by the English establishment. Cormac King (the disguised king who relinquished his monarchical position on the shores of Inishowen) wants a Republic because he firmly believes the Monarchy to be undemocratic and exploitative. However, Cormac's dream for an elective 'monarch' based on the ancient Irish system and modelled on the election of a king on the Blaskett Islands, is not one that is achieved in the novel: 'I am a thorough Republican, you know. If you have a monarchy at all, it should be elective. As the old Irish used to choose the ablest man as Tanist to their chief.'[11]

In *Glimpses of Erin* Alice Milligan and her father complained that 'Royalty is represented in Ireland by deputy'.[12] *A Royal Democrat* rights this wrong when a positive 'national marriage' is forged between Ireland and England; an arrangement secured by the new presence of monarchy in Ireland. Not only does the real king of England maintain his disguise and continue to live in Ireland as a married man; but his cousin (who was forced to take the throne in his absence) maintains strong links with the country where she frequently spends 'quiet weeks of summer in the peaceful retirement of her beautiful castle in County Wicklow'.[13] The ex-leader of the Irish constitutional party, MacNamara, becomes a minister of the Crown under this new regime:

> This young sovereign always cherished a love for the country where her dear cousin lived with his beautiful young bride. She saw them both sometimes,

for she frequently came to preside at the openings of the Irish parliament, and held court in Dublin on such occasions.[14]

The conclusion to the novel in which a dual monarchy is fully functioning is prepared for by earlier discussions that take place between characters. Even the Irish-American leader of the militant Sunburst Band Sir Cahir (Tom O'Doherty) envisages a monarchical presence within an independent Irish nation state. Cormac King asks him: 'And when Ireland is free, how will you govern it? England has found that hard to do, and I fear it won't be an easy task for anyone. Would you have a republic?' Sir Cahir answers in the negative:

> 'Not if I know it,' said the freeborn American. 'There's more style about a monarchy, and I think in the end it would come as cheap. There would be awful ructions in this country over a Presidential election. No; give me a King.'[15]

During the 1940s as the story unfolds, the English policy in Ireland is to depopulate the Irish from their lands (through eviction and increased emigration) and replant the land with English manufacturers.[16] The country is exploited as a service industry and a touristic playground for the English: the futurist nightmare Alice and Seaton Milligan in *Glimpses of Erin* were indirectly warning might come to pass if a change in relations between the two countries was not imminent. *A Royal Democrat* begins:

> At the time our story opens, the misery of the land had been consummated by a terrible famine, and the population of the country was barely three million. There was on foot for the salvation of Ireland a plan, in the formation of companies of rich English Capitalists. The linen and woollen trades were to be developed; Ireland was to supply the London markets with meat, butter, and eggs, and serve as a health resort and shooting ground for the British nobility and plutocracy.[17]

These are concerns expressed several times throughout the novel. A Donegal man named 'Con' explains to Cormac how the English are buying up land and waiting for the Irish to be driven off completely before they begin to develop it. Con regards living in his home in Donegal an act of political resistance that he encourages his contemporaries to emulate:

> They say the land round here's goin' to be sold over to some rich English people, that'll start the mills an' work the quarries … they say there'll be

nothing done till they're red of the most of us. They're waitin' on a bad year or a hard time when we get behind hand to get the chance ov puttin' us out ... It isn't much wud make me think of goin' to Amerikay meself ... I wudn't like to satisfy them by goin' away; That's what I sez to the boys when they're talkin' about goin' off to push their fortunes. 'Stay in yer own country,' sez I ... These Englishmen are wild to get us out of the way ... Ireland's so near hand to England they'd have it like their own country in no time, with their ships, an' quays, an' quarries, an' big towns ...[18]

The presence of the disguised monarch foregrounds the discourse of shared democracy between England and Ireland. Yet Kildare, the young would-be Irish politician, tells Cormac (his tutor) that there can be no unity between the two nations while England pursues its policy of depopulation:

Don't talk to me any more about peace and union between the democracies; we all naturally hate the Saxons. Your Radicals and Republicans have often been our worse persecutors, and at heart the English people all think that the best cure for Ireland's woes would be the gradual expatriation of the Celtic race, and the peopling of the country with Saxons. Famine and pestilence they look upon as blessings in disguise. It has always been the way. You remember how the poet Spenser wrote about us; and then Cromwell, England's liberator, was Ireland's greatest foe.[19]

Milligan's Irish characters describe English policy in Ireland in terms of systematic colonial depopulation, eviction, emigration and plantation. In the House of Commons the character MacManara, leader of the Irish Parliamentary Party shouts to the Tories opposite him: 'We understand now the kind of prosperity which you wish for Ireland. It is the enrichment of the English capitalists by the employment of English labour in a land from which the celts have been driven.'[20] These ideas would have been an integral part of the Land League's political discourse under the leadership of Michael Davitt. Although Milligan's fiction deals with the 1940s, it is a landscape that was deeply familiar at the time of its publication in 1890. Milligan's novel was published in the midst of the Land League's 'Plan of Campaign' when the kinds of evictions described in the novel were common. As the book was being reviewed in March 1890, reports about 'Royal Patronage in Dublin' were being printed alongside court sessions detailing evictions during the 'non rent protests' (later re-enacted in Northern Ireland during the 1980s Non Rent Payment Protests). Clearances that take place in the novel are associated with the seventeenth-century Cromwellian Plantations of Ireland. In fact, throughout the first months of 1890, the *Donegal Independent* (produced in the west of Ireland where so much of the novel's action takes place) actually began to publish extracts from the newly released seventeenth-century 'Donegal Plantation Papers'. The newspaper thus made parts of this historical archive democratically available to the local population for the first time. These archives detailed the systematic destruction of local Irish culture and the remapping of Gaelic society by English military settlers: a story that would be reimagined for stage in Brian Friel's play *Translations*. Milligan narrates plantations, evictions, mass immigration, imprisonment, fear of racial genocide into her futurist vision of Ireland. Yet the briefest survey of local and national newspapers reveals just how current a nightmare this future was for the Irish at the start of the last decade of the nineteenth century.

Political and cultural epiphanies

The language in *A Royal Democrat* that describes the unearned rights of 'the wealthy', 'the landed classes', 'the plutocracy', 'the upper classes' and 'the monarchy' carries a double meaning and a contemporary resonance in Ireland: these are the terms denoting inequality and hierarchy through which Milligan writes about the unionist Protestant populations and the Anglo-Irish elite whose wealth and status in Ireland derive from sources of historical connection and colonial reward. The 1940s plantations in *A Royal Democrat* are a replay of the plantations of the 1640s. Milligan's novel is full of references to the seventeenth-century settlement of Ireland, to Cromwell and to the execution of Charles I. In fact, Cromwell haunts the prison dreams of Cormac as he awaits execution in London. It is vital that the most forceful anti-establishment views expressed in the novel are articulated by the king himself: like Milligan, Cormac King speaks against 'the other' from the position of 'the other'. The English settlers in the novel have reached a moment (in the 1940s) when their plantation of the land in Ireland is brought to a halt.

The imminent decline of the ruling classes that dominates the novel's narrative trajectory, chimes with the situation facing many Protestant settler families at the end of the nineteenth century when their position in Ireland was seemingly threatened by the Irish land wars and the Home Rule movement. In a 1909 article published in the *Leader*, Milligan recalled the widely held perception that the land wars of the 1880s were righting the wrongs of the Cromwellian plantations:

> In my own memory (as lately as 1891 even) this traditional feeling took the form of believing that as a result of Home Rule the natives would get back their own, and that the Catholic clergy had gone so far as to hold raffles for

allotments of land. My own ancestral farm at the time of the 1886 Home Rule Bill was reported to have reverted to a Catholic country tailor-man, who lived at the Lough side.[21]

Milligan's first novel allowed the English a heroic role in finding a political resolution that marks the end of colonial expulsion of the Irish from their land. By setting the novel in the 1940s, Milligan takes the land wars out of both their historical and contemporary context. Cormac's feelings of emancipation in part derive from the liberty of travelling around the unknown futures of Ireland. But in her second novel, *The Cromwellians* (written between 1891 and 1893), Milligan looks back into history for a portal into the future. The English traveller who arrives in Ireland is not a disguised King but a military settler who is rewarded with Irish land for his loyalty to Cromwell. Unlike Cormac King's marriage to Nola Shane, the soldier's 'national marriage' in *The Cromwellians* to a native Irishwoman ends in mutual exile and displacement. Milligan's novel explores the historical 'original' moment of colonial sin when the Irish were literally expelled from their homes by English military planters. In Augusta Gregory's play *Dervorgilla* the roots of the primal moment of colonial 'sin' are rooted even further back in history. The idea of retribution haunts *Dervorgilla* in the play: 'I dreamt last night that the people knew me, that they knew my story and my sin; that they knew it was for my sake the wars were stirred up and the Gall brought into Ireland. They seemed to curse and to threaten me. They stooped like this, to take up stones to throw at me, knowing me at last as Dervorgilla.'[22] It is from this idea of an exact datable moment of simultaneous dispossession and occupation, that terms such as 'ancestral farms' and ideas about how 'the natives would get back their own' derive. But at a distance of 250 years, 'ancestral' ownership and claims of one community being more 'native' to Ireland than another are extremely complex.

Yet these were the confusing terms of belonging through which Milligan would be forced to negotiate her own identity as a Protestant Irish woman during the Revival period and again after Partition. In the 1920s, she told Dublin's *Evening Telegraph* how a hierarchy of social place and 'belonging' were present even in the rural landscapes of her childhood:

> I was a small girl in the county Tyrone, riding a shaggy pony along a country road. A hired boy who rejoiced in the name 'Roddy' held the rein. He was the first native Irishman I remember to have conversed with … It was he who interpreted for me the words 'Home Rule for Ireland,' which appeared in white painted letters on a grey stone wall, and why the harp rudely shaped was there without a crown.[23]

In describing 'Roddy' as 'the first native Irishman' she ever encountered, Milligan reveals that she did not consider herself 'native' to the country of her birth. The words and drawings the young Alice Milligan saw on a wall in Tyrone were to her as incomprehensible as the script of a foreign language. The graffiti is only made meaningful by the presence of the 'native Irishman' ('hired' on her Uncle's farm) who can decode the meaning of this nationalist iconography.

Milligan interrogated the historical origins of discord between Protestant and Catholic, between settler and native in *The Cromwellians*. In this unpublished novel, events centre around 1 May 1654, the last 'day of grace' offered by Cromwell to the native and old Irish to leave their homes 'voluntarily'. For Milligan and many other Protestant Irish women novelists of the late nineteenth century, this date became a symbolic fictional motif. In the 1890s, a series of plantation novels written by women represent an early example of the Irish 'Big House' fiction usually associated with the rapid decline of the Anglo-Irish during the Irish Civil War. In these Cromwellian novels, homes and estates are taken over by settlers; those daughters of the dispossessed re-inhabit their homes only after they are made 'other' through religious and social transformation of intermarriage.

With the forced colonial transfer of land and property, Catholics are either wedded to their Protestant oppressors or locked in sectarian battle. All these gendered conflicts are staged in the contested symbolic 'home' space that is at once a private tragedy and a metaphor for the national struggle. As the Protestant ascendancy started its rapid decline in Ireland, women writers such as Emily Lawless, Mary Marks and Lily MacManus began to contemplate how the story would end by looking back into history for its beginnings. Elizabeth Bowen's memoirs and fictions are a later version of this genre that began in the 1890s. During the Irish Civil War, southern Protestants were reduced from ten to six per cent of the population as their extensive homes were burnt to the ground.[24] In *Bowen's Court*, Elizabeth Bowen writes a biography of the 'Big House' her family occupied which she traces to a seventeenth-century military adventurer.

Milligan never published *The Cromwellians* as novel but she rewrote the manuscript as a historical stage melodrama. A mode of signification that is essentially popular in its form, melodrama offers a clear emotional codification of drama with schematic oppositions and a manichean dualism of vice and virtue. It is a popular drama of sensation and sentiment that reveals recurring attention to the struggles of the oppressed or marginalized. As David Grimstead puts it, melodrama is the 'echo of the historically voiceless'.[25] Home in any Irish story is never just a place where people live. In Ken Loach's recent film about the Irish Civil War, for instance, homes are embattled sites for being and belonging: at the start of *The wind that shakes the barley*, Damien (played by Cillian Murphy), a politically naive medical student from Cork, attempts to leave Ireland for a career in England. By the end of the film, every idea of a homeland or a home space he held at the start of his journey is completely ripped apart. Damien has to learn what 'home' means – and this apotheosis happens when he encounters first hand the racism, injustice and violence of an occupying army.[26]

'Insistent that our politicians should ever be mindful of the lessons of history and that our poets and dramatists should not be forgetful', Milligan actually republished her Cromwellian novel as a melodrama at the start of the Irish Civil War.[27] As this preface to her play indicates, Milligan felt that the issues dividing the Irish against each other in the early 1920s were rooted in the sectarian politics engendered by the seventeenth-century colonial planters. All the way through Loach's Civil War film (and in Milligan's fictional treatment of the Cromwellian settlements) homes are contested: they are invaded, burnt to the ground, filled with starvation. They are places of mourning, violence and humiliation – but they are also places of resistance. While the homes depicted in the film are vulnerable to indiscriminate daily attacks by British troops, they often double up as unofficial underground meeting places where members of the Flying Columns and later the anti-Treaty republicans seek refuge and exchange information. Home is also the site for the fetishization of the family in the new state. It is the unit by which Irish society is to be reconfigured. In Milligan's novel, resistance is enacted in the home space not by men but by the expelled daughter who returns from enforced exile.

As a student of English history at King's College, London between 1886 and 1887, Milligan was taught by the leading seventeenth-century historian S.R. Gardiner whose publications included a multi-volume work on the Commonwealth and Protectorate period 1649–60. Historian Micheál Ó Siochrú suggests that Gardiner's work was unique in tone and methodology:

> He was scrupulously even-handed as a historian. Despite writing at the height of the Victorian era, he avoided the nasty cultural stereotypes normally associated with English writings on Ireland, and was meticulous about his research, visiting obscure archives, long-forgotten battle scenes (on his bike apparently).[28]

Gardiner's views about Cromwell and Ireland are very similar to those expressed by Alice Milligan and her father in *Glimpses of Erin*. Gardiner famously wrote: 'That Cromwell should have been guilty of the slaughters of Drogheda and Wexford is a matter for regret, not for surprise.'[29] Milligan's studies in London give an added insight into the history that informed her fictional re-assessment of the seventeenth century and its impact on contemporary identity politics in Ireland.

This is particularly relevant to her enquiry into the historical landscapes of Ulster: as Lionel Pilkington has pointed out, although the Irish fictional 'Big House' novels focus on the decline of the Anglo-Irish, this group represented only a tiny part of Protestant communities in Ireland.[30] In contrast, the north contained the largest population of Protestant settler communities and subsequently became the main geographical location of unionism and Protestant loyalism. Milligan knew from the outset of the Irish Cultural Revival, that the movement's ultimate national success would depend on the radical inclusion of the north's political, religious and social makeup. *The Cromwellians* represents Milligan's first fictional attempt to re-imagine the history of Protestantism in Ireland and its colonial legacy.

The Cromwellian plantations were a seminal event in Irish history: thousands of people from the 'old' and 'native' Irish communities were dispossessed after Cromwell compensated loyal soldiers with Irish homes and land. Hundreds of Irish people were deported as slaves to work on the sugar plantations in the Barbados; thousands were executed or starved to death; others were re-housed on the stony, inhospitable farmsteads of Connacht in the west of Ireland. This particular narrative of colonial settlement recurs in several Milligan texts, emerging in different genres and publication contexts but, as Milligan explained in 1904, the novel itself was never published:

> A fact at which I do not wonder, as I had gone to immense trouble to write it throughout in archaic English prose, and while I was engaged in writing it I read nothing but Elizabethan drama, Milton's prose works and other books of that sort and, of course, Prendergast's 'Cromwellian Settlement', and Gilbert's 'History of the War in Ireland' from which I took the basis for facts.[31]

Milligan recycled characters and incidents in several of her short stories. She then re-wrote the novel as the stage melodrama, *The daughter of Donagh* which was rejected in 1904 by the newly opened Abbey Theatre as it had too many ambitious set changes that included a moving boat scene.[32] In all the different versions of this narrative, Milligan consistently deals with scenarios of dispossession, colonial occupation and betrayal.

Although only nine pages of the novel's final chapter have survived, this small fragment contains the moment of revelation that is crucial to the novel's plot.[33] The Cromwellian soldier Hosea Greatreax has expelled Onora Cavanagh from her father's lands. The Minister Tobias Morton, reminds Master Eleazor Parkes that: 'The Lord Protector is desirous above all things, to keep the godly stock lately planted in Ireland, free from all communication with idolaters'.[34] Aware that marriage between settler and native was an offence punishable by seizure of land and transplantation to Connacht, Onora fakes a religious conversion in order to marry the soldier who has occupied her home. She strategically divulges her real identity at a social gathering, knowing that this disclosure will destroy her husband's standing in the settler community. Conscious that the minister, Tobias Morton, is observing her every move, Onora performs devotional actions that identify her as a Catholic. The minister privately confides his suspicions about Hosea Greatrex's wife to his neighbour:

> She hath a Papist face and a proud heart and her beauty such as it is, is of the devil … Truly I myself saw the woman make the sign of the cross upon her breast and upon the babe and doubtless she purposes secretly to rear him in the Romanish superstition though openly she professeth our purer faith.[35]

At the end of Milligan's play version, *The daughter of Donagh*, settler and native, man and wife are expelled from their own communities and alienated from one another. Milligan re-examined the historical role of Protestants in Irish history in order to further understand and realize the potential of her own contemporary position. Mark Poster has argued that the present can only be fully understood by reference to the past: 'Historical reason must retrace the projects of the past and only by doing so can it present history as the arena of human choices.'[36] Milligan's journey back into the historical narratives of the seventeenth century was as personal a project as the diary she kept. The state of dispossession that is depicted in her fictions is something that Milligan herself experienced on multiple levels when her own political and cultural allegiances shifted. In a 1904 letter to the *United Irishman* Milligan claimed that the act of writing *The Cromwellians* was synonymous with her own personal formation. She also references the co-democracy alliances that she had explored in *A Royal Democrat* (and which lost momentum after the death of Parnell in 1891):

> It was written at the time that the breach occurred between Irish Nationalism and English Democratic Puritanism. In the long period devoted to working on it, my own political opinions became clearly and firmly defined, and the bulky manuscript has ever since been preserved as a memorial to my own political development.[37]

After 1890 Milligan never once mentioned her first two publications. It was as though *Glimpses of Erin* and *A Royal Democrat* belonged to another writer altogether. What are the reasons for this extraordinary literary abandonment?

their midst. Onora feeling the eyes of Tobias
Morton upon her, and noting how he peered
through his fingers, crossed herself and
moved her lips as if in prayer. This she
did twice or thrice ere they rose from their
knees, also she crossed the babe's brow
and murmured over it, Tobias all the time
spying eagerly.

Of this simple act, she was well aware
question would afterwards be made and rightly
she judged, for Morton, riding homeward by
the side of the minister, took occasion to tell
of what he had seen and Mistress Parkes
being ill content with this Onora's queenly
pride gave earnest heed to this evidence
against her.

"It is I fear as you have surmised my
brother" said the minister, shaking his head.
"Yea the woman hath a wicked and a mocking eye.
Ere my exhortation had been continued an hour,
she wearied of it and sighed as if she longed for
me to make an end of all godly discourse."

"Sighed indeed!" put in his good wife,
"The jade yawned twice or thrice, for I was by
her side and saw well enough, though she laid
her hand upon her lips. She hath a Papist
face and a proud heart and her beauty such
as it is, is of the devil. Such black eyes

15 'She hath a Papist face', extract from three surviving pages of Alice Milligan's
unpublished novel *The Cromwellians* written between 1891 and 1893. The novel
provided the narrative for her play, also set in 1654, *The daughter of Donagh*.

Milligan could well have been embarrassed by her cruel treatment in *A Royal Democrat* of the Irish Parliamentary Party and the Land League whose leaders only became 'real' for her when she encountered them face to face in Dublin during 1891. In addition, the liberal rhetoric of negotiation and moderate Home Rule that dominate Milligan's first two publications had a very quick 'sell by' date after the demise of the Irish Parliamentary Party in the early 1890s. Seaton Milligan continued to propose a form of constructive unionism right through to his death in 1916; but after 1893 his daughter stopped looking to find models of benevolent English political good will that could change the fortunes of Ireland. Instead, she self-consciously placed a strong female character at the historical scene of the crime when the sectarian lines where first drawn. In *The Cromwellians* Milligan gives the strongest part to the one character who is dealt the weakest historical, political and social hand of all: the dispossessed, homeless Irish woman is given both voice and agency with which to resist the colonial new order of assimilation and annihilation.

Milligan stated that the act of writing *The Cromwellians* between 1891 and 1893 was integral to her own 'political development': it is essentially her reconsideration of the historical background to Protestantism in Ireland that is so fundamental to her personal growth. After she defined herself as a 'staunch nationalist' in 1893 Milligan's own 'versions' of her Protestant upbringing were, to some extent, 'performed' for the Revival and for post-Partition audiences in particular. Because she was a Protestant it was assumed that she had derived from a staunch unionist background; to be a Protestant was to be simplistically aligned with the Big House tradition and the Anglo-Irish elite. But the Anglo-Irish only represented a socially self-isolating and very small percentage of the Protestant population in Ireland. Yet people who wrote about Milligan's cultural output and her political activism usually required a known discourse through which to understand her.

When Seamus MacManus published a selection of her poetry in 1951 he described her as a poet, 'who had smashed off the shackles of alienism whereunto she was born'.[38] Commentators on Milligan's role in the Irish renaissance (particularly in the American press) often began by outlining her unusual cultural (and therefore religious) credentials. In 1905 the San Francisco *Leader* celebrated Milligan's recent employment as a Gaelic League lecturer:

> She is a Protestant Nationalist, a rather unusual combination, but an excellent one when it exists, for none are more sincere when they join the Irish ranks, and by doing so cut themselves off from all the prizes within reach of the Ascendancy Party.[39]

The *Leader* claims that Milligan's Protestant heritage binds her automatically but not irrevocably to the privileges of Ireland's upper classes. Yet the 'prizes' of the Ascendancy – political power, wealth, social status – were never realistically within reach of the Milligan family. Like her contemporary, William Butler Yeats, Milligan was the product of a middle-class upbringing.

Assessments of Milligan's work usually lauded her as a nationalist who sprang from the stony ground of northern unionist Protestantism. Republicans viewed her as a writer identified with an alien culture, a generation of colonial outsiders who descended from plantation stock. Celebrating Milligan's seventy-fourth birthday in 1940, 'Cormac MacAirt' in the *Ulster Examiner* conceived of Milligan's commitment to the Irish cause as deriving from a sentimental nationalism that was organically rooted in a naturally unified land:

> Alice Milligan is a Tyrone woman, the child of a typical Ulster Methodist family, who was reared in the usual Ulster Protestant atmosphere of distrust of their own fellow-countrymen. I remember once asking her how she, nurtured and educated as she was, became a Nationalist. Her answer was a surprising one. 'Frankly, I don't know,' she said. 'Instinctively, since I was a child my heart went out to my own nation. In spite of all I heard, I knew that Ireland was my country and that its people were my people.'[40]

As Milligan was herself only too aware, in a colonial paradigm, national identity, community and the soil are hotly and, at times, violently contested terms.

In his 1991 essay 'Cannon fodder: literary mythologies in Ireland', Seamus Deane contends that any declaration of identity – whether religious, racial or regional – constitutes an active compliance with the logistics of subjugation:

> The moment you stabilize your identity you have done part of the job of the imperial system. Imperial systems are about mapping, about geography, about stabilizing, about characterizing people within certain fixed limits.[41]

Religious designations, in a colonial context, serve the interests of the occupying power. In Ireland, national identity became inextricable with religion: Protestants were associated with the colonial plantations while Catholics endured their historical role as oppressed representatives of an authentic Irish identity. Milligan sometimes chose to fix the limits of her own identity almost as a way of giving others in the Revival a language through which to understand her. That is not to say that the autobiographical narratives she wrote about herself were untrue: only that the positions of otherness required of her became more extremely defined as the Irish political situation became more divided along sectarian lines.

Her poem, 'When I was a little girl' is the most striking example of a Milligan text which critics have cited as a work of autobiography. The poem concerns a Protestant nurse who scares children into submission by invoking the threat of a Fenian invasion. Milligan herself explained the contexts in a letter to *The Leader* in July 1909:

> In the poem, 'When I was a little girl', I tell the tale as "twas told to me. The Loyalists and Orange people of the North have assuredly imbibed the belief that but for a late and terribly severe winter, including snow, the Fenian rising would have been a repetition of what they call 'the great Ulster massacre of 1641'. This feeling of apprehension had been, doubtless, engendered, and, increased by heredity; generation after generation of Northern land-owners and land-tillers since the time of the plantation must have gone to bed nightly with an uneasy feeling that the rightful occupiers of the land were prowling around in the dark outside.[42]

Milligan proposes that in late nineteenth-century Ireland, Protestants still regarded themselves as interlopers, even though their ancestors had settled in Ireland over two centuries earlier. As a means of sustaining an identity distinct from 'the Irish', unionists frequently invoked the spectre of Catholic reprisals that haunted the Protestant imagination. According to Milligan, unionist discourse implicitly recognized the dispossessed Catholics as the 'rightful occupiers' of Ireland. Milligan insists that the central issue of the poem is the utilization of the myth by a Protestant community aiming to promote and sustain sectarian ascendancy. Milligan is suggesting in her letter to the *Leader* quoted above, that she is interested not in factual detail but in the cultural power that is invested in the representation of events. The 'truth value' of both historical instances derives not from what 'actually happened' but from belief systems which shaped these occurrences as evidence. 'When I was a little girl' tackles the question of how such myths can be 'engendered' and reified. Certain historical dates are integral to a 'Protestant massacre theory' dating back to 1641 – a discourse re-activated at crucial moments in Irish social and political history.

'When I was a little girl' expresses the siege mentality of Ulster Protestants through the eyes of a child who identifies not with the Unionist ideology of the family nursemaid but with the imagined community of the Fenians:

But one little rebel there,
Watching all with laughter,
Thought 'When the Fenians come
I'll rise and go after.'

Wished she had been a boy
And a good deal older –
Able to walk for miles
With a gun on her shoulder;

Able to lift aloft
That Green Flag o'er them
(Red-coats and black police
Flying before them)
                                    (45–56).

In 'When I was a little girl', the 'fiend' does not lurk in the hills beyond the nursery but is an invisible monster that inhabits Protestant nightmares. The poem implies that it is not only the imagined Fenian who qualifies as a rebel but also the individual who dares to look beyond the fence that separates one community from another.

The Protestant nurse who scares children into compliance first appeared in Milligan's column 'Notes from the north', published in the *Irish Weekly Independent* in January 1895. Milligan urged her readers to 'record contemporary narratives of the '67 movement' and herself contributed a 'Northern narrative of the Fenian time'.[43] Beginning with an allusion to 'the state of terror prevalent up in these Orange dens' when the French attempted to land in Ireland during the 1790s, Milligan contends that those who are considered heroes within Irish Republican history are perceived as terrorists by Protestant unionists. In the *Irish Weekly Independent* Milligan maintained that in the 1860s the word Fenian had replaced the evil spectre of Napoleon, the 'terrible Boney':

In much the same way the word Fenian was used in the north in my nursery days, and its resemblance to the word fiend made it very effective and suggestive in this capacity. The following anecdote told at the nursery fire, on a wild winter night, when the stormy shrieks of the blast and the clattering of the window panes made us imagine that a yelling, murderous band were clamouring round the house, shaking at the windows and doors, in a wild longing to cut Protestant throats, especially those of small children who were noisy and rebellious against nurses or parents.[44]

'When I was a little girl' was interpreted as a straightforward account of Milligan's childhood and remains the verse which people still quote as an example of her longstanding commitment to the Irish national movement. In her insightful 1994 essay, 'Glimpses of Erin Alice Milligan: poet, Protestant, patriot', Brighid Mhic Sheáin concludes:

> In a sense this particular poem was a characteristically light hearted declaration, in retrospect, of her vocation. A vocation is a call to a certain way of life and Alice Milligan thought herself called to dedicate her life to the cause of Ireland.[45]

As we have seen, George Russell identified the fictional speaker in the poem with the poet herself. In a private letter to Milligan in 1908, Russell mocked her anxiety that the poem might cause offence to the Catholic Church: 'I have too much respect for that little girl who chases the black coated police to oust her because a bigger girl is terrified because of black coated priests'.[46] In 1930 Pádraic Colum republished the verse commenting how it 'tells us that in the midst of Belfast distrust of Irish Nationalism she was a little Nationalist'.[47] Seamus MacManus placed an asterisk by 'When I was a little girl' in his 1951 collection *We sang for Ireland* explaining, 'The poet was born into a British-descent family.'[48] Milligan encouraged such biographical readings, chronicling in numerous contexts her break with the unionist traditions that accompanied her Protestant upbringing. Despite being publicly disseminated as a work that identified extreme familial political differences, Alice Milligan actually included a hand decorated copy of it in a collection of work presented by the Milligan children at their parents' golden wedding anniversary in 1912.[49]

Milligan's explorations of a Protestant childhood in Ireland are similar to the experiences recorded later by other northern Protestant artists such as James Cousins and Louis MacNiece. The landscape painter Paul Henry recalled the anti-creative and hostile religious environment of his upbringing:

> Life in Belfast I knew had nothing to give me ... The urge to get away became more and more intense. I had been brought up in the most narrow and arid religious atmosphere, and the longing to get away from home and its atmosphere was stifling me. I had to smoke in secret, drink in secret, and think in secret ... I was the caged bird that had to be set free.[50]

In the 1930s Milligan was asked to write the script for a radio broadcast about her career by her friend Áine Ceannt. Accordingly, Milligan wrote a short autobiographical sketch that recounted how her first experience of the Irish language came from listening to labourers on her uncle's farm. Drawing upon the poet's memoir, Ceannt introduced the programme by explaining Milligan's Anglo-centric upbringing and education:

> At school in Omagh and later in Belfast nothing was taught about Ireland except that it was conquered in 1154. Of the famine one of her school books taught that it was sent by God for the Irish people's good as they were too poor and too many in the land of their birth. Mixing among the country people in the fields and by the river sides and from the real servants in kitchen and nursery she learned other things. Her poem 'When I was a little girl' represents this period.[51]

In contrast to 'When I was a little girl', which portrays an already formed sympathy for Irish insurgency, the narrative of nationalist consciousness offered by Milligan to Ceannt confirms that her political transformation was a process rather than a sudden awakening.

The complex liberalism of her northern upbringing (which had resulted in *Glimpses of Erin* and *A Royal Democrat*) had also created a house of children who went on to represent the extremes on the Irish political spectrum. Every one of her siblings considered themselves Irish and claimed Irish culture actively as their heritage. But Irishness and unionism in late nineteenth-century Ulster did not carry the same political meaning as they did after 1891. Members of the Milligan family did indeed go on to join the British Army; some moved to live permanently in England; two of Milligan's siblings were awarded the OBE for their loyal services to the English crown. Yet in the last two decades of the nineteenth century, the Milligan family may well have considered themselves to be Irish, Protestant, English, northern and Methodist. They may also have felt European given that at least two daughters studied music at the conservatories of Milan and Germany. Alice Milligan herself spoke fluent German and in the early 1920s drafted a German opera.

In the 1880s when they had newly moved to Belfast, the family self-educated themselves in areas of Irish history and culture; they participated in multiple educational forums such as lectures put on by the Workingman's Institute (in part founded by Seaton Milligan) or tours given by the Belfast Naturalist Field Club. They collected lost manuscripts (of Bunting and Fergusson) and placed them in public libraries. What the Milligan family learned about Irish archaeology and music, they immediately made available to the public in self-published journals and articles; they participated regularly in social public cultural forums that they both joined and established. In short, the Milligan family members worked

16 'While in a tram going up O'Connell Street I turned into a Parnellite';
view of O'Connell Bridge.

collaboratively on many cultural projects, they published in the same Revival
journals (such as the *Irish Homestead*) and collected rare Irish folk music in
Co. Tyrone.

Yet after 1891, Alice Milligan came to regard Irish culture in a radically different
way from her parents, siblings and their liberal unionist northern community.
Irish culture for Milligan's family represented something historically valuable but
politically non-dynamic: poetry, music and literature were like the archaeological
finds that rest under the earth's surface in *Glimpses of Erin*; they are to be excavated
and placed under glass in a museum as further evidence of Ireland's legitimacy as
a historically important civilization. Culture was celebrated by the family and their
community as another example of their northern Protestant enlightened
liberalism. So when they staged tableaux in their drawing rooms it was in the
tradition of a bourgeois costumed parlour game. In contract, when Alice Milligan
staged tableaux (after 1897) in the fields of rural Ireland, the pictures were a form
of cultural politics in which democracy and community were enacted both on

stage and off. Milligan and her comrades cleared the fields, built the stages, made the costumes and performed the narratives. Their tableaux were not commemorative effigies to honour a dead culture, they were living breathing images of a nation projecting itself into the future. For Alice Milligan, Irish culture was a dangerous live explosive that could utterly transform the political and social fabric of the world she had been born into: she realized at the beginning of the 1890s that it was within the powers of a new community of cultural activists to change Ireland's status and future possibilities.

As the nuanced politics of her earliest publications suggest, there was no one moment of epiphany for Alice Milligan. Her biographical reflections of national self becoming were not like those recorded by her contemporary Lily MacManus in a memoir that states the exact moment, 'I turned from one flag to the other'.[52] What Milligan astutely called her own 'political development' was a process that was in constant transformation. But Dublin, Parnell and the year 1891 were three major components of the sea change that would determine the rest of Alice Milligan's life. In 1891 Milligan arrived in Dublin to study Irish after working full-time as a teacher in Derry and before going on to sit her formal teaching exams in Liverpool. Dublin was a city in which Milligan was looking for something and she frenetically involved herself in everything that was political, social, literary, occultist and intellectual. She found herself intrigued watching Yeats compose verse in the National Library of Ireland; she walked out to Michael Davitt's house to introduce herself; she followed Parnell's campaign as though her life depended on it. Milligan had written so much about travellers in Ireland and their moments of political transformation that it is no surprise that she recorded in her diary how a private moment of political conviction came upon her suddenly in the most public of spaces while she herself was literally in transit: 'While in the tram going up O'Connell St I turned into a Parnellite. The conversion was sudden and almost unaccountable – perhaps it won't last'.[53]

As though uttering the first words of a foreign language, Milligan tentatively put her new political allegiances to the test: 'Tuesday – up Sackville St – Said something hesitatingly in favour of Parnell.'[54] The very fact that Milligan calls Dublin's main thoroughfare by both its colonial name (Sackville Street) and its nationalist one (O'Connell Street) is a further indication of a divided political consciousness. The Parnell split marked a stage in Milligan's own conversion from being a supporter of constructive unionism (as articulated in *Glimpses of Erin* and *A Royal Democrat*) into an ardent champion of Irish self-determination. Her diary entries reveal a writer for whom the personal and the political are one and the same thing. Reading the newspapers was not enough for her and she intended to encounter Parnell directly so as to judge whether he was absolutely the correct

17 Sketch of Parnell by Alice Milligan in her diary, June 1891.

leader for her: 'If I had seen his face, perhaps I would know whether to trust him.'[55] When she did finally observe the party leader at Harcourt Street station in Dublin, her reactions were emotionally charged. She recorded how 'sad & silent' he appeared: 'I stood up on the tram steps waving my handkerchief wildly excited ... I will never forget the sad downcast expression ... the ghastly pallor of his face.'[56]

Charles Stewart Parnell refused to stand down as leader of the Irish Parliamentary Party after his adulterous affair with Katherine O'Shea was made public, but was subsequently subjected to a campaign of slander and vilification when members of his own party assailed his integrity.[57] His private life was exploited to destroy his political career and damage the Irish Parliamentary Party's campaign for Home Rule. After seeing him face to face, Milligan (like Yeats) decided that Parnell was an 'impossible leader'[58] and she went on to support Justin McCarthy's opposition. Comparing Parnell with Samson (and repeating word for word a speech given by the character Kildare in *A Royal Democrat*) she wrote angrily in her diary, 'What does he mean like Samson to pull down the edifice ruining himself, enemies &

all.'[59] It had been easy for Milligan to kill Parnell off in her 1890 prose fiction: at that stage in her life Irish contemporary politics held as much meaning and consequence for her as the futurist year '1948'. But in 1891, even though she had no vote, Milligan behaved as though Irish politics was the oxygen she needed in order to breathe.

From May 1891, she sketched Parnell over and over in her diary: his distressed bearded face (that 'sad downcast expression') would later reappear as a ghost in her sketch of Roger Casement that she drew in the London courtroom as he was sentenced to death in 1916. But it was Parnell's death, his funeral and her inability to leave Belfast that really had an impact on Milligan's psyche and on her cultural production. Her diary reveals that newspapers were the very first port of call for Milligan during moments of major political upheaval. Milligan hears about Parnell's death from her sister Charlotte: 'I received a shock – "Parnell is dead – he died suddenly at Brighton last night." I dressed hurriedly & went to town for the evening paper & brought it to the library.'[60] Milligan chooses to read about Parnell in a democratic shared space in Belfast; a choice that rhymes with her conversion to Parnellism on a tram in Dublin. A woman reading in public space would have been a relatively new sight because the city library in Belfast had only opened a year earlier. (The National Library of Ireland, which was to feature so prominently in the creation of the Cultural Revival and in the lives of Milligan, Yeats, Joyce and their contemporaries, similarly only opened its doors in March 1890.)[61] In her diary for October 1891, Milligan picks up on the irony of a mistake caused by a unionist newspaper getting mixed up with her nationalist one. This unwittingly leads to the nationalist leader being lauded as a 'respected' member of the community in the unionist stronghold of Belfast:

> Some papers concerning the death of Marsh the biscuit manufacturer had got in amongst the account of Parnell's career after starting the foundation of the Land League, it went on to say 'the deceased was widely respected in Belfast' etc.[62]

After Parnell's death, Milligan immediately began to connect with an imagined community by publishing in the very newspapers she lived so much of her life through. From 1892 to 1895, she published historical ballads in the national Parnellite papers in Ireland at the time, the *Irish Independent*, the *Irish Weekly Independent* and *United Ireland*. Her verses appeared in the same pages as those of Katherine Tynan, whom Milligan viewed as Ireland's 'Parnellite poetess'.[63] When John O'Mahony, the literary editor of the *Irish Weekly Independent*, asked her to write a poem about Parnell to commemorate the second anniversary of his death,

Milligan considered his request as proof of her own ascent to national fame: the preference of the editor filled Milligan with pride; 'my writing preferred to any other'.[64] Asked for the poem on Tuesday, she was 'Busy writing Ode' by Wednesday and it was 'finished and dispatched' within two days.[65] Her systematic approach to the production of poetry evidently won admiration from the papers and Milligan was soon posting off more than three verses a week.

Commemorating Parnell's death in Dublin's nationalist newspapers connected Milligan with many other figures involved in the Irish Literary Revival which emerged in the aftermath of his fall. The *Irish Weekly Independent* began publication in April 1893. To mark its launch the paper republished poems from *United Ireland* about Parnell and commissioned some new works including the following: 'One who judged him' by Katharine Tynan, 'In Memoriam' by Dora Sigerson, 'The dead chief' by Anna Johnston and 'Mourn – and then onward' by W.B. Yeats. Parnell's name served as a screen behind which Milligan articulated the anxieties of Protestant figures that were politically and culturally aligned to the de-colonization of Ireland. Her poem 'Ode for 6 October: dedicated to the memory of the dead and the cause that shall not die' is less an assessment of Parnell's career than an exploration of a Protestant female child's alienation from Irish national culture and history:

> Throughout the toilsome hours of my schooling days,
> No mention of thee was made unto me, save only
>> By speakers in heedless scorn or in harsh dispraise.
> No word was told me at all of thy burdening sorrow,
>> No tale of thine ancient warfare yet was heard. (I. 6)

The child's knowledge of Ireland's 'fight for freedom' (I. 8) is articulated as an unspoken rebirth. In a line that forecasts Milligan's much later autobiographical reflections of how 'the soil cried out' to her, the understanding of Ireland's struggle in this poem does not come from intentional learning but reaches the Protestant child in 'a way beyond reach of mortal knowing' (I. 9). Ireland and Parnell are interchangeable signifiers in this poem. As the child's imagination 'awakened for war for thee' (III. 46), the gender of the female Protestant dissolves into a 'warrior iron-armed' (IV. 48). Milligan not only wrote a poem to mark the second anniversary of Parnell's death, she also sent a wreath from Belfast that she funded by selling off her Shelley Society books that she had purchased as a student in London.[66] She remained privately convinced that the *Irish Weekly Independent* drew public attention to her flowers: 'my *chaplet*, taken for a heart & fully described as being laid right on the centre of the mound – allusion to delicate fingers and black north.'[67] Two years after his death, Parnell clearly still haunted Milligan's writing as well as her unconscious: the week of the second anniversary she recorded 'dream of Parnell vividly'.[68]

Parnell's political credentials acted as a precedent which influenced and shaped Milligan's conversion. He was a Protestant leader of the most significant contemporary constitutional Irish nationalist movement. In 1895 Milligan added his name to her roll call of Protestants who had united with the Irish in an anti-colonial struggle since 1798.[69] In 1899, she rather defensively invoked his name as evidence that Protestant non-Irish speakers could participate in the Irish cultural movement, declaring 'Parnell never troubled himself about the Irish language'.[70] Despite her earlier criticism of Parnell as a destructive Samson-like figure, Milligan considered that the struggle for an independent Irish Parliament had died with its main advocate. She wrote on 8 October 1891: 'The last vestige of independence is gone, except some new man come to the front, or the spirit of the people becomes strong enough to take the stand that Parnell took.'[71]

In Dublin Milligan had secretly expressed her awe for Yeats, Davitt, Parnell: after October 1891, she stopped looking for great men to admire and emulate and started to envisage herself as an agent of political and cultural change. The Revival made it possible for 'the spirit of the people' to become 'strong enough' to envisage a future that they collectively participated in creating. According to John Kelly, the divided Irish Parliamentary Party and the death of their discredited leader acted as catalysts for cultural revival in Ireland:

> The atmosphere, so uncongenial to cultural enterprise in the 1880s, suddenly altered after the fall of Parnell, and this change was self-conscious from its beginning: contemporaries were astonished at the speed with which cultural awareness developed after the split, and as early as 1892 the terms 'Irish Literary Revival' and the 'Irish Renaissance' were in frequent use.[72]

Parnell's dramatic demise became the symbolic moment for Milligan's own delivery into an Irish nationalist cultural movement. But it was less his death than his funeral that brought out Milligan's most profound emotional articulation of her altered sense of national identity. Parnell's funeral produced one of the largest public gatherings in Dublin. It was a day that would go down in history and in the private histories of Milligan's contemporaries.

Milligan had experienced what it was to live for a short but intense time in Dublin where she felt part of an emerging dynamic cultural world that was infused with political energy. In Belfast people within the unionist community went about their business as usual on the day of Parnell's funeral. On the night of

18 Magic Lantern slide showing a photograph of Parnell's funeral procession through Dublin, October 1891.

his death she had noted that her own family went to the theatre to see a Gilbert and Sullivan show, *The Yeoman of the Guard*. On the evening of the funeral Milligan went with them to another show after which she expressed political estrangement and cultural alienation for the very first time. In her diary she wrote:

> We spent last night at Knock & came in for a matinee of *The Gondoliers* & concert. Heard Alice Gomez & L. Johnson – not a very suitable way to spend days of national mourning – but I'm in the enemies camp – if I had but the money I would go at once to Dublin to be among the people who feel as I feel.[73]

MUSEUM DUBLIN. 2501. W.L.

19 View of the National Library of Ireland where Milligan first encountered Yeats and many of her friends and colleagues who would create Ireland's Cultural Revival.

In her diary Milligan longs for a community of solidarity that she does not have in the north but that she had experienced in Dublin. After Parnell's funeral her own relation to Belfast was transformed. From 1891 she repeatedly described the unionist stronghold as an oppressive place for those with Irish national affiliations. In July 1895, for instance, she informed readers of the *Irish Weekly Independent* that Belfast was a city 'where even to be an open and avowed Parnellite and no more, bespeaks a certain amount of manly courage and uprightness which is not necessarily possessed by everyone who flaunts the most advanced views amidst safe surroundings'.[74] In other words, to participate in national Irish culture in Belfast was more difficult than in other parts of Ireland. As we shall see in the next chapter, Milligan chose not to move to Dublin to participate in the emerging Revival but instead nurtured the cultural revival from within the more difficult territory of 'the enemy's camp'.

The 'enemy's camp' for Alice Milligan was the city of Belfast because of its dominant and uncompromising majority unionism; but it was also her own family; her own past; and the colonial legacy of Protestants in Ireland. Suddenly in October 1891, Milligan found she was no longer 'at home' in her own home; she would never again be at 'home' anywhere. Milligan's alienation from home was intensified after 1922 when she wrote of herself as being 'practically interned' by a family and the new state of Northern Ireland. As soon as Alice Milligan made the conscious decision to step outside of the dominant politics of her family and her community, she began to occupy the liminal space that Thomas MacDonagh described as the key to understanding her radical Irishness and her nuanced cultural production.[75] She was a northern, Protestant, woman who renounced the political unionism of her upbringing: as such, Milligan occupied multiple identities that could not be fixed or easily defined. But just as Milligan left one community, she was never fully embraced by the communities she affiliated with: as a member of the '98 Executive many nationalists discriminated against her gender. In the early days of the Gaelic League she found herself chastised on public platforms in Donegal for not being a native Irish speaker.[76] As we shall see in later chapters, Milligan's feeling of never quite belonging made her acutely aware of the need to create forms of cultural production (such as tableaux) that were inclusive of people's complex identities (their gender, politics, region and religion). Milligan also attempted to build cross-community dynamics into the organizations she established. This was a standard set first by the Irish language group in Belfast and then by the Gaelic League in August 1893 when it made membership available to both men and women; and to everyone who wanted to join regardless of their politics or religion.

But certainly as a northern Protestant (who was not a member of the Anglo-Irish elite) Milligan found it necessary throughout her life to find narratives that could translate her otherness into a language understandable (and acceptable) to others. This narrative was most often autobiography and it was a story she would relate in public interviews and through poems such as 'October ode' and 'When I was a little girl'. These poems and narratives helped 'explain' the radical position of 'otherness' that she had felt growing up in the Unionist community she ideologically left behind. They also articulate her sense of alienation from the nationalist communities that required (and often provided) such explanations of national becoming. Autobiography was the way Milligan conveyed what it meant for her (and more broadly) for other northern Protestants who were raised in Ireland with no sense of Irish cultural identity and yet who did not consider they should be excluded from that identity. In a lecture entitled 'The north and the national movement' Milligan described in detail the education of the 'Ulster Protestant' for the Irish Literary Society, London in July 1896. Her remarks caused J.K. Bracken, the founder member of the Gaelic Athletic Association in Tipperary, to write to the *Shan Van Vocht* and explain his contrasting experiences of the pro-Irish education he had received as a southern Catholic 'at his mother's knee, where duty to God and to Ireland were inculcated together'. Milligan reported his letter:

> As a child he had seen true men in Tipperary go to make confessional for death, and then march away in arms in their hands ready to die for Ireland in the glorious '67. He had, however, faith in the North, which had it done no more than give Ireland a man like John Mitchel had given them grounds for gratitude and hope.[77]

John Paul Sartre argued in the 1940s that, 'there is no reality except in action ... man is nothing else but what he purposes, he exists only in so far as he realizes himself, he is therefore nothing else but the sum of his actions, nothing else but what his life is.'[78] Sartre developed his political theories only after he renounced the bourgeois presumptions endemic in his family class background about the direction his life should take. In *A Royal Democrat*, Cormac King finds in Ireland an opportunity to experience a life different from the one ordained for him by birth: 'He was free, liberated suddenly from bonds which he had deemed were to bind him for life.'[79] Cormac's reflections about the imprisoning limitations of a preordained life, articulated Milligan's own anxieties about the colonial strictures of a historically imposed identity.

Alice Milligan's writings from 1888 to 1893 are a kind of journey in which she restlessly paces up and down, tracing and retracing the footsteps of historical, colonial, fictional and imagined travellers who have passed (and who are passing) through the country of her birth. Milligan's Ireland in the years before the Revival was a place in which nobody is quite at home either with themselves or with each other: English tourists are also Irish voters; military settlers illegally fall in love with the native Catholic 'other'; in doing so they find themselves 'othered'; dispossessed daughters return 'home' only to re-enact expulsion; girls constantly 'wish' they'd been boys; children secretly long to escape the family nursery and run with the rebels; kings don't want crowns, politicians look too vulnerable to be leaders of people; then there are 'the Irish' who are 'native' and 'the Irish' who are not.

If Milligan had started out exploring the otherness of English travellers in Ireland, she entered the Revival movement a traveller herself. Over the next decades 'she found herself' (literally and metaphorically) journeying into the heart of Ireland's complex communities physically, in newspaper print, through private letters, in fictions, lecture tours, magic lantern and theatre shows. There would be

19a Magic lantern projection, from 'Lanterne de projection à deux objectifs à lumière oxyhydérique', *La Nature*, 391 (1880), 2, courtesy of Mervyn Head.

no more private diaries after 1893: everything she thought and felt would be communicated in the public arena of newspapers or in private discourse of letters. Every journey begins from home. And from the moment Milligan understood that Belfast was 'the enemy's camp', she knew that the north was the centre of the Irish Cultural Revival's radical beginnings. If Susan Mitchell viewed Milligan as the 'nursemaid' of the early Revival, Belfast was the experimental nursery.

CHAPTER THREE

Identity

The cultural movement of 1890s Belfast is a part of history that is difficult to trace and uncover: it is a fractured unknown story that only barely comes to light through memoirs, newspaper reports, interviews and private letters. Milligan was actually the key figure in a chapter of the Revival's history that has disappeared from our understanding of Ireland's most revolutionary cultural movement. There is therefore a disparity between the celebrated narrativized, multi-perspectival views we have of the Revival as it unfolded in Dublin: this disparity is Belfast. Everything that was achieved in Belfast in the 1890s was immediately contested by a whole range of oppositions: by unionists who objected to Irish cultural nationalism; by nationalists who opposed republicans; by men and women who contested the political feminism of Milligan and others. The organizations and cultural initiatives established largely by Milligan in the 1890s were so thoroughly undone almost as soon as they were founded. In part this was because of the extraordinary pace of Milligan's own shifting identity and of the endlessly transforming and international nature of the organizations that she set up across the city.

But the problem of cultural disappearances also arose out of political negligence: the rich cultural legacy of late nineteenth-century Belfast was utterly erased from the records of history by the systematic lack of acknowledgement by both the state of Northern Ireland and by the Free State. The Revival was not seen as a significant part of the new Northern state's historical cultural legacy after 1921, while the Free State most often only celebrated the part of Irish cultural history that had taken place in the south. The cultural organizations and initiatives that took place in Belfast and across the north in the 1890s were therefore not considered worthy of research or space in the state archives of either country.

When Milligan and her associates set up cultural alliances and printing presses and commemorative public events in the north, they did so with a consciousness that the north had a different political dynamic to the rest of Ireland. Milligan was acutely aware of a Protestant unionist politics that dominated one of the most industrialized sites of capitalism in the empire. The Irish language classes, the Irish Women's Association, the McCracken Society and the *Northern Patriot* defined themselves as separatist organizations that aimed to combat 'Ulster's colonial isolation' from the rest of Ireland. Milligan overcame this severely limiting atmosphere in her second journal, the *Shan Van Vocht* and through her increasing

20 Photograph of Belfast in the 1890s, the period in which Milligan was founding cultural organizations and journals across the city.

allegiance to the culturally nuanced possibilities released by the Gaelic League's democratic membership policy and branch system. In the 1890s, Milligan hoped to generate a vibrant set of culturally active and engaged communities in the north that could integrate fully into the broader national and international Revival movement.

The narrative of this movement was simply impossible to include either as part of the history of Ireland as a whole or of Northern Ireland. It is therefore not only hard to find these broken airbrushed pieces of Ireland's history (and of Alice Milligan's life story) but it is difficult also to know which part of the jigsaw they ever belonged to. Milligan's story in this decade is the story of the forgotten women's movement in 1890s Ireland; it is the story of the Irish language and the Gaelic League's northern origins; it is the story of a radical Irish publishing venture that was achieved by two northern women whose religious and political

"Ꞡoꝺ sᴀᴠe ᴀll heꞃe & bless the ᴡoꞃᴋ;
Sᴀᴜs Roꞃᴜ,of the hill."

Uɴᴅᴇʀ this heading we shall record from month to
    month what is being done in different departments
of work for the advancement of Ireland's cause, and for
the cultivation of her people.   We shall be pleased to receive, from Literary Societies throughout the country,
complete reports of each month's meetings.

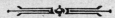

21 'For the Old Land', column reporting all the work of emerging cultural groups,
Shan Van Vocht, 1897.

backgrounds make such a union visionary. By charting Milligan's life in the 1890s
we are able to see how simultaneous groups and alliances were formed and how
individuals became part of a collective movement that we now call the Irish
Cultural Revival.

Alice Milligan and the Irish language

In the mid-1890s, Milligan wrote with urgency that 'it is in this generation the
Gaelic League will be lost or saved'.[1] The statistics even for Belfast justified
Milligan's assessment and proved the success achieved by her generation in just ten
years. In 1891, 900 people living in the city identified themselves as Irish speakers;
by 1901 that figure had increased to 3,587. Given her northern Protestant
Anglicized educational upbringing, Irish was clearly not an obvious choice for
Milligan. It is therefore all the more extraordinary to realize how early Milligan
understood that the Irish language was vital to the survival of Irish culture, to the
emergence of a new modern political movement, and to her own identity as an
artist and an Irish woman. The first act of collective becoming for Milligan in the

Irish language was 1892 when Francis Joseph Bigger founded an Irish language class. This was a significant development because it meant that she (and many others) did not have to travel elsewhere to learn Irish. As we know, Milligan had initially heard Irish spoken by farm workers in Co. Tyrone, she had won a scholarship to Donegal in the 1870s, and in 1891 she studied Irish in Dublin at unofficial lessons delivered by the secretary of the Royal Irish Academy.

In 1892 all isolated private dispersed study came to an end for Milligan. Taught by Patrick J. O'Shea (whose pen name was 'Conan Maol') in a room inside the Belfast Museum, the class was affiliated to the Belfast Naturalists' Field Club, an organization Milligan had been part of since the 1880s. She later recalled how pupils attending the informal Irish language classes were thrown into contact with the traces of Belfast's revolutionary history: 'we hung our cloaks and laid sticks and umbrellas against the cases holding cocked hats and green uniforms that had figured in many a Volunteer muster'.[2] The group's interests strayed beyond pure linguistics as they worked to 'revive Irish music and the Irish tongue'[3] in a city where there existed few 'opportunities of cultivating a taste for Gaelic'.[4] It was through the Belfast language groups that she first encountered figures such as Anna Johnston ('Ethna Carbery'), Francis Joseph Bigger, Patrick MacGinley, John O'Donovan, Michael Hussey, Dermot Foley, William Gray, T. Ward and Sinclair Boyd. Each of these now almost forgotten figures were themselves to become workers in the Gaelic League and contributors to the revival. These individuals would form the backbone to everything that followed in the north for the Gaelic League.

From 1892, Milligan undoubtedly became a major figure who helped save the Irish language from extinction: what is remarkable is that she did so from the position of not being a native speaker and of being a life-long learner. Often she was facilitating events that she could never fully participate in. Sometimes this could result in very uncomfortable moments such as when she was forced to apologize 'for speaking the Saxon tongue' from a platform in Donegal.[5] Yet she remained determined that Irish identity should be nuanced enough to include everyone regardless of their proficiency in Irish. Could she or could she not speak and write in Irish? The evidence about whether she did or did not speak Irish is hard to assess. In 1904 she wrote that she had been permanently 'left behind' by her contemporaries in the Belfast class as she had not attended for the best part of (what turned out to be) a crucial year for study. Yet in 2007 an old country doctor in Co. Fermanagh told me how Milligan often visited his school in Donegal and was frequently heard speaking fluent Irish with his school teacher. It could also have been the case that Milligan was initially hampered by the poor quality of early Revival Irish language text books. It is likely she had another attempt at learning when more books became available for Irish language learners. Certainly she received letters in Irish and she translated poetry on several occasions into Irish.

Throughout her long life Milligan was absolutely committed as a learner to facilitating others to learn. The language classes were taken often by people who, like Milligan, had to learn the language from scratch. W.P. Ryan explained how Irish communities could set up new Gaelic League branches and suggested how they could cope with the vastly different levels of Irish within local communities:

> In other places we have simply at first a few enthusiasts (or even one) who must learn the language from the beginning, and then teach others … In several places will be found native speakers – in certain cases people who can talk but cannot read or write Irish. Their assistance will be very valuable in the matters of pronunciation and in giving students a good knowledge of the spoken language. Also, those who only speak Irish can themselves be very soon taught to read it.[6]

Milligan may not have been a native speaker; she may not have achieved absolute fluency or developed the confidence to speak and write in Irish. On the other hand, she may have been proficient in Irish and chosen not to write or speak the language often. Milligan may also not have had the opportunity to speak Irish in the north at the very time when she was being remembered most: in the 1930s she felt isolated in Northern Ireland where Irish was treated as a 'foreign' language. Milligan created an interspace for Irish in all her literature and through all forms of textual and non-textual cultural production she engaged with. We see this, for instance, in her plans for including Irish in the second Belfast-based journal that she edited at the time when there were few outlets for the Irish language in the press. In 1896 she wrote to the co-founder of the Gaelic League, Eoin MacNeill: 'I am going to try to have in the *Shan* a brief leader in Irish every month after the new year. It is for the News most people buy newspapers & it is the news of the day should be put into Irish. I would like to see all the paragraphs about the progress of the language given in Irish with the English; side by side.'[7] Milligan dedicated decades of her life to creating the cultural conditions that would give the Irish language new meaning and a social context in which it could begin to exist: she helped establish Irish teaching colleges in Letterkenny, Donegal and Antrim; founded numerous Gaelic League branches across Ireland and Britain; and promoted the language movement abroad in places such as the US and Argentina.

Milligan provided valuable documents describing the early days of the League through her journalism and autobiographical memoirs which she published in the Irish language papers. She also later became the voice and the memory of the early League in the post-Partition years when she began to republish poems from the *Shan Van Vocht* that had been written in the 1890s by key language activists. The attitudes of the Northern Irish authorities after 1922 reveal just how subversive an act of commemoration and re-memory this process of contextual republication actually was. After 1916 all the work that Milligan and her associates did in saving the language from extinction and sectarianism was undone. By the 1930s just fifteen teachers in Belfast were trained to teach in Irish. In 1937, the parliamentary secretary to the ministry of education in Northern Ireland spoke of Irish as a 'foreign tongue' in the six counties. In the year that the ministry in Northern Ireland withdrew the £1,500 payable in fees for the teaching of Irish, the ministry of education in the Free State paid £2 per head to 3,960 children in Donegal for efficiency in Irish as their home language.[8] As Gordon McCoy explained:

> From the 1920s until the 1970s the Irish language movement had little relationship with the unionist-dominated Government. There was no point in having one anyway, as Irish was effectively banned from public life; the Irish restricted the language to the private domain and Catholic schools … While unionist officials regarded Irish speakers as seditious, lack of support for the language was justified on modernist or utilitarian grounds, which appeared to be less politically partisan. The Regional Director of the BBC refused to produce Irish language broadcasts, writing in 1940 'there are no Gaelic speakers in Northern Ireland, by which I assume is meant Erse or Irish'.[9]

The crisis point in the Irish language that was reached in Northern Ireland by the 1950s was intensified by the sectarian politics that underpinned so much of the country's social policy. One hundred years after Milligan began her campaign to save Irish, the Belfast Peace Agreement had to begin the same process all over again. The 1948 Declaration of Human Rights and funding from the European Community helped re-animate the contemporary Irish language movement in the six counties. Yet language activists in the North also took great energy and hope from the earlier work of Alice Milligan and her generation: organizations such as Ultach and human rights bodies recognized that they had much to learn from those who had managed to regenerate a minority language within a non-sectarian dynamic after centuries of colonial censorship.

Liminality was a deliberately nuanced space that Milligan intentionally opened up in her own work. The silence of the tableaux made national theatre and the national language movement available to people at very different stages of Irish language learning. Her early theatre productions often included bi-lingual programmes and bi-lingual storytelling: in fact, in 1898 Milligan convinced Belfast's *Irish News* to give over their printing press to produce the first bi-lingual theatre programme for their Irish cultural festival. The emphasis on gestural theatre made it possible for audiences who did not have Irish to understand what was being enacted in Irish on the stage. Milligan published all her plays in Irish newspapers and she prefaced each with the instruction, 'To be translated into Irish'. She often sent her plays to school teachers to assist with translation: Irish versions of three of her plays were published in the last two decades of her life when they were specifically marketed for schools. In 1897 after writing a poem and a narrative based on the story of Brian of Banba, Milligan wrote: 'I hope to get my narrative translated into modern Irish'.[10] Being in English did not make these plays any less Irish but this was a contention that she had to fight continually with language purists such as Patrick Pearse who argued that: 'If we once admit the Irish-Literature-In-English idea, then the language movement is a mistake'.[11] The copyright for her plays was always given over to the Gaelic League and she worked with schools, colleges and branches of the language movement across Ireland to stage Irish plays and theatre.

As an Irish woman at the dawn of a new national history where language was a site of conflict and as a woman forgotten by that history, Alice Milligan occupies an in-between space. This was reflected in her cultural production and in her legacy that could not be envisaged or fully researched until after the contemporary Irish peace process began in the 1990s. The Gaelic League issued quotations by famous Irish writers on most of their teaching material. One such pamphlet began with words by Thomas Davis: 'A nation without a language of its own is only half a nation.'[12] Was an Irish person without Irish only half a person? Milligan's liminality was often expressed through her relationship with language: as a subject Milligan was never unified in Irish or English; instead she tried to imagine a cultural space that encompassed both at the same time. Moreover, the north and the traditions of unionist Protestantism seemed to contest the Irish language, particularly in the twentieth century when the language was increasingly associated with politics and with religious identity. This sectarianism was already making its presence felt at the end of the nineteenth century within the Gaelic League. Despite the League's policy of non-sectarianism, some members of the organization increasingly associated the Irish language with Catholicism. Gaelic League activist Fr Peter O'Leary publicly declared that the League was a Catholic organization and that allegiance to its project should 'override all other associations'.[13] Douglas Hyde confided to his fellow Gaelic League founder, Eoin

MacNeill that this proposal was 'simply monstrous' because it seemed to exclude non-Catholics.[14]

The poet and translator T.W. Rolleston informed Hyde that if O'Leary were allowed to continue speaking his views in the name of the League, Protestants would be forced to establish a separate language organization of their own: 'there are over a million Protestants in Ireland – they cannot be driven out'.[15] The debate about whether the Gaelic League could remain politically neutral raged from 1893 into the new century. In 1906, for example, the Church of Ireland rector James Owen Hannay (who wrote fiction under the pen name of George A. Birmingham) announced: 'When they say that the League is non-political they mean that it is, and will continue to be, a society which anyone may join without prejudice to his political convictions.'[16] Under pressure to abandon his non-partisan stance in 1914, Hyde declared that 'the language is not the monopoly of the League but the possession of the nation'.[17]

Towards the end of the decade, Milligan found herself in the midst of a very complex argument: while she wanted to promote the Irish language, she did not want those who could not speak Irish (that is, the majority of Irish Protestants) to be excluded from the essence of the cultural movement and the broader project of decolonization. When the Irish language was in danger of being completely aligned with Catholicism, Milligan was quick to show that Protestants had made a major contribution to the national anti-colonial struggle even though they had not been Irish speakers. In a lecture entitled 'Nationalism and the Gaelic League', Milligan insisted that a Revival movement should not alienate non-Irish speakers from involvement in the cultural and political national movement. She pointed out the absurdity of the views being propounded by some of her contemporaries in the Revival who dismissed the work of Ireland's most revered revolutionary thinkers and activists:

> The policy of United Irishmen is attacked, the Young Ireland movement is derided. We have lived to hear Wolfe Tone & Robert Emmet as [not] being Irishmen at all because they did not talk Irish – & the work of Thomas Davis set at naught.[18]

In an attempt to dislodge Irish identity from the precondition of speaking Irish, Milligan suggested that '*No nation; no language* is being carried too far'.[19] Concluding that, 'in the Gaelic movement, everyone is a worker', Milligan resisted the view that a person's voice should only be heard if it carried words in the Irish language.[20] This was a practical view that Milligan would later restate in her defence against Pearse's opinion that 'since she was not a fluent speaker of Irish she should not be employed as an organizer by the League. This objection she countered by remarking that her job was to raise money and not to teach the native language.'[21]

The place in which this policy of inclusivity achieved most success was in the local communities she worked within; in the moments of cultural communication, and in the development of theatrical productions. Such aspects of Irish cultural history are hard to retrieve because so much of their energy and meaning was contained in the act of becoming; they existed in moments of recognition within specific receptive communities. These unofficial language classes clearly provided a significant meeting ground for a range of cultural activists in the north at the beginning of the 1890s. The Irish language class that started in Belfast may have been small, but its impact was lasting. The first branch of the Gaelic League was established in Dublin by Douglas Hyde and Eoin MacNeill in 1893. This was an organization that Milligan gave her absolute commitment to as she explained to an audience in London in 1899: 'I am heart & soul with the Gaelic Movement … it is at present giving new life to the National movement in Ireland … no better medium than the Gaelic League has appeared in Ireland in my lifetime.'[22] The second branch of the Gaelic League was set up in Belfast in 1895; a significant development in the Revival that was immediately successful in large part because Milligan and her fellow cultural workers had already established a receptive Irish language learning community within the city. According to Milligan, 'the steady growth of this club necessitated the formation of the Belfast Gaelic League in August 1895'.[23]

This class enabled all the people who would become key workers in the League to gather together for the first time and to form a collective activism. These early members and founders were also the people who initiated the different spheres of the League's northern social and educational network. Establishing the Irish language as a spoken living language was clearly not just about learning grammar or publishing helpful text books (although the League did this also). The Gaelic League members quickly realized that the Irish language would only take shape if they were able to give life to a thriving economic, textual, oral and cultural environment. This is what 'Sliabh Liagh' meant in 1917 when she wrote: 'The Gaelic League has done good work in keeping alive the spirit of Nationality amongst the people.'[24] Milligan and her associates staged bi-lingual theatre productions in Derry and Belfast; fundraised for the establishment of Irish Teacher Training Colleges such as Cloughaneely in Co. Donegal; they founded the Ulster Union of the Gaelic League in 1906 'to unify the various Irish language and cultural activists in the north'.[25] Their first Festival of the Glens in 1904 has been described by Richard Kirkland as 'the high watermark of the Northern Revival activity'.[26] This unique cultural festival became a meeting ground for an extraordinary range of political and cultural activists that included: Alice Milligan,

Roger Casement, Bulmer Hobson, Margaret Dobbs, Ada McNeill, Francis Joseph Bigger and Alice Stopford Green.

One of the most inspired interventions of the Gaelic League was its immediate emphasis on the equal and democratic rights of both 'Irish men and women' to be members and workers in the language revival. This mixing of the sexes was, of course, one of the main problems the Irish Catholic church had with the Gaelic League. Sydney Brooks noted in his 1907 social history, *The new Ireland*:

> At Portarlington the parish priest, though himself the President of the local branch of the League, fought it violently over the question of mixed classes. The laymen insisted that men and women should attend the classes in Gaelic together. The priest wanted the men to go for their instruction to the Christian Brothers School, and the women to the local convent. There was a terrific contest with denunciations from the pulpit, the expulsion of the priest from the League, his effort to start a rival branch, which headquarters refused to recognize, his appeal to the Irish priesthood to 'rig' the elections to the Council, and, finally, the meeting of delegates from all the branches throughout the country, and their overwhelming election to the Executive Council of the very man who had led the struggle against him.[27]

The anxiety of the priests may also have been an objection to the disempowerment of the church in local communities and to the prominent inclusion of women in a national cultural organization. Participating in this early language group and the Gaelic League increased Milligan's circle of female colleagues to include such figures as Margaret Hutton, Rosamond Praegar, Agnes Farrelly, Ada McNeill, Alice Stopford Green and Mary Spring Rice. Women not only founded a huge percentage of the Gaelic League's branches but they also filled many of the (unpaid) teaching posts. Alice Milligan and Anna Johnston were the first founding women members of the Belfast language class: 1892 signalled the beginning of a working friendship that was to have a profound impact on the cultural direction of both women's lives and on the Revival movement as a whole. But in the early 1890s, the lack of women present at the Belfast group immediately heightened Milligan's awareness that there was a need for an alliance that women could both organize and participate in. Her solution was to found the Irish Women's Association in 1894.

The Irish Women's Association

The Irish Women's Association was the first public formalized articulation of a feminism that was at the heart of Milligan's career: she quickly understood that within society and within Irish politics, women were doubly discriminated against. Ireland had no parliament of its own and women (in Milligan's own words) 'were not called upon to have any opinion whatsoever' about decisions made in Westminster.[28] Women were therefore denied a vote within the empire as well as within their own country at national and local level. In the 1890s, Milligan developed a position amounting to a total rejection of parliamentary politics that was both a response to the discrimination she faced as a woman and to the undemocratic lack of an independent Irish government. She first articulated this position in 1896 after she commissioned four articles from James Connolly, the founder of the Irish Socialist Republican Party. While she completely supported Connolly's objectives, Milligan's editorial strongly opposed his recommendation for Irish people to vote Irish socialists into the British parliament:

> Whilst in full sympathy with Mr Connolly's views on the labour and social questions, we are absolutely opposed to the scheme he puts forward for the formation of an Irish Republican party in the British Parliament. Any conscientious Republican would stick at the oath of allegiance and no reliance could be placed on what John O'Leary calls 'double-oathed' men. John Mitchel allowed himself to be returned as a representative, but absolutely refused to entertain the idea of claiming his seat. He looked upon his election merely as a declaration in favour of his unalterable rebel principles. We would like to have this question debated.[29]

In October 1897 Connolly invited Milligan to lecture to the Irish Socialist Republican Party in Dublin. She agreed but in turn invited him to participate in a public debate with her about the issue of Irish parliamentary representation in England stating that: 'In advocating the formation of a democratic party in Parliament they are taking the broad road that leads to destruction, as such a party would inevitably be in alliance with the English labour party.'[30]

Milligan also opposed Irish parliamentary politics because political parties usually banned women members. This was an exclusion that extended to the Irish cultural organizations that were often affiliated to political parties. By 1894, the Young Ireland Society had long been considered to be the only northern organization affiliated with the cultural Revival. But this Society was actually a branch of the Irish Parliamentary Party and as such meetings were limited to the party faithful, and to men only.[31] Feminism was embedded within all of Milligan's activities and in the types of cultural production she engendered and participated in. Her feminism existed at the level of formal separatist organizations that she established (the Irish Women's Association and the Irish Women's Centenary

Union) and joined (*Inghinidhe na hÉireann* – Daughters of Ireland). Milligan created strong female characters in her prose fictions, poetry and plays. She also forged life-long alliances and friendships with women at home and abroad who themselves were involved in multiple aspects of Ireland's cultural and political history: the Revival movement, the Easter Rising of 1916, the Irish War of Independence, the Civil War and the anti-Partition campaigns.

But in the early days of 1894 Milligan would not have viewed herself as part of a nationalist or a cultural movement. Yet she was aware that there were other women like herself who were articulate, educated and politically engaged. Alone they remained isolated from each other and from the broader public sphere of cultural politics, yet collectively they could make an intervention and build alliances of solidarity. Irish cultural activism became the signature of the Revival. Irish women wrote their names into history by finding forums through which their voices could be heard. In this decade large numbers of women began to learn Irish, express themselves through both languages orally and in print (in large part through newspapers), they wrote poetry, produced Irish music, wrote and staged plays. They became educationalists, actresses, playwrights, printers, artists and editors. They also became founders of journals and members of organizations and committees. Like all the associations that were founded in the Revival, the women conducted their associations and organizations as though they had already won their independence at every level. The cultural revivalists printed membership cards, drew up manifestos, elected presidents and secretaries, kept detailed accounts and professional minutes: they were the nation in waiting ready to take the power they already sensed at their fingertips. Virginia Woolf interpreted women's enthusiasm for professionalized committees as a symbol of the power they desired and that society denied them. In her diary in 1918 she recorded her thoughts after attending a Women's Guild meeting in London: 'the Guild ... it does somehow stand for something real to these women ... they have a deeply hidden and inarticulate desire for something beyond the daily life; I believe they relish all the pomp of offices and elections because in some way it symbolises this other thing.'[32] In their enthusiasm for committees, Woolf observed that women also ran the risk of bureaucratization. She herself avoided attending committee meetings because she viewed them as a drain on her creative energies.

Because so many women were involved in the Revival movement, we tend to think of it as a democratic and inclusive movement. The Gaelic League was open to both men and women; the 1916 Declaration (written by those at the forefront of the Revival) was addressed to 'Irishmen and women'; the 1916 insurrection against the empire was fought by women such as Constance Markievicz; Maud Gonne was the first women in Europe to be voted into parliament in 1918;

Hanna Sheehy Skeffington was appointed to the first executive of Fine Fáil in 1926; the Abbey Theatre was funded by a woman; one of its key directors and playwrights was a woman; women led the way in union rights in Belfast textile industries. Throughout her long and varied life, Alice Milligan came to know all these women personally: she admired their achievements and acknowledged the struggles Irish women had faced historically; she not only read what her female contemporaries wrote, she sought out material from them to publish; she attended their talks and created forums for women to speak publicly.

Yet her male contemporaries often would not have necessarily taken it for granted that Irish women should have equal membership or equal rights within the organizations and events that defined the Cultural Revival. There was much discrimination for instance, in the Henry Joy McCracken Literary Society's treatment of Alice Milligan and Anna Johnston. Despite being the founders and editors of the Society's journal the *Northern Patriot*, they were denied the basic rights given to other (less senior) members. Even though she had been elected vice-president of the Society, Milligan found herself most often barred from decision-making elections and denied keys to the Society office. This was a form of discrimination she encountered repeatedly after she was elected onto the executive board of the 1798 Centenary committee.

In arguing in 1897 that 'Ireland's rights should be won before that of any other radical reform was agitated', Milligan was defining herself as a radical nationalist. The 'other radical' reforms that would have to wait included the democratic rights of women. Yet it was not at all guaranteed that women's human rights would be fully awarded by a new Irish government of a united Ireland. Post-Partition and after the Free State was declared in 1921, women largely disappeared from the cultural and political radar altogether. This earlier period of feminist activism, of which Milligan was a part, was completely forgotten and went unrecorded for the best part of a century until a new generation of historians began to reclaim these archives. In the 1890s Milligan clearly did not believe that women could achieve democratic rights within the context of an undemocratic system of national governance. Yet she was also conscious that women were being excluded from the very organizations that were set up to challenge this system. Irish women during this period joined many of the Revival's organizations and were leading figures in cultural events. But they were also very quick to establish separate organizations to make sure they had a place within the national movement as it took shape. For instance, both Milligan and Maud Gonne established organizations on the basis of 'women only' membership as direct responses to the exclusion of women from nationalist organizations. In her autobiography Gonne claimed that she had been inspired to establish *Inghinidhe na hÉireann* in Dublin in 1900 on behalf of 'all the girls who, like myself, resented being excluded, as women, from our national organizations. Our object was to work for the complete independence of Ireland.'[33] The 'Daughters of Erin' aimed to project women into the forefront of nationalist political consciousness.

Six years earlier Alice Milligan had set up the Irish Women's Association (IWA) in the three heartlands of northern unionism: Belfast, Portadown and Moneyreagh. This organization was much more politically nuanced than Maud Gonne's later Dublin-based initiative: the latter could take for granted that its members would also share socialist, feminist and generally republican views. But in the late nineteenth century context of northern politics, Milligan's IWA was an attempt to create a new cultural platform for Irish women who were living within the patriarchal heartlands of Protestant unionism. As the poem by Thomas Davis printed on their membership card proclaimed, the IWA was forthright about its policy of inclusivity: 'What matter that at different shrines we pray unto one God! / What matter that at different times your fathers won this sod!' [Plates 7 and 8]. This quote demonstrates a consciousness within the IWA that it was an organization set up to connect women of very different backgrounds who may have never joined anything independent of their families. The IWA did not aim to separate feminism from politics or history from tradition, but it did want to extract Irish cultural and political history from sectarianism.

Milligan's views expressed from the position of her presidency may have been more forthright than those held by other members. According to the *Irish News*, Milligan insisted in March 1895 that the role of the IWA was to challenge unionist versions of Irish history and identity:

> The main argument against Ireland's demands for nationality was the opposition of Ulster. This opposition was supposed to be colossal and unconquerable ... The Women's Association could do something towards breaking down the forces of intolerance, ignorance and bigotry, which kept Ulster apart from the rest of the country ... Their association established itself, so to speak, within the very stronghold of Unionism, and it was possible for them, though few in numbers, to spike the guns from which these missiles are discharged.[34]

Among the regular participants were women who would not have considered themselves nationalist or republican in the sense of desiring separatism from the Union. But they clearly did want to explore the possibilities for women in social politics and to engage with the meaning and production of Irish culture. The IWA in this sense was similar to the non-nationalist Gaelic League. Members included the novelist Moira Pender and her daughter Nora, the feminist Quaker Mary Hobson (whose son Bulmer would become revolutionary republican activist and close friend of Alice Milligan in later life), and several of Alice Milligan's sisters who participated in meetings, especially when there was an opportunity for them to perform Irish music.

Milligan suggested, rather disingenuously, that the Irish Women's Association had been 'established under very happy auspices'.[35] But as soon as the IWA was launched in November 1894, a major unionist Belfast paper, the *Northern Whig*, attacked the organization relentlessly until the end of the year. The paper viewed the IWA as a symbol of everything that needed to be suppressed: it was nothing more than an uncouth example of the 'weakness' of women who 'venture without much experience on the stormy sea of politics'.[36] They suggested the women should stay by their 'own firesides' and leave politics to 'their fathers, husbands, and brothers' who 'may be expected to know something' on the subjects that women could know very little about.[37] They also exploited the launch of the IWA as another opportunity to marginalize the support for nationalists in the north. Belfast, the *Northern Whig* stated, 'returns four Unionist Members of Parliament, and if we had an equitable system of redistribution of seats … it would return two more'.[38] They ridiculed the association as being mainly made up of men, dismissing 'Milliken's' role as president of the organization because she was an outsider (having only lived in Belfast for fifteen years): 'the few ladies present [at the launch] were not recognised as Belfast ladies at all'.[39]

After Milligan invited Louise Swan to talk about the issues she had faced in establishing women's organizations in the north of England, the paper refused to call the IWA anything but the 'Women's Home Rule Union'. The press derided the Women's Association as nothing more than an extension of Lady Aberdeen's British Liberal Home Rule Federation. Following two weeks of relentless criticism, Milligan replied that by objecting to Swan's presence in Ireland, the *Northern Whig* was subverting its own loyalist, Anglo-centric principles: 'The lady in question being an Englishwoman, you treated her mission to Ulster as an intrusion'.[40] Milligan denied that the IWA was connected to the British Liberal Party, claiming 'No affiliation with the English Women's Liberal Federation was ever suggested or intended.'[41] Although Milligan had helped Lady Aberdeen to set up a Derry branch of the Irish Industries Association in 1893, she soon dismissed Lady Aberdeen's work in Ireland as a dangerous example of: 'English philanthropists under royal, vice-regal, and aristocratic patronage'.[42] It is not hard to understand why Milligan's patience with Lady Aberdeen's version of the aims of the Irish Revival was so short lived. In her November 1893 pamphlet *Why we should encourage Irish industries*, the Lord Lieutenant's wife explained exactly why Irish workers were in dire need of paternalistic aid from England: 'How can peasants in the west of Ireland know what will be wanted during the coming season at London and Paris and New York?'[43]

The idea of 'Home Rule' – with its implication of domestic servitude and political isolation – was a prominent feature in the public opposition to the IWA. The women responded by debating the roles women should adopt in the national struggle. The poet Mary Hobson suggested in a paper entitled 'Social and political work of women' that Irish women should not simply attend to 'domestic duties' within the home:

> It is the duty of every woman to take an interest in the country in which she lived, to know something of its history, past and present, and, if in the conditions under which she and her sisters are placed are likely to lead to a fair development, she should be prepared with the experience she has gained through many years to extend her help and sympathy outside her own home.[44]

Hobson envisioned that the IWA's 'duty' lay in bridging 'the sectarian differences which have so much separated the people in the past, and making the name of Irishmen and Irishwomen a title of honour in the land of their birth'.[45] The novelist Moira Pender similarly called upon the IWA to create a united front of women from various backgrounds. For Pender, the IWA's central objective was 'to draw together the women of Ulster, without distinction of class or creed or politics, into a loyal and loving sisterhood, pledged to do all that women might do on a common platform for the common good of their dear native land.'[46]

As a trained teacher, educational imperatives were at the heart of all cultural initiatives that Milligan helped to activate in the north during the 1890s. Community education programmes were also something that she carried through to her work for the Gaelic League movement. The Irish Language Society, the Irish Women's Association and later the Henry Joy McCracken Literary Society offered lectures, reading groups, access to literature and shared spaces for the discussion of ideas at a time when adult education classes were not widely available. Furthermore, for many who joined these groups, it would have been the first time they were able to gain access to national and nationalist literature, history books, to listen to and produce Irish music and participate in public cultural discussions. This was particularly the case for Protestant members like Alice Milligan whose access to Irish cultural history or Irish culture as a living dynamic would have been limited. Mary Hobson concluded one of her talks by stating that 'the aims and objectives of the IWA are not entirely political, but in large measure social'.[47] Each meeting, she argued, should be 'educational in the sense of providing an opportunity of improving ourselves by writing, reading, etc., on subjects in which we are all interested'.[48]

The women met in Belfast's Unitarian Church School in Rosemary Street where the United Irishmen secretly met in 1795. By meeting in the place where the United Irishmen had met a hundred years before, this subversive feminist alliance consciously forged a connection with Belfast's hidden revolutionary history; in doing so they released ideas embedded in the architecture of the city. The IWA thus reclaimed and re-animated the city's suppressed Irish cultural politics. In this historically charged space, they delivered talks, read new poetry and extracts from plays, performed Irish music and planned their responses to the political issues of the day:

> Mrs Hobson read an extract from Ruskin's 'Sesame and Lilies' on the education and influence of women. Miss Milligan read a ballad by Clarence Mangan and an original one on the 'Captivity of Red Hugh'. Mrs M.T. Pender having referred to the recent demand for reprieve in the case of John Twiss, in which the association had joined, read with great feeling a powerful ballad on 'Myles Joyce', which was listened to with evident sympathy and interest of all present. Miss Nora Pender contributed an Irish song, 'The Coulin' and Miss Eveleen Milligan sang to a guitar accompaniment 'A Spinning Wheel' words by A.P. Graves and 'The Skye Boat Song' a Jacobite ballad.[49]

From this one report in Belfast's *Irish News*, we see how the women were engaged in a complexly layered politics: multiple forms of imprisonment were expressed through several genres of song, poetry, and prose. They explored the incarceration of women in society and historical Irish conflict, as well as the plight of contemporary prisoners. This is the first instance we have of Milligan's preoccupation with Irish political prisoners in both her literature and in her public protests. Milligan reworked her poem about the imprisonment and escape of Red Hugh O'Donnell into a play in 1901, by which time his escape was considered a metaphor for Ireland's liberation from English rule. In 1917, she reworked the image from the play into a poem about de Valera's escape from Lincoln Prison.

The IWA took great interest in the 'miscarriage of justice' case of John Twiss, a Kerry farm labourer and 'moonlighter' who was to be executed for the murder of a tenant farmer. They publicized his plight at meetings and wrote to Dublin Castle requesting his reprieve.[50] In the face of protests from the nationalist community across Ireland, Twiss was tried and executed in 1895 in what was widely seen as a judicial murder. The ballad read by Pender at the IWA meeting commemorated Myles Joyce who was similarly executed in 1882. Myles Joyce, like John Twiss, was interrogated in English even though he only spoke Irish. The breakdown in communication that cost Myles Joyce his life was viewed in 1907 by his namesake James Joyce as an appropriate emblem of the poor translation of Irish culture and politics through foreign media. In 'Ireland at the Bar' he argued:

> The figure of this dumbfounded old man, a remnant of a civilization not ours, deaf and dumb before his judge, is a symbol of the Irish nation at the bar of public opinion. Like him, she is unable to appeal to the modern conscience of England and other countries. The English journalists act as interpreters between Ireland and the English electorate, which gives them ear from time to time and ends up being vexed by the endless complaints of the Nationalist representatives who have entered the House, as she believes, to disrupt its order and extort money.[51]

It is precisely the refusal and inability of the Irish to find personal and national articulation in the English language (and by implication, under English rule) that Milligan expressed later in her work through the tableaux form. In this dramatic mode, the still body protested censorship through silence: the national body awaiting speech. The Irish language activist Peadar Ua Laoghaire (Peter O'Leary) also refers to the problems encountered by Irish speakers in an English-speaking court: 'in any kind of legal affair, the man with English was able to turn black into white on them and they had no means of defending themselves'.[52] At their weekly meetings, the IWA foregrounded the human rights of prisoners and re-imagined the role of women in public space. They sought historical, literary and political examples of how such issues had been explored previously in Ireland.

Marcus Ward publishing company produced the IWA's membership card which bore the same motifs he had engraved in Alice Milligan's first publication *Glimpses of Erin*. The company began as a family paper-making business in 1802 under the management of John Ward. Throughout the nineteenth century it became one of the most successful Irish publishing houses that specialised in colour lithography and copybooks. Artists such as John Vinycomb and Kate Greenaway were employed to produce designs for cards and books. In the 1870s Marcus Ward boasted the firm as 'publishers, wholesale stationers and manu-facturers, lithographers, artistic designers, illuminators, engravers, dye sinkers, embosses, bookbinders'.[53] Ward would have been sympathetic to Alice and Seaton Milligan's early publications and projects as he too had participated in Irish language classes in Belfast in the 1870s. In both *Glimpses of Erin* and *A Royal Democrat*, the harp, round tower, wolfhound, and monastic ruin recur. However, a significant new element has been added to the scene on the IWA membership card: the sunburst first appeared on the Fenian flag during the insurrection of 1867 (and later provided the background to the *Shan Van Vocht* masthead in 1896). By contrast with *Glimpses of Erin*, the membership card did not present a physical female personification of Erin. Instead of being visualized as national emblems, female identity is recognized in the organization's epithet; actual women's names fill the spaces left for membership identification and the secretary's signature. Six years after *Glimpses of Erin*, women are no longer rendered visual icons but through the IWA they have been transformed into an active body.

The IWA established a network of 'Home Reading Circles' at which each member bought and read a recommended text before circulating it to the other members.[54] Austen Morgan noted that Mary Hobson was the mother of Bulmer Hobson, the Belfast republican Quaker who founded the Ulster Literary Theatre in 1901: 'Milligan and Hobson's mother were joint secretaries of the Irishwomen's Association, and a home reading circle met in young Hobson's house.'[55] Hobson also went on to subscribe (as a schoolboy) to Milligan's later journal the *Shan Van Vocht*, which he cited as key influence upon his work. This early context provides the foundation for Hobson's later commitment to Milligan during the Irish War of Independence, the Irish Civil War and in the years immediately following Partition.[56]

Milligan had been at pains to prove that the Irish Women's Association was not simply an Irish version of the British Liberal Home Rule movement. After Milligan's presidency ended, the IWA became an organization that, for the most part, avoided overt expressions of Irish nationalist politics. She sought out a different kind of organizational collective through which she could express a more forthright agenda and reach a larger audience. Milligan was also aware that her political ideals could not be fully realized solely within a gender segregated organization. Milligan therefore founded another organization in Belfast that aligned itself much more with political commemoration and with contemporary politics. But the cultural politics that Milligan seemed to be seeking in 1895 would not find its most articulate voice until 1896 when she founded the *Shan Van Vocht*. This was a journal edited by two women who themselves transcended the sectarian divides and embodied a new millennial energy. In the second half of this decade, Alice Milligan (a Protestant) and Anna Johnston (a Catholic) established and edited two of the most important journals to come out of Ireland in the nineteenth century. The first of these, the *Northern Patriot*, grew out of Milligan's involvement with the Henry Joy McCracken Literary Society.

Regionalism

In January 1895, Milligan helped to set up the Henry Joy McCracken Literary Society. Named in honour of the Presbyterian United Irishman who led the northern republicans in the Battle of Antrim in 1798, the society boldly asserted its political affiliations. Like the IWA, the McCracken Society was based in Belfast and concentrated its energies on promoting nationalist activities. As its revolutionary name suggests, this second organization established by Milligan was much more explicit in its regionalist nationalism. The more assertively political organization, the Henry Joy McCracken Literary Society, strove to make Ireland 'national in literature, and national in art, language and song'.[57] The Society fulfilled its educational aims through a series of lectures on Irish art and antiquities and a planned Irish language class.[58] To establish symbolic affiliations between contemporary Belfast and its political history, the Society structured their annual programme of events around 'Anniversary Commemorations' of nationalist 'martyrs' and insurrections such as the birth of Robert Emmet, the battle of Antrim and the death of Edward FitzGerald. After one such commemorative gathering, Society member James O'Donovan explained the intimate connection between the act of remembering Ireland's anti-colonial past and a re-envisioning of alternatives: 'These anniversaries of ours are no empty celebrations. We mean not alone to honour the dead but their principles that live as well.'[59]

Where the Irish Women's Association reading programme took the form of private discussion groups, the McCracken Society facilitated access to Irish national literature for its Belfast members by opening a reading room. Milligan invited supporters (including Francis Joseph Bigger and Maud Gonne) to donate books 'of a national character'[60] to the library, which she personally adorned with portraits of Edward Fitzgerald, Theobald Wolfe Tone, Hugh O'Donnell, Owen Roe O'Neill and John O'Leary. This library allowed Society members to encounter what Milligan termed 'works of sound national tone in the departments of history, biography, fiction and poetry'. The books in their collection were divided into periods representing the republican struggle in Ireland. 1798 was represented by *The life of Wolfe Tone*, Teeling's *Personal narrative*, *The life of FitzGerald*, R.M. Young's *Ulster in Ninety-Eight*, Madden's *Literary relics of the United Irishmen*, Barry O'Brien's *Tone's autobiography*. Works such as *The poems and essays of Thomas Davis*, Gavan Duffy's *Young Ireland*, John Mitchell's *Last conquest*, *Jail journal* and *The life of Meagher* represented the Young Ireland Movement while the 1867 Fenian Period was covered by *Speeches in the dock*. The fiction section included *Lily O'Hartegan*, *The last monarch of Tara* and Emily Lawless' *Eblana*. Maud Gonne and Francis Joseph Bigger also donated books. A

22 Henry Joy McCracken Society advert of *Christmas story* by Alice Milligan (Iris Olkyrn), from the *Northern Patriot*, December, 1895.

rural home reading scheme was simultaneously established to reach members who could not attend its lectures or discussion groups.[61]

The only information we have about the Irish Women's Association and the McCracken Society comes from Milligan's own weekly *Irish Independent* column entitled 'Notes from the north'. After eight months of McCracken Society activity, however, Milligan's journalism could no longer provide sufficient space for reporting the Society's events. She complained, too, that the nationalist press in Ireland gave limited space to revivalist events in the north:

> We have no national paper within the borders of Ulster, to speak for us to the rest of Ireland; and in the Dublin press we have no claim to more than a brief notice of anything we attempt.[62]

This is a fascinating statement not least because Milligan picks up on the south subconsciously forgetting or abandoning the north. To guarantee greater coverage of northern cultural events, the McCracken Society launched its own monthly journal in October 1895, the *Northern Patriot*, which was jointly edited by its only female members, Alice Milligan and Anna Johnston. In their first editorial the women declared that the journal would serve as: 'the voice of a body of staunch and energetic nationalists, speaking out boldly' from 'the darkest part of the land, surrounded by an overwhelming majority of opponents'.[63] In its use of fiction and poetry to explore and re-engage Irish nationalist history and culture, the *Northern Patriot* reasserted the educational agenda of its parent organization. The short stories, poems and songs that dominated its pages were largely contributed by Milligan herself (under the pseudonym 'Irish Olkyrn'), leading one reader to proclaim that 'another "Speranza" has come amongst us'.[64]

In their timetable of lectures, recitations, reading clubs and 'original nights' where participants read from their own work, the Irish Women's Association and the McCracken Society were similar to other revivalist organizations of that period such as the London and Dublin Irish Literary Societies. However, as Milligan had already learned through the IWA, Belfast's distinct political orientation presented northern cultural activists with challenges unmatched elsewhere in Ireland. In March 1895, Milligan asserted that in 'the very stronghold of Unionism' the Irish Women's Association would 'do something towards breaking down the forces of intolerance, ignorance and bigotry, which kept Ulster apart from the rest of the country'.[65] The Henry Joy MacCracken Literary Society was similarly set up to fulfil Belfast's 'great need … for a national literary educational society'.[66] By organizing cultural events in the north, Milligan and her associates thus set themselves in explicit opposition to unionism. As the public reception of the IWA demonstrated, the tension provoked by such nationalist statements became manifest in a series of highly public conflicts.

The IWA and the McCracken Society were alienated from the broader revival not only by their clashes with northern unionist opposition but also because of their own insular hostility towards cultural nationalists outside the north. The *Northern Patriot* December 1895 editorial offered a caustic seasonal greeting to 'Irish friends' beyond the invisible border:

> A Christmas greeting to Ireland round and round out of the North; and, added to this, a heartfelt hope that in the years to come our brother patriots of the other three provinces will drop a tone of distinction which they too frequently adopt, and cease to speak of the North, as if it were an alien-colonised district of Ireland, which is gradually being absorbed into union with the nation proper ... this assertion of Ulster's colonialism is exaggerated vastly.[67]

While the paper claimed to be the 'meeting-ground of many who differ in opinion as to the methods by which Ireland may be best served, but who have in the end one absorbing life purpose, one final goal, one common foe',[68] the journal's commitment to nationalist solidarity was severely undermined by its obsession with the north's cultural isolation. The 'common foe' depicted in the *Northern Patriot* included not simply the undemocratic rule of empire but also Irish nationalists outside Ulster.

In a celebratory Christmas letter to Milligan, John Clarke ('Ben More'), secretary of the McCracken Society, boasted that their journal had been successfully 'distributed all over the country'. He hoped that 'loving the common cause' would 'cement' Irish nationalists in a resolute political harmony.[69] But the cement was not long dry before cracks began to appear. Indeed, when she received Clarke's letter Milligan already knew that she was leaving the paper because the first edition of her new monthly journal, the *Shan Van Vocht*, was on sale by mid-January 1896. After only three editions, the democratic principles on which the *Northern Patriot* was apparently established were showing signs of strain. In his debut editorial for the *Northern Patriot*, 'Rollicks M. Quinzey' (probably pseudonym of John Clarke) announced that Milligan and Johnston had been dismissed on political grounds:

> We were reluctantly compelled to take this step in order to keep our journal from becoming the weapon of any particular party in Irish political life. The

THE

Northern ✳ Patriot

"How is Old Ireland?
And how does she stand?"

No. I. Vol. I.   Belfast: Monday, Oct. 15, 1895.   Price—Twopence.

CONTENTS.

Our Northern Patriot—J. O., ...   1
H. J. M'Cracken Literary Society, ...   2
The Betrayal of Clannabuidhe—ETNA CARBERY, ...   3
Selected Poetry—Edward Molloy, ...   4
Anne Devlin : An Irish Heroine, ...   5
William Warwick, Hanged 15th October, 1798, ...   6
William Orr, Biographical Sketch—H. C., ...   7
The Month's Martyrs, ...   9
Our Reading Room, ...   11
Our Story : The Dark Rose of Rathmullan—IRIS OLKYRN,...   12
Members' Column—Lord Edward, and Let Erin's Sons Re-
      member, and Thinkin' Long, ...   14

The Northern Patriot.

Here in the stronghold of the North,
   In brave M'Cracken's native town;
We, who have known the patriot's worth,
   Would wake the news of his renown.

The hill-top where his life was vowed,
   Stands fair against our northern sky,
And daily do the heedless crowd
   Pass where unmarked his ashes lie.

Up from the very street they tread,
   The martyr mounted to his fate,
On steps that to the scaffold led,
   One summer eve of ninety-eight.

But, oh, the cause for which he fought,
   And, oh, the land he died to free;
Though many died, have perished not,
   But wait the dawn that yet shall be !

And we, whilst clouds of darkness lower
   In Ireland's night of sternest fate,
Speak words to cheer the vigil hour
   Of all who for the sunrise wait.

We speak from records of the past,
   Of all who fought, of all who fell;
Of Ireland's martyrs, not the last —
   We have more cheering news to tell :

For in this city, 'neath that band,
   Where Ireland's sons in union met;
Our aim shall be the hopes to speak
   Of Northern patriots toiling yet.

ᙍE have chosen as the motto for our paper the
      questioning words of an old ballad, which was
sung in the streets; nay, I should say, secretly, in the
homes of Belfast nearly a hundred years ago. The
battle at Antrim had been fought and lost. The brave
young leader of that forlorn hope, had yielded his life

on the scaffold at the Market House of his native town.
True men and fair women who lamented his fate, wore
the green as mourning to honour his memory, and out
of the Lough, away over the Irish Sea to the shores of
France, the exiled United Irishmen fled from the
vengeance of the oppressor. In Paris they were met
by other exiles who had gone before them ; there was
the gay and gallant Tone, and many another patriot,
eagerly awaiting news from Ireland ; hoping to hear
that in spite of defeat, and disaster and death her spirit
was unconquered, and her star of hope still shining. We
all know the historic answer to the exile's question :—

" 'Tis the most distressful country that ever yet was seen,
   For they're hanging men and women for the wearing o' the green."

And now after nearly a hundred years, in that same
Belfast, M'Cracken's native town, which has grown
into a great city, we repeat the question :—

" How is old Ireland and how does she stand ?"

We shall not dwell upon the shame and sorrow and
treachery, far worse than English oppression, which
within late years has fallen to Ireland's lot ; making
some pause to ask themselves whether it is worth while
carrying on the struggle for freedom, when so many of
our race have shown themselves willing slaves.

From that black page in our history, we turn away
our eyes to read in the records of the past the names
of those who have fought and fallen in Ireland's cause,
and pined and died in prison for her sake—soldiers,
patriots, martyrs—during the long lapse of seven
centuries ; and the record inspires us with confidence
that the land for which they died is reserved by God
for some high destiny. We learn another lesson of hope
from history's pages, one which will sink deep in the
hearts of those who have founded, and who will work for
THE NORTHERN PATRIOT steadfastly and with unwavering earnestness, feeling that however humble they may
be in the world's eyes, it may be given them to achieve
much for Ireland. Within the last fifteen years we
have seen world-wide reputations built up by Irishmen,
whose talent, whose eloquence, is undoubted. We
have heard high boasts of what they were to accomplish
for their country by their marvellous talents. We have
seen those great reputations crumble into dust, when

23 The first issue of the *Northern Patriot* edited by Alice Milligan and
Anna Johnston, 1895.

Northern Patriot is a journal of the people; we shall never allow it to become an organ of faction.[70]

Milligan claimed in a letter to the *Irish Weekly Independent* that she had left the *Northern Patriot* and the McCracken Society on good terms and urged unity amongst northern nationalists: 'We part with our former associates, expressing a farewell hope that, though no longer banded with them, they will remember that Irish men and women should look but toward one foe, and that a strong one which all our efforts are required to combat.'[71] Writing to Francis Joseph Bigger in January 1896, John Smyth Crone, editor of the *Irish Book Lover*, viewed this new discord between northern nationalists as part of an inevitable trend in Irish history. He declared that it was 'the same sad old story of every Irish enterprise whether political, religious or literary – divide, divide'.[72]

The multiple reasons why Milligan and Johnston left – or were sacked – from the *Northern Patriot* are buried in an acrimonious battle that was fought out in the letters page of *United Ireland*. The conflict undermined Milligan's position within the McCracken Society, further exemplifying the internal warfare that stunted the organizational continuities of the northern revival. The Society's very first internal struggle emerged within a month of its establishment, when members of the McCracken Society Council undemocratically expelled most of its founding members. Initially run from the National Workingmen's Club on Royal Avenue, the Society began as an unofficial offshoot of the Belfast Amnesty Association (led by Anna Johnston's father, Robert). Owner of a timber yard in Belfast, Johnston's activities were monitored by police spies who were wary of his participation in the 1860s Fenian insurrection and of his ongoing involvement with the Irish Republican Brotherhood. Following un-timetabled summer elections, members of the Amnesty Association were ousted by the McCracken Society council in July 1895. The remaining members of the Society further cut ties with the National Workingmen's Club by immediately relocating its offices to another part of the city. After Anna Johnston and Alice Milligan became editors of the society's monthly journal, the *Northern Patriot*, the breach between the Belfast Amnesty Association and the McCracken Society was intensified.

These political tensions impacted negatively upon Anna Johnston's relationship with the McCracken Society, whose members refused to communicate directly with her. During an interview in the 1940s, Milligan revealed the anxiety aroused by the discovery of 'Ethna Carbery's' real name:

When some of the more squeamish members of the club learned that the joint editor of the club's paper, Eithne Carbery, [Anna Johnston] was in

THE

ꞹꝏtꞩern ꝓatriot:

A VOLUNTEER JOURNAL.

———◆———

RATES OF SUBSCRIPTION
(Post Paid).

				s.	d.
Quarterly,	...	...	...	0	7½
Half-Yearly,	...	...	...	1	3
Yearly,	...	...	...	2	6

All Contributions to be addressed to the Editor.
Subscriptions to the Secretary.

———◆———

Offices : IVEAGH CHAMBERS, NORTH STREET, BELFAST.

24 Advert showing subscription rates of the *Northern Patriot*.

reality the daughter of a Fenian, they wrote to Miss Milligan asking her to dissociate herself from Miss Carbery and to request Miss Carbery to leave the club.[73]

In February 1896, Milligan alleged that her co-editor was never formally invited to edit the *Northern Patriot* from the society's offices and that neither she nor Johnston were given keys to their editorial rooms or allowed access to Society mail or funds. She also recalled how 'the opportunity was taken at Miss Johnston's first appearance in their [McCracken Society council's] midst, to open an attack of a personal character.'[74] While Anna Johnston simply withdrew from the Society, refusing to attend lectures and meetings, Milligan confronted the Society's secretary John Clarke, warning that 'if these dissensions were persisted in he was to understand that I considered myself bound on the side of those they were opposing'.[75]

Differences between the editors and the Society manifested themselves again when Fenian Anniversary celebrations held separately by the McCracken Society and Amnesty Association were reported together in the journal. Milligan claimed that during one Society meeting:

> Strong objections had been made to the insertion in the December number, side by side, with a McCracken society report, of another Belfast meeting, at which some of her [Anna Johnston's] relatives and friends took part, and at which I was one of the chief speakers.[76]

The main lecture at this McCracken Society meeting was given by the Fred Allan, whose ascendancy as vice-president finally precipitated the resignation of Milligan and Johnston. For Milligan, Allan's rise within the McCracken Society inevitably compromised her own editorial independence. This particular rift isn't at all obvious as there were many similarities between the old and new vice-presidents. Both Allan and Milligan were Irish Methodists who had renounced the unionism of their educational upbringing. Allan became a key figure in the outlawed Irish Republican Brotherhood (IRB): by 1895 he was on its supreme council; he had founded the Parnellite newspaper the *Irish Weekly Independent* (to which Milligan was a writer between 1891 and 1894); and he was a major figure in the Amnesty movement (an association that Milligan was also committed to supporting). With such a background, Milligan and Johnston should have welcomed the involvement of Fred Allan in the McCracken Society.

But their disaffection (and the personal attack on Anna Johnston) was in fact generated by 'the bitter split' within the secret society and that resulted in the leading IRB organizers becoming radically 'estranged' from each other;[77] in fact, Anna Johnston's father was on the opposite side to Fred Allan. The ascendancy of Allan in the McCracken Society not only posed a challenge to Milligan's own position as vice-president, his attempt to take over editorial control of the *Northern Patriot* was an indirect attack on the faction of the IRB he was opposing, to which Anna Johnston and Milligan were affiliated. In February 1896, Alice Milligan was compelled to explain to readers of *United Ireland*:

> The cause of our resignation was that, without consulting or informing us, an addition had been made to the council. As editors we were responsible in the eyes of the public for the paper, and should have been informed of any addition to the numbers of those who owned the paper.[78]

From October to December 1895, Milligan and Johnston had continually attempted to disentangle the *Northern Patriot* from the clutches of its McCracken Society sponsors. In the journal's first number they stated that just one page of the *Patriot* would represent 'contributions from the members of the society which has been instrumental in starting the journal'.[79] In the November edition, the editors were more forthright: 'whilst the society has undergone the risk and expense of starting the paper, it hopes to put it in a quite independent position'.[80] Dissatisfied with the terms offered by the McCracken Society council Anna Johnston resigned in December 1895. Milligan held out for new editorial terms by submitting a 'code of rules' to the Society, 'with a view to securing the continued existence of the *Northern Patriot*, apart from the McCracken Society'.[81] However, despite John Clarke's insistence that the rules had been unanimously accepted on 1 January 1896,[82] Milligan followed Johnston's lead and resigned her position as a member of the McCracken Society and editor of the *Northern Patriot*:

> Naturally I had no intention of letting my literary services, given freely in the cause of Ireland, be directed by a set of men of whom I practically knew nothing; nor of earning money for them to spend; nor of building up a paper for them to retain.[83]

Milligan's split with the Henry Joy McCracken Literary Society and the *Northern Patriot* was the result of acrimonious feuding that went on for months behind the scenes and was eventually fought out in the pages of the national press. The involvement of secret societies and the lack of documentation make it difficult to be absolutely clear about what happened. But it is worth trying to summarize events: the divisions began when the McCracken Society split from the Belfast Amnesty Association in October 1895. Matters were complicated by the fact that Robert Johnston was involved in the latter while his daughter (disguised under her pen name) was involved in the former. When the McCracken Society launched the *Northern Patriot*, Milligan and Johnston believed that as editors they would be able to publish the journal as a separate cultural venture. The McCracken Society sponsors brought in Fred Allan as a major figure who could overshadow the views of the editors and curtail the political direction Milligan and Johnston were taking the journal. While the story of the conflict can be in part traced in the public letters fired off to the press, insight into what Milligan and Johnston were up against can also be found in the pages of the *Northern Patriot* throughout 1896 when it ran for a year under new editorial control.

Milligan's opposition to party politics was a key part of why she walked away from the McCracken Society and its journal. As soon as she was gone, the Society became affiliated with the Irish Parliamentary Party, whose rising star Joseph Devlin was described by the *Northern Patriot*'s new editors as a great man of 'energy and genius'.[84] The journal had, in fact, become an organ for Devlin's associates: the new editor published constant reports of the Young Ireland Society, the cultural association affiliated with the Irish Parliamentary Party from which women were banned. The *Northern Patriot* spoke indirectly to the Young Ireland Society by addressing: 'the young men of Ireland today';[85] 'young Ireland today'.[86] The journal was kept afloat by Fred Allan whose *Irish Weekly Independent* was part of the press that 'stood by us manfully'.[87] Anna Johnston complained to Francis Bigger that the new team at the *Northern Patriot* kept trying to poach subscribers from the *Shan Van Vocht*: 'Charlie has been asking nearly all our contributors to help the *Northern Patriot* – even Miss Gonne has been written to by him.'[88] The journal openly celebrated its new 'manly' nationalism and delighted in the lack of women members and writers: one editorial urged its contributors to 'avoid the feminine in literature and thought'.[89] A letter of praise from one reader unmanned the editor into displaying a 'rosy blush': 'since Mr Quinzy [John Clarke] put his hands to the helm of the *Northern Patriot*, it has become a veritable oasis in the desert'.[90] The new editors used the letters page of the journal to indirectly accuse Milligan of 'wire pulling'; of using her 'imagination' rather than facts to explain the fall out; of writing 'word-twisted epistles' to the press.[91] The male nationalist response to Milligan and Johnston's new-found independent voice tapped into an anxiety that was widespread in the late nineteenth century about disenfranchized, highly articulate and literate women taking over the presses.[92]

The launch of the *Shan Van Vocht* marked the end of this incredibly discordant period of conflict. Yet in the midst of all this public turmoil Milligan proved herself to be an extremely active figure: by 1896 she had established feminist and nationalist organizations in the very city she had feared only three years previously. In 1893, she had warned Lady Aberdeen to avoid the sectarian anti-Home Rule disputes in Belfast and instead urged her to set up the Irish Industries Association in Derry. The hostile reception Milligan herself received in Belfast from both unionist and nationalist men and women proved that her earlier anxieties had been well founded. This part of the north's cultural history had been completely erased from accounts of the Revival. Yet the story of Milligan's career in the 1890s (particularly the first part of the decade) provides a unique example of how complicated things were for Irish cultural activists in the north.

Milligan faced a very different set of issues than her counterparts in the south. These challenges were about how to include Protestant women in an Irish cultural educational movement; how to promote the inclusion of the north in the broader national Revival project; how to protest against Belfast's regional cultural isolation without creating further exclusion. In December 1893, Milligan had warned Yeats that the new Irish art of the Revival should not 'be produced in some quiet paradise apart'.[93] Instead, she argued for a more politically committed (not necessarily textual) art that replicated the pre- and post-famine ideals of the

Nation: 'the so called Irish Literary revival had stopped short because it had proceeded on purely literary lines and lacked the national spirit which fired the country in '48'.[94] Milligan's story could have ended at Christmas 1895 amidst the negative public fallout with the McCracken Society and the *Northern Patriot*. What is extraordinary, is that Alice Milligan and Anna Johnston quickly dusted themselves off and moved in a completely new direction. The *Shan Van Vocht* became a central forum not only for Milligan's own literary and political writings, but the editors made it the major local, national and international vehicle for the promotion and construction of the Irish Cultural Revival.

The Shan Van Vocht

In February 1896, a time capsule was discovered under the foundation stone of the old Linen Hall library in Belfast during building works. The glass bottle held words written by the Irish Volunteers of 1782 in which they described the 'long oppressed' condition of Ireland that they hoped would be 'completely liberated' by the time their words were unearthed. The eighteenth-century Volunteers wrote as though speaking to a future population in Ireland that had won independence and to whom they offered the example of their own 'firmness and unanimity … if in future times there should be an attempt made to encroach upon the liberties of this country'.[95] Alice Milligan was intrigued by this document and by the aura of the event. Recalling how in 1893 A.J. Balfour marched with eight thousand anti-Home Rule Ulstermen over the spot where the secret message was buried, Milligan viewed the prematurely released words as a 'strange prophetic warning of aftertimes'.[96] Reading Anna Johnston's surviving copy of the *Shan Van Vocht* in the National Library of Ireland is like opening another time capsule written a century later in Belfast.

The *Shan Van Vocht* was so different in tone and outlook from the *Northern Patriot* that it is almost as though it belongs to a different era of cultural politics altogether. The contrast between the two journals could not have been stronger. This was a transformation in tone, outlook, agenda: the rupture with the past was deeply feminist, it was visual, political and cultural. It is hard to believe that just three weeks existed between the women's departure from the *Northern Patriot* and their launch of the *Shan Van Vocht*. When Milligan and Johnston took over their own journal they did not just become 'the voice of a body': they helped engender the body, facilitated a new voice and gave rise to a new community and audience.

In 1896 when Milligan and Johnston founded the *Shan Van Vocht*, they effectively set up a local, national and global arena for multiple voices to engage with each other. They demonstrated that the Revival was not the 'disparate' phenomenon that the journalist and novelist William Patrick Ryan (1867–1942) had lamented in his 1894 book *The Irish Literary Revival: its history, pioneers and possibilities*. Ryan had argued that 'literary Ireland does not know itself' because the autonomous groupings existed merely as 'fragments, very far apart and very strange to one another'.[97] In the pages of the *Shan Van Vocht* the Cultural Revival suddenly existed as a complexly multi-dimensional localized, national and international movement that was made up of an extensive network of organizations. Like Ardono's constellations, a seemingly unconnected set of cultural events cohered into a community through the pages of this new Belfast journal. Milligan was very self-conscious about what the Revival was and could achieve. She referenced the actions that her present generation 'will look back on' as embodying the memory that could shape the future. In the *Shan Van Vocht* Ireland's future was not already written; the 'poor old woman' was only almost dead:

> We have good hopes of the various movements now for the revival of Nationality through study of Irish literature, music, language, and the celebrations of our patriot dead. We believe they will achieve much, and that before long we will look back on the work of the past few years, and be in a position to say that a new soul had been breathed into Erin.[98]

The *Shan Van Vocht* was not just a textual publication, it was a community: a vibrant, animated cultural revival in and of itself. It was literature, history, contemporary international politics, political commentary; it was a diary, a network, a place for learning, a library, an invitation to a bi-lingual, anti-sectarian dialogue. There were a number of ways in which Milligan and Johnston created this dialogue and the increasing sense of a movement. There is an urgency articulated by Milligan and her generation that made the Revival, as Luke Gibbons has pointed out, 'as much about survival as "revival"'.[99] Responding to Douglas Hyde's powerful (and now famous) rallying call, 'The De-Anglicisation of Ireland', Milligan urged Irish people to take immediate control of the cultural and economic means of production:

> Let us realize our responsibility at this crisis in our country's history and act up to it, so that when the time comes for judging the work of this generation it may be said of us: 'They saved the Gaelic race from expatriation, and the Gaelic language from extinction.'[1]

The reanimation of Irish culture became for some (like Milligan and James Connolly) a foundational part of the process of decolonization, of preparing the

Yes Ireland shall be free
From the centre to the sea,
And hurrah for Liberty
Says the Shan Van Vocht.

VOL. I.—No. 1.   BELFAST, 15TH JANUARY, 1896.   PRICE TWOPENCE.

The Shan Van Vocht.

THERE is news from o'er the sea,
 Says the Shan Van Vocht ;
There is news from o'er the sea,
 Says the Shan Van Vocht ;
And this message o'er the sea,
From the land of liberty,
Brings the best of news for me,
 Says the Shan Van Vocht.

Ere the dying of the year,
 Says the Shan Van Vocht ;
From a land that's far but dear
 To the Shan Van Vocht ;
In a voice that laughed at fear,
There rang forth defiance clear,
Let us send an answering cheer,
 Says the Shan Van Vocht.

And a cloud is glooming now,
 Says the Shan Van Vocht,
O'er our haughty tyrant's brow,
 Says the Shan Van Vocht ;
Whilst like thunder bursts afar,
Where her sons and daughters are,
The din of dreadful war,
 Says the Shan Van Vocht.

But there's light behind that cloud
 For the Shan Van Vocht ;
And that thunder roaring loud,
 Says the Shan Van Vocht ;
Though it strikes the weakling dumb,
Shouts in tones of joy to some
That the dawn of Freedom's come
 To the Shan Van Vocht.

But tell me who is she
 Called the Shan Van Vocht ;
And if other name there be
 For the Shan Van Vocht ;
Yes ! immortal is her fame,
She's the queen no foe could tame,
For old Ireland is the name
 Of the Shan Van Vocht.

The Boy From Barnesmore.

(A STORY OF '67). BY IRIS OLKYRN.

THE train had stopped an unusually long time at
Strabane Station. Trains in Ireland are rarely in
a hurry ; indeed, when you come to think of it why
should they be, as some wit remarked "there is more time
to spare than there is of anything else in this distressful
country." And to-day there was every excuse for delay,
and plenty to divert my attention whilst we waited, for
that day had been the great spring hiring market in
Strabane, and the crowd upon the platform was an interesting and picturesque one.

Here were the wives of strong farmers in all the
flaunting bravery of their new spring bonnets, gorgeous
in scarlet and purple, and emerald green ribbons with
wondrous flowers, fresh from the milliners' hands ; whilst
in paper bags they carried the head-dresses in which
they had come to town that morning. Their crinoline
distended skirts, their gay fringed shawls, their loudly
creaking boots, were objects of wonder and envy to the
simply dressed country girls of Donegal, who had
entered into six months service with them that day, and
who had left homes among the mountain glens up by
Stranorlar and Glenties, and far away in Gweedore, to
do housework and field work on farms in Tyrone. I
could not help admiring the picturesque simplicity of
their plain kilted skirts of grey or dark blue
homespun ; the bright kerchiefs knotted simply over
their neatly braided locks as compared with the tawdry
grandeur of their newly found mistresses. The men were
shouting and talking excitedly, running this way and
that, and calling to their women folk to follow to the
seats they had secured in the carriages. Through the
swaying, surging crowd, with quiet sauntering step passed
two or three straight military looking men, easily recognised as members of the police force in plain clothes.
I thought nothing of their passing up and down and

25 First issue of *Shan Van Vocht* edited by Alice Milligan and Anna Johnston, January 1896.

country and its people for an independent Republic. To create and participate in culture was in fact to already control the reigns of power. This is precisely what the collectivist cultural gatherings were aiming to achieve; this is what the music festivals and tableaux shows were about, this is what the magic lantern lectures were – they were participatory acts of imagination experienced within and created by multiple communities. They were literary, cultural, economic and metaphorical projections. Moreover, imagining or picturing a Republic required a shift of agency through which Irish people could take control of their own national destiny.

At the time Milligan was producing the *Shan Van Vocht* it would have been impossible for her to offer a measurable, quantifiable definition of its cultural impact or the audiences it would reach and create. Yet looking back, it is clear that the impact of the Revival's cultural production was nothing less than revolutionary. The statistics of the language movement speak volumes: in 1901 there were 21,000 Irish speakers in Ireland; by 1906, 100,000 people were learning Irish in national schools, 3,000 in secondary, and 1,000 branches of Gaelic League had been established. Milligan argued that Ireland's political fortunes would not be transformed unless Irish people took responsibility for the changes they wanted to achieve at the most local level of individual choice. Praxis was the key to all her cultural work in this decade: if she felt women were excluded from politics, she responded by setting up a feminist alliance; if she could not get the publishing outlets for the northern cultural activists through other journals, she set up her own. Her phenomenal achievements were attained within a community of shared effort. It was this communal generosity of spirit that the Cork poet 'Tórna' (Tadhg Ó Donnichadha) remembered so warmly when he wrote to Milligan in the early 1940s:

> I, myself remember Ethne Carbery & yourself at the Oireachtas in the early days, when it was grand to be alive & everybody was so enthusiastic. How different things are today! Nobody will stir hand or foot unless he or she gets paid for it![2]

The local, for Milligan, was always a broader metaphor for the larger national transformations that would follow: 'In self reliance is our only hope. We can achieve a great deal for our country without appealing for the change of a single law.'[3] She not only appealed to people to take responsibility for changes that were within their powers, but she viewed their daily support for the Revival as the key to activating a new social era. Milligan called for a boycott of English products and Irish products marketed to England; she urged Irish people to acknowledge that some parts of daily life were a choice. Even within a colonial paradigm people could adopt a different way of thinking and living: she therefore asked her readers to give, and to become, audience to each other and themselves. So while her generation had no proof that their present actions could change the future, Milligan argued that a radical act of faith could be achieved through practical choices in the immediate present:

> Whose fault is it that Irish industrial products are not more used? That Irish literature has to be published in England to have any chance of a single success? Has English tyranny anything to do with the disruption of the GAA, or does it compel the Irish race to limit the organisation which exists for the salvation of the Irish language to an income that would not be considered a respectable sum for the winter coal fuel of a fourth rate English city.[4]

As this forthright editorial suggests, Milligan and Johnston were determined to make their new publishing venture not only the voice of the north but also an integral part of the broader pan-Irish revival. Proclaiming itself as 'a national journal', the *Shan Van Vocht* espoused a less regionalist agenda than the *Northern Patriot*. Thus, at the same time as they were producing the *Shan Van Vocht*, the two women attended regular private meetings in Dublin, London and in Belfast to discuss the aims and progress of the paper with members of organizations such as the National Literary Societies and the Gaelic League. They then reported back on the: 'Informal consultation as to the best means to advance the paper as a literary factor in the national cause.'[5] Acting as sole editor for the first year, Milligan declared from the outset her intention to run the paper as a collective venture that would unite Irish cultural activists in nationalist solidarity:

> I shall regard myself, though proprietor of the paper, as responsible to the contributors whose writings form its capital, and I shall render an account of expenditure to them monthly. We will then be in good truth a friendly band of volunteers, working for Ireland's sake alone in mutual confidence and with growing enthusiasm, according as our efforts are crowned with success.[6]

While the bulk of the journals political comment and literary material came from Milligan and Johnston, other contributors included historians, language activists, poets, political commentators, writers and cultural activists. The list of contributors includes names that may be familiar and many, like Milligan herself, whose names and achievements have been forgotten to history.[7] [Plate 9]

Local historian, solicitor and amateur archaeologist Francis Joseph Bigger (1863–1926), had a very unique relationship with the journal as he supplied invaluable research materials to Milligan and Johnston for their stories and articles. The three had, of course, formed friendships through the early language classes Bigger had helped to establish. Bigger fostered similar intellectual friendships with many cultural activists in the north that helped to draw connections between people. His house in Belfast, 'Ardrigh', (knocked down by Belfast city council in 1979) became an unofficial meeting place and research centre for cultural nationalists: this was where Milligan first met Roger Casement. Bigger's library of books and photographs supplied information for much of their work. Moira Pender, for instance, would write asking to consult historical books for background information for her novels; the artist J. Vinycomb requested images to transfer into staged tableaux: 'Maclises or Madrises picture of the marriage of Strongbow & Eva – have you a copy of this. Some friends of mine are getting up living pictures in Bangor and want to see this picture to set out tableaux. Could you lend it?'[8] Bigger not only wrote secretly for the *Shan Van Vocht* but he generously supplied documents and materials that Milligan and Johnston required for illustrations, factual details and historical context.

The letters from Milligan to Bigger offer a flavour of her energetic boldness and the speed at which the paper was produced. Always looking for ways to save money on the publication of the journal, Milligan wrote to Bigger for images of the 'Down Rising': 'Have you any illustrations that could be introduced – it would be an additional attraction – any '98 pictures would do – just to head the article. We can't afford to get pictures just yet and they are a great attraction.'[9] She often sent messages across the city at very short notice: 'We have only tomorrow to prepare our June number & want special information as to the location of graves also to hear what you can give us yourself & some information to enable me to write a story about Wolfe Tone's sea fight.'[10] Another letter gives further insight into how Milligan and her associates gained information in the years before public libraries were well stocked with accounts of local Irish national history: 'Would you let me know if you have any facts or names connected with preparations for landing of the French in Lough Swilly ('98) as I have a story in hand must be finished this week.'[11] The women even ask Bigger for flowers out of his garden for the grave decoration events that they organized!

The paper was run from offices at 65 Great George Street, Belfast and published by J.W. Boyd at 1–9 Academy Street, the same printer the women had used to produce the *Northern Patriot*. Milligan and Johnston had a complex relationship with Boyd who often left vital contributions out of forthcoming editions without warning them. Anna Johnston explained the situation in a letter

26 Accounts of the *Shan Van Vocht* submitted to Alice Milligan from J.W. Boyd, publisher.

to Bigger when she wrote to thank him for the flowers and to apologize for holding over an article he had sent in. This letter offers a very rare glimpse of Johnston's character as so few communications by her have survived. She writes about how the amount of errors by Boyd the printer have become a standing joke, and she tells Bigger to look out for a real error inserted by her and Milligan as part of the joke:

> Our printer means well no doubt, but somehow he is confusing. For instance, he can never tell the complete contents of the SVV beforehand and at the eleventh hour when Miss M went over in desperation to know if everything could go in – he said 'all except that little essay', pointing to O'Neill Russell's Irish Poem which is one of the features of this month's issue, & the omission of which would have made him almost our enemy. I have kept your MS all right as you decided, and I corrected the proofs most carefully so if you see mistakes, you must remember that the printer disregarded the corrections – even in my own work it is the same. Mr O' L' Castio amused himself correcting the errors last month. This month there

is a joke, a real joke, in the reports at the back, and I wonder will he see it ... As for your request that we should tell no-one that you are writing for us, of course we shall respect it ... Now I hope you are not offended, but will understand and forgive my apparent rudeness. I am really powerless in these matters, and as Mr Boyd does our work much more cheaply than any other printers would we cannot afford changes at present.[12]

The local, national and global reach of the women's vision was reflected in the subscriptions lists achieved across Ireland, Britain, Scotland, Mexico, Paris, Argentina and the US: 'The same sum 1 ⅓ will take the paper post free to your friends in America or abroad.'[13] John McBride forwarded a list of subscriptions from Johannesburg that included the members of the Irish National Foresters and the South African Amnesty Association. By 1897, 400 papers were being distributed across America by their distributor, M.J. O'Brien whose offices were at 195 Broadway, New York. Milligan and Johnston also ran a series of competitions in which they exchanged book prizes for subscription lists. Writing to an Irish miner in Colorado Milligan proved that the paper had literally gone underground in search of readers: 'Thanks for your subscription; thanks also to the brother miner who dropped the *Shan* down your shaft!'[14] In February 1898, the secretary of the '98 Committees of Scotland, J. Brolly, wrote to Anna Johnston with a list of subscriptions from Irish associations in Glasgow, Greenock, Motherwell, Paisley and Coatbridge and requested Milligan to visit on a lecture tour:

> All of these places have flourishing clubs and are working hard establishing others all over the country ... If she can find time she might let us know what date she would be likely to come. There are some of the '98 clubs in the country wanting her and as the saying goes she could kill two birds with one stone.[15]

Across the Atlantic, the Irish-American press fervently supported the *Shan Van Vocht*. The Crime Special Branch in Ireland filed a copy of a New York paper, the *Irish Republic*, which carried an editorial celebrating the 'two patriotic Ulster ladies who have taken on their shoulders the labour of preaching the undiluted gospel of nationality' in Belfast. The paper urged Irish-Americans to:

> help the one magazine that is doing genuine work for the common cause. Don't let it perish. Show some of the old spirit of Irish chivalry towards the two brave young ladies ... struggling with foreign tyranny and – worse still – domestic apathy.[16]

27 Alice Milligan (standing) and Anna Johnston, photograph taken from Christmas 1897 edition of the American Catholic Irish literary journal *Donahoe's Magazine* (Boston), p.584.

The complex circumstances in which the *Shan Van Vocht* came into being signalled the break Milligan made with the fractured nationalistic regionalism increasingly promoted by the McCracken Society: this was a politics that Milligan and Johnston had been under pressure to reproduce in pages of the *Northern Patriot*. The confidence of tone they achieved in the paper was only possible because of the cultural foundations laid in previous years. The *Shan Van Vocht* became the 'voice of a body' that the *Northern Patriot* (with its chauvinistic abuses of its female editors) had only aspired to promulgate. Until Milligan and Johnson were forced to strike out alone, 'body' and 'voice' were radically detached and remained disparate. The name of the journal was the phonetic spelling of the Irish *An tSean-bhean Bhocht* meaning, 'The poor old woman'. (The original title of Yeats' play, *Cathleen Ní Houlihan*.) The name derived from the title of a late eighteenth-century song that connected the imagined Irish Republic of the United Irishmen with both the French and American revolutions. The voice of the future is repeated over and over as a refrain in the song by 'the shan van vocht' who is both a prophetic visionary and the memory through which hope can be achieved.

The contemporary Irish poet Eavan Boland lamented in her 1995 essay 'Outside history' that the Poor Old Woman was reduced in Irish literature to an empty 'mouthpiece ... a sign' that lacked agency of her own.[17] Yet in the original Gaelic versions the poor old woman had the sovereignty of Ireland at her disposal. Boland berated how personifications of Ireland in poetry made the female body and the female experience 'passive, decorative, raised to emblematic status ... where the nation became a woman and the woman took on a national posture ... as fictional queens and national sibyls.'[18] Suggesting that as an Irish poet, she had no female poets or articulate literary iconographies to gain inspiration from. Yet in the Revival period Irish women such as Milligan found many other women to look back to as inspirational writers, political activists and cultural practitioners. The *Shan Van Vocht* published essays about the lives of women such as Anne Devlin and republished women's writings such as Mary McCracken's reflections about the United Irishmen. The nineteenth-century poet 'Speranza' was also an inspiration, not least because she, like Milligan herself, had derived from a non 'native Irish' cultural background. Speranza's life story was published by Alice Milligan as an example of how the production of new publishing outlets can make a change in the imagination of the next generation:

> A girl educated far beyond the most advanced education then given to women, but whose studies had never in the slightest degree treated of Ireland, her people, or her history ... The Library of Ireland series of Thomas Davis' poems transformed Jane Francesca Elgee into a Nationalist.

She came to understand that she had a country ... she began to think how best she could serve and further the interests of her country.[19]

Milligan not only looked back on traditions of Irish women but she also derived energy from other women writers who were her contemporaries and whose work she commissioned: these included Alice Furlong, Edith Dickson, Maud Gonne, Kathleen Knox, Charlotte Milligan Fox, Moira Pender, Winifred Pattern as well as members of the Irish Women's Association. Rather than rejecting 'the shan van vocht' as an outmoded trope of a patriarchal nationalism, Milligan and Johnston re-embodied the voice of this historical allegory. They not only printed old versions of the poems but they commissioned new versions: the famous refrain from the song, 'says the Shan Van Vocht' was repeated and echoed after editorials, reports and commentary throughout the journal. Thus Milligan and Johnston's editorials, fictions, discussion forums, reports and reviews became the words newly spoken by the *Shan Van Vocht*. The poor old woman was speaking out and speaking back against colonial occupation, cultural Anglicization, and the factional unionist and nationalist misogyny Irish women encountered.

The female body as nationalist allegory was therefore not a disempowering idea to Irish women such as Milligan and Johnston. In fact, by bringing the 'shan van vocht' back into circulation from the era of the United Irish movement, the women were able to tap into a known national and international political consciousness that was at once popular and specific. It was at the level of the known, the familiar and the popular that most of Milligan's cultural activities reached out. The banner of their journal, 'The Shan Van Vocht' was set against the sunburst which was an obvious emblem of hope as well as a coded visual nod to the revolutionary politics of Fenianism. 'The Shan Van Vocht' was a song that came out of an Irish revolutionary eighteenth-century movement that was informed by a European discourse of republican sentiment. In the late nineteenth century, Milligan reanimated the song and placed the poor old woman that was Ireland in a new context of international revolution:

> We are not at liberty to preach revolution, but there is no restraint put upon our reporting the doings of revolutionists, insurgents, conspirators in Matabeleland, Johannesburg, Cuba, Canada, and elsewhere ... We have a perfect right to do so and shall henceforth avail ourselves of that right ... In a few pages we can monthly compress a record of every incident which is of permanent importance to 'the cause' and which will give our readers a right understanding of the events of the day as they effect the destiny of Ireland.[20]

This discourse of rights, the questions, the forthright expressions of opinion that were articulated by Milligan in the journal signalled a new moment of becoming for her. In 1945 the Abbey actress Máire Nic Shiubhlaigh who had performed Milligan's early plays wrote an article about the *Shan Van Vocht* in which she praised the achievements of Johnston and Milligan. As the title of her article 'Women pioneers' suggests, Nic Shiubhlaigh was at pains to convey to Irish readers in the mid-twentieth century just how courageous and visionary Milligan and Johnston were in setting up a new journal in Ireland in the heartlands of northern unionism:

> It was like the voice of Ireland herself crying out words of hope and encouragement to those who loved her, words of warning and defiance to those who thought she had been broken forever by the political disagreements brought about by the success of the enemy's plot for the destruction of Parnell. Rooney wrote for it, and Lionel Johnston, and James Connolly, and many then unknown whose names became famous in the land. A Maynooth priest in the making said of it afterwards in a lecture to his fellow students: 'The paper was as a friend to all who held the doctrine that Ireland should be Irish in language and life and feeling. Its columns were full of hope, of sympathy, of encouragement. It was the outward manifestation of a deep and abiding love of Ireland, such as is given to few to possess. Month by month it became more precious to those who read it, to none more so than the exiles who were forced to walk hard streets in far countries.' Alice Milligan and Ethna Carbery had both been blessed with the gift of song and with lavish generosity they devoted precious blessing to the awakening spirit of Irish Nationality in Irish minds and hearts. And their days and nights were not passed in song alone. Even a monthly paper cannot be produced and distributed and paid for without hard work, and everything connected with the regular appearance of the *Shan Van Vocht* was done by their own working hands. They wrote most of it, they prepared it for the press, corrected the proofs, sent out subscription copies by post after writing the addresses in all the wrappers, furnished bills … Honour forever to the fearless pioneers who raised up the flag of Irish Nationality from the mud where it had been trampled under the feet of warring factions, and placed on the heights where it could be seen again by the young people of Ireland … Honour forever to Alice Milligan and Ethna Carbery who raised that flag in the heart of Anglicised Belfast and drew men's thoughts again to the vow that was spoken one morning long ago on the summit of Cave Hill![21]

As Nic Shiubhlaigh points out, the journal gave over large spaces to 'Different voices': they commissioned arguments about the Revival movement from figures as diverse as T.W. Rolleston and James Connolly. Controversial essays were thus published about methods of saving the Irish language, and the role of politics and socialism in the Revival. Henry Dixon got the ball rolling when he asked: 'Do the Irish people mean to preserve the National tongue or not? If they do mean to preserve it, what do they do to preserve it?'[22] The concept and policy of the language movement was monthly thrashed out in the pages of the journal. The women also set up an exchange of adverts across Irish language presses as soon as any new Irish journals were established. This is an example of one such letter to the editor of the *Gaelic Journal*: 'Dear Sir, I enclose an advertisement of our paper the *Shan Van Vocht* which I would like to exchange for one of the *Gaelic Journal*. We have a fair circulation in Irish speaking districts ... Kindly translate into Irish & insert as an exchange advert in the *Gaelic Journal*.'[23]

Milligan invited James Connolly to use the pages of her journal to promote and explain his 'ideas on the programme of political and social reform' of his new Socialist Republican Party. The Revival, in Connolly's view, was a process to facilitate 'public opinion ... ripening ... impending the arrival of the propitious moment of action.'[24] This was a view that Milligan also held: 'A day will come when more than the poet's thoughts, more than the patriot orator's moving words, Ireland will stand in need of arms strong enough to strike, and feet swift to pursue.'[25] It was in the *Shan Van Vocht* that Connolly first defined what would become the text of the 1916 Rising: 'the Irish Republic might be made a word to conjure with – a rallying point for the disaffected, a haven for the oppressed, a point of departure for the Socialist, enthusiastic in the cause of human freedom.'[26] He also outlined his own personal commitment to the achievement of the Republic, a commitment that would be tested to the full by his involvement in 1916 and his subsequent execution: 'As a Socialist I am prepared to do all one man can do to achieve for our motherland her rightful heritage – independence; but if you ask me to abate one jot or tittle of the claims of social justice, in order to conciliate the privileged classes, then I must decline.'[27] Milligan had commissioned four articles from Connolly without even meeting him, so impressed was she by his political presence in Ireland. This was a life-long respect that she felt for Connolly, as her 1938 pre-'Bloomsday' homage to him in the *Irish News* made clear. On this day, Milligan recollected her own voyage through Dublin of 1897 that she had made with Connolly where they had walked around the city, past the post office and along the river.

The educational aims of the journal were as strong and forthright as all Milligan's other earlier cultural ventures: the editors provided regular detailed summaries in book reviews of new publications by Irish publishers such as the New Irish Library and the Shamrock Library Series; they gained the rights to reproduce extracts from history books that readers may not otherwise have access to. In the section called 'For the old land' the editors recorded 'from month to month what is being done in different departments of work for the advancement of Ireland's cause and for the cultivation of her people.' The women asked for reports of lectures and events undertaken across Ireland, Britain, Scotland, America, South Africa, Mexico and Argentina. They published cultural events by a diverse and growing set of organizations that included: the Young Ireland League, the National Literary Societies, the C.J. Kickham Society, Edmund Burke Debating Society, the People's Rights Society, the Amnesty Association, the Irish Women's Association, the Irish Literary Reading Circle (also initiated by Milligan), and the Belfast Naturalist Field Club.

The editors commissioned new works from writers such as Douglas Hyde, Nora Hopper, Edith Dickson, William Rooney, Seamus MacManus, and Maud Gonne. Poetry and prose were often published in Irish and accompanied with English translations: it was these poems that Milligan would later return to and republish in the 1930s as an act of political and cultural re-memory. As editor Milligan took the decision from the outset to avoid making the journal a newspaper: 'We were prompted to preserve this silence, partly from a desire to stand aloof from the fray of party politics, which for some years back, has so bitterly divided the people of Ireland.'[28] Instead, she wrote a monthly political overview and analysis of events that she felt had a direct bearing on the Irish national struggle for independence. In her writings Milligan therefore added a new radical context for the revival as it emerged in the pages of her journal. Because of the very direct and chatty style of the editors and the ever-present sense of dialogue unfolding, the paper developed a tone of a movement that was gathering force from multiple sources and arenas.

The paper ran for three years and covered key events associated with the Revival: indeed, the *Shan Van Vocht* was instrumental not just in reporting organizations and events, but also in actually creating them. As we shall see in the next chapter about commemoration, the *Shan Van Vocht* rallied and promoted the 1798 Centenary from January 1896. The journal was a vital force in supporting the Gaelic League to construct its national and international branch system. The editors used their office to fundraise for a range of cultural initiatives such as the language movement, the restoration of nationally important but neglected graves, and the erection of public monuments to commemorate the past that had been written out of Irish national history. In addition, the journal was a major forum for Milligan and Johnston to publish their own writings. An extensive part of my research has involved simply locating the many short stories, poems, plays and other writings of Alice Milligan that she published across six decades in over sixty different newspapers and journals. But between 1896 and 1899 the *Shan Van Vocht* was the main repository for Milligan's fictional writings.

The *Shan Van Vocht* represents the most substantial book Milligan published in her life time. Its value was known intimately to those who worked on the paper. It was the voice of the north in the Revival and as such it did not need to state its case in a regionally caustic manner. The journal became a vibrant intellectual force that promoted literary and social networks of ideas within communities of national and international solidarity. In other words, while it was produced in Belfast and contained an unapologetically local northern historical and regional flavour, the editors self-consciously connected Irish cultural events across vast terrains of separation that were at once geographical, political, linguistic, gendered and religious. In 1951, the playwright Pádraic Colum praised the journal's distinctive achievements, ascribing them to the collaboration between the 'daughter of a Presbyterian business man' (Milligan was in fact a Methodist) and an 'Ulster Catholic' woman (Anna Johnston):

> With a freshness that came from its femininity, the *Shan Van Vocht* went to a nationalism that had never been parliamentarian, the nationalism of Wolfe Tone and that idealistic band that had been largely recruited from the Ulster Presbyterians of Scottish descent, the United Irishmen.[29]

Their responses to readers who sent in poems and stories and articles for publication was always democratic and sincere: the women responded to creative writing both in the journal's main pages and through personal letters. Indeed, it was the 'personal' element of trust and one-to-one communication that was the key to much of the success of the Revival movement. It was this hands-on personalized approach that won Milligan and Johnston such an audience and that made this journal (above all others) stay in the minds of their contemporaries. In a 1927 memoir about his late wife, Anna Johnston, Seamus MacManus affection-ately recalled how the paper was produced in cottage industry fashion in Belfast:

> For three and a half years these two girls edited the magazine, and managed it. They themselves wrote almost all of the magazine ... They read the proofs. They kept the books. They sent the bills. They wrote the letters. With their own hands they folded and addressed every copy that was to go out, and licked every stamp ... Many and many a weary day they spent drudging in the office – and on many and many a weary evening they trudged home to Ethna Carbery's father's house in Donegall Park (on the

outskirts of Belfast), there to swallow their supper, and … sit down on opposite sides of the table, turning out story and poem for the next issue.[30]

The women dissolved the journal in 1899 but, as Press Ombudsman John Horgan has pointed out, Milligan and Johnston did not just let the paper disappear; the editors gave over the subscription list to Arthur Griffith and his new journal *United Ireland*.[31] By 1899, Milligan and Johnston felt that the cultural climate had changed substantially from when they were first impelled to make their intervention. When they first began publishing together in 1895 there were few outlets for cultural events in the north to make themselves heard of; there were limited forums to promote and support the Irish language movement; there was little unified connection between Irish national and international cultural initiatives. By 1899, the Cultural Revival was well underway with a successful and articulate language movement, an emerging national theatre movement, an extensive and growing body of Irish literature and a confident, growing, participatory culture of commemoration. This movement was represented in an array of newspapers and journals that were able to target specific audiences with specialized interests. The language movement had its own papers; the Irish co-operative movement was finding voice in the *Irish Homestead*; the national theatre movement would find articulation through journals such as *Uladh* and *Beltaine* as well as being reviewed and debated in all the daily presses.

A key driving force in establishing a journal from Belfast was to put that city and the north on the map of the Revival. By 1899 that aspiration had been achieved in a non-sectarian, non-regionalist manner. Milligan and Johnston dissolved their journal at the exact moment when cultural events in the north were once again becoming negatively regional in tone. In the *Shan Van Vocht* Milligan had achieved a national and international consciousness and while she certainly supported the Ulster Literary Theatre and its journal, *Uladh*, the defensive regionalism of Hobson's agenda would have sounded old hat to Milligan; an echo from an argument that she'd had years before. It was within national local communities that Milligan aspired to project her cultural ideas. Milligan's desire to connect the language movement and the theatre movement in a national context would be achieved most successfully through travel, community theatre performance, magic lantern lectures, the national(ist) presses and the national railway systems. In 1899, Milligan and Johnston parted ways only to meet each other again on the stage in Dublin as members of the feminist organization *Inghinidhe na hÉireann*. The stage shows that they constructed and performed were only made possible by the Centenary they had been so prominent in constructing. The next chapter will look in more detail at the event which marked a pinnacle in the Revival movement: the 1798 Commemoration.

CHAPTER FOUR

Memory and commemoration: 1798 in 1898

> And as Irish men and women progress to a truer appreciation of correct
> social and political principles … the stones rejected by the builders of the
> past have become the corner-stones of the edifice.
>
> <div align="right">James Connolly, <i>Labour in Irish history</i>, 1910.[1]</div>

On New Year's Eve 1897, Alice Milligan led a delegation up Cave Hill, the
symbolic birth place of the United Irishmen, overlooking Belfast. At the top they
lit a bonfire and pledged their loyalty to principles that had been envisaged on the
same spot one hundred years before:

> 1. We declare the right of Ireland to freedom. 2. That on this historic spot
> where Tone and his co-patriots pledged themselves to Ireland, we re-iterate
> our right to Irish national independence. 3. That we pledge ourselves never
> to desist from the struggle until Ireland is a nation.[2]

The celebratory events that marked the anniversary of 1798 were invested with
intense political significance for nationalists, cultural practitioners and politicians
in late nineteenth-century Ireland. The centenary became a key rallying point for
the development of the cultural movement and in the broader political anti-
colonial struggle: Milligan was at the forefront of this movement years before it
even began to take shape. The commemoration of 1798 tapped into an already
present resource of activism: by 1897 (when planning for the centenary began in
earnest) many Irish people were already participating in a number of cultural
projects that linked them with ideas of national becoming.

Gaelic League branches were a feature that defined Irish communities and
included Irish language classes as well as a range of educational and social outreach
programmes. Reading was an established way of imagining communities; Irish
artists chose to distribute their ideas and literature through the mass circulation of
Irish newspapers. In addition to the Gaelic League branches, by 1898 many other
Irish educational, literary, cultural, co-operative and political organizations existed
in Ireland and abroad. As an event, the centenary had the potential to infuse the
Revival with a political radicalism and to further unify the collective national
consciousness of a generation. Milligan described the symbolic resonance

28 Photograph of Cave Hill, Belfast.

communicated by their actions on New Year's Eve when she and her colleagues reignited the past as a coded signal to the future: 'we lit on the topmost peak of M'Art's Fort the beacon fire that throughout Ireland was to welcome in the Centenary of '98. To Belfast, to Carrickfergus, to the low-lying green hills of Castlereagh opposite, the signal flashed from the very spot whereon Wolfe Tone stood when he made his vow to win our country back her independence.'[3] So what exactly did 1798 mean for Alice Milligan? And to what extent was she involved in the Commemorations?

This chapter will seek to answer these questions with reference to her publications and her activities in the lead-up to the centenary. The United Irish movement was the most critical dynamic in Milligan's political thought and cultural aspirations. This was a historical movement that inflected the very issues of gender and northern Protestantism that preoccupied her work and her life: how could the north be included in the national movement? What was the role of women in Irish political and cultural life? How had Protestant settlers managed to unite with Catholics under the United Irish banner? Was such radicalism possible one hundred years after their defeat? The centenary was a remarkable phenomenon in Irish cultural history not least because of its national formal organization and planning: Irish communities at home and abroad set up committees, executives, local branches and international '98 organizations. They published new work and republished material from the annals of history; they collected counter-narratives of oral memories from the oldest in their communities. They marched in costumed uniforms, took over cities and villages for formalized parades, and through a series of national lecture tours and magic lantern shows disseminated the meaning of 1798 [Plate 10]. Those who had fought and died in the insurrection of 1798 were suddenly thrust into the limelight of commemoration: forgotten and poorly-kept graves became sites of pilgrimage; the names of United Irishmen were reanimated as national bodies of '98 organizations. The activities in Ireland were part of a broader commemorative energy connected with the *fin de siècle* idea of symbolic dates that was present right across Europe.

Milligan and her colleagues repossessed public space in all manner of ways: they renamed and marked the landscapes of the dead; they took to the streets and reclaimed the exact days and spaces of particular battles and executions. They literally re-embodied history by erecting public monuments of the United Irishmen. The unveiling of the foundation stone for the Wolfe Tone statue in August 1898 was a centrepiece of the Revival: it was an event suggested by Alice Milligan and she was one of the key figures who symbolically carried the stone from Cave Hill in Belfast to Dublin. This piece of rock hewn from the hillside of Belfast belonged to a forgotten chapter of Ireland's history. That foundation stone from Cave Hill symbolised for Milligan and her colleagues the corner-stone of the new nation state they were trying to imagine and create.

The ideals of the United Irish movement in Milligan's work

Long before the centenary, Milligan was a passionate advocate of the events of 1798 as representing the idealism essential to propel the Cultural Revival. In this section of the chapter I want to give a flavour of the sheer number of lectures, public talks and publications that Milligan delivered in the build-up to 1898. She collected and published oral histories, wrote fictions and plays, became an elected member of all the official '98 groups, and set up her own organizations when women were again excluded by male nationalists. In multiple forums, through a diverse set of genres and locations, Milligan attempted to prove again and again that there was a different version of Irish history. In this alternative view of the past, Protestants in the north had been an integral part of developing republican political consciousness and culture in Ireland. Milligan tried to demonstrate that many of these Protestants had come from the north: the very same place that was quickly becoming the industrial bulwark of empire in Ireland; a bastion of Protestant loyalism, unionist politics and Anglo-centric culture. The enlightened and inclusive politics advocated by the United Irishmen at the end of the eighteenth century was informed by a radical European Republicanism. It was through her re-examination of this politics and its northern Protestant connections that Milligan sought to connect the Ireland of her own time with a new anti-colonial cultural movement.

From 1893 it seems that Milligan tried to engage everyone she met on the topic of 1798. In a diary entry for November 1893, for instance, she recorded the first of several trips made with Yeats to Cave Hill, where in 1795 the United Irishmen had famously pledged their unwavering commitment to Irish independence. Yeats, Milligan noted, did not share her enthusiasm for this symbolic site: he 'didn't warm the least at the mention of '98 & when we got up in the open, & paused to look at the view, seemed grateful to turn.'[4] Maud Gonne similarly recalled how trips to Cave Hill became a regular pastime: 'I used often to stay with Anna Johnston in her father's house on the Antrim Rd. and with Alice Milligan we used to go to Cave Hill, and talk of the old legends and Wolfe Tone, and sometimes Willie Yeats was with us.'[5] In February 1893, Milligan's nervous experience with her first public lecture revealed the strength of popular sentiment that could be inspired by those who, as the celebrated song declared, did not fear to speak of '98: 'I read my paper on historic Ulster in the museum to a crowd of people and hosts of gulls in flock … I was not applauded till I came to Belfast & '98.'[6]

Milligan argued repeatedly at public meetings that it was through reconnecting with Belfast's hidden history that a new dynamic of cultural politics could be achieved. At a meeting of the Irish Women's Association which she chaired in February 1895, Milligan introduced a paper by the novelist Moira Pender entitled 'Some men and episodes of 1798' with the claim that 'no period of Irish history should be of greater interest to the people of Belfast'.[7] It was not just the northern associations of the eighteenth-century revolutionary movement that interested Milligan: the religious makeup of the organizations offered the first example of a political unity that went against the sectarian divisiveness advocated by the English colonial administration in Ireland. In June 1895, the *Irish News* reported the following statement made by Milligan at a lecture in Belfast:

> The history of '98 referred to a time when Protestants and Catholics were united in a great national organisation. There was but one period in Irish history in which that had happened, and that was '98. Up to that period the national cause was mainly the Catholic cause.[8]

Milligan suggested on this occasion that colonial education had suppressed the scale of northern Protestant involvement in the militant and intellectual struggles of the previous century. According to the *Irish News*, Milligan commented that most of the audience 'were already acquainted with the principal events of 1798; but many, especially Protestants, had been brought up in utter ignorance of the simple facts connected with the history of that time and required to be enlightened upon the subject.'[9] In September 1895, Milligan delivered a lecture to the Henry Joy McCracken Literary Society on the subject of the Battle of Antrim. During the question session which followed her talk, a Revd Lyttle highlighted the instructional value of discussions of 1798:

> The teaching of Irish history, and especially of the history of the period with which Miss Milligan had dealt that night, would, he believed, remove the prejudices of Ulster Protestants and bring them into line with the rest of Ireland in the demand for self-government.[10]

One member of the audience pointed out that in Belfast they were practicing the non-sectarian values that they preached: that night the platform had been shared by 'speakers representing the Presbyterian, Unitarian, and Wesleyan sections of Protestantism as well as by a Catholic'.[11]

By the mid-1890s, Milligan was a long way from the views she had expressed in 1888 about the insurrection led by the United Irishmen. In her earliest publications Milligan did not look to the north but instead highlighted the sectarianism that plagued the southern-based United Irishmen. In *Glimpses of Erin*, Alice and Seaton Milligan asserted that:

> In the North of Ireland the religious question was not the cause of the rebellion, and the Society of United Irishmen embraced all creeds. But in Wexford and the South, where the most menacing outbreak took place, the religious question alone incited the people. Their leaders were priests like Father John Murphy, Michael Murphy, and Philip Roche.[12]

The Wexford insurgents were also depicted as religious extremists in 'Wexford Bridge. A story of '98', a poem by Alice Milligan included within *Glimpses of Erin* that takes the side of Protestant prisoners held in Wexford gaol during 1798. After United Irishmen have executed some of their captives on Wexford Bridge, 'Bold Father Corrin' consecrates their deed:

> He spake, and signed the holy cross against the fiery West,
> 'Brothers, the work you do this day must now by heaven be blessed;
> Then kneel and pray the words I say. For a holy cause you fight,
> To free beloved Ireland and our Church's wrongs to right.'[13]

Milligan's early, pre-Revival, account of the role played by the priests in Wexford drew upon sectarian interpretations of the rebellion by historians such as Richard Musgrave and George Taylor. Milligan may have been influenced by W.H. Maxwell's 1845 history of the rising, which portrayed the insurgents as a sectarian 'rabble' rather than as enlightened radicals. Maxwell argued that in Wexford during 1798, 'the rabble power had become predominant – and all persons of superior rank, or a different faith, were denounced by the wretches who associated crime with religion, and slaughtered in the name of God.'[14] In his foreword to the issue of Musgrave's *Memoirs*, David Dickson suggests that his interpretation of the rebellion propounded a sectarian view of the United Irishmen: 'throughout a simple message echoes: the insurrection of 1798 had been in essence a Papist rebellion, sided of course by Protestant dupes and Presbyterian republicans, but a Papist rebellion with deep and sinister ultra-montane roots.'[15] Milligan may also have looked at the Methodist historian, George Taylor for a narrative of the rebellion that implicated the Catholic priests in torture of Protestant prisoners.[16] Fifty years after these views were expressed in *Glimpses of Erin*, '98 commemorations were outlawed by the state of Northern Ireland. In 1938 Milligan travelled to speak from public platforms in Wexford where the anniversary of 1798 became, for her, a protest against Partition.

After 1893, instead of seeking divisions and sectarianism within the eighteenth-century republican movement, Milligan focused instead upon their promotion of social cohesion. In her article, 'The north is up!' she juxtaposed Wolfe Tone's revolutionary plans with Patrick Sarsfield's earlier struggle for Irish independence, explaining that the United Irishmen established a precedent by their advocacy of religious unity. Thomas Davis, the poet who most influenced Alice Milligan, presented a view of Sarsfield's heroic venture in his poem: 'The Battle of Limerick': 'Oh, hurrah! for the men who, when danger is nigh, / Are found in the front, looking death in the eye, / Hurrah! for the men who keep Limerick's wall, / And hurrah! for bold Sarsfield, the bravest of all.'[17] Milligan explored the difference between Sarsfield and Wolfe Tone:

> In aiming at the national independence of Ireland and the subversion of the English yoke, Tone merely took up the cause for which Sarsfield had struck the last blow on Irish soil on the shattered walls of Limerick. But in recognising the fact that the future liberty of Ireland depended on the abolition of creed distinctions and the promotion of union amongst all whose homes were in the land, he struck a new note.[18]

This view that 1798 was the first moment of national unification between settlers and natives was an interpretation Milligan had first expressed in June 1895: 'Up to that period [1798] the national cause was mainly the Catholic cause; when the last blow was struck for Ireland at Limerick under Sarsfield the leaders and soldiers of the army were Catholic.'[19]

Milligan thus argued that the United Irishmen activated the first coherent struggle against English colonial rule that was in part led by an enlightened Protestant input. The establishment of this inclusive organization indicated to Milligan that by 1791 the terms 'Protestant and foreigner' were no longer 'synonymous':

> The foundation of the United Irish societies implied that a section of the descendants of the Protestant colonists planted here had thrown in their lot with those of the Catholic Irish who still cherished the ideal of Nationality. The mass of these Protestants were Dissenters, Presbyterians of the North of Scottish descent, but many of the leaders were Episcopalians.[20]

In *Partners in revolution: the United Irishmen and France* historian Marianne Elliot examines the intrinsic role Protestants had played in constructing the insurrection: 'It was within the Protestant community, rather than among the discontented

Catholic majority, that revolutionary nationalism developed spasmodically and took off in the last two decades of the century.'[21] In late nineteenth-century Ireland, this was a crucial history for Milligan to publicly connect with. The United Irish movement provided the political philosophical background to her writing and to her cultural activism in the north. As a northern Protestant, this narrative also gave her an alternative 'family' tree through which to explain and express her origins and to project her ideals.

The revolution of 1798 was eventually suppressed and a series of executions, arrests and deportations ensued. The Irish parliament of College Green was dissolved in 1800 and all powers transferred to London. In *Glimpses of Erin* Milligan and her father refused to discuss the period following the 1800 Act of Union. Its consequences, they suggest, were too contentious to be given space in a text that aimed to strengthen bonds between Ireland and England. They explain that this part of Ireland's colonial past could not so readily be consigned to the realm of 'safe' and distant history:

> On both sides we can talk calmly now about the Plantation of Ulster or the Cromwellian settlement; but it would be impossible in the present day to speak of the union without becoming a politician.[22]

Revising her views when she became a Parnellite in 1891, Milligan began to focus upon Protestant involvement in the republican and nationalist political movements that emerged in the wake of the Act of Union.

Giving the inaugural address for the Irish Women's Association in March 1895, Milligan stated that nineteenth-century reforms such as Catholic emancipation displaced what she viewed as the key issue – Ireland's claim for 'national freedom':

> Ireland's rights should be won before that of any other radical reform was agitated. It was possible that Ireland would be in a better position to-day had agitation for Repeal of the Union taken a prior place to that of Catholic Emancipation, Church disestablishment and land reform.[23]

The belief that the repeal of the union should have preceded any other form of agitation and legislation was also a view offered by Thomas Davis, the editor of the *Nation*. In an 1846 article entitled 'History of to-day' Davis asked:

> Yet what was Emancipation compared to Repeal? The one put a silken badge on a few members of one profession; the other would give to all trades the rank and riches which resident proprietors, domestic legislation, and flourishing commerce, infallibly create.[24]

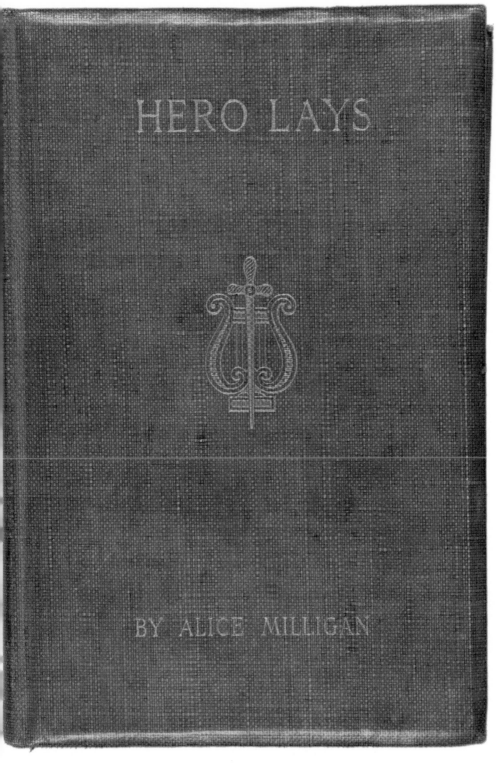

1 Front cover of *Hero Lays*, poems by Alice Milligan edited by George Russell in 1908.

2 Front cover of *Sons of the Sea Kings*, children's novel by Alice Milligan and her brother
Seaton Milligan, 1914.

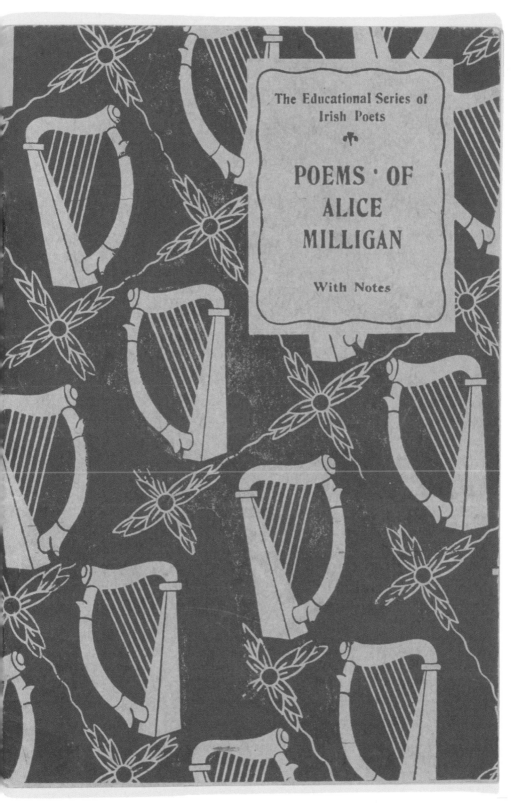

The Educational Series of
Irish Poets

POEMS · OF
ALICE
MILLIGAN

With Notes

3 Front cover of *Poems of Alice Milligan*, Educational Series of Ireland, *c.*1923.

Supplement to "The Republic," February 26th, 1921.

"CARSONIA"
THE GREAT BETRAYAL!

ULSTER POPULATIONS ACCORDING TO LAST RELIGIOUS CENSUS.

AREAS	PROTESTANTS (INCLUDING NATIONALISTS)	CATHOLICS (ALL NATIONALISTS)
Province of Ulster	891,881	689,816
Province of Ulster, excluding City of Belfast	597,176	597,573
Province of Ulster, excluding City of Belfast and its adjoining counties of Antrim and Down	303,245	493,337
"Carsonia" (the six counties and two cities separated from Ireland by Government Bill)	821,371	429,161
Nationalist Areas separated from Ireland by Government Bill):—		
Tyrone County	63,650	79,015
Fermanagh County	27,096	34,740
Derry City	17,857	22,923
	108,603	136,678
Ulster Counties separated from "Ulster" by Government Bill):—		
Donegal County	35,316	133,021
Cavan County	16,002	74,271
Monaghan County	18,992	53,363
	70,310	260,655

Key to Map

THE EXISTING PROVINCE OF ULSTER is shown inside Heavy Lines.

"CARSONIA"
Counties with Large Protestant Majorities

Counties with Narrow Protestant Majorities

Counties with Nationalist Majorities

Counties to be excluded from "Ulster" — WHITE

DONEGAL (In Southern Ireland)

DERRY CITY — **ANTRIM**

LONDONDERRY

TYRONE — **BELFAST**

CARSON'S HOMOGENEOUS ULSTER — **DOWN**

FERMANAGH — **ARMAGH**

MONAGHAN

CAVAN

RAILWAYS TO DONEGAL

CONNAUGHT

NEW REPUBLIC OR CROWN COLONY

GALWAY

DUBLIN

LEINSTER

LIMERICK

WATERFORD

MUNSTER

CORK

Threefold Treachery!

Sir Edward Carson—not an Ulster man but a Dublin lawyer, and a late member of the National Liberal Club—has climbed to power by preaching and practising treason. Treason not alone to the "Empire"—about which he boasts so loudly—but treason first, to the Unionists of the South of Ireland and, then, to the Unionists of Donegal, Monaghan and Cavan to whom he was bound by the "Solemn League and Covenant" of "Ulster."

A few characteristic utterances and their consequences are sufficient to establish Sir Edward's position as an exponent of treason.

An Invitation to Lunch.

On August 27th, 1913, the "Belfast Evening Telegraph" (the official evening Unionist paper) announced:—

"Sir Edward Carson had the honour of being invited to lunch with the Kaiser last week at Homburg."

"Don't be Afraid of Illegalities."

On September 11th, 1913, Sir Edward Carson said: "The Ulster Volunteers are an illegal organisation, and the Government dare not interfere with them. Don't be afraid of illegalities"!

Illegal Landing of German Rifles.

On April 24th, 1914, under cover of a test mobilisation of Ulster Volunteers, 30,000 German Mauser Rifles and supplies of necessary ammunition were landed at Larne and other ports, while the Volunteers "held up" the police and coastguards.

"A Betrayer of his brother."

On September 26th, 1913, at Londonderry, Sir Edward Carson said: "Let no man make light of signing the Covenant. Any man who having taken this pledge goes back upon it OR, FAILS AT THE CRITICAL MOMENT, let him beware. He is a betrayer of his brother."

"One Jot of your Rights."

On July 17th, 1913, Sir Edward Carson, speaking at Belfast to representative "Covenanters" from Donegal, Cavan, and Monaghan, said: "I tell them that if they attempt to take away one jot of your rights as British citizens, I will once more call out the Ulster Volunteers."

The Final Act of Treachery.

And now—the culminating act of treachery: Sir Edward Carson refuses even to walk into the Division Lobby to save his fellow-Covenanters of Donegal and Cavan and Monaghan from the destiny which the "Solemn League and Covenant" was intended to avoid. Truly, "a betrayer of his brother!"

Homogeneous Humbug!

In the sacred name of "homogeneity" the British Government—forced thereto by the logic of events and the pressure from Sir Edward Carson—have produced the most fantastic conceivable series of proposed frontiers and groupings of administrative units.

Why the Scheme is proposed.

These frontiers and groupings are adopted by the Government in response to the "Ulster" claim that they enclose communities which are "homogeneous" in respect of the religious opinions of their constituents.

The first test is to be applied—however disagreeable it may be to the liberal habits of thought—most therefore be to ascertain whether in fact the Government's scheme secures sectarian homogeneity? If the scheme fails to pass this test it must fail altogether.

Some Facts and Figures.

A reference to the adjoining map and table of populations will reveal the following important facts:—

Ulster outside Belfast is Catholic.

(1) That Ulster contains more Catholics than Protestants if the City of Belfast be omitted from the calculation.

(2) That, if the City of Belfast and its two immediately adjoining Counties of Antrim and Down be omitted, the population of the remaining Seven Counties of Ulster consists of 493,336 Catholics and 303,000 Protestants.

(3) That the whole province, as it exists contains roughly 689,000 Protestants and 890,000 Catholics—so enabling 820,000 Protestants, if so disposed, to unite with the Catholics and vote Belfast into union with Southern Ireland.

(4) That "Carsonia" (the six counties shaded and coloured red on map) has been artificially constituted, in defiance of all historical groupings, and all administrative convenience, in order to secure an artificial and permanent anti-national majority in the new state.

The Really "Homogeneous" Areas.

(5) That the really homogeneous Protestant populations of Ulster are confined within the City of Belfast and its adjoining Counties of Antrim alone.

(6) That such a grouping would avoid many administrative absurdities including that which, under the Government's scheme, would compel the Southern Governments to communicate with one of its constituent counties by railways crossing the territory of the Northern Government.

"Partition" confined to these two counties, however objectionable, would incidentally preserve the common headquarters of the Irish Protestant and Catholic Churches—the City of Armagh—within Ireland; and it would bear the general semblance of fair play and sincerity, so obviously outraged by the present proposals of the Government.

Ulster's Protest against Partition.

The British Government, having suppressed and ruined our industries, devastated and depopulated our country, starved and theorised our educational development, and overtaxed and impoverished our people, now proposes, in the exercise of its assumed authority, to consummate the ultimate crime against Ireland of partitioning her. It proposes doing this in defiance alike of history, economics, and commonsense, and in opposition to the opinion and verdict of the vast majority of the Irish people as expressed in every way open to them. Ireland has been since the beginning of modern European history a legal, social and economic unity, and has always been treated as such even by England. The Act of Union purports to be a treaty between two sovereign States. The economic life of the whole of Ireland is based upon a common focal point. The ecclesiastical systems of the country are all national in structure. Land Acts and Coercion Acts have been the same alike for Tyrone and Kerry, and Mr. Lloyd George's own Government, when attempting to enforce conscription, made no distinction between the men of Antrim and the men of Clare. "Partition" is, therefore, a purely political device designed to weaken the Irish nation and break its unity, and is so abhorrent to the view and wishes of the vast majority of the people of every province in Ireland that the British Government dare not take a plebiscite on this question in any area in the country. The propagandists who are hired to distort the facts of the Irish situation in the hope of screening the iniquities of the English tyranny base their arguments for partition on the allegation that the people of Ulster are so different from those of the rest of Ireland that they constitute in fact a distinct nation. How grotesque is this assertion may be learned from the fact that nine-tenths of the area of the nine County Council chairmen and the Mayor of one of the only two cities in the province are appended to this statement. Exclusive of the City of Belfast, there is a substantial Anti-Unionist majority in Ulster, and whilst the minority approves of the union system of Government, he would be an audacious man who would dare argue that they do not form part and parcel of the Irish people. In the five counties which have returned Nationalist Councils the proportions of the population are about 70 per cent. to 30 per cent. non-Catholic; and in the whole of Ulster,

with the exclusion of the Borough of Belfast, the proportions are 60.08 per cent. Catholic to 49.884 per cent. non-Catholic. (The actual figures of population being 597,573 to 597,176 respectively—Appendix I. In the area comprising the counties of Tyrone and Fermanagh and Derry City there is a Catholic majority of no less than 79,015—Appendix II.) No Nationalist would admit that an unglamorate minority possesses the right to secede from the nation of which it forms a part any more than an American would admit the right of one of the areas in the West or South in which there is a German or negro preponderance of population to cut itself off from the United States. But, if the existence of such a right were arguable, it would only apply to the City of Belfast, and even in that borough there is a Nationalist minority of almost one-fourth.

Against this attempt, therefore, to partition our country, we, the undersigned, elected as we have been by the people of Ulster and representing every county and city in the province protest before the world. We own no allegiance save to the sovereign people of Ireland, and will give no willing obedience to any Government not sanctioned by them. We declare our determination to resist by every possible means the British Government's iniquitous proposal and, conscious of the justice of our cause, we crave the goodwill and sympathy of all civilised peoples in our struggle to prevent the dismemberment of our motherland.

Dated the eleventh day of November, 1920.

Signed,

Hugh C. O'Doherty, Mayor of Derry City.
John M'Hugh, Chairman Fermanagh County Council.
Alex E. Donnelly, Chairman Tyrone County Council.
T. Smith, Chairman Cavan County Council.
Thomas Toal, Chairman Monaghan County Council.
P. T. Ward, T.D., Chairman Donegal County Council.
Archibald Savage, Member Belfast Corporation.
Louis Walsh, Member Antrim County Council.
M. Derry, M.D., Member Armagh County Council.
James Mullan, Member Derry County Council.
Henry M'Grath, Member Down County Council, and Chairman Downpatrick, R.D.C.

A GRAPHIC PRESENTATION OF THE HISTORY AND MEANING OF THE GOVERNMENT OF IRELAND BILL, 1920.

4 'Carsonia: the Great Betrayal', supplement to *The Republic*, 26 February 1921.

At The Castle.
June 26

To Aine bean Eamon Ceannt.
who brought me there and to one who
welcomed all.

Where we have come see the tri-colour flying
None wore the Khaki or redcoat on guard,
Wide, as in welcome the Gates that we drove through.
(Once was a time, they had got to be barred.)

Up where I come from, if flown were those colours
Or wound among flowers for a grave in the grass
Dearly you'd pay for the like of such boldness
As did the True-men beside Money glas.

You at my right hand, who enter beside me
Stricken, but brave gave your dearest of all;
She on my left, for both husband and brother
Mourned, but was proud that they issued the call.

Now, have we captured the Castle of Dublin?
Hoist up the flag with its Watchword of Old:
Now:— or it's "Never"—Yes Now! Then for ever
Ireland,— all Ireland, to have and to hold.

Hush! Who has captured the Castle of Dublin?
To whom have surrendered the Garrison Crew?
Not alone to the living high honoured amongst us:—
The faithful departed are triumphing too.

5 'At the Castle' poem by Milligan, June 1936.

6 Front cover of paperback edition of *Glimpses of Erin* by Alice Milligan and Seaton Milligan, 1888.

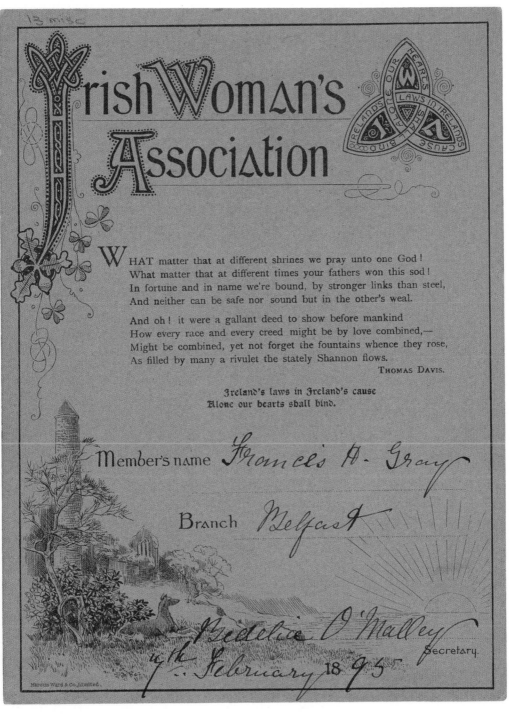

WHAT matter that at different shrines we pray unto one God!
What matter that at different times your fathers won this sod!
In fortune and in name we're bound, by stronger links than steel,
And neither can be safe nor sound but in the other's weal.

And oh! it were a gallant deed to show before mankind
How every race and every creed might be by love combined,—
Might be combined, yet not forget the fountains whence they rose,
As filled by many a rivulet the stately Shannon flows.

THOMAS DAVIS.

Ireland's laws in Ireland's cause
Alone our hearts shall bind.

Member's name *Frances A. Gray*

Branch *Belfast*

Fedelia O'Malley
Secretary.

14th February 18 95

7 Front cover of only surviving membership card of the Irish Women's Association
founded by Alice Milligan in 1894.

WOMAN'S MISSION.

"It is within what is more properly her own sphere woman can serve her country best. Her mission is to awaken the apathetic to a sense of duty; to shame the wavering into action; to lighten the toil of the true and brave."

C. J. KICKHAM.

PROGRESS.

"What is a man born for but to be a reformer, a re-maker of what man has made, a renouncer of lies; a restorer of truth and good, imitating that great nature which embosoms us all, and which sleeps no moment on an old past, but every hour repairs her self, yielding us every morning a new day, and with every pulsation a new life."

EMERSON.

WHAT IRELAND WANTS.

"To get her peasants into snug homesteads with well-tilled fields and placid hearths; to develop the ingenuity of her artists and the docile industry of her artizans; to make for her own instruction a literature wherein our climate, history, and passions shall breathe; to gain conscious strength and integrity, and the high past of holy freedom,—these are Ireland's wants."

THOMAS DAVIS.

SECURITY FOR THE FARMER.

"Since my boyhood I have always looked with a sort of veneration upon an independent farmer cultivating his small demesne, who aspires to no lot but labour in his own land, and takes off his hat to no superior but God Almighty. Tenant-right, fee-farm, call his tenure what you will, only let him be sure that, where he sows, he or his shall reap, eat, and be satisfied."

JOHN MITCHELL.

RULE BRITANNIA!

"As far as concerns England and the Colonial Empire she has created, I say, cordially, 'Rule Britannia;' but Ireland is not a colony of Great Britain, but an ancient kingdom, entitled to its distinct nationality, and determined to have it."

SAMUEL FERGUSON.

Our Motto:

"Ireland's laws in Ireland's cause
Alone our hearts shall bind."

JOHN O'HAGAN.

8 Back cover of Irish Women's Association membership card.

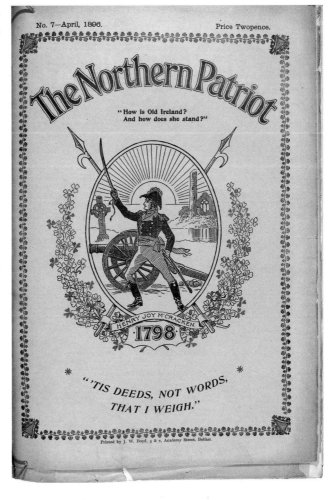

9 Alice Milligan's copy of *Shan Van Vocht* gifted to Brother Allen of O'Connell Schools containing this list she wrote in October 1951 in which she decodes some of the pen names used by writers throughout the journal.

10 Front cover illustration of the *Northern Patriot*, Apr. 1896.

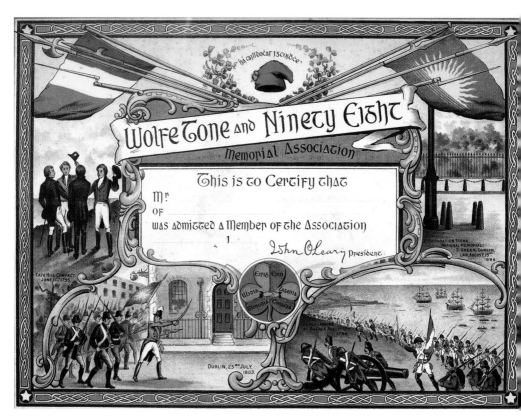

11 1798 association membership card. Milligan was a member of the '98 Executive Committee, founded in 1897.

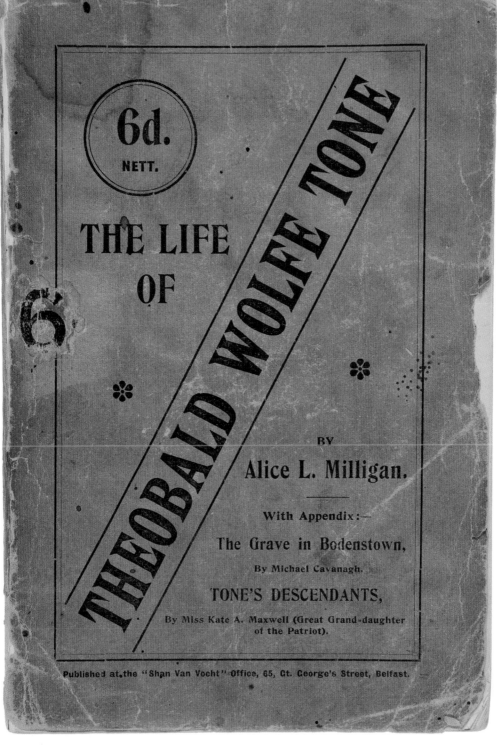

12 Front cover of Alice Milligan's *The life of Wolfe Tone*, published in Belfast in 1898.

13 Grave decoration image from *Weekly Freeman*, 26 June 1897.

The Daughter of Donagh . .

By Alice L. Milligan.

MARTIN LESTER, LTD.

14 Front cover of *Daughter of Donagh,* published by Bulmer Hobson in 1920

The Last Feast of the Fianna

A Dramatic Legend

By

Alice Milligan

London : David Nutt
57–59 Long Acre
1900

3234

15 Front cover of *The last feast of the Fianna*, performed by the Irish Literary Theatre at the Gaiety Theatre, February 1900.

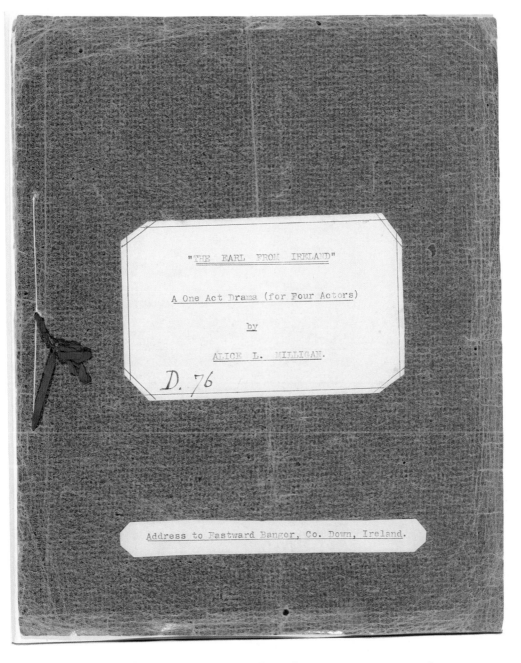

"THE EARL FROM IRELAND"

A One Act Drama (for Four Actors)

by

ALICE L. MILLIGAN.

D. 76

Address to Eastward Bangor, Co. Down, Ireland.

16 A hand typed, hand sewn manuscript play Milligan sent to a newspaper to be published (date unknown).

17 'Stand to the guns! Henry Joy McCracken leading the rally at the Battle of Aughrim', by Walter C. Mills, *Irish Weekly Independent*, December 1895, NLI HP 1798 (32).

18 'Rejoice Oh Greatly', *Weekly Freeman*, 4 June 1887.

19 'At their mercy', *Weekly Freeman* supplement, 8 April 1882.

20 'The Land Bill mirage', 19 March 1881, *Weekly Freeman*.

21 Sketch by Milligan for costume design of Queen Meave *c.*1898–1901.

22 Milligan's sketches for costumed tableaux.

23 Jack B. Yeats, 'Communicating with Prisoners', *c.*1924. Oil on canvas, 46 × 21 cm. Courtesy of The Model Home of the Niland Collection. © Estate of Jack B. Yeats. All rights reserved, DACS 2011.

24 Elizabeth Young as Deirdre in play of the same name by Æ (George Russell).

25 Photograph by Ros Kavanagh of part of the Alice Milligan and the Irish Cultural Revival exhibition curated by Catherine Morris at the National Library of Ireland. The exhibition was opened by Fiona Shaw in November 2010 and ran until March 2011.

"LET US REALISE
OUR RESPONSIBILITY
AT THIS CRISIS
IN OUR COUNTRY'S HISTORY
AND ACT UP TO IT."
ALICE MILLIGAN, 1898.

26 Gaelic League teacher in Connemara using Froebel spheres to teach mathematics. Postcard created by National Women's Council to celebrate the Alice Milligan exhibition on International Women's Day, 2011

27 Ronan McCrea, *Projective techniques* (1994). An installation at the Pearse Museum, St Enda's, Rathfarnham, Dublin. The image shows a detail of the installation made at the museum using a magic lantern belonging to the Pearse family, and illustrates the kind of machinery Alice Milligan would have been familiar with. The drawing on the wall is based on an image of Killarney from Pearse's Gaelic League glass slide collections. As part of the installation the artist applied cut-vinyl lettering on the window quoting from Pearse's sister's diary: 'Once Padraig brought down a cinematograph operator to Connemara and gave an entertainment in an adjacent school ... It was the first time that anything like it had ever been seen in the district ... One old woman tried hard to get behind the screen to see the real people! Her remarks should be quoted in Irish to give the real full value ...'

"AT THE OUTSET MY PRESENCE WAS OBJECTED TO:
'THIS IS A MEETING OF THE ELECTION COMMITTEE.
WE DO NOT EXPECT LADIES!.'"
ALICE MILLIGAN, 1897.

28 Postcard created by National Women's Council to celebrate the Alice Milligan exhibition on International Women's Day, 2011. Photograph shows Anna Johnston looking at camera from her desk in the reading room of the National Library of Ireland, 1900.

"FREEDOM IS AS YET
A FAR OFF THING;
YET MUST WE WHO DESIRE IT
WORK FOR IT
AS ARDENTLY
AND AS JOYOUSLY
AS IF WE HAD GOOD HOPE
THAT OUR OWN
EYES SHOULD BEHOLD IT."
ALICE MILLIGAN, 1896.

29 Woman carrying turf in Donegal c.1898. Postcard created by National Women's Council to celebrate the Alice Milligan exhibition on International Women's Day, 2011.

Milligan argued that the breach between Protestants and Catholics throughout the nineteenth century had overshadowed the progressive accomplishments of the United Irishmen:

> Unfortunately they had never united since to so great an extent. Since Catholic Emancipation came about they seemed to separate, and when their religious disabilities were removed, the Presbyterians passed from the struggle.[25]

After 1800, many Protestants, Milligan suggested, had been dissuaded from committing themselves to an anti-colonial agenda because of sectarian interpretations of the revolution: 'Since '98 there has never been such a large and active body of Protestants identified with the furtherance of the national cause, and in the eyes of the ignorant Orange faction the words nationalist and papist are still synonymous.'[26]

Adamant that the national cause should not be regarded in exclusively Catholic terms, Milligan championed the Protestants who had supported Irish self-determination in the nineteenth century. On 7 June 1895, the *Irish News* recounted how Milligan won 'great applause' from a Belfast audience when she tackled Protestant republicanism after '98: 'We have since had isolated cases of Protestants leading and helping in the National cause, and there was an increasing number joining with their fellow Catholic countrymen.'[27] She identified four of the Protestants who had served as standard bearers for the nationalist cause after 1798: 'Since then the names of Emmet, Davis, Mitchel, Parnell are sureties for the fact that the cause of Ireland is no longer merely the Catholic cause.'[28] Her use of the word 'merely' in this context was not derogatory: Milligan was trying to emphasis that the struggle for democracy that was so integral to those most discriminated against (that is, Catholics in Ireland) was also a struggle historically shared by some Protestants. It was a point that she made at great personal cost in a social landscape of conflict and animosity.

In his memoirs, the poet James Cousins recorded that the Protestant unionist community in Belfast regarded Alice Milligan as one of the 'isolated cases' of Protestants who had joined in the national struggle for democracy. Cousins recalled that this 'red-headed nationalist' was a figure of gossip and controversy in *fin-de-siècle* Belfast where she was branded a 'black mark' on her family's reputation.[29] The Belfast unionist press shared this view of Alice Milligan as a 'black mark'. Under the headline 'The '98 microbe in Ulster', the *Belfast Evening Telegraph* labelled as 'discontents' those Protestants who commemorated 'the futile rebellion of '98'.[30] The editorial of this unionist paper argued that the inequalities which had led to the United Irish uprising had been dismantled after 1800 by the progressive wave of reforms:

> Those who are now exultant over the futile Rebellion of '98 are the discontents who seek the re-establishment of a Parliament in Dublin and the ascendancy of the Roman Catholic church in Ireland. We may remind them that had there been no rebellion in 1798, the Irish Parliament might never have been taken away. The men who are now causing such a furore … are merely fomenting strife and keeping up party feeling.[31]

The paper also invited readers to contribute verses on the topic of '98: one correspondent re-wrote the lines of the famous '98 verse: 'Afraid to speak of ninety-eight? / Nay, but we blush to hear the name / When Irish pseudo patriots prate / And glory in defeat and shame.'[32]

In the early 1890s, Milligan attacked what she saw as the 'alienation and colonial spirit of the vast mass of Irish Protestants'.[33] In one of her 'Notes from the north' columns she traced the origin and deployment of the '98 song 'The Wearing of the Green', recounting how this verse had shaped her own perception of Ireland as a nation rather than as a colony:

> This song was in earliest recollection the first that ever touched me with real Irish life and feeling, just as it came to me at a time when the songs and tunes I knew best were 'The Protestant Boys', 'The Boyne Water', and others of that sort breathing a feeling of murderous hate, and threatening to slit and slaughter Papists and roll them under Orange drums.[34]

This is another version of epiphany recalled by Milligan: it was music that had a profound impact upon her in this instance, and it was through literary culture that she would explore some of the more complex anxieties latent in commemorating 1798. The short stories Milligan published in the *Shan Van Vocht* between 1896 and 1898 work through the conflictual currents that define Irish Protestant republicanism. In these stories of contested identities, religious determinants are disengaged from political affiliations. Their protagonists are frequently forced into a reckoning with the ramifications of 1798 – which provoke estrangement and alienation. For example, Dr Carr, narrator of the 1896 story, 'A boy from Barnesmore', agrees to help an Irish-American Fenian smuggle arms into Derry, despite knowing virtually nothing of the man or his mission. Attempting to rationalize his automatic willingness to take part in the hazardous venture, Carr evokes the powerful memory of his grandfather's exploits at Ballynahinch:

> Forgetful of everything, I, a sensible, settled, middle-aged doctor, an elder
> of the Presbyterian Church, was on the point of promising this boy from
> dear knows where! – Baltimore, more likely than Barnesmore; that I would
> do anything I could to oblige him. I was going to become guilty of high
> treason, or treason felony. 'My grandfather was with Monroe in '98,' I said,
> 'and you may confide in me anyhow'.[35]

Carr's unquestioning loyalty to the ideals of his grandfather makes it plain that the
cause for which the United Irishmen fought is an ongoing process of cultural
memory rather than a contained and completed fragment of history. The 1897
story 'The little green slippers' also invokes the memory of a heroic father-figure
as a means of activating and justifying a (female) Protestant's allegiance to
republican ideals.[36]

'A rebel's wooing', published in 1896, is actually set in the turbulent period of
1796–8. Randal MacAllister leaves his home in the 'little village of Cushendal' to
fight as a United Irishman. Milligan describes the scenes of battle, significantly
naming historical figures and northern towns:

> There were thousands of good men and true fleeing for life and liberty over
> the hills of Antrim and through the glens that summer of '98. He had been
> through the fight in Ballymena, carrying himself like a very hero, ever in the
> front encouraging his comrades to sterner strife around the burning Market
> House. Then he had gone up to Slemish and met there the fugitives from
> the Battle of Antrim with their leaders, Henry Joy McCracken and staunch
> Jamie Hope, the latter an old friend and the very man who had sworn
> Randal into the brotherhood.[37]

John Macauley, an especially contradictory father figure, is a Catholic property
owner who is devoted to the ascendancy and opposed to the United Irishmen.
Macauley's political beliefs, however, are irrelevant to the loyalist soldiers who
destroy his house and then burn his cattle. After the Battle of Antrim, Macauley
is visited by the defeated United Irishman, Randal MacAllister, who is
romantically involved with Macauley's daughter Rosie. When he reaches their
house, Randal contemplates the irony of John Macauley's plight:

> Rosie's home was roofless and desolate. Stables and byres were burned, and
> no living creature stirred about. The yeos, in their rage of massacre and
> plunder, made no allowances for John Macauley's loyalty, no inquiry into his
> principles. He was a papist and had a rich house to plunder and fat kine to

slay. That was enough … He would have done better, he and others like him, to have struck boldly in defence of home and motherland. But for a section of such loyalists Ireland might that day have been on the high road to freedom.[38]

John Macauley is technically on the winning side of the battle, yet his farm and home have been lost to him in an attack by those who emblematize the principles he supports.

Milligan argued in all of her writings throughout the 1890s that the establishment of the United Irishmen in 1791 enabled a religious and national unity that ended a century of sectarian division. Milligan urged late nineteenth-century cultural activists to look upon the United Irishmen movement as a precedent for their own ideals. It would be difficult to overstate the importance of United Irish insurgency for Milligan's literary and political career. Over a decade she produced three plays, four short stories, numerous ballads and poems which are set in, or refer directly to, the 1790s. Indeed, as the last chapter indicated, it is hard to imagine the 1898 centenary taking place without the energy and support given to it by the *Shan Van Vocht* from 1896. Milligan's regular articles for the *Irish Weekly Independent* also provided a platform for the discussion of the northern leaders and battles. Newspapers were especially important to Milligan because they enabled information about '98 to be distributed to a wide audience at relatively little cost. By mapping the development of Milligan's convictions concerning the significance that the 1790s held for the 1890s, it is clear that her writings from the period 1888 to 1898 qualified Milligan for the high profile role that she was elected to perform in organizing the Centennial of '98.

Conflict and commemoration

The commemorative agenda for the centenary year had been plotted well in advance. In March 1897, Young Ireland established a network of organizations to plan the Centennial in conjunction with the '98 Executive, which co-ordinated local events at a national level. The Irish Republican Brotherhood (IRB) activist, Henry Dixon, stated that the new Executive would include only those 'who do not fear to speak of '98, and who would join in paying tribute to the United Irishmen without assuming the role of apologists for their principles or actions' [Plate 11].[39] As its title suggests, the '98 Executive was structured by a complex hierarchy that included two vice-presidents, six treasurers and ten elected represen-tatives of Ireland and ten elected representatives for Britain, Scotland, Wales and France. There were also six honorary secretaries.[40] This dense official structure is another example of how the anti-colonial movement in Ireland organized itself as the nation waiting to step into public office. As though forming a 'shadow' administration, everything was carried out with a heightened air of democracy and officialdom: votes, multiple committees, minutes, local administrations, delegations, speeches, newspaper reports, membership cards, uniforms, names and regiments. But the complexity of the Executive lay not just in its elaborate Borgesian labyrinthine structures but in its political makeup.

The tensions that surfaced during the Commemorations were embedded in old animosities between parliamentarians and anti-parliamentarians; secret militant republicanism and those who favoured constitutional reform; and between Irish women who once again were forced to fight for inclusion and representation in organizations to which they had been democratically elected to serve. The northern members of the Executive had an added set of bitter twists to complicate their set of conflicts: Milligan faced opposition on the Executive not only because she was a woman, but all the old rifts with the McCracken Society over the *Northern Patriot* and the *Shan Van Vocht* resurfaced. In addition, Milligan also had to face many public battles with the fiercely confrontational Irish Parliamentary Party in Belfast who resented her endless opposition to politicians who took the oath in Westminster. At the start of 1898 spies for Dublin Castle reported that, 'Strenuous efforts are being made by leading agitators to combine all parties in a united body, but at present there is nothing but disunion and dissension in every direction.'[41] Ironically, the conflicts and the political complexity of the north made it the place in Ireland that had the greatest number of '98 clubs. These associations sprang up across the country and rapidly gained a sizeable membership. Police files compiled in 1897 and 1898 show that while the 28 clubs in Dublin had 1,465 members, the 20 clubs established in Belfast drew a membership of 4,020. The north also became the most worrying site of protest for the authorities. British agents working for Dublin Castle expressed surprise at the strength of the northern interest: 'It is remarkable that more life appears to exist in the '98 movement in the northern counties than those in the middle, West and South of Ireland.'[42]

Milligan did much work in boosting these northern membership numbers and in defining their political historical consciousness. With a decade's worth of '98 lectures and publications to her name, Milligan was one of the five chosen from Belfast to represent Ulster on the Executive. Anna Johnston took over the business of the *Shan Van Vocht* while Alice Milligan travelled to Dublin where she expected to be elected. She wrote to Francis Joseph Bigger: 'A meeting to elect a Committee for the '98 centenary will be held tonight in the City Hall, Dublin … Miss Milligan has been invited to speak and left this morning'.[43] In September 1897, Milligan was elected to three of the five sub-committees (the Literary and Exhibitions Committee, the Memorial Committee, the Tours & Hotels

Committee) set up to bolster the effectiveness of the centenary. While serving on the Dublin-based executive, she continued as secretary of the Belfast Centenary Committee, and as proof of her strong rural connections Milligan was also elected the representative for Letterkenny's '98 Centenary Association.

As editor and proprietor of the most prolific literary and political journal in Belfast, Milligan held an influential position among nationalists in Ireland and abroad. From 1896 to 1898, the *Shan Van Vocht* carried Milligan's personal agenda for the centenary, presenting her opinions and blueprints to Irish nationalists in Ireland, Scotland, London and America as though they were part of the executive's plans. Her provisional outline for the Ulster procession of '98 Clubs proves how difficult it was to separate Milligan's voice as editor from her role as elected spokesperson for Ulster. In August 1897, she envisaged a 'marshalled' parade in which participants were to assemble in military fashion:

> Each club should decide on some one pattern of home made manufactured material to be recommended, if not actually insisted on, as a uniform to be provided at the member's own expense before next year.[44]

She suggested that each '98 Club should carry four banners – designating the club's title, region, the battles fought locally between 1797 and 1798 and the names of its dead martyrs.[45] Milligan's editorial in the *Shan Van Vocht* described how one such procession held in Derry on St Patrick's Day in 1898 avoided overt association with political parties:

> The banners carried in the procession all did honour to the illustrious and sainted dead; from St Patrick and Brian Boru to Tone and Emmet. In the interest of harmony no banners with portraits of living politicians were carried. The procession was not only in honour of Ireland's patron saint, but of many of her Protestant patriots. It was therefore, in no sense of the term, a 'party' procession.[46]

Each member was asked to wear two badges: one to display their club's emblem, the other exhibiting its colours. Milligan implored the '98 Clubs to assert their allegiance to the ideals which had inspired their revolutionary predecessors. A pageant, ordered by a rigid dress code with banners, badges and bands, would have a tremendous impact on 'onlookers' and participants alike: 'The march past of Belfast clubs in this way would illustrate the history of Belfast in '98'.

The complex political geography of late nineteenth-century Belfast made it difficult for followers of the commemoration to display their support. Minister Lavery of the Ards District Lodge urged resistance to commemorative parades,

29 Photograph of Grafton Street with union jacks waving *c.*1898.

demanding that his congregation heeded the following question: 'Were the sons of those who conquered at the Boyne lightly to allow the descendants of Irish rebels to plant their standards in our midst?'[47] In the light of the possible clashes that would inevitably ensue between Orangemen and nationalists, Milligan cautioned against the Belfast '98 procession planned for 6 June 1898:

> About this procession we have a word to say. We do not think that when the protection of the police force and military is necessary for the carrying out of a demonstration, it should be persisted in. We understand that the Chief Secretary for Ireland has authorised the police to protect the '98 demonstrations in the north. In that case it is the Orangemen who will be in the position of the rebels, and the only gain will be to the British Government, which will have succeeded in rekindling the long-slumbering fires of party hatred.[48]

The absence of a large and vocal Orange Order in Dublin meant that the '98 commemoration proceeded smoothly, its marches, memorial dedications and parades meeting with no violent opposition. Dublin Municipal Council officially supported the celebrations, declaring the unveiling of the Wolfe Tone foundation stone a public holiday on 15 August 1898. Dublin Corporation offered the site on the corner of Stephen's Green – at the top of Grafton Street – for the foundation stone to be laid.[49] Milligan described how northern nationalists revelled in this unobstructed demonstration of republican ideals:

> The presence of the northerners from Belfast, Derry, Armagh, Tyrone, and Donegal in such vast numbers must be accounted for by the fact, that to share in such a great national demonstration, uninterrupted by Orange affrays, is for them a rare pleasure.[50]

Believing that all supporters of the commemoration should exhibit their unity, Milligan attempted to counter the bitter factionalism she associated with nineteenth-century Irish politics. In her retelling of *The life of Wolfe Tone*, published in 1898, she argued that sectarianism was a colonial policy that aimed to thwart a unified national struggle for self-determination:

> The memories which will be awakened will save us from falling a prey to England's insidious policy, well summed up in the dictum – DIVIDE AND CONQUER.[51]

Milligan advertised her work on Tone in the *Shan Van Vocht*: 'It aims at giving a striking narrative of the great patriot's life and times, some account of his friends and associates, and a clear exposition of his principles and methods.'[52] On 15 August 1898 thousands attended the procession in Dublin that preceded the laying of the foundation stone for the Wolfe Tone statue. From the platform John O'Leary made reference to Milligan's work on Tone: 'To know how Tone felt during that sad period, you must read his diary, and this you can now easily do in the little sixpenny book, by Miss Milligan, where this is well epitomised.'[53] A copy of this speech was kept by Dublin Castle [Plate 12].[54]

Though she hoped that 1898 would promote political solidarity, Milligan hardly anticipated that the greatest obstruction to this goal would not be the 'ignorant orange faction' she protested against in 1895.[55] Instead, she found that conflicts between nationalists also provided a formidable barrier to unity. The '98 Clubs in Belfast had to contend not only with loyalist opposition, but with dissent among nationalist ranks. Milligan asserted that such members of the Irish

30 Magic lantern glass slide showing 1898 Centenary Commemoration march through Dame Street to St Stephen's Green. On this procession, Milligan and her colleagues carried a rock from Cave Hill for the laying of the foundation stone of the Wolfe Tone statue.

Parliamentary Party (IPP) as Joseph Devlin, John Dillon and William O'Brien did 'not represent all the nationalists in Belfast' and they in turn dismissed the '98 Executive as 'not representing all the nationalists of Ireland'.[56] Every account of the '98 Executive in the *Irish News* was contested by the Irish Parliamentary Party in protest against the exclusion of political parties from the Executive.

In September 1897, a bitter dispute arose between Milligan and the leaders of the National Federation and National League (NFNL) – a branch of the IPP.

Members of this organization, she claimed, were infiltrating the '98 clubs in order
to win support for nationalist politicians in the forthcoming Belfast municipal
elections. In his detailed study of the fractured nationalist response to the '98
Centennial, Timothy O'Keefe draws attention to the ways in which the IPP
utilized the commemoration as a potential vote winner: 'Because of their diminished
prestige, the party leaders became increasingly defensive and suspicious of
anything which threatened to capture the nationalist imagination. The '98
Executive', he suggested, 'was considered a potential danger by the contending
leaders of the Irish Parliamentary Party'.[57] The Irish National Federation League
formed the United Irishmen '98 Centennial Association and set out to form their
own branches of '98 Clubs. Letters of criticism suddenly began to appear in the
Belfast newspapers that drew attention to the disorganization of '98 clubs across
Ulster. Regarding the official programme of events surrounding the American visit
to Ireland, 'A '98 Man' complained: 'The South of Ireland takes a leading part in
the programme and yet no mention is made of the North at all … Is the Northern
Capital – which from the beginning threw itself heartily into the movement – to
be left unvisited?'[58] A second correspondent was concerned that no '98 Clubs
existed in Antrim, Down, Lisburn, Saintfield or Portaferry.[59] It was later revealed
that these letters to the press were orchestrated by the Ulster Centenary
Committee (a branch of the Irish Parliamentary Party) to underline their general
discontent with the work of the '98 Executive.

The *Times* (London) reported one meeting at which IPP opposition to the '98
Executive surfaced:

> A private conference first took place, at which resolutions approving of the
> action of the 'men of '98' and asking for unity among the Irishmen carrying
> out the celebrations were adopted.[60]

The resolutions were afterwards proposed at the public meeting by Mr
T. Harrington, MP, who condemned the action of the '98 Centenary Committee
(a kindred organization) in excluding from its ranks Irish members of Parliament
because of their taking the oath of allegiance on entering the House of
Commons.[61] Milligan attracted some of the hostility that existed between the
Parliamentary Party and the '98 Executive when she began to defend the Dublin-
based organization. In March 1897, she urged supporters of the '98 Executive not
to allow party factions to jeopardize the united aims of the Centenary organization:

> Let us not address ourselves to any political organisation, nor enrol men
> under our Sunburst banner, as Parnellites, anti-Parnellite or the like. We do

not want to know what any man thinks of Dillon, Redmond, or Tim Healy. We can answer that question in the polling booths.[62]

In September 1897 she turned up uninvited to a meeting of the Irish National Federation and National League in Belfast and tabled an amendment to their agenda. The *Irish News* noted that both Milligan and Anna Johnston had proposed, uncontroversially enough, that yet another committee should be established to discuss the '98 Convention. Although Timothy O'Keefe dismisses Milligan's participation at the meeting as 'a futile protest', her own response to the proceedings makes it clear that much was at stake. In letters to the press, Milligan claimed that the organizers had attempted to discriminate against her gender:

> I may say that at the outset my presence was objected to, and that a
> gentleman who afterwards took an active part in the meeting told me –
> 'This is a meeting of the Election Committee. We do not expect ladies.' He,
> however, immediately acknowledged that the business of the evening was
> the '98 Centenary, and I claimed to be present either as a member of the
> Executive of Ireland or a representative of the press. In spite of objections
> from some of the most prominent local politicians present, a courteous
> hearing was claimed for me by the majority of the audience. The report of
> the proceedings mentions Miss Johnston as having been present. This is
> totally inaccurate.[63]

Milligan argued that the nationalists had exploited membership of '98 Clubs solely for the advancement of party politics. The Parliamentary Party responded to Milligan's unrelenting accusations against Westminster's Irish MPs by displaying tremendous public hostility towards her place on the Executive. In April 1898 bids between Milligan's friends began for a copy of a controversial letter she had written criticising O'Brien and the Parliamentary Party. Francis Joseph Bigger was asked: 'Is it true that you are offering £20 for a copy of Milligan's withdrawn letter. I am going to wait till the price goes up.'[64] In July 1897, Douglas Hyde sympathetically acknowledged her general position: 'I see your hand is being forced by William O'Brien.'[65] Milligan's letter to the *Irish News* and her subsequent analysis in the *Shan Van Vocht* suggest that she acted as the main spokesperson of the group. The difficulties Milligan faced in confronting the Irish Parliamentary Party were characteristic of the problems that prevented women from taking part in any male-dominated political struggle. She was repeatedly barred from constitutional political party meetings because of her gender. According to a report in the *Irish News*, a member named McCabe blocked her contribution to an Irish Parliamentary Party meeting by declaring its irrelevance:

A representative of the IPP denounced the present executive, and added they would take no dictation from Dublin, but work on the lines of Wolfe Tone. Miss Milligan informed the speaker that Wolfe Tone was a Dublin man who came down to Belfast and educated the people. He [Mr M'Cabe] did not think he could benefit the '98 Association by detaining them any longer on the subject.[66]

Joseph Devlin also attempted to silence her criticism of party involvement in the centenary:

Miss Milligan claimed that they could accomplish union by standing by the '98 Executive; that the two organisations in question did not represent all the nationalists in Belfast. An exceedingly grave division at present existed among nationalists in Belfast, and the '98 movement should be guarded from being involved in it. Mr Devlin protested that this last remark was an insult to the nationalists of Belfast and said Miss Milligan should not be heard. He objected to any man from Dublin coming down to interfere in Belfast. Miss Milligan observed that Wolfe Tone was a gentleman from Dublin who came down as secretary of the Catholic Association, and who interfered to such an extent that he transformed Belfast politics, and founded the United Irish body.[67]

It is ironic that while Devlin and Milligan both argue for de-centralization, the former perceived Milligan as a tool of the Dublin Executive. Milligan herself argued continually for a more diverse structure in the '98 Executive. In the columns of her own paper she too displayed irritation in the central location of the Executive in Dublin. While Milligan never actually suggested Belfast as an alternative capital city to Dublin, she was always circling the radical and far reaching possibilities of such an idea:

WHY NOT HOLD THE NEXT CONVENTION IN BELFAST? We believe that the cause of Ireland would be served and the '98 organisation would spread if the conventions were not held invariably in the City Hall, Dublin. Why not hold a convention in Belfast, Cork, and Athlone or Galway alternately in order to awaken the provinces to take action in the matter?[68]

After months of dispute she warned that only 'the enemy' could possibly benefit from these 'insane internal divisions'.[69] Milligan's new year editorial in the *Shan Van Vocht* stated:

> This base mistrust of the integrity of each other's motive has been our bane
> in the past, and, sons of Ireland, if you will but study your country's history,
> you will recognise the truth that this fault of ours has done more harm to us
> than the strength of the enemy could ever have achieved unaided.[70]

The strife did indeed prove advantageous to the colonial administration that
vigilantly monitored all activity connected with the commemoration. The Crime
Special Branch revelled in the implications of discord among nationalists: 'The
disunion and distrust which exists amongst Irish nationalists, both at home and
abroad, renders it very difficult for them to successfully organise any important
matter at present. So far as can be foreseen the actual demonstrations give no
serious cause for anxiety save in the case of Belfast.'[71]

Conflicts continued to dominate the commemorative agenda throughout 1897
and into 1898. In January 1898, Milligan argued that the divisions among
nationalists and republicans in Ireland played into the hands of Ireland's colonial
rulers: 'If the Centenary of '98 should pass by and leave us still engaged in
internecine warfare, then we will have given proof that we are slaves indeed.'[72]
Fearful that opportunities for cultural unity would be destroyed, in April she
concluded that the only way to quell the factional dissent was to amalgamate the
Irish Parliamentary Party and the '98 Executive:

> On May 23rd a meeting will be held in Dublin to inaugurate the
> Monument Fund. It is hoped that for this occasion it will be found possible
> without sacrifice of principle to amalgamate all existing organisations
> working for a common end, the honouring of the dead of '98, and agreeing
> to ignore political differences.[73]

The eventual merger took place in May 1898 and was welcomed by Milligan in
the *Shan Van Vocht*: 'This news will be greeted with heartfelt pleasure by everyone
who desires to see the Centenary celebrations carried out with unanimity and
success'.[74]

Despite her vital contribution to the planning of the commemoration, the
presence of nationalist MPs on the Executive forced her to accept a more marginal
position. For example, Milligan proposed that a statue of Wolfe Tone should be
erected, a project which formed a crucial part of the centenary calendar:

> An important resolution, which was carried without opposition, was that of
> Miss Alice Milligan, Belfast, which ran as follows: – That a fitting way in
> which to honour the men of '98 would be by the erection of a monument

to the memory of Wolfe Tone in a prominent position in the metropolis and that a fund be opened for that purpose.[75]

However, Milligan was excluded from the select group of speakers chosen by the Executive to mark the unveiling of the foundation stone in August 1898. While John O'Leary, William Butler Yeats and Maud Gonne were among the dignitaries on the platform, having delivered the stone from Belfast Milligan watched the huge procession leading to the ceremony from the Gaelic League office doorway on Middle Abbey Street.

Women, nation, memory

In 1898 Milligan watched as she and other Irish women were sidelined and occluded from public space. Women and secrecy, official and unwritten histories were all bound together in the centenary commemorations. The counter-revolutionary discourse that emerged in the wake of the Act of Union of 1800 had similarly suppressed the story of female participation in the United Irish project. Dáire Keogh and Nicholas Furlong suggest that the role of women in the United Irish movement was written out of the published record constructed by male historians:

> No aspect of the 1798 rebellion has been so neglected as that of the women's role in the events of that year. Contemporaries drew upon their experience, but for the most part the women's voice was smothered beneath the partisan priorities of the commentators. There was little enthusiasm in the immediate aftermath of the rebellion for an accurate record of events since both loyalists and the vanquished attempted to play down the politicisation of the 1790s. The former sought to interpret the rising as a jacquerie or popish plot, while the latter attempted to minimise their culpability, presenting themselves as 'reluctant rebels' or moderating elements in a spontaneous rebellion provoked by unrelenting terror.[76]

During the centenary Milligan experienced how her contemporaries (especially elected politicians) were already beginning to write women out of this next phase of history. Milligan had two principal objections to the appropriation of the '98 commemoration by career politicians who took an oath of allegiance in the English Parliament. First, she felt that this encouraged factionalism and, second, women were excluded from the institutional political process supported by politicians. In October 1897, Milligan established the Irish Women's Centenary Union in Belfast to ensure that women could actively participate in the '98 celebrations. She put the following question to readers of the *Shan Van Vocht*:

> Is it too much to ask … that the women of Ireland, who are not called on to have any opinion whatever as to who has the right to speak for Ireland in the British Parliament, should form that Union which a historic occasion demands? The existing committee, in Dublin … is threatened on every side from within and without, with forces which may mar and shatter it.[77]

Milligan claimed that one aim of the Women's Union was to offer women in politically sensitive circumstances a 'secure and neutral ground'[78] regardless of their political, religious or familial affiliations. Echoing the role of the Ladies' Land League formed in 1880 when the male members of the Land League were imprisoned, Milligan also suggested that this women's organization could continue the centenary work if the '98 Executive was impeded by the British state machinery:

> The government may find it expedient or necessary to forbid some of the demonstrations which the men's committees will organise. No power of law exists to prevent the celebration of '98 in the form which the department under women's management is to be arranged.[79]

Milligan's suggestion that her women's organizations will operate as a front for the Irish Republican Brotherhood recalls the historic precedent of the Ladies Land League and raises the intriguing question of whether Milligan was, like Maud Gonne, a sworn in member of the IRB. As the examples below demonstrate, she certainly was closely in touch with many of the organization's key figures.[80]

Dublin Castle regarded the '98 Executive as 'mainly Fenian': 'The excitement consequent on the '98 Centenary is being availed of by the old Fenian leaders to revive and re-establish local circles of the IRB.'[81] The Crime Special Branch held records of at least four members of the Executive – John O'Leary, Fred Allan, Henry Dixon and Maud Gonne. Milligan may also have been a sworn member of the IRB, a fact which would further explain her prominent role in, and defence of, the '98 Executive. In 1919 she told Sinéad de Valera that she had been 'sworn into the Republican Movement'.[82] Furthermore, senior IRB members were part of her close circle during the early 1890s: Fred Allan was an editor of the *Irish Weekly Independent* when Milligan was awarded a weekly column from 1893. Mark Ryan of the London wing of the IRB was one of her regular correspondents and she lectured at their headquarters in 1898. Ryan was later to win admission for Milligan to the trial of Roger Casement in 1916. The *Shan Van Vocht* was produced in Robert Johnston's Belfast timber yard from 1896 to 1899. Johnston had taken a prominent role in the insurrection of 1867 and had extensive Fenian connections in America that were monitored by the Crime Special Branch. He was father to 'Ethna Carbery', Milligan's main colleague, and his house on the

Antrim Road in Belfast provided a meeting place for the Amnesty movement and other political groupings. The proposal to establish the Irish Women's Centenary Union was put to the '98 Executive by IRB member Henry Dixon. Further evidence of her continued allegiance to IRB members can be found in her letters to Áine Ceannt, whose house in Dublin she considered her 'political head quarters' after Partition. In 1937, Milligan wrote to Ceannt lamenting that she had not visited her friend Henry Dobbin before his death in February of that year: 'How sad I didn't see Dobbin. I worked with him for years and years 1895 till 1918.'[83] The *Irish Press* reported that Dobbin had been 'one the founders of the IRA in Belfast'.[84] Milligan's involvement with secret revolutionary societies was like her knowledge of the Irish language: an unquantifiable unknown that she kept ambiguous in a radical and self-conscious way.

Gender became the most revolutionary site of commemoration in 1898. In her 1919 book *Women of Ninety-Eight*, Helena Concannon asserted that 'One more pious duty the women of 1798 took upon themselves, and that was to guard the memory of the fallen, and to keep bright their names' [Plate 13].[85] Milligan foresaw such a role for the women during the Centenary, urging them to continue the work of their fore-sisters. She argued that women merited a central role in the commemoration because they served Ireland as the guardians of its cultural memory:

> To them we entrust the moulding of the minds of growing generations of the Irish race, and they should exercise their influence. So that old quarrels pass away with the makers of them, and so that those who are to work for Ireland in the new era should be able to do so untrammelled by old feuds and hatreds.[86]

By locating women as the nurturers of culture Milligan privileged them as the principal architects of history and nation. She addresses Irish women as a homogenous group, irrespective of the divisions of religion, region and class. By her determination that women would not be excluded from centenary events, Milligan herself provided a map of alternative possibilities for women to transform Ireland's identity and culture.

By designating women as the sole agents of memorialization, she re-directed three of her Executive posts – literary, tours, and exhibitions – to women. Her ideas were a continuation of the work she had recommended to Irish women in a column entitled 'Decoration day' published in the *Northern Patriot*.

This column advocates that Wolfe Tone's birthday in June should be commemorated by home grown flowers being laid to decorate 'patriotic graves'. The carrying out of this ceremony in this way, as it can only be done in summer time, would nourish patriotism in the home, and make the names of our holy dead familiar to the women, the girls, the little children of Ireland, who could share in the beautiful and pious custom, the observing of which is now in the less capable hands of men.[87]

Countess Markievicz's later gardening column for *Bean na h-Eireann* similarly defines cultivation of the land as a metaphor for the national debate.[88] Aware of the commercial possibilities created by the centenary, Milligan also envisaged an active economic role for women in 1898. The *Shan Van Vocht* advertised jewellery, handkerchiefs and badges which displayed '98 motifs, and Milligan informed readers that, 'we can dispatch to friends abroad any of the '98 badges and jewellery advertised on our cover, and can recommend them as thoroughly artistic and most suitable as gifts for the New Year '98'.[89] It was this initiative that provided the context for Milligan's already cited attack on Lady Aberdeen. Milligan insisted in 1898 that the organization of the tourist trade in Ireland could be 'more fitly undertaken by patriotic Irishwomen than by so-called English philanthropists under royal, vice-regal, and aristocratic patronage'.[90] During the Centenary year, Cook's Travel devised an enterprising scheme in which US citizens were invited to take a 'cheap trip' to Ireland for the celebrations. In the *Shan Van Vocht*, Milligan welcomed the scheme: 'Our Irish-American friends will be disposed to spend their money generously', she proclaimed enthusiastically, recognizing that the influx of revenue from America would benefit Irish home industries and promote the Irish Women's Centenary Union.[91] Dublin Castle considered that the war against Spain would preoccupy Americans, leaving them unwilling to travel to Ireland: 'It is asserted that numbers of Americans will visit the country during the summer and autumn. If the war continues, however, it is very improbable that this will take place, as money will be very scarce and American Irishmen will have enough to do at home.'[92] The Special Branch had little fear of the type of American visitor Milligan anticipated: 'The expense would be enormous and the class of American-Irish whose visit to this country would cause anxiety could hardly afford to give up their work in America to attend demonstrations in Ireland.'[93]

The Irish Women's Centenary Union welcomed into its ranks women who were directly connected with historic revolutionaries. These included Theobald Wolfe Tone's great granddaughter Kate Maxwell (to whom Milligan dedicated her *Life of Wolfe Tone*) and the sister of the Irish revolutionary and journalist John Mitchel. For Milligan these two women symbolized the union between past and present that she was attempting to establish through the '98 Executive:

> To
>
> Miss KATE A. MAXWELL,
>
> Of Brooklyn, New York, U.S.A.,
>
> Great Grand-Daughter of
>
> THEOBALD WOLFE TONE,
>
> This sketch of his life is dedicated by the Author.
>
> ────────
>
> " *Béidʰ Ulanh fós gan bhrón*
> *Ag cuimhnuighadh ar Wolfe Tóne.*"

31 Dedication page of *The life of Wolfe Tone*. Kate Maxwell's copy of this book is now in the American Irish Historical Society archives, New York.

It is surely a hopeful and healing sign to see a number of Irishwomen working together on a high and patriotic platform above strife and turmoil. Mrs John Martin, sister of the most honoured patriot that Ulster has produced since '98, is giving active help in forming the committee and has secured for it the addition of the name of one of John Mitchel's daughter's.[94]

Martin and Maxwell were celebrated as 'sympathizers' and 'patriots' because their male relatives had fought against the colonial system. Maintaining that the divisions in the republican movement during the '98 centenary derived from the interference of Irish nationalist politicians, she attempted through the formation of the Women's Union to offer an alternative politics that was untainted by Westminster or Party wrangling.

As she engaged in such grassroots political organizing, Milligan used fictional forms to explore the intricate compromises besetting gender and nationalism. One of the major plot devices in her 1898 short story, 'A rebel's wooing', involves a woman misunderstanding the motives of her lover when he informs her that he must leave her because of a greater commitment. Without mentioning that he is a United Irishman, Randal MacAllister speaks of his devotion to the republican cause as if he were describing another woman who had stolen his affections:

'This hand is not mine to offer you, it was pledged elsewhere, long, long before I saw that face or loved it.' Rose shrank from him in dismay, and at the next her heart was stabbed with jealous fear, for his head was raised

32 Adverts in *Shan Van Vocht* showing *Life of Wolfe Tone* alongside James Connolly's
new journal *Workers' Republic*, 1898.

proudly, and he was not looking on her tenderly as before; but away over the
mountain tops as if there was someone there that he remembered and
longed for. 'Oh, yes,' he said, 'I am pledged and bound in honour, and
though it has silenced the love I may have spoken and must not speak to
you, I shall never repent.'[95]

Randal's avoidance of the word 'nation' produces confusion for Rosie who has been
excluded from all knowledge of the revolutionary movement. He feminizes the
Ireland which inhabits both his memory and all that he sees before him. The
republic is simultaneously 'remembered and longed for', like a lost state which
requires restoration. The affections Randal had previously showered on Rosie are
displaced by his preoccupation with this intangible other. Despite his secrecy, Rosie
finally discovers that Randal is not 'wedded to another' but is in fact a member of an
outlawed political society. Rosie is elated with pride at her lover's activities. Her show
of faith in the republican struggle proves that she is not simply a follower of her
father's loyalist principles as Randal had automatically assumed.

With the conservative Protestant ascendancy strengthened by the republican
defeat of 1798, women were consigned to liminal spaces within Irish public and
political life. 'The little green slippers', set in December 1798, is another short
story by Milligan that concerns a Protestant woman's struggle to affirm her
personal and political identity. Jessica Huston defiantly and heroically rejects the

unionist agenda of her mother and stepfather in favour of a vision of republican democracy. With the growing dominance of a military state, Jessica's widowed mother decides to marry a wealthy businessman who is loyal to the English crown. Retaining her commitment to the republican ideals of her dead father, Jessica refuses to acknowledge Cuppage as a valid father figure, and also spurns the suitor appointed by her mother and stepfather. On the way to the Christmas ball, Hansard speaks to Cuppage about the outrageous behaviour of Irish women who parade through Belfast wearing the outlawed colour green:

> 'You would be surprised to know with what daring the people have been displaying mourning for the rebel, McCracken ... I have seen young misses walking down Castle Place in twos and threes past the faces of the soldiers with green and black bonnet strings or spencers, such as little Miss Mary McCracken has been wearing ever since.'
>
> Mr. Cuppage shook his head, sagely. 'I have no patience with these female politicians. That young person you speak of cannot have, I fear, fine feelings of any sort. I believe she was lately responsible for her brother's folly, and encouraged him in every way. And then the way she went wandering round the country without escort or chaperone after the Antrim business was shockingly improper'.[96]

Fear and a kind of awe inform the disdain the two men demonstrate against the actions of Irish women. Elaine Showalter asserts that hysteria was regarded strictly as a 'female malady' by nineteenth- and twentieth-century European psychoanalytic theory and practice:

> During an era when patriarchal culture felt itself to be under attack by its rebellious daughters, one obvious defence was to label women campaigning for access to universities, the professions, and the vote as mentally disturbed, and of all the nervous disorders of the *fin-de-siècle*, hysteria was the most strongly identified with the feminist movement ... In literature, too, the women who aspired to professional independence and sexual freedom were denounced as case studies in hysteria and degradation.[97]

The pro-ascendancy view, articulated by Cuppage and Hansard, stigmatizes Irish women who support the United Irish movement with the characteristics of hysteria. Their behaviour is considered politically misguided and decidedly un-feminine ('improper'). Cuppage and Hansard disparage the opinions expressed by these Irish women through a series of adjectival qualifications that construct their politics as a problem stemming from their immature age and lack of marital status. Those who stage protests are described as 'young misses' and 'Miss McCracken' is a 'little mortal'. What Hansard calls 'daring people' are in fact young, single women. Mary McCracken has questioned the legitimacy of the colonial legal system. In travelling without escort, she has posed a challenge to bourgeois patriarchal tradition, displacing the function of the 'chaperone'.

At the ball, Jessica declares her antipathy to Cuppage and Hansard by donning a pair of green slippers. Through her gesture of defiance Jessica disrupts 'the settled order of things' and refuses complicity with the loyalist allegiances of her mother, stepfather and unsuitable suitor. It is crucial that Jessica's father is not a republican martyr of 1798, as he died of a fever. Jessica's 'wearin' of the green' is not a direct reference to a brother, lover or father. Milligan knowingly appropriates the well-known myth of Cinderella and renders it within an overtly Irish republican context. The Cinderella fairy tale is a narrative of female transformation that ultimately sustains a conservative ideology of female suppression. Cinderella plays the passive role of victim while her godmother transforms the props of this neglected daughter's poverty into finery. In contrast, the female protagonist in Milligan's retelling actively rebels against the reactionary agenda of her parents and the emerging state. Milligan's work here seems to anticipate feminist revisions of fairy tales in the 1980s and predates Augusta Gregory's revision of Grania in the early twentieth century. Marina Warner argues that 'fairy tales give women a place from which to speak, but they sometimes speak of speechlessness as a weapon of last resort'.[98]

A narrative related by Milligan in her newspaper column 'Notes from the north' during 1895 indicates that her fictional story was inspired by an actual pair of green slippers worn by a Belfast woman in the wake of the defeat of the United Irishmen:

> A near relative of my own is the fortunate possessor of a relic of this McCracken mourning, in the shape of a dainty pair of emerald green slippers or half boots, which were the property of a lady whose people were in sympathy with the cause. What a picture they suggest of the Belfast High Street in the good old days, with patriotic citizens defying the authorities from behind the green wood work of their shop windows, measuring out green silks and bonnet strings to the ladies, who were all eager to show their pity and sympathy for the brave and handsome youth, who had gone, with his sister by his side, to die on the scaffold at the market house. We can imagine them holding their heads high and walking with a pretty air of scorn and defiance past the officers of the line and yeomanry, who thronged

at the street corners, having been brought in to awe this rebellious town into
subjection. As for the fair owner of this particular pair of green slippers, be
sure that it was to a very tiny and prettily shaped foot that she ventured to
draw attention by adopting this particular method of wearing the green.[99]

Francis Joseph Bigger added a hand-written note to this section of Milligan's
article: 'Given by Dr Wheeler who had them from Miss Spencer, an old lady of
Belfast. Mr Wheeler gave them to Mr Robert Young for his collection.'[1] Robert
Young was a historian of Belfast. Milligan and Bigger's additional footnotes gives
further insight into how important it was to reanimate history through fiction; to
re-inhabit actual shoes with new bodies imagined one hundred years later when
women were once again being scorned in public space and being urged to return
to the fireside.

   As her 'Notes from the north' article about the origin of her 'green slippers'
story indicates, Milligan very often reanimated oral histories and historical
ephemera in her fiction and journalism. Throughout her life, she placed a high
value on unofficial histories because these were the stories of the marginalized, the
dispossessed, the voices of those most forgotten in official colonial histories of
Ireland. Women were the most dispossessed in colonial history; they were
therefore most receptive to hearing and remembering and relating the voices of
those similarly dispossessed. This was a trait that defined Milligan's journalism: she
inflected the contemporary political landscape found in newspapers with stories
and memories that she had heard and witnessed. In the 1930s, she battled against
poverty, censorship, state misogyny and political discrimination. Yet her
newspaper articles and letters to the press endlessly countered the politics of
Partition with memories of Ireland's revolutionary past and the voices of the
Revival movement. This was a signature of her journalism that began in the early
1890s. A good example of how Milligan wove unofficial oral histories into her
newspapers articles can be seen in 'The north is up' published in the December
1895 in the *Irish Weekly Independent*. Under the name of Iris Olkyrn, she relates a
unique story about Henry Joy McCracken walking through Belfast in disguise
after the Battle of Antrim:

> A friend of my own has told me that her father, when a mere lad, was
> playing marbles in front of a shop on the Shore road near Whitehouse. A
> group of workmen passed along, one carrying a carpenter's tool bag. The
> proprietor of the shop, shook his head, and remarked to a companion,
> 'There goes young McCracken. Dear, dear; but he is very badly disguised!
> He hasna the walk of a workin' man at all! Ye would know him anywhere'.[2]

For three years Alice Milligan and Anna Johnston made sure that the *Shan Van Vocht* was devoted to the publication of personal narratives of '98, stories and songs collected locally by the editors and their readers. The paper took a keen interest in securing copyright to serialize previously unpublished materials concerning the 1790s. For example, one report noted:

> Miss Anna Johnston … was pleased to inform us that she had secured through the generosity of the representatives of the late Dr Madden, historian of the United Irish Movement, the MS [manuscript] of the memoirs of Henry Joy McCracken as originally compiled by him from information and documents received from Mary McCracken, James Hope, and others.[3]

In July 1897 Milligan called for stories from readers 'which still live upon the lips of the people'.[4] Milligan believed that those struggling to achieve a new democracy had an obligation to record unpublished narratives out of the past in which their struggle was rooted. Two months after her first appeal to readers for stories, Milligan again urged people to produce the unwritten chronicles of the United Irish struggle:

> We invite our friends throughout the country who are acquainted with unpublished traditions of the times, to communicate them to us. It is the sacred duty of all who are in sympathy with the cause of Irish freedom, to revive the memory of the humbler and almost forgotten heroes of the strife.[5]

In 1919 Helena Concannon made use of narratives taken from the pages of the *Shan Van Vocht* for her history of the *Women of Ninety-Eight*. Concannon suggests that the north had a greater investment in collecting narratives and tokens of 1798 than other parts of Ireland: 'For some reason … the North has kept a richer record of the sufferings and heroism of its obscurer women in 1798 and 1803, than other parts of the country. Some very precious relics have been gathered up in the pages of the *Shan Van Vocht*, and make of them a most valuable repository of patriotic memories.'[6] Milligan argued that the past was not dead and that the dead were not forgotten. She and her comrades committed themselves to locating the unmarked graves of those United Irishmen and women who had fought and died in the 1798 insurgency. They decorated these graves with new flowers and delivered contemporary political orations as an integral part of the '98 movement. But decorating the graves of those who had fallen in 1790s was a contentious issue in the north. The Special Branch recorded disturbances around the site of Betsy Gray's grave in May 1898:

Around Ballinahinch, in the County Down, feeling between Protestants and Catholics runs high as a result of the decoration by '98 sympathisers of the grave of Betsy Gray, who fell while fighting amongst the insurgents. The gravestone was afterwards destroyed, – presumably by the Orange party – and many exciting incidents took place, culminating on the 12 ult, in a riot between the opposing parties.[7]

Commemoration was at the heart of the Irish Cultural Revival: in fact, the two ideas were totally connected. In the 1890s, Milligan looked back to 1798 as the first moment when Protestants and Catholics had united together in the national struggle for independence. The United Irishmen had placed high value on Irish culture, music, language and literature. The ideas that animated the eighteenth-century movement were interconnected with the republican ideals that similarly energized the French revolution. In her second novel, *The Cromwellians*, Milligan focussed on 1654 when Protestant settlers first occupied the homes and land of Irish Catholics: this was a narrative defined by conflict, sectarianism, colonial occupation, gender separatism, and native dispossession. But 1798 offered Milligan a much more positive historical lens through which to envisage the role of Protestants in Irish history and in the contemporary national cultural movement. From the early 1890s she channelled all of her time, all of her writing, her magic lantern lectures, the *Shan Van Vocht* and her theatre productions to disseminating the contemporary significances of 1798. She viewed it as her role to educate herself and others into a better understanding of a history that had been airbrushed from official accounts of the empire. Milligan also saw the commemoration as an opportunity to rally a mass movement; a way to bring the north into dialogue with the rest of Ireland; a chance to gain an articulate public space for women.

The consequences of 1898 centenary were complex and lasting. The mass political movement it had engendered did indeed become a solid cornerstone of the new edifice. The mass mourning that followed the downfall and death of Parnell in 1891 was initially channelled into a multifaceted cultural movement. The centenary further consolidated the Revival movement (in all its different forms) into a political independence movement. For Alice Milligan, 1898 was an opportunity to create nuanced communities of solidarity at a local level and to reclaim civic Irish space from the colonial authorities. But it was also a time of great conflict among the broad coalition of Irish nationalists in which factional (misogynistic) infighting came to the fore. The fracas of '98 must have reminded Milligan of the tensions she had encountered in Belfast from 1893: the trenchant unionist opposition to cultural nationalism; the anti-feminism directed against the Irish Women's Association; the disputes between the McCracken Society and the

Amnesty movement that led her to leave the *Northern Patriot* and set up the *Shan Van Vocht*.

James Connolly had argued in the *Shan Van Vocht* that the Revival had to pin its political colours to the mast. In 1897 he warned that in order to survive, the brilliant and multifaceted movement that was the Irish Cultural Revival needed to unite its various constituencies under a more politically focussed set of ideas. In Connolly's view, the Revival was in danger of breaking its energies in reified commemoration. His vital point was that 'worship' of the past could also be a way of escaping, rather than confronting, the mediocrity of the present. The centenary, Connolly believed, could have no emergent potential unless it was aligned to the ideals of socialist republicanism. He therefore urged Milligan and her readers to connect their ideas about national culture with 'vital living issues':

> In Ireland at the present time there are at work a variety of agencies seeking to reserve the national sentiment in the hearts of the people. These agencies, whether Irish Language movements, Literary Societies or Commemoration Committees, are undoubtedly doing a work of lasting benefit to this country in helping to save from extinction the precious racial and national history, language and characteristics of our people. Nevertheless, there is a danger that by too strict an adherence to their present methods of propaganda, and consequent neglect of vital living issues, they may only succeed in stereotyping our historical studies into a worship of the past, or crystallising nationalism into a tradition – glorious and heroic indeed, but still only a tradition. Now traditions may, and frequently do, provide materials for a glorious martyrdom, but can never be strong enough to ride the storm of a successful revolution. If the national movement of our day is not merely to re-enact the old sad tragedies of our past history, it must show itself capable of rising to the exigencies of the moment. It must demonstrate to the people of Ireland that our nationalism is not merely a morbid idealising of the past, but is also capable of formulating a distinct and definite answer to the problems of the present and a political and economic creed capable of adjustment to the wants of the future. This concrete political and social ideal will best be supplied, I believe, by the frank acceptance on the part of all earnest nationalists of the Republic as their goal.[8]

The quarrels that defined the '98 commemoration grew into polarities that would mark the Irish cultural movement right through to 1916: the Irish Parliamentary Party opposition to the Irish Republican Brotherhood; nationalists' disunion with republicans; men who objected to the public status of women;

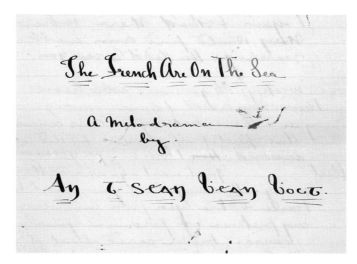

33 The front page of Milligan's lost melodrama *The French are on the sea*.
She signs this An tSeanbhean Bhocht – (the Shan Van Vocht). Roger Casement
also signed some of his literary works and articles with this name.

unionists' opposition to all of the above groups. Indeed, the schisms engendered
by the centenary were even more clearly marked after the founding of the two
states in 1922.

James Connolly's final play, staged in Liberty Hall just three weeks before the
1916 Insurrection, asked in its title the very question he had asked Milligan's
readers in 1897: *Under which flag?* One of the key forums for the political
dissemination of this question was theatre. The centenary brought Irish theatre
onto the streets: it would only be a matter of months before Yeats and many others
reclaimed the energies and visual rituals of commemoration for the stage. And it
is to drama that the next chapter of this book will now turn. Milligan argued that
the '98 parades in Belfast would be like history illuminated; the centenary
commemoration was all about projections. It was a foundation stone not just of a
statue of Wolfe Tone, but of a new democracy that re-imagined a place for the
ideals of the United Irishmen in Irish public space, culture and thought. The final
scene of Milligan's '98 melodrama is a literal projection in which the action of the
drama stops still and all movement is suspended. The picture is held captive like
the audience who experience the image as it propels itself from the stage into a
shared collective space in which nation is both 'remembered and longed for'.[9]

The French are on the sea concludes with a tableaux which functions as a form
of symbolic metacommentary upon the specific issues articulated through the
drama. Only the last act of this unpublished and undated manuscript survives, but

A faint roseate glow brightens the sky.

McCabe. It is near the dawn. Make haste

David. It is an omen Rose dear. look. The sky shines o'er our going. We will see brighter days.

Rose. You & I, yes Heaven grant it — we may — but David — Let this be our last prayer on Irish soil, that the Sun of Freedom may yet rise on Ireland

Final tableau.

Putnam McCabe stands leading Mrs Gordon at entrance, the boat seen behind him. Rose in centre of stage, with clasped hands raised. David, taking off his hat stands beside her. The peasants kneeling by the body of Gilbert raise their hands as if ceasing to pray for the dead & joining in her prayer.

(Music from Band. Fainne geal an lae

"The dawning of the Day)

Curtain.

34 The final tableau of *The French are on the sea* — this is the only surviving part of this unpublished manuscript play.

it could very well be either the 'bloodthirsty melodrama of the '98 period' that Milligan informed Yeats she was writing in 1893 or the play she wrote as an entry for J.W. Whitbread's competition for '98 plays.[10] The final tableau involves a scene of departure by boat. English soldiers shoot dead a United Irishman, Gilbert, in a cave where he shelters with his fellow republicans. When the soldiers leave, Gilbert's comrades emerge from their hiding places to fill the mouth of the cave. Led by the Belfast man William Putnam McCabe, the republicans prepare for exile. As they do so, the action on stage is frozen into a tableau that shows Rose Adair bringing everyone together in prayer:

> Final *Tableau*
> Putnam McCabe stands leading Mrs Gordon to the entrance, the boat sail behind him. Rose in centre of the stage, with clasped hands raised. Davis taking off his hat stands beside her. The peasants kneeling by the body of Gilbert raise their hands as if ceasing to pray for the dead & joining in her prayer.
> (Music from band *Fainne Geall an Lae* 'The Dawning of the Day') Curtain.

Rose's prayer inspires her nationalist brethren to turn their eyes from the failed rising, symbolized by Gilbert's corpse, and to look instead to future possibilities for solidarity. The living picture allows the apparently vanquished and colonized Irish a moment of heroic transcendence, suggesting that the republican ideal will be reinvigorated and re-envisioned by Irish exiles in the coming century.[11]

CHAPTER FIVE

Drama

The swift upspringing of a dramatic literature and art in a soil that seemed sterile has something mysterious about it. Thirty years ago there did not seem a people in Europe less visited by the creative fire. Then a girl of genius, Alice Milligan, began to have premonitions of a dramatic movement, and she wrote little plays to help the infant Gaelic League, and she went here and there, an elfish stage manager, with a bag crammed with fragments of tapestry to be used on the actors in order to create the illusion of a richly robed ancient Irish romance.

George Russell, 1926.[1]

Focusing on Milligan's multifaceted engagement with drama from 1893, this chapter will explore her attempts to realize a vision for Irish theatre that was decentred and democratic. Milligan responded with such passion to the medium of theatre because of the opportunity it provided her to work directly with a community of players, themselves drawn from local communities. The production of history through drama thus activated a powerful charge of immediacy and involvement. The critical intervention of Alice Milligan provides a unique lens through which the traditional narrative of Ireland's national theatre can be refocused to take account of forgotten modes of cultural practice. Her theatrical enterprises differed substantially from the dominant currents within the 'canonized' textual national theatre of Yeats, Synge and Gregory. An alternative story of localized community drama emerges out of Milligan's uncollected letters, multiple play reviews, newspaper articles, her published and unpublished plays, the fragments of her lost theatre scripts, rare photographs, tableaux sketches, notes for performances, private diaries, and through memoirs written by those who both witnessed and performed Milligan's theatre shows.

This rich and untapped archive reveals an animated world of national drama that was taking place across Ireland from the last decade of the nineteenth century. It is through Milligan's scattered papers that we glimpse the involvement of a whole raft of unnamed workers in the Revival movement. We suddenly discover that Ireland's national theatre was not just the extraordinary story of the Abbey Theatre; it was a movement experienced and envisaged by school teachers, women's alliances, Gaelic League workers, community groups, children, emerging

35 Photograph showing community theatre and audience benches being created in
County Antrim, *c.*1904.

actresses, playwrights and directors. Milligan's ideas for national theatre emanated
from within the actual moment of conception and realization, in the dialogue of
planning and in the community of performance and production. Her plays and
tableaux were staged in school halls, on city streets and in fields where they were
watched by audiences on benches carved out of felled trees. And these audiences
were not passive, ticket-buying anonymous people; those who watched were those
built the stages and sewed the costumes; those who performed the shows had
sourced the props and invented stage effects out of local materials.

The creation of an Irish National Theatre, for Milligan, anticipated Brecht
in its rejection of the colonial (imported) spectacular: her theatre practice
forged connections between people and developed a sense of history through
contemporary politicized cultural activism. Milligan was determined that people
should not feel disempowered by lack of resources, buildings, scripts, trained
actors, spectacular stage machinery or unaffordable elaborate costumes. The stories
she brought to the stage were taken from traditional songs, contemporary protest,

and familiar images from legends and tales that were then re-performed by local people. Belief in the past was connected to belief in the future and both intersected during the Revival: so the local school teacher was also Brian Boru; the farm worker could transform into a Fenian warrior; the school child could be Queen Maeve. This is what Susan Mitchell meant in 1919 when she reflected: 'so great is the power of mind, her audiences saw the plays as she intended them'.[2] It was through the 'power of the mind' – the collective imagination – that decolonization was first achieved. In the years following 1916 Milligan received letters from Irish political prisoners who recalled how their own national consciousness was awakened by these early local experiences of national theatre. The stories that Milligan staged were articulated through people's own words, their own voices, the inflections of their own accents, the gestures of their own bodies: no longer would the Irish stage be the domain of English actors and hired props from abroad. Staging the nation at the most local level was, in Milligan's view, the greatest step towards creating an independent nation: 'in the Gaelic movement', she argued, 'everyone is a worker'.[3]

Towards a national theatre

In the 1890s Irish theatres were dominated by English imports. With Dublin and Belfast as provincial stops on the regular itineraries of English stage productions, Irish playhouses were 'flooded with the third rate overflow of the London stage'.[4] Stephen Watt maintains that under colonialism Dublin was rendered 'a cultural satellite of the London stage, a status shared by English and Irish provincial towns alike'.[5] The establishment of an Irish national theatre was accordingly a pressing concern for the revitalized cultural movement of the period. Ernest Boyd declared in 1916 that the 'creation of an Irish National Theatre was the most familiar and most popular achievement of the revival'.[6] Figures as diverse as William Butler Yeats, Augusta Gregory, Edward Martyn, Maud Gonne, Douglas Hyde and Milligan herself perceived theatre as an especially vital forum for the consolidation of political and cultural identity. By no means a single-focus initiative, the new national theatre movement was energized by various groups – including the Irish Literary Theatre, the Irish National Theatre Society, the Cork National Players, the Irish Players Society, the Gaelic League, *Inghinidhe na hÉireann* and the Ulster Literary Theatre Society – who nonetheless shared a core set of values regarding the purpose of theatre in modern Ireland. In particular, their work was impelled by an anti-colonialist agenda that called for the dramatization of Irish subjects through Irish speech on Irish stages.

It is not at all surprising that so little is known about Milligan's extensive involvement in Irish drama: her intense focus on the immediate, the unscripted and the pictorial was antithetical to documentation. Milligan's conception of an Irish national theatre was not confined to a single group, place or building. She argued instead for a healthy pluralism, in which numerous literary and political organizations would collaborate in the production of Irish plays. Her main aim was to bring theatre to diverse communities across Ireland, in places that lacked dedicated venues, and to this end she worked in conjunction with all groups engaged in the Revival project. Milligan was not simply a playwright but a total woman of the theatre who from 1898 involved herself in every aspect of stage production. Besides writing plays, she designed and made costumes, constructed theatrical sets and props, published and distributed scripts, and even acted. In 1919 Susan Mitchell remarked in the *Shamrock* that Milligan was the first Irish playwright and theatre producer to help make drama possible for many Irish people and groups who were involved in the early Irish Cultural Revival. Milligan clearly viewed herself less as a named author or specialized director then as a practical facilitator. As Mitchell recalled, the meaning of her plays resided in the community process of production and in the actual moment of performance:

> There was no end to her contrivances for the staging of the plays. Ancient Irish chariots were made out of rocking-chairs, Gaelic crosses out of bits of brown paper. Nothing daunted her … and she was the most successful producer of plays before the Abbey Theatre started on its triumphant way.[7]

Milligan very self-consciously and unashamedly celebrated amateur theatre at local level and in rural districts: she did everything in her powers to facilitate community participation in Irish drama at its earliest stages. She published essays and articles in local journals and newspapers detailing how Irish plays could be staged and how costumes for all periods could be made cheaply, giving detailed guidance on sourcing props. In March 1904, for example, Milligan published her essay 'Staging and costume in Irish drama: some practical hints' in *Ireland's Own*. The article details her 'long and varied experience' in the Irish theatre movement for amateur groups and her encouragement of them to stage plays of 'an ancient, historical, and legendary character'.[8] Insisting that lack of resources need not impede imaginative theatre production, Milligan suggested that plays set in early Irish history could be produced with minimal expenditure if props were sourced in Ireland rather than imported from England. Milligan attached instructions about the costumes to her published dramas such as *The wearing of the green* (1898) and *The deliverance of Red Hugh O'Donnell* (1901). Her description of the latter accompanied the 1902 publication of the play in the *Irish Weekly Freeman*: 'The costumes may be made more cheaply and suitably than hired ones, and need

Province Hotel,
· Cavendish Row,
Dublin.

2. grey wigs.
1 curly auburn
1 curly brown Cavalier
1. Red Comic
1. long fair curly childs
1 long fair womans
1. long black tangled
1 Short shaggy black —
7 Plaits
6. Beards

1. grey womans
1 white front
2. white men's court
1 ladies grey court
1 auburn ladies'
1 Curly fair.

36 List of costume wigs for tableau and drama show by Milligan, Dublin, 1901.

not be elaborate, except in the case of the governor.'[9] She urged Irish people to work as a collective and use the skills of the community to produce Irish theatre at little financial cost:

> When we go back to more remote times … we find ourselves in the fortunate era, when all garments, including those of royalty, were home made, and when neither dressmakers nor tailors were required to cut out and stitch up close fitting garments. In our reproductions we can also dispense with the aid of skilled cutters or machine stitching.[10]

Revealing all the tricks of her trade, Milligan details the particulars of how a theatre apparel can be assembled on a meagre budget: sunburn is created by mixing ochre with vaseline while tan-coloured tape or dress binding provide credible alternatives to genuine leather. Integral to her conception of stagecraft is a commitment to buy theatrical supplies from shops in Ireland: 'To complete your weapons you will require a set of lustre paints. Ristona lustre, which is made by M'Caw, Stevenson, and Orr, of Belfast, is supplied in several tints … Gold tissue gauze necessary for gold ornaments is purchasable at Liberty's agencies in Belfast and Dublin.'[11]

Her pragmatism was further shown in her readiness to seize the opportunities afforded by newspapers as a means of cheaply disseminating play-texts to amateur theatre groups. Eight of her eleven dramas appeared in Irish nationalist newspapers like the *Shan Van Vocht*, the *United Irishman*, the *Daily Express*, the *Weekly Freeman* and *Sinn Féin*. Her practical approach to access is clarified in a letter to T.W. Rolleston, president of the Irish Literary Society in London and a literary editor of T.P. Gill's *Daily Express*. In 1899 Milligan asked Rolleston to print her new play *The last feast of the Fianna*, because she needed multiple copies urgently for an impromptu amateur production:

> I would be forever grateful if this could be published on Saturday. I have promised Mr & Mrs [Standish James] O'Grady to try to get up an inaugural gathering of the Belfast Gaelic League before they go & they would like best to see a theatrical performance. This scene I could get up very quickly as I have nearly all the costumes, & suitable actors in view. The delay would be in copying out the play and actors' parts. If it was in Saturday's Express I could get a number of copies & distribute among my actors to learn at once as I am to see them all on Saturday afternoon as they are asked to meet Mr O'Grady. There would then be no delay & we could have the play in three

weeks. I trust to you to do what you can for me in the matter. Mrs O'Grady is most eager to see it & will be helping me.[12]

To ensure that some of her plays remained available, Milligan published them more than once and also republished several in book form. *The daughter of Donagh*, first published in the *United Irishman* in 1903, was reissued as a book in 1920 [Plate 14]. *The last feast of the Fianna* was first published in the *Daily Express* (23 September 1899) and was published as a book by Alfred Nutt a year later. Joseph Holloway observed in 1912 that *The last feast of the Fianna* was performed far more often than Milligan's other two Ossianic plays – a factor encouraged not only by its performance by the Irish Literary Theatre but also because the script had been preserved as a book in 1900 rather than in obsolete newspapers [Plate 15].[13] Milligan's life-long use of newspapers to publish her literature underlines her commitment to the principle that national theatre should be widely available, and could be produced by non-professional, community-based drama groups.

Milligan, however, offered no coherent overview of what such a theatre practice might achieve until 1909, when she joined a debate inaugurated by the Gaelic League activist Henry Mangan concerning proposals for a national theatre. The first dialogue between Milligan and Mangan began in 1909 when the latter wrote to *Sinn Féin* arguing for the establishment of a subsidized and professionalized travelling theatre company for Ireland:

> The historical dramatist in Ireland must have a vehicle – a company of trained actors, with cultured voices who are capable of something more than peasant plays. The average amateur is hopeless for this purpose ... If Ireland cared for a National Theatre it could have it by next Samhain. No great building in Dublin is required, because the real function of a genuine National Theatre would be to tour through this country – not through England ... As to actors, there are several Irishmen on the professional stage who might be induced, if reasonable prospects were afforded, to join such a venture ... There are also some members of the Theatre of Ireland and of the National Players who might be available ... £500 would go a long way towards securing the establishment of a really National Theatre, if there were five hundred people whose interest could be translated into £1 shares.[14]

Mangan cites Alice Milligan's 1903 play, *The daughter of Donagh*, as a work that should be acted in the first tour of his proposed company. His idea of raising money for a professional theatre company through shareholders echoes how Yeats, Augusta Gregory and Edward Martyn formed the Irish Literary Theatre. In *Our*

Irish theatre Gregory recorded how they sent letters to certain individuals asking for a donation: 'We asked for a guarantee fund of £300 to make the experiment, which we hoped to carry on for three years.'[15] Mangan published a similar idea in 1907:

> To form a genuine Irish National Theatre, a professional company is necessary, as Mr Yeats has shown. Such a company should tour Ireland as the Abbey Theatre has toured England, they should produce plays in Irish as well as in English, as the Abbey Theatre company has not done … A federation of existing dramatic societies, including those of Cork and Belfast etc. should be possible.[16]

While she too opposed the idea that Irish national theatre should reside solely in the commercial centres of Dublin and Belfast, Milligan rejected Mangan's blueprint for a professionalized theatre company, insisting that local communities should retain a primary role in the production of Irish plays. She ultimately propounded a more eclectic, decentred and inclusive national theatre movement, urging support for existing community theatre companies because they were more fervently dedicated to the promise of theatre than the 'mechanical performances of trained troupes of second rate professionals.'[17] Rather hypocritically, Milligan also opposed Mangan's plans because she believed that the 'life of a strolling player' was unsuitable employment for 'our young women of spirit and talent who are workers in the national cause'.[18] This was a strange point for Milligan to make, given that she herself had lived the itinerant life of a travelling theatre producer and Gaelic League lecturer for over a decade. Yet Milligan could well have been sensitive to the very public issues relating to female 'virtue' within Gaelic League ranks given the vocal opposition articulated by the Catholic Church in relation to mixed sex Gaelic League social meetings.

Spurning Mangan's elitist conception of theatre as a remit of 'cultured voices', Milligan championed instead a de-centred, democratic and collective grassroots movement. Milligan claimed that her view of national theatre was inspired by appeals from community drama groups, confiding that: 'scarcely ten days of my life have elapsed in the last ten years without my receiving letters asking for information and advice. As a matter of fact I am only able to answer about half the letters I get.'[19] The documents Milligan received and kept certainly are a fascinating record of early amateur drama being generated in Irish committees during the Irish Revival. One such letter came from a teacher in Co. Louth who asked Milligan to write a play for pupils of their national schools. The request is a good example of the extent to which Milligan was prepared to work towards and within the practical restrictions amateur groups operated under: 'It is the girls of our national schools here who are going to act the play. We have them of all ages from sixteen down, with a couple of eighteen years of age so I don't want to cramp your energies by asking you to write a play for any special age whatever.'[20] Eamonn O'Neill was also aware of Milligan's reputation for organizing Irish stage performances. In January 1902 he asked her to join a collaborative ensemble of people to help bring his Irish language play to performance:

> You have heard about our (Central Branch) William Rooney Commemoration Concert to be held on Saturday 25th inst. The little play of mine is to be produced, and I have partly rewritten it. We have already the cast selected and trained, this being done by Miss Curran who knows Irish, and has considerable experience in getting up theatricals and teaching elocution. With reference to scenery, staging etc we are not in a good way. It was suggested to me by Mrs Power, and I was also thinking myself of it, that we should ask you to come to Dublin, and give your invaluable help, and advice. Your experience of such things is considerable, and you would know just what we want, and how to get it in the easiest and cheapest way. We may be able to get a loan of some scenery, or may have to get it painted … I earnestly hope you will come down, and help us through. The matter is really very urgent.[21]

Milligan later described some of the costumes and sets that she had helped design for this show. Such instructional articles were published by her for the benefit of theatre groups who may also wish to produce the play in a different part of Ireland: 'At a play staged by Miss May Curran of the Central Branch Gaelic League, Hugh O'Neill and his son wore a modification of Irish costume, large hanging sleeves and upstanding collars to the cloaks, giving a more modern, and, I believe, historically accurate touch.'[22]

While Mangan stressed the financial impediments to the founding of an institutionally sanctioned touring bi-lingual National Theatre, Milligan was more concerned with the difficulty of co-ordinating the various local organizations. In her estimation, the main priority of genuinely national theatre was to make drama practicable for groups with motivation but no resources. Her principal recommendation was for a theatre library, stocked with scripts and costumes that could be transported across the country for use by dramatic groups:

> What we really need is a bureau of information, and loan of costumes, also a dramatic library … I have it in serious contemplation to start a dramatic

bureau, publishing small plays, or supplying typewritten copies of them, with sketches of requisite costumes … Everywhere through Ireland there are small amateur companies ready to act.[23]

Milligan's plea appears not to have secured support for a travelling library – indeed, she was still calling for such a scheme in 1913. In a letter to the *Weekly Freeman* entitled 'National drama for country districts', Milligan designated responsibility for organizing the library scheme to the language movement: 'I am strongly of the opinion that the Gaelic League should prepare and hire out from headquarters well-designed costumes, simple scenery, and properties.'[24] Several of her contemporaries suggest that Milligan herself fulfilled this role around the turn of the century. In 1926 George Russell recalled in the *Irish Statesman* how she moved through the country with 'a bag crammed with fragments of tapestry to be used on the actors in order to create the illusion of a richly robed ancient Irish romance'.[25] In 1939, Lennox Robinson similarly praised Milligan's ability to transform 'A bit of cardboard tacked on the wheels of a country cart' into 'an ancient Irish chariot'.[26]

'Half Irish at best': the published plays

One tangible reason for the neglect of Milligan's contribution to Irish theatre is the difficulty of actually locating her dramatic works. Three of her eleven plays remain unpublished, while the rest languish in the unindexed columns of Irish newspapers. *The harp that once*, performed in August 1901, derived from the 1898 short story of the same name but was never printed as a play-text. The type-script of the previously unknown *The earl from Ireland* was donated to the National Library in 1980 while only the last act of *The French are on the sea* survives in manuscript form [Plate 16]. It is not yet known whether the play versions of *The French are on the sea*, *The earl from Ireland* and *The green upon the cape* were ever staged. Another reason Milligan's work is so difficult to trace is that she focussed so much of her time on non-textual forms of cultural production. Milligan worked extensively with *tableaux vivant*, a form of dramatic enterprise in which the immediacy of performance outweighs the significance of text. The tableaux developed in part from the magic lantern performances she gave on behalf of the Gaelic League. In fact, Milligan raised funds from America for the first Gaelic League lantern. Few, if any, of the League's portable lanterns or glass slides have survived. Furthermore, the essence of Milligan's living picture shows depended on music and image rather than published written scripts. Resistant to documentation, such material is easily marginalized in written histories; Milligan's tableaux left virtually no visual or photographic traces.

Milligan's plays are, self-consciously, moments torn from the pages of history. With the exception of the Ossianic trilogy, which deals with the mythological transition from Paganism to Christianity, they explore the discord fomented by the colonization of early modern Ireland. *Brian of Banba* (1904) takes as its subject the Irish expulsion of the Danes in the eleventh century; while *The deliverance of Red Hugh O'Donnell* (1901) and *The earl from Ireland* (date unknown) are both set in the sixteenth century. The earliest stages of Elizabethan colonization form the backdrop to *The last of the Desmonds* (1904), while *The daughter of Donagh* (1903) deals with the displacements provoked by the Cromwellian plantation in Munster. Three plays – *The green upon the cape* (1898), *The harp that once* (1901) and *The French are on the sea* (date unknown) – take as their subject matter the rebellion of 1798.

The linguistic vibrancy of Synge's elegiac paeans to a vanishing Irish community and culture is not a realisable option in Milligan's plays. They are populated, instead, by figures who struggle to forge a communicative union with others in the face of political and cultural barriers erected by colonization. Rather than cementing social cohesion, language consistently provokes blockages and miscommunications at multiple levels. These difficulties with language emblematize broader problems besetting the definition of cultural and national identity in a divided land. Milligan is drawn repeatedly to figures who straddle the cultural opposition of colonizer and colonized – 'renegades' who encounter social estrangement whichever history they choose to defend or whichever language they speak. Three plays – *The green upon the cape*, *The deliverance of Red Hugh O'Donnell* and *The last of the Desmonds* – demonstrate how Milligan's dramatic works pivot around scenarios in which characters battle for national and social belonging in a fractured landscape of unstable definitions.

The green upon the cape, published in the *Shan Van Vocht* in April 1898, is a short one-act drama that allows Milligan to express her frustration at the 'internecine warfare' between Irish republicans and nationalists that jeopardized the 1898 centenary commemorations. The play centres upon a meeting between United Irishmen John Tennant (a Belfast Presbyterian) and Theobald Wolfe Tone in a French boarding house in 1797. The encounter is complicated immediately because, never having met before, neither man is able to recognize the other as a fellow republican. Tennant cannot trust that Tone is who he professes to be, while Tone fears that Tennant himself may be a spy. Their dilemma is crystallized by problems with language. Tennant poses as a German and Tone as a Frenchman, but neither can actually speak the language of their assumed identities. Tone mutters in an aside: 'I've half a mind to pretend I'm a deaf mute.' Fearful of disclosing their true allegiances, the two men stumble through a melange of

THE
Shan Van Vocht

(An t.Sean Bhean Bhocht).

"Ireland shall be free from the centre to the sea,
And hurrah for Liberty, says the Shan Van Vocht."

VOL. III.—No 4.   BELFAST, 4TH APRIL, 1898.   PRICE TWOPENCE.

HENRY JOY M'CRACKEN.
Born in Belfast 31st August, 1767.
Died for Ireland 17th July, 1798.

The Green upon the Cape.

A SHORT PLAY FOR THREE PERSONS.

Dramatis personæ—Wolfe Tone; John Tenant, a United Irishman from Belfast, Ireland; Fanchette, a waiting maid.

Time—The autumn of 1797.

Scene—At an inn, one day's journey outside of Paris, where Tone and Tenant, travelling to Paris to meet each other, both put up for the night. It is here assumed that they had no previous acquaintance.

Tone stands on the hearthrug. The table is laid for his dinner. Fanchette enters carrying a tray with extra glass, knife and fork as the scene opens.

Fanchette—Milles pardons m'sieu! Mais il n'y a qu'une salle-a-manger. Il faut que le monsieur qui vient d'arriver dinera avec vous.

Tone—Sacré au nom d'un chien! Mais qu' importe! Il est Allemand n'est ce pas? Et bien, je reste content— (aside) So that he doesn't turn out to be some low English spy who has got on my tracks and wants to report my interview with Tenant. I must restrain my naturally confiding nature and be on my guard. Above all, I mustn't let him see that I am not a Frenchman born, and with my shaky knowledge of the language *that* will puzzle my wits, I've half a mind to pretend that I'm a deaf mute.

Fanchette (returning to the door calls back shrilly to the porter to carry up the gentleman's luggage to his room)— "Jacques! Apportez le baggage de monsieur au numero cinque au troisieme—(curtseys to the traveller and invites him to enter). Si monsieur veut bien entrer. Le souper sera pret tout a l'heure. Il n'ya qu'une personne ici et M le general est fort agreable je vous le jure.

Tone (aside and laughing)—The little minx tries to assuage my wrath by raising me a step in the army—general no less. I wish it may be prophetic. She pays me the compliment, too, of finding me "fort agreable," though I haven't been here beyond fifteen minutes.

(The stranger advances and throws aside his wraps, says not a word, but stares suspiciously at Tone.)

The Stranger (aside)—Hang it all! Here's a pretty fix! Napper Tandy's very last words to me were, 'Above all don't let yourself be taken for an Englishman or you'll be arrested as a spy." Now here am I tête-a-tête with a general, a member of the Ministry maybe. If I open my lips in French I'm lost. Now I have it! I'll pass myself off as a German. Ten to one he doesn't know the language.

Fanchette (places the chairs to the table and asks the stranger what he will have to drink)—Monsieur que veut il a boire? du vin blanc—du cidre—du vin de Bordeaux?

The Stranger (gruffly)—Lager bier! Ich verstehe kein wort—no vord. Vielleicht verstehen sie English—oder Deutsch. Ich spreche kein Franzosich. Not French— only Engleesh and Deutsch. (Aside)—Brilliant idea! When my German gives out I can speak broken English. That scoundrelly looking fellow will be none the wiser.

37 *The green upon the cape*, Milligan's first scripted play published in
Shan Van Vocht, April 1898.

broken French, faltering German and bastardized English; the Irish language is itself a defining absence amidst this turmoil of miscommunication. Frustrated at the inability to connect with a potential comrade, Tennant attempts to escape his quandary by feigning sleep.

Only then does Tone feel sufficiently secure to declare his political identity and, significantly, he manages to do so through the medium of music rather than words. As soon as Tone begins to play 'The wearing of the green' on his fiddle, Tennant awakens and heartily unites with Tone for the second verse. Tone and Tennant lack a sustaining cultural bedrock upon which they can lay the foundations of communication. As Irish republicans without an Irish republic, they are consigned to a furtive existence in which loyalties must be disguised and speech suppressed. Lacking the confidence to communicate openly, Tone and Tennant direct their words not to one another but to an imagined other. These problems of speech and connectivity are most explicit in the play's tactical use of the aside, a dramatic strategy that is grounded in the fragmentation of discourse. Even though they physically inhabit the space, neither man is able to access the secret articulation of his republican brother. This device is also a prominent feature in *The daughter of Donagh*, which has twenty-three asides.

Milligan prefaced all of her plays with the instruction 'to be translated into Irish' and in a way she was trying to open up a bi-lingual space of possibility for the dramas she published and produced. Her only play to include an Irish-speaking character was the 1901 *The deliverance of Red Hugh O'Donnell*. Significant parts of the dialogue were rendered into Irish by Fr Glendon of St Malachi's Priory, Dundalk for its 1902 publication in the *Weekly Freeman*.[27] The play was staged in the Antient Concert Rooms in August 1901 by *Inghinidhe na hÉireann* and the Fay brothers' amateur theatre company, the Ormond Players. Dudley Digges played Red Hugh and Frank Fay took the part of Martin. It was a great success among nationalists and influenced the second phase of the Irish Literary Theatre. Yeats who commented, 'I came away with my head on fire', heralded the production of the drama.[28] He immediately formed the Irish National Dramatic Society with the Fay brothers who had helped to produce the event. Frank Fay recalled the rehearsals some years later:

> The production of these plays was put into my brothers hands, & to act them he had the assistance of an amateur company which he had organised in Dublin during the years he spent in the theatrical profession … In the plays, referred to above, which he produced for the Daughters of Erin, the chief members of his company were supplemented by members of The Daughters of Erin Society and an associate Literary Society. At the

performances of these plays, Mr Yeats was present & said to the writer one evening at the fall of the curtain 'I like the grave acting of your company'. The mystic poet and painter George Russell (Æ) also saw these plays and entrusted my brother with the production of his three-act play, 'Deirdre'.[29]

The deliverance of Red Hugh was advertised by the *United Irishman* as 'the first play produced in Dublin by Cumann na nGaedael'.[30] It was influenced by a lengthy 1889 historical drama, *Red Hugh O'Donnell*, by Standish O'Grady, which tells the story of the Ulster Chief in fourteen acts. Milligan's version centres not on Red Hugh O'Donnell, however, but on the prison guard, Martin, who facilitates his escape from Dublin Castle in 1591.[31] The critic Una Ellis-Fermor dismissed *The deliverance of Red Hugh O'Donnell* in 1939 as an 'old rattle-trap type' of melodrama.[32] But Ella Young recalled that at the turn of the century when first performed in a 'little shabby room' in Dublin, Milligan's drama was a 'prime favourite' among amateurs and audiences. Young suggests that nationalists interpreted the work as an anti-colonial resistance play, reading Red Hugh's liberation from captivity as 'the symbol of Ireland escaping'.[33]

As in *The green upon the cape*, language is a critical issue in *Red Hugh*. The Governor of Dublin Castle declares the 'heathenish jabbering' of Irish to be the language of infiltrators, informers and enemies. 'Speaking it here is strictly forbidden,' he tells Martin, 'except by those that are being trained as spies.' But Martin himself secretly communicates with the Irish prisoners in both languages:

> Martin (*in English*): Alas, it is among the English I was brought up, and their speech that I know best. I am but half Irish at best, and what there is in me of that race is my mother's gift. It was not willingly she was married to an English soldier, but being carried away by him for her beauty, was glad enough at length to be called his wife, but for her own sake and mine. Thus I came to be English named, but am Irish in heart and loyal to a prince of my mother's people.

The play parallels the travails of the Irish and the plight of Martin's mother, highlighting the extent to which both are the victims of colonial exploitation. The product of a union between the colonizer and the colonized, Martin supports the Irish captives in their jailbreak but cannot escape with them. Through his actions, the renegade prison guard alienates himself as a member of both communities.

The importance of language to the affirmation of Irish cultural identity is further emphasized by *The last of the Desmonds*.[34] Published in the *United Irishman* in 1904, this play centres upon the political and marital union of tribal chieftain Hugh O'Donnell and Joan Desmond, the only living female scion of one of

38 'The symbol of Ireland escaping', illustration of prison guard in Milligan's play *The deliverance of Red Hugh*, from the *Weekly Freeman*, March 1902.

Ireland's most ancient and most glorious families. The plot makes clear that this marriage is itself essential to safeguard Ulster from the threat of invasion by Elizabethan military forces. Because they live under the patronage of Sir George Carew, the English overlord of Munster, Joan and her brother James Desmond are keen to deny their Irish lineage. For example, when Carew asks him which language is best suited to a new national battle cry, James replies: 'anything at all but Irish. It is vulgar – only fit for the mountain people.' By relegating the Irish language to the liminal realms of the dispossessed and the disenfranchized, James Desmond effectively disavows his own familial heritage in order to cement his allegiance to the ascendancy of the colonizer.

The most intriguing figure in the play is Mary Sheehy, Joan Desmond's old nurse and the go-between in her courtship with Red Hugh. Sheehy performs the role similar to that of the nurse in many of Shakespeare's plays and of the tutor and nanny in Victorian novels: she has a mediating position and embodies an ancient symbolic power. When the play was staged by Cork National Theatre Society in the Assembly Rooms, (advertised as a 'Shrovetide performance' in March 1905), the production contained some Irish speech – leading Joseph

Holloway to designate it a bilingual drama in his 1912 dictionary of Irish plays.[35]
However, the *United Irishman*'s version prints Mary Sheehy's words in English
with the instruction 'speaks in Irish'.[36] Milligan's choice of name for this voice of
national memory recalls Revd Nicolas Sheehy (1728–66), the executed 'Whiteboy'
priest of Clonmel, Co. Tipperary. The name would also have carried a contemporary resonance because Mary Sheehy, mother of Hanna Sheehy-Skeffington,
was an Irish feminist and republican activist well-known in Ireland at the time
when Milligan's play was published and performed. Milligan's character Mary
Sheehy acts as the guardian of tradition, conscience and memory. When Joan
confesses that she has 'forgotten the Irish tongue', the nurse reprimands her by
insisting that failure to keep faith with the Irish language amounts to a willing
embrace of colonial suppression:

> Daughter of Gerald, the Earl, can it be that you forget your father's speech
> and that I must be speaking to you in the language of the enemies? Ah,
> cailin, if you forget the Irish, there are other things you will be forgetting
> with it. You will be forgetting the wrongs of Ireland and your race. You will
> be forgetting the cruelty of the English and their dealings with the house of
> Desmond. You will be forgetting the wasting of fair Munster with fire and
> sword.[37]

The presentation of Joan Desmond throughout the play exemplifies the
nursemaid's warning about the sacrifice of cultural integrity: she is a shallow figure
who is disconnected from her Irish roots, vainly accepting the patronage of the
English administration.

The heroic figure of Red Hugh is a striking absence in *The last of the Desmonds*,
his displacement from the drama opening up possibilities for the tracing of an
alternative history focalized through a woman of conflicted loyalties. By centring
her plays upon peripheral figures like Martin and Joan Desmond, Milligan deflects
history away from the canonical figures that conventionally give it meaning.
Milligan's drama repeatedly defines language as essential for the affirmation of
national and cultural identity. The complex bilingual terrain that Milligan
mediated as a key figure within the Gaelic League reflected a national dilemma.
Nowhere are these critical problems with language better exemplified than in the
Ossianic trilogy.

Milligan's Ossianic trilogy: a native Irish drama?

Stimulated by the publication of Douglas Hyde's groundbreaking study *A literary history of Ireland* in 1899, Milligan launched a rigorous campaign for the (re)establishment of an authentic Irish drama. Hyde maintained that the colonial occupation of Ireland had impeded the flowering of the dramatic potential incipient in the early dialogues and prose sagas featuring the bard Oisín:

> I have already observed that great producers of literature as the Irish always were – until this century – they never developed a drama. The nearest approach to such a thing is in these Ossianic poems. The dialogues between St. Patrick and Ossian – of which there is, in most of the poems, either more or less, is quite dramatic in its form ... But I think it nearly certain – though I cannot prove it – that in former days there was real acting and a dialogue between two persons, one representing the saint and the other the old pagan ... But nothing could develop in later Ireland. Everything, time after time, was arrested in its growth. Again and again the tree of Irish literature put forth fresh blossoms, and before they could fully expand they were nipped off.[38]

Milligan proposed that the Ossianic dialogues were more than simply dramatic recitals, but were the first example of a native Irish drama. In 'The dramatic element in Gaelic literature', an article published by the *Daily Express* in September 1899, she insisted that the dramatic qualities of this poetry did not reside in the text but in the process of reading aloud to audiences. With its spatial disposition of speakers, its scenic design, its dialogic rapport of narrator and audience, the oral context encouraged a dramatic process instead of a strictly literary one:

> When we recollect that they were not composed to be read in the study, but to be recited in the chieftain's hall by troops of bards and bardic pupils, we will comprehend that the recitals must have taken a dramatic form, especially at those parts where narrative was discontinued and dialogue took its place. The reciters would naturally identify themselves in voice, gesture, action, and expression with the characters represented.[39]

The structure of the Abbey Theatre (playwrights, actors, patrons in a national building) and the inclusion of songs, music, costume and stylized performance were also very close to this ancient tradition Milligan was pointing to. Declan Kiberd highlights the importance for Synge of 'the function of the ancient bard'

Cluiċeooiri·na·h-Eireann

SECOND PERFORMANCES OF THE SEASON | The Cast includes Maire Nic Shiubhlaigh,
THE ROTUNDA (Large Concert Hall), | Honor Lavelle, Eibhlin O'Doherty, Joseph
Thursday, Friday & Saturday, March 21, 22 & 23, | Goggin, Proinsias Mac Siubhlaigh, E. Keegan,
At 8.15 p.m.   Admission 2/-, 1/- & 6d. | Thomas R. Madden, Fred A. Macdonald, etc.

39 Front of postcard advertising 1907 Theatre of Ireland production of *The last feast of the Fianna*, Joseph Holloway Papers, National Library of Ireland.

and the bardic poetic tradition that Alice Milligan made a case for in 1899: 'Synge was not a revivalist in the sense of someone who wanted to restore some previous form of poetry or society: rather, he believed that it was the task of the radical traditionalists to unleash and liberate spurned but still potent possibilities.'[40] Milligan's ideas on bardic recital may well have enriched Yeats' ideas on psaltery, as well as the Abbey's iconic theatre practice.

Inspired by the belief that the Ossianic poems provided the originating moment of a national Irish drama, Milligan put her ideas into practice with three plays published in the *Daily Express* in 1899 – *The last feast of the Fianna* (September), *Oisín in Tír na nÓg* (October) and *Oisín and Pádraic* (November). The 1899 published plays organize Oisín's exploits as a linear and chronological narrative. In *The last feast of the Fianna*, the mythological poet Oisín agrees to leave both Ireland and the Fianna, a warrior-band. With the fairy Niamh he travels to the land of immortality and forgetfulness. *Oisín in Tír na nÓg* relates how the warrior bard eventually recovers his political and social consciousness and returns to Ireland. However, as soon as he touches the soil of his homeland, Oisín loses his protection against physical decay. He is left to mourn rather than redress the changes he witnesses in Ireland. *Oisín and Patrick*, the final part of the trilogy, presents the dialogues between the poet and the missionary. Oisín is impelled to reflect upon the vanished splendour of a pagan, non-sectarian Ireland.

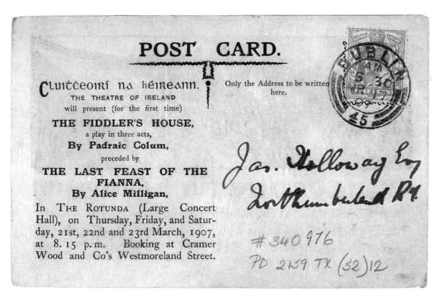

40 Reverse side of postcard addressed to Joseph Holloway.

With this trilogy, Milligan conceives of the cultural renaissance literally, suggesting that her plays breathe new life into an older form of indigenous culture:

> At a time when the literary talent of our country is being invited to inaugurate a revival of the drama in Ireland, it will be well for us to understand the effort is not being wasted to introduce an exotic art. An acquaintance with even the translated editions of our native literature will show us that, though the dramatic form is not represented, the dramatic element is strong in every one of the old tales and poems.[41]

At the turn of the twentieth century many cultural nationalists were eager to differentiate 'Irish' literature from 'foreign' influence. By contrast, disgusted by the provincialism of the Irish Literary Theatre's second season of plays, James Joyce in 1900 urged Irish playwrights to look to Europe for literary models: 'A nation which never advanced so far as a miracle-play affords no literary model to the artist and he must look abroad.'[42] Yeats and the Fay brothers did indeed turn to European models of national theatre and drama. But Milligan chose instead to look back into Ireland's history for her ideas about national theatre practice and for the subject matter of her plays and tableaux. When Milligan sent the script of *The last feast of the Fianna* to T.W. Rolleston, she elaborated this point: 'I wrote it as far as possible in the style of the dialogues so as to represent what a Gaelic drama would have been like if it had been developed further.'[43]

By valorizing both the dramatic potential and the cultural integrity of the
bardic stanzas, Milligan was directly challenging the blank verse style favoured by
Yeats. Blank verse was inappropriate, she argued, because it was an importation
from European and English theatrical traditions. In the same letter, Milligan
objected to the adoption of blank verse for the first Irish play staged in
Letterkenny in November 1898: 'I don't like the sound of it; besides it is alien …
The Gaelic medium for drama would be stanzas – not blank verse lines like
French'.[44] Her introduction to *Brian of Banba*, published in the *United Irishman*
in April 1904, similarly identifies the stanza as the only appropriate vehicle for a
native drama:

> Blank verse, in the manner of Shakespeare, is unsuited to a Gaelic medium
> of drama, and mere prose lacks in literary style and concision. Something in
> the style of the quatrains used in the Ossianic dialogues should be used and
> made the customary medium in legendary or ancient historic plays.[45]

Despite such bold pronouncements, Milligan never adequately pursued this
purist conception of a native drama – either in theory or in practice. Even though
she asserted that the Ossianic narratives could not 'be equalled nor expressed in
translation', she herself accessed them through English language versions published
in the *Transactions of the Ossianic Society* (1855–60).[46] Just as the Ossianic trilogy
was taken from previously published sources, so *Brian of Banba*, published in the
United Irishman in June 1904, was taken directly from translations by James Todd
in *Wars of the Gaedhill and the Gaill* (1867). Milligan openly acknowledged her
debt to previous translations and argued that the latter was a seminal text that
depicted Brian as 'the Napoleon of our history, rising up to rival the established
royal dynasty of the house of Conn'. In an essay review in *All Ireland Review*
published in 1900 she elaborated this point:

> Let me briefly enumerate some of the books of our historic literature, which it
> is essential to read. I mention only those which have been published and edited.
> *The Book of Rights*, dry as it is, is a storehouse of delight, to anyone with a deep
> interest in early Irish history, genealogy, and topography … *The Wars of the Gall
> and Gael* (which, in reality recounts the life of Brian Boru) is one of the most
> important Gaelic publications, from a historical point of view.[47]

Milligan repeatedly averred that the trilogy was intended for translation into
Irish, admitting that it would otherwise remain an unfinished work. Her footnotes
to both the trilogy and *Brian of Banba* state that the plays were 'written with a
view to translation into the Irish language in the Ossianic stanza'.[48] A year later

Milligan dedicated the published play-text of *The last feast of the Fianna* to Irish language activist Fr Eugene O'Growney, explaining that because he had produced drama 'for translation into Gaelic', her play was 'written after his example, with the same aim'.[49] The *United Irishman* welcomed the Irish Literary Theatre's production of *The last feast of the Fianna* as the first step towards an indigenous Irish language drama: 'Miss Milligan's play is in itself with the breath of the Ossianic legends, as near perfection, from a Gaelic standpoint, as anything not written in Gaelic can come.'[50] The paper later stated, 'The primal object of the drama was its translation into Irish. That done, an incalculable service must result.'[51] Frank Fay referred to the play as 'a little gem'.[52] A contributor to the paper suggested that an Irish version would symbolize a landmark in the unity of the linguistic and literary revivals: 'Is there any chance of it being translated in time for rendition at the coming Oireachtas? A recital in character would be a striking evidence of the progress which the past twelve months has seen.'[53]

Over three decades would pass, however, before any of the plays were actually translated – an Irish language version of *The last feast of the Fianna* by 'Fiachra Eilgeach' appeared in 1930, and the poet Tadhg Ó Donnchadha, 'Tórna', published a translation of *Oisín in Tír na nÓg* in 1944. Aodh de Blácam commended this literary collaboration as 'the best thing done in the Irish revival in recent times'. He believed that the English and Irish texts captured a lost narrative of Ireland's poetic heritage: 'Young people who recite this Milligan-Tórna play will be going back to the Irish culture instead of dressing English culture in Gaelic words. They will be reviving the poetry that used to be chanted in strong male voices.'[54] De Blácam is referring perhaps to the problem with Young Ireland verse: what was Gaelic in the poetry looked ungainly in English publication. He also suggests that the translation of Milligan's work offers a revival of forms not just of themes. That the Ossianic trilogy was a dramatic narrative more appropriate for 'young people' was an observation made by a reviewer in the *Irish Independent* who described it in 1944 as 'poetic play for children' that 'should be popular with school drama classes'.[55]

Milligan's insistence that the plays were destined for translation was perhaps in part a defensive response to what Terence Brown describes as 'one of the most fraught debates of the period 1880–1930'. According to Brown, Irish cultural activists were split on the question of:

> whether a distinctive Irish identity might be forged in the English language (the mother tongue of most of the island's inhabitants) or whether the revival of Irish was a 'necessity' (in Douglas Hyde's formulation) if the idea of Irish nationhood was to be anything more than a political expediency.[56]

Even non-native Irish speakers like Frank Fay, Arthur Griffith and George Moore believed that a truly Irish culture was impossible without the native language. Frank Fay confessed that he could not 'conceive it possible to achieve this [native drama] except through the medium of the Irish language'.[57] Arthur Griffith agreed that Irish literature was of a 'higher, purer type' than anything written in English.[58] Despite not knowing a word of Irish, George Moore responded to criticisms of the Irish Literary Theatre by promising never to speak English again. The *Daily Express* mockingly reported that Moore 'announced his intention of expressing himself in future in Gaelic, a language he has yet to learn'.[59]

While Arthur Griffith's paper lauded Milligan's aim to have the plays translated, the Gaelic League's Irish language press was more scathing about the very idea of an 'Irish' drama written in English. After the 1900 productions of *The last feast of the Fianna* and *Maeve*, a reviewer in *An Claidheamh Soluis* (in all likelihood Patrick Pearse) levelled a crushing insult at Milligan and Edward Martyn. While allowing that the writers had aspired to produce plays that furthered the Irish cultural renaissance, the paper concluded that neither was capable of achieving this goal:

> They are not only idealists, but Irish idealists, and have as much of the Irish spirit as it is possible to have without the Irish speech. But when is the Irish Literary Theatre going to deserve its title by producing an Irish play – that is to say – a play written in the Irish language? *At this stage of the day few intelligent people will be found to hold that works written in the English language are Irish literature.*[60]

The *Freeman's Journal* was similarly unimpressed, commenting that 'Miss Milligan and Mr Martyn have apparently to learn this – that the mere mention of a few Irish names does not and cannot make an Irish drama'.[61]

In his study *Postnationalist Ireland*, Richard Kearney argues that similar complaints were made against the establishment of an Irish Literary Theatre:

> Yeats was deeply disappointed by the fact that the Irish Literary Revival inaugurated by himself, Synge and Lady Gregory had been spurned by the Catholic middle classes, the Gaelic Leaguers and many of the republican nationalists. Pearse, for example in a letter in the journal *An Claidheamh Soluis* in 1899, had declared that … 'Against Mr Yeats personally, we have nothing to object. He is a mere English poet of the third and fourth rank and as such he is harmless. But when he attempts to run an "Irish" Literary Theatre, it is time for him to be crushed'.[62]

41 Milligan's sketch of John O'Leary who she cast as one of the Fianna warriors when *The last feast of the Fianna*, was staged by the Irish Literary Theatre at the Gaiety in Dublin, February 1900.

Kearney suggests that the pre-Christian plays and narratives such as the Ossianic legends were a way of Protestant cultural activists to transgress the dichotomous analogy between Catholicism and Irishness:

> The recourse of Yeats and Lady Gregory to the legendary images of Celtic mythology may thus be read as an attempt to make peace between the opposing interests of class, creed and language. It was a plea for a unifying notion of identity and sovereignty, based upon an 'ancient Irish sect' which preceded all contemporary dissension. In its way, it was an endorsement of Wolfe Tone's ideal of non-sectarian Irish tradition.[63]

Alice Milligan's drama *The last feast of the Fianna* came under attack not only for its avoidance of Irish speech but also for its dramatic imperfections. Augusta Gregory, playwright and co-founder of the Irish Literary Theatre, noted in her diary that: 'Miss Milligan's tawdry little piece was well staged, but Finn and Usheen both very bad – & the language in the piece is to me intolerable – however it was very short and applauded.'[64] Gregory also recalled the defensive attitude of Milligan when she refused to allow George Moore to amend certain parts of her text: 'Dined Ly.Layard, & on to a party at Yeats' to meet Miss Milligan

– whose play, or a part of it is going to be performed – but there was nearly a row
as George Moore, who is resolving himself into a syndicate for the re-writing of
plays, wanted to alter hers, & she refuses to let any hand touch it but her own.'[65]
George Russell wrote to Milligan in November 1899 informing her of the
rehearsal schedule for *The last feast of the Fianna*. He raised the issue of where the
large quantity of men was to be found to perform the role of warriors. In the letter
Russell reveals how George Moore considered Irish performers inferior to any
shipped over from England:

> All the rehearsals will be done in London except for about three days in
> Dublin before staging. Your advice of course will be taken about costumes
> etc. and Martyn would like very much to see you here about this & other
> matters you refer to. He will be in Dublin all this week. His address is
> Kildare Club. He would of course like a supply of athletic warriors who
> would not make fools of themselves as the question of supplies is a local one.
> There would be no use in bringing over a supply from London.[66]

In the end Milligan engaged members of the Dublin Gaelic League in her play
and included ex-Fenian prisoner John O'Leary as one of the warriors. Charlotte
Milligan Fox wrote an original orchestral score for the play that was performed
from the wings of the theatre.

While Gregory dismissed *The last feast of the Fianna* as a 'tawdry' failure, other
contemporary responses suggested that the form and conception of the play owed
more to the *tableaux vivant* tradition of theatrical spectacle than to realist
dramaturgy. The *Freeman's Journal* reviewer described *The last feast of the Fianna*
as a 'full-dress recitation of a pleasing and nicely written poem', arguing that it was
not drama so much as a 'series of very pretty animated pictures' that had 'no claim
for the slightest toleration on the stage'.[67] James Cousins raised a similar objection
in an article for the *Leader*, announcing that: 'I, for one, refuse to call by the name
of "drama" the dialogues of Usheen and Patrick, or Miss Milligan's beautiful and
cruelly maltreated *Tableau Vivant, The last feast of the Fianna*.'[68] Milligan's stylized
characters, Cousins believed, were not part of the 'speaking, feeling, moving
throng' that drama should aspire to reproduce. More recently James Flannery
echoed the earlier critique that *The last feast of the Fianna* was 'far more a pageant
than a play', with music and spectacle assuming 'more dramatic importance than
character, plot, or dialogue'.[69]

For James Cousins and the *Weekly Freeman* reviewer, tableaux are considered
inappropriate in the new Irish drama because of their association with popular
traditions. They identify the living picture as an inherently debased form; they can

42 The only surviving photograph of members of the Gaelic League performing the first Irish-language play in Donegal, 1898. The two women in the picture are Anna Johnston and her sister.

only conceive of Milligan's adherence to the tableaux mode as a failure to achieve 'proper' dramatic expression – rather than allowing that she may be attempting an alternative conception of theatre. The archival evidence suggests that Milligan deliberately devised *The last feast of the Fianna* as a combination of *tableaux vivants* and drama. By yoking together these opposed representational modes, she created an 'impure' theatrical form that knots together enactment and stasis, speech and spectacle, polemic and pictorialism. The play's contested identity exemplifies the hybridity that characterizes so much of Milligan's cultural production. In her work and in her life, Milligan straddled many seemingly contradictory political and cultural identities – as a northern Protestant who had relinquished the unionism of her upbringing, as an Irish nationalist activist excluded in the eyes of many from the native language, and as a woman engaged energetically and ubiquitously in the public sphere.

'Pretty animated pictures': tableaux in drama

Given the fact that Milligan began her extensive involvement with 'living picture' shows shortly before commencing work on the Ossianic trilogy, it is hardly surprising that reviewers likened *The last feast of the Fianna* to a *tableau vivant*. In May 1898 she helped the Belfast Gaelic League to stage a series of tableaux as the finale to its annual Irish music festival. In November of the same year she took part in an unprecedented theatrical event in Letterkenny in Co. Donegal, organizing the *tableaux vivants* that were performed before and after *The passing of Conal* – the first drama to include 'an act written in Gaelic by a Gaelic poet'.[70] Working for the Belfast Gaelic League, Milligan repeated scenes from this 'popular entertainment' in April 1899, at St Colum's Minor Hall in Derry. The *Derry Standard* described one of the contributions, *St Patrick at Tara*, as 'an impressive tableau' that took 'a musical character, embracing songs … and recitations in Gaelic'.[71] In a letter written in December 1898 to Eoin MacNeill, co-founder of the Gaelic League, Milligan credited the 'training and experience' she gained from developing these presentations in Belfast, Letterkenny and Derry as a prime influence upon her conception of the Ossianic plays.[72]

In the same letter Milligan outlined her plan to present a dramatization of the dialogues of Oisín and Patrick at the 1899 Dublin Oireachtas. The letter provides an unusually detailed account of how the interplay between tableaux and drama could be negotiated in a single performance. Crucial to Milligan's conception of the event was a schematic use of stage space. Oisín and Patrick, she notes, should convey their conflicting interpretations of Irish history on the periphery of the stage while, behind a curtained boundary, an inner sanctum displayed emblematic representations of Oisín's memory and projections of his imagination:

> There would be an outer stage on which Patrick his clerics & the aged Oisín would appear: & selections translated from the dialogue would be given by them. An inner curtain rising after every description, to show tableaux of the scenes described by Oisín, Tír na nÓg, Hunting scenes &c.[73]

Milligan discussed this prospective production further in 'Literary drama and the Gaelic League', a letter she published in the *Daily Express* in January 1899:

> A few members of the League in Dublin, who have considerable elocutionary power, should impersonate the aged Oisín, Patrick and his clerics, and that from the old version of the dialogues some of our poets should condense the most important parts, embodying Oisín's laments for his lost comrades, Fin and the Fianna, a narrative of the elopement of

Diarmuid and Grainne, and his own wanderings to *Tir-nan-oig*. During the narration, Oisín, by magic art, is to summon up for the benefit of the astonished clerics visions of the chief scenes in his heroic youth. These in a series of beautiful tableaux, appearing behind a gauze curtain in an inner stage, will form the chief feature of the entertainment.[74]

Milligan was principally concerned with tableaux within these theatrical presentations. In the spatial configurations of the stage, tableaux occupy the interior realm – a magical zone that offers access to the cultural memory of the nation. The Irish music, dancing and recitations that accompanied many of Milligan's *tableaux vivants* entertainments further affirmed the vitality of indigenous culture. By suggesting that the dialogues between Oisín and Patrick could be adapted from published sources, Milligan underscores the extent to which they are peripheral to the central process of memorialization. The Oisín and Patrick debate that Milligan staged and writes extensively about is also a debate about the difference between oral and written culture; the unofficial and the official at the centre of the Irish/English colonial encounter. Her symbolic division of the stage establishes two opposed imaginings of Ireland: while the conflictual dialogues of Oisín and Patrick occupy the outer borders, the core affirms the glories of a heroic and communitarian past. Through Milligan's theatrical work the tableaux mode conveys the inner realm, articulating an 'unofficial' culture in which the national finds articulation.

The chronology of Milligan's published trilogy is linear: Oisín leaves the Fianna, travels to Tír na nÓg and returns to Ireland after four hundred years. In contrast, tableaux enabled Milligan to produce a more complex narrative in which memory and identity were visually present in the stage structure and in the iconography of performance. It is through living pictures that Oisín reviews, remembers and re-envisions Ireland's heritage. In November 1900 Milligan staged the trilogy as a silent series of *poses plastiques* in the Belfast Museum. The 1900 series of tableaux relied upon a sequence more in line with the published trilogy than the more sophisticated demonstration of tableaux and drama described above. An off-stage orator replaced the voice of Oisín by explaining the *tableaux vivants* to the audience. *An Claidheamh Soluis* reported how the story was performed: 'The next series had for subject Oisín the Bard, whose meeting with Niamh while out hunting with the Fianna, his departure for Tír na nÓg, and his subsequent return to Erin and conversion by St Patrick, made a set of beautiful pictures.'[75]

In 1917 Frank Morrow, a key figure from the early days of the Ulster Literary Theatre, staged a revival of Milligan's Ossianic trilogy as a homage to its author –

43 Sketch by Milligan (*c.*1897) showing inner and outer regions of stage. In the distance
would be performed tableaux often behind a gauze curtain.

who by that time symbolized a past era of cultural activism. Advertised as a 'bardic
pageant play' with 'full band, chants and dances', *The return of Oisín* was staged at
the Ulster Hall in Belfast.[76] The Ulster Orchestra provided the music for this
production with members of St Anne's Cathedral, St George's Church and the
Ulster Male Choir. Although the play was part of a double bill featuring Margaret
Dobbs' comedy, *The doctor and Mrs Macauley*, Milligan's drama received most of
the acclaim and publicity. Oisín's mythical journey through an unrecognisable
homeland in search of lost comrades carried a particular resonance in the context
of war-torn contemporary Ireland. The *Irish News* report makes clear the
importance of pageantry and tableaux to Morrow's stylized rendition of the
Ossianic saga, which integrated scenes from all three plays into an approximation
of the processional mode Milligan practised from 1898:

> Two scenes are introduced showing the most interesting of Celtic periods –
> the pagan and the Christian eras. In the first we are shown the land of 'Tir-
> na-nÓg', that fairyland of Irish legend where Oisín sojourns forgetful of his
> own country, and later he is carried across to his native, 'Glenasmoil', where
> he finds St Patrick has planted the faith among the people.[77]

In 1944 Milligan recalled how Morrow staged Oisín's discovery that his son Oscar
is dead. Milligan's recollections were published as an attachment to the first Irish
language publication of her play. At the age of seventy-eight Milligan connected

44 Sketch of Oisín leaving Tír na nÓg, *c.*1900.

Oisín's experience of deciphering the coded ancient ties of kinship with ideas which were for her embedded in the early years of the Cultural Revival:

> The ogham stone was carried in on the bier by the mourners, and as they grouped around with arms raised in lamentation the stone was set up, and the procession moved along disclosing it to Oisín, who stood well to the front of the stage. On reading the name of his son on the stone, his memory is aroused, he cries aloud for vengeance declaring he will return to Eire. The visionary procession then passes away with the stone concealed in a mantle.[78]

Milligan's letters of the late 1890s and the reviews of the 1900 production of *The last feast of the Fianna* make it clear that she conceived the trilogy as a deliberate hybrid of dramatic and tableaux modes. Although crucial to the staging of the Ossianic plays, living pictures were never formally scripted into the published versions. Milligan's plans for staging the Ossianic trilogy defined a key opposition between a 'peripheral' enactment of history through spoken dialogue and a 'core' that depicted the imaginings of an Irish nation through *tableaux vivants*. A similar tension between the tableaux and the dramatic modes of representation informs *The daughter of Donagh*. The play incorporates three living pictures that interrupt the flow of enactment, inviting the audience to contemplate the political and cultural oppositions they emblematize.

A reworking of Milligan's 1893 novel *The Cromwellians* (discussed in chapter two), *The daughter of Donagh* was published in four separate acts in the *United Irishman* throughout December 1903.[79] Set in 1654, concerns the attempt of a dispossessed Catholic woman, Onora Cavanagh, to avenge herself against a Cromwellian soldier, Gabriel Fairfax, who executed her father and usurped their property. As the newly wedded Onora and Fairfax prepare for transportation across the river Shannon, she defiantly announces herself to be the daughter of the man he murdered: 'I came again unto my home, designing vengeance. And in wedding and thus ruining you, I wrought my vengeance.' Shortly after this declaration the stage is frozen into an allegorical spectacle that provides an emphatic conclusion to the play:

> (Final *Tableau* – Onora stands at the prow of the boat with hands crossed over her breast. Seaghan slowly swings the oars. The boat moves very slowly. Gabriel kneels with his face hidden in his hands.)

The design of the tableau invests the scene with ritualistic and religious overtones that contest the sectarian authority of the Cromwellian regime. As a Celtic figurehead at the prow of the boat, Onora towers above the penitential soldier who kneels beneath her at the river's edge. The picture is prepared for by an exchange between Onora and Fairfax. As she leaves him on the shore, Onora tells her husband that the river that separates them symbolizes the 'deeper gulf between us, between your race and mine'.

Milligan's two multi-act historical melodramas, *The daughter of Donagh* and *The French are on the sea*, focus on the seventeenth-century plantations and the United Irish revolution of 1798. In both plays, tableaux have a different rationale than the living pictures summoned, as if by 'magic art', during the Ossianic dialogues. In the scripted melodramas they disrupt the dramatic process, charging the scene with broader cultural and historical resonances that reach far beyond the specific intrigues of the stage narrative. These two concluding scenarios of escape and departure are set at the physical boundary of Ireland, on the shore that simultaneously delimits the land and connects it to the rest of the world. In each instance, the final tableau translates defeat into a celebration of the empowerment of the dispossessed. The living picture reaches beyond its dramatic context, pointing towards new horizons for a nationalist future that exceed the conceptual and physical boundaries of the colonized nation. Thus where the dramatic narrative submits the characters to localized extremes of emotion and injustice, the tableaux scenes show that they are part of a bigger picture – transforming them into mythic players on the national cultural stage and symbols of the ultimate nationalist triumph. There is a latency in Milligan's work that sees possibilities inherent in the defeated seemingly dead past. Her characters and her cultural work look so deeply into the present that the shape of a future becomes discernable.

Through its strategic juxtaposition of enactment and tableaux, Milligan's theatrical work established a dialogue between the particularities of the dramatic process and the wider discourses of nation. The Irish Revival may have been united in its aim of regenerating a national drama, but the search for an appropriate language and subject matter wrought tremendous discord and confusion. As an Irish cultural nationalist who was both an English-speaker and a Protestant, Milligan combined within herself a multitude of conflictual identities and allegiances. Her plays deal with characters locked within struggles to consolidate their political and cultural affiliations; besides mirroring Milligan's own conflicts, they also connect with more general divisions and tensions besetting the Irish revivalist project. Milligan's interest in tableaux was not restricted to the dramatic contexts examined thus far. Instead, she worked with living pictures as a form in their own right – and in so doing moved increasingly from the dominant tendencies of a cultural renaissance that prioritized literary rather than pictorial values. Milligan's fervent commitment to living pictures was intrinsically related to her concern with 'voicelessness': articulate in its very muteness, the *tableau vivant* offered her a valuable space beyond the contested terrain of language.

CHAPTER SIX

Republican tableaux and the Revival

> Those who were in B Wing, Kilmainham, during the summer of 1923 will
> ever remember Angela Doyle as Robert Emmet ... Angela chose Robert
> Emmet and to all of us who had ever visioned Emmet, Angela seemed to
> embody every idea of ours. Young, pale, fair, tall, with an earnest sad
> expression in her eyes, she seemed the ghost of the hero of 1803.
>
> Death notice of Angela Doyle (1907–25),
> *Cumann na mBan*, September, 1925.

In 1923 Irish women prisoners on hunger strike in A Wing of Kilmainham Jail
staged for their comrades in B Wing a series of costumed *tableaux
vivants* that
evoked their republican heroes Robert Emmet and Anne Devlin. With its roots in
English and French state-censorship of spoken language in theatre, the voiceless
form of *tableau vivant* also proved, because of the suppression of Irish, to have a
special potency in the colonial (and immediately post-colonial) context of Ireland.
The women who staged these tableaux in 1923 were responding to their memory
of how 'living pictures' had been radicalized during the Irish Cultural Revival by
Alice Milligan. In fact, many of the prisoners had actually been trained in the
making of tableaux by Milligan through her association with the Gaelic League
and *Inghinidhe na hÉireann*.[1] 'Living pictures' was a particularly appropriate
theatrical mode to enable these women prisoners to display their allegiance to
historical forebears whose legacy was, like their own experience, one of disempowerment, bodily torture and silence. Their enactment of these tableaux in such
circumstances is an example of what Declan Kiberd has called 'an attempt to
release the still-unused potential buried in past moments'.[2]

Tableau vivant is a hybrid of theatre and pictorial art; its political implications
can only be fully recognized in relation to other pictorial representations. The
1923 performance enabled the confined prisoners to transform themselves into a
community. This was characteristic of the Irish Revival in general; its aim was to
produce a communal consciousness by creating the 'past' through street parades,
collecting folklore, staging and publishing Irish legends and histories, initiating
art and museum exhibitions, and by travelling with theatre productions and magic
lantern shows. Milligan was essentially concerned with how this emergent
nationalist culture depicted itself in public space as both an act of and a search for

45 Sketch of two women on their way from Mass in Donegal, by Alice Milligan, *c.*1888.

self-representation. In particular, her theatre work explored how the body itself became the subject of repressed history in nationalist iconography and commemoration. Visual culture in this period of radical transformation offered a site for the rehearsal and performance of possible identities. Irish public space was reclaimed and redefined in print culture, in performances enacted on official and unofficial stages, in the opening up of theatres, galleries and cinemas. The unwritten story of Milligan's political mobilization of visual culture is located in a wide range of archival materials such as photographs (nicknamed 'the mirror with a memory' in the 1890s), magic lantern slides and travelling lantern shows, illustrated fiction, theatre posters, newspapers and journals, *tableaux vivants* (also

46 'The lament for the dead'; woodcut by Seaghan MacCathmhaiol from *Four Irish songs*
by the Milligan sisters, 1910.

known as 'living pictures' and '*poses plastiques*') representing scenes from well-
known Irish melodramas, public commemorations, costumed pageants, banners
carried at public demonstrations, murals, paintings and public monuments, street
theatre, sculpture and film reels. In this chapter I want to investigate some of the
contexts that will help us better understand the latent visual community dynamics
that fired Ireland's national theatre and Irish language movement.

After 1894, Milligan began to argue that Ireland should empower itself from
within and that culture was a central decolonizing agency. According to the *United
Irishman*, the highlight of her April 1901 theatre show staged in Dublin with the
Fay brothers and *Inghinidhe na hÉireann* was, 'the introduction for the first time
in the metropolis of a cottage céilidh scene representing the actual everyday life –
the amusements and occupations of the people of the Irish-speaking districts'.[3]
The theatre critic and architect Joseph Holloway reveals in his famous diary the
inclusive nature of the new Irish theatre in which the rural worker and the urban
bourgeoisie sat side-by-side. The man sitting next to Holloway, for instance, was

so engaged with the theatrical performance of a scene from rural life that he commented upon minor discrepancies in its realism:

> The céilidh (caly) or Irish social gathering round the fireside in the cabin was well carried out, (though a countryman beside me said that the woman who rocked the cradle should have done so with the foot instead of her hand if she were an industrious girl & also that countrymen never light their pipe with matches but with a lighted coal or bit of turf).[4]

It was precisely these aspects of private Irish social life that were given a prominent visual part in the new Irish national theatre. In his introduction to *Songs of old Ireland*, A.P. Graves argued that Irish music represents:

> The various characteristics of the people, from which they sprung. Thus, glimpses into the lives of the Irish peasant, fisherman, and mechanic are given through the Lullabies, the Love Songs, the Lays of Sport and Occupation, and the Lamentation for the Dead.[5]

Music was a key component to how Milligan re-imagined the hidden aspects of Irish cultural life on stage: a tableau reconstruction of the killing of Brian Boru provided Milligan with the opportunity to stage the first actual performance of the caoine or keen, the collective female vocal lament for the dead. The *United Irishman* reported in April 1901 that:

> The rendering by the choir of that beautiful old Irish tune, 'The Return from Fingall', in which the fierce cry of victory and the wild wail of sorrow for the slain monarch, so wonderfully mingle, was excellent ... The mournful strains of the Irish caoine, which followed the death of Brian, was weirdly impressive.[6]

The tableau performed scenes not usually witnessed in public that were familiar and domestic; thus, hidden aspects of the cultural landscape of Ireland were shared collectively for the first time as national. Milligan also helped to introduce the language movement as radical anti-illusionist theatre. In 1901 she arranged for a special appearance of the Gaelic League's co-founder, Douglas Hyde [An Craoibhin], on the stage where a domestic cottage scene was being performed as tableau. Hyde was 'recognized' in the audience by the 'cottagers' on stage and invited to join them in their home. His movement from one space (in the theatre audience) into the imagined cottage scene (on stage), connected both. 'As the man of the house looked out through his door who did he see coming up the road but An Craoibhin, and when Douglas Hyde appeared on the stage with his big Irish frieze coat and with a fine Irish blackthorn in his fist the audience cheered him enthusiastically.'[7] In May 1905 Milligan depicted the significant role taken by women in the language movement in a tableau, 'The Gaelic League (Miss Hanna Cotter) instructing the youth of Ireland', in St Mary's Hall, Cork.[8] The relationship between the actualities of Irish life and the stylized rituals of the tableaux was being reconfigured on and off the stage [Plates 21 and 22].

Magic lanterns and tableaux

Milligan and her associates seized upon the popular tableau form to reanimate a history that had been for too long buried and suppressed. Their tableaux offered a counter-narrative to officially sanctioned cultural entertainment. 'England is monopolizing the eye of our public', claimed the *United Irishman*. It was only by taking control of visual culture that 'the character of the country will be altered'.[9] As early as 1843 Thomas Davis had stressed the importance of visual culture for the formation of national identity in Ireland. He believed that the pictorial arts had an instructional and commemorative duty: 'art is biography, history, and topography, taught through the eye'.[10] Like Davis, Milligan stressed the capacity of the pictorial arts to re-imagine the 'illustrated history'[11] of a people whose contested past was not officially recorded or taught. Milligan's complaint in 1901 that 'there was no Irish art worth speaking of'[12] echoed an appeal she had made some years earlier for Irish artists to depict and popularize Ireland's nationalist history in painting.[13]

Milligan was consistently drawn towards visual forms of cultural production – magic lantern shows, photography, tableaux and melodrama – because they enabled her to reach a wide range of audiences. Her commitment to the educational efficacy of *tableaux vivants* was encouraged by her earlier experiences of delivering magic lantern slide lectures; indeed, lantern slides and tableaux were combined on many occasions. A member of the Belfast Naturalists Field Club and the Antiquarian Society from the 1880s, Milligan photographed many Irish historical sites. She then transferred these images onto glass slides, which were projected onto a wall by a magic lantern.

Under the auspices of the Gaelic League, which she joined in 1895, she presented numerous lantern lectures in Ireland and Britain. Initially, she relied on a hired gas lantern and operator; in 1898 she complained that her lecture tour of Donegal had been seriously impeded by the lack of a mobile magic lantern:

> It is not possible to get a lantern for a lecture in Donegal without entailing the expense of hiring one and paying an operator from a distance. Lecturing in Letterkenny in January I met with this difficulty. A man had actually to

be brought from Belfast to operate. I would like to establish a good lecture lantern and set of slides in the control of some energetic Gaelic worker in Donegal. The explanation of the slides could be supplied in Irish, and it would not take an orator or a Gaelic linguist to give an interesting Gaelic lecture. You would attract the young people in crowds to such an entertainment. The sum of £3 10*s*. would, I understand, purchase a first class lantern working by oil light, an instrument which in the average schoolroom would show slides as well as needs be.[14]

She soon convinced an American sponsor in 1898 to donate a portable oil lantern to the Gaelic League which was itself sometimes called 'the Shan Van Vocht' as a salute to Milligan and Anna Johnston's newspaper of that name. The *Derry Journal* reported how Gaelic League workers donated magic lantern slides that could be used for educational lectures as well as for local fund-raising events. The mobility and independence of the lecturers to reach remote areas in Ireland was a critical factor in Milligan's plan to do away with the type of magic lanterns that depended on hired gas cylinders:

> At Mountcharles that evening a case was opened containing a splendid magic lantern, presented by a friend of the cause to the *Shan Van Vocht*, Belfast. This lantern is to be used at meetings and entertainments through Donegal, where the lecture and description of slides is given in Irish … Miss Milligan presented a set of historical slides dealing with the lives of Red Hugh O'Donnell and Hugh O'Neil. It had been intended to use the lamp in Glenties the following evening, but as the case was only opened now for the first time no one had time to learn to operate with sufficient dexterity. It has however, been promised to that town for an early date to be exhibited at an entertainment on behalf of the Cathedral building fund.[15]

When she was officially employed as a travelling lecturer by the Gaelic League in October 1904, Milligan began to journey across Ireland with her own portable magic lantern and a camera that she used to collect pictures for slides. These photographs were both projected and accompanied by storytelling, public talks or music. Milligan worked with local communities to re-embody the pictures as theatre and devise new scenes for the stage from local folklore, the cultural life of the community and from Irish songs and legends. Milligan's official appointment by the League simply gave structural and economic recognition to the localized cultural practices (such as magic lantern and theatre shows) that she had already engaged in for over a decade. Writing in the *United Irishman* in 1900, Milligan made a forthright case for the suitability of magic lantern and tableaux shows for

47 Patrick Pearse's magic lantern and glass slides, St Enda's, Rathfarnham, photograph by Brian Crowley, curator of the Pearse Museum, Dublin.

the advancement of the Gaelic League's educational remit. Moreover, she suggested that theatrical entertainment combined with lantern shows could be used effectively to raise historical consciousness and to draw in revenue for the language movement:

> Magic lanterns and tableaux could be pressed into service for teaching history, and even if these attractions cost something, they will be found to be self-supporting and frequently profitable, whereas the lecture on the ordinary lines is purely a source of expense. People are rarely charged for entrance, and in some cases it would look as if they expected to be paid for coming.[16]

After the April 1901 performances in Dublin, Arthur Griffith acknowledged how useful the tableaux were in conveying narrative without language. The bi-lingual programme and off-stage orator meant that it was possible for people to have an experience of Irish and be inspired to learn more:

> The performances this week have done splendid service to the national cause. People who never studied a line of Ireland's history in their lives and who thought nothing about their native language went away from the Antient Concert Rooms determined to study both.[17]

In the 1890s, Milligan took photographs of Gaelic League workers and projected them as magic lantern slides to Irish communities abroad. She displayed and further enriched the new context of the Cultural Revival by connecting emigrant Irish communities (most often in places such as Scotland, Liverpool and London) with those involved in the revival of language and culture 'at home'. It was essential that the audience recognized the figures they saw on screen. The power of the image was crucial in the formation of a community.

An Claidheamh Soluis (The Sword of Light) published a report of one of Milligan's lectures, delivered in London, called 'In the Gaelic speaking country'. The magic lantern show was very similar to the structure of a tableau performance: the images that were projected onto a screen for people to see were accompanied by stories provided by an off-stage narrator (in this case Milligan herself). Live Irish music was also an important component of these shows. In London in 1900, Charlotte Milligan Fox (founder of the London Irish Folk Song Society) provided post slide-show music for her sister's talk. Live music and singing from the audience often accompanied such pictures as they were projected from the magic lantern or performed as tableaux on stage:

> Every available seat was occupied, and many were unfortunately unable to obtain admission ... Miss Milligan, who received a great ovation, immediately began her lecture, which she delivered in a chatty, pleasant, and very interesting manner. She had a magnificent set of views shown by the magic lantern as the groundwork of the lecture ... Photos of Gaelic League gatherings, groups of Irish speaking people and of prominent Gaelic workers, beauty spots in the Gaelic country, old seats of piety, power and learning, were flashed on the screen, each being appropriately referred to, and the whole so skilfully blended and interwoven as to make the subject interesting to all, and to bring the members of the league in London into still closer touch with their friends in the movement at home. Each picture on being recognised was greeted with enthusiasm, and often with an Irish blessing ... A picture of Thomas Concannon received a very hearty greeting ... The vote of thanks to the lecturer was ... seconded by W.B. Yeats. After Miss Milligan had suitably replied, a selection of Irish airs was exquisitely played ... Miss Charlotte Milligan Fox next played on the piano her own beautiful arrangement of the grand old war song, 'Cath Ceim an Fheidh' and also of a charming Jacobite ballad.[18]

Fundraising was a key part of this cultural project: in October 1904, Milligan herself was appointed by the League to present slides and 'living pictures' of 'Irish historic and literary subjects' in order to 'propagate the cause and get in funds'.[19] Milligan's 'living pictures' were therefore performed as fundraisers for Irish cultural and political groups with limited resources. For example, the entrance fees raised by *Inghinidhe na hÉireann*'s tableaux show in April 1901 funded the publication of *Poems and ballads* by William Rooney (1873–1901). Money collected by Milligan on her touring tableaux productions was 'sent forward to the language fund'.[20] Milligan organized the Gaelic League in and around Cork with Thomas MacDonagh and helped set up League branches and raise funds in the north with Roger Casement. As has been noted earlier, with Ada MacNeill, she toured Donegal and the Glens of Antrim to raise money for the establishment of an Irish College in Co. Donegal.[21] When the college was opened in October 1906 it was reported that 'Eilis Ni Mhaeleagain [Alice Milligan] delights students, visitors and country people with *tableaux vivants* illustrating Irish history.'[22] As late as 1910 Milligan informed Margaret Hutton that she had once again assisted in the production of *tableaux vivants* to raise 'some money for the building fund'.[23] In the post-Partition era, tableaux were used to connect Irish communities in a United Irish agenda and to raise funds for their opposition campaign work.

Image, vision, culture

Milligan radicalized Thomas Davis' ideas about visual culture in her work with a broad range of Irish cultural activists in Ireland and abroad and by making theatre in local communities. Her theatrical pictures were not just about teaching 'through the eye'; they were participatory, communitarian and localized. By creating for the stage pictures in which people embodied representations of Irish history, she helped to release this history from the frozen official narrative. Milligan's own ideas about tableaux seemed to have developed from her participation in the unofficial cultural activities conducted for the '98 Centenary. Street parades and other public events constituted a form of radicalized commemorative art. She declared in the *Shan Van Vocht* that decorated banners were infinitely more effective for young people in conveying national history and forging anti-colonial resistance than any textbook. In a report on the Wolfe Tone procession held in Dublin, she commended participants from the north for their 'magnificent banners' portraying the United Irishmen. She asserted that the pictures of 'Wolfe Tone and his comrades on Cave Hill; McCracken at Antrim's fight; Tone's interview with Napoleon; McCracken's execution' would act as 'illustrated history lessons to the young people in the black north' [Plate 17].[24] As a member of the Gaelic League's Tableaux Committee from 1902, Milligan also co-ordinated costume pageants of Irish history for the annual Irish Language Week parades in Dublin's city centre. The 1902 language demonstration included 'picturesque' and 'emblematic tableaux' paraded through the streets of Dublin.[25] In 1907, *An Claidheamh Soluis*

48 Front cover of Feis Ceoil programme, Belfast, May 1898, a music festival for the Gaelic League that featured tableaux shows staged by Milligan and her colleagues in the Irish language movement.

reported how the festival was an integral part of developing the revival of the language as a living movement. Costumed representations of Ireland's historical and mythical past were an intrinsic part of this project. Groups participating in the language parade were invited to choose a scene and perform this as a tableau on the day, while moving through the city streets. These were events that had a profound impact on the formation of the national cultural movement and the cohesive development of the language societies:

> As long as they remained a viable means of public appeal, the language processions provided revivalists with a unique way to bring their cause in to the streets of the capital. By drawing on traditions of civic pageantry, the League addressed Dubliners through a familiar medium that allowed unions and trade societies, temperance organisations, friendly societies, and other advocacy groups to align themselves opportunistically with the language cause. In practice, therefore, pre-existing associational networks, the socioeconomic conditions of the city, the condition of the League as an organisation, and the spectacle of the processions themselves all combined to affect how people interpreted and internalised the League's linguistic nationalism.[26]

In 1938 Milligan was invited to judge the tableaux presented at the Feis in Omagh. She told the *Derry Journal* that she readily accepted the offer because the event resonated with her extensive 'experience in organizing tableaux in places as far apart as Carndonagh and Skibbereen, in Dublin and in Belfast, in spacious premises like the Antient Concert Rooms and the Ulster Hall and often in tents at Feiseanna and little country school-houses'.[27] Milligan was here recalling how in the late 1890s and early 1900s, tableaux had been crucial to her political activities. Following a highly successful exhibition of 'living pictures' in Belfast in May 1898, staged in conjunction with the city's Gaelic League and Arts Society, she was inspired to mount further shows in Derry (1899), Belfast (1900) and Dublin (April and August 1901). She subsequently took *poses plastiques* to schools and Gaelic League branches across Ireland, tailoring her visualizations of national history to suit the demands of local constituencies. Tableaux were accessible for three main reasons: they readily engaged their audiences, they could be produced by groups with limited funding, and they could be performed by those with modest dramatic skills. Thus local communities, language groups and small-scale political and cultural organizations were able to participate directly in the theatrical memorialization of national identity. There are accounts written by those who witnessed the tableaux shows. The actress Maíre Nic Shiubhlaigh remembered 'living pictures' directed by Milligan that re-enacted scenes from history or legend:

> William Rooney's 'Dear Dark Head', or, perhaps, something out of Moore's 'Rich and Rare' in which would appear a lady, richly bejewelled and garbed in silks, wooed by a glittering Sir Knight to the accompaniment of appropriate choral music.[28]

In 1949, Pádraic Colum recalled more precisely how the living picture shows were a hybrid of music and narrative in which 'statuesque groups [were] introduced by some familiar piece of music … holding their pose for some minutes – an elementary show in which costume, music, and striking appearance were ingredients'.[29]

Milligan herself expressly conceived of the *tableau vivant* as a vehicle for communal and national unification. Milligan and Ada McNeill worked together during the 1906 Feis in Cushendall. This was the occasion when Roger Casement took the initiative to clear a disused overgrown field after a unionist landowner refused the League access to a site on his land. Milligan helped choreograph 'The Mask of the Nine Glens' which was both a *tableau vivant* and a procession that formed 'a unique open-air spectacle … headed by the Irish War Pipes and by the artistic banners'.[30] The music was provided by Francis Joseph Biggar's Belfast Pipe Band. The ceremonial, processional pageantry, which involved music and Irish language recitation, became Milligan's trademark in the Gaelic League movement.

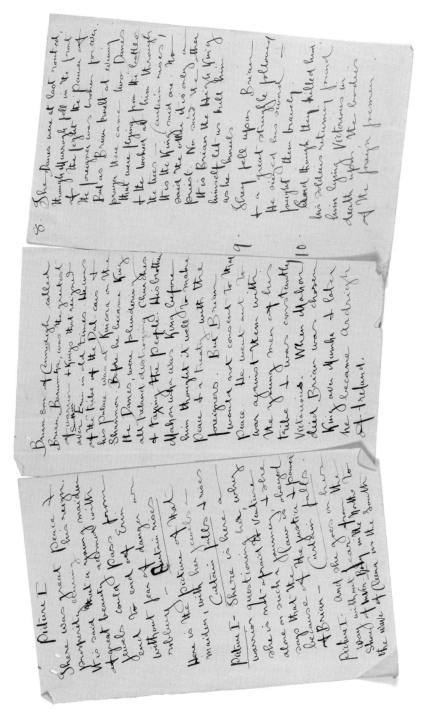

49 Only surviving script of a tableaux show. In this manuscript Milligan shows what the
off stage orator or storyteller would say in describing each picture as the Brian Boru
series is enacted on stage.

Tableaux vivants became the central focus of her work with amateur groups because they were easier to stage than dramas; as Kirsten Gram Holstrom observes, 'living pictures' did not make 'excessive claims on the talents of the participants'.[31] An especially illuminating insight into Milligan's nurturing role for amateur theatre groups is provided by the letters she received in 1899 from Mary Spring Rice. As president of the Foynes Branch of the Gaelic League, Spring Rice viewed Milligan's theatre practice as a vital way to create an Irish language community. Because her language group was eager to stage 'living pictures', Spring Rice wrote to Milligan requesting assistance with costumes and scenery:

> I think they would hardly be up to acting *The Last Feast of the Fianna* but we had thought of having tableaux [drawn] from the Fianna, one of the murder of Brian Boru, one of Malachi and the collar of gold, the last two the same as the ones they had in Belfast in May ... The people here are getting so keen about the Irish that they would be very much interested in anything of the kind.[32]

Milligan suggested that it would be possible to devise a coherent series of tableaux, centred upon the Brian Boru narrative. In response, Spring Rice explained:

> I agree Brian Boru would be so much better in a series than isolated ... But I'm afraid we have no one good enough for Brian ... You say Oisin is simpler ... of course I see it would be so much better to have several tableaux on the same subject, just changing the pose and position; besides being more historically instructive to the audience than several of different ages and periods altogether.[33]

The overarching consideration, as Spring Rice makes clear, was to ensure that the presentation was 'historically instructive'.

Women and nation

Milligan accorded Irish women more dynamic roles in public space, on stage and behind the scenes. It is important that these shows were performed in public arenas rather than in elite drawing-rooms and by women who often identified themselves as part of a cultural collective. The silence of the tableaux was a political act. Women, Milligan complained, 'were not called upon to have any opinion whatsoever' in constitutional politics.[34] Their silence, when staged, became a form of speaking back. Milligan produced tableaux with women who were artists, educators, community, cultural and political activists. The very first major show of tableaux Milligan helped produce in Belfast took place under the auspices of the Gaelic League in 1898 at Belfast's Exhibition Hall, with leading cultural activists such as Anna Johnston, Mary Hutton, Edith McCann and Rosamund Praeger taking part.

The silence of these shows was important in opening up an inclusive space, particularly in contested areas such as Belfast. Women could work together on the production of tableaux despite holding (and indeed, sometimes, because they held) opposing political views. Tableaux made it possible for a radical nationalist such as Anna Johnston to work alongside the staunch unionist sculptor Rosamund Praeger. Praeger designed the sets for the 1898 show that Johnston performed in and Milligan was central to. Women usually contributed to such events without defined titles; they produced and performed in unscripted shows in which they remained largely unnamed, where their roles were contributions to a whole. It was in essence a collective 'event'. At issue in the debates about native language and national theatre was the question of who had the right to speak for the Irish nation and how that nation could be spoken for. The Gaelic League wasn't just about reinstating the Irish language: it was part of the Revival project to create the cultural conditions that would give the Irish language and national theatre meaning. In this context, the tableau was a symbol of the national body awaiting speech. At the turn of the century these living picture shows were crucial for the huge numbers of people who didn't have Irish but who wanted to participate in the formation of 'national' theatre. Tableaux were vital in forging communities, for women in gaining space in the public life of the nation, for connecting people in difficult political contexts, for learners at different levels of Irish language training, for the inclusion of northern Protestants, like Alice Milligan herself, whose upbringing led them to believe that Irish was not their native language or their national culture. Silence represented a halfway house, a space, a means of crossing borders and transgressing the barriers erected by years of colonial occupation.

In addition, *tableaux vivants* were clearly significant in providing a cultural platform for women who were often banned from nationalist political organizations. Milligan aligned her work with Irish feminist organizations such as *Inghinidhe na hÉireann* (Daughters of Ireland) that had been founded by Maud Gonne in April 1900. The tableaux had already proved a major forum for the Irish Women's Association in Belfast. After witnessing the 1900 series of tableaux in Belfast, Maud Gonne sought Milligan's aid for a show she was planning for Dublin with *Inghinidhe na hÉireann*:

114   THE SHAN VAN VOCHT.

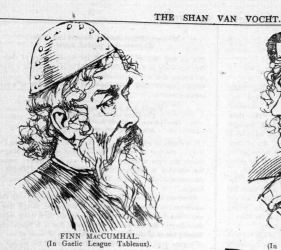

FINN MacCUMHAL.
(In Gaelic League Tableaux).

DIARMUID.
(In Belfast Gaelic Tableaux).

NOTES AND NEWS.

"How is Old Ireland, and how does she stand?"

THE OIREACHTEAS.

The Oireachteas, which took place in the Rotunda, Dublin, on 24th May, was a distinct success, and was even more strongly supported than last year.

In regard to the prize awards, we would point to the fact that the men of Munster, and especially of Co. Kerry, have carried all before them.

The Munster roll of honour includes — P. J. O'Shea (Belfast Gaelic League), 2 prizes, for original stories; J. J. Doyle (late Glasgow, now Belfast Gaelic League), prize for humorous tale; James Fenton, prize for story and special prize for folk-lore; Dermot Foley (Newry), prize for essay on St. Columba; Michael Martin (Dingle, Co. Kerry), prize for folk-lore; Jas. Fenton, prize for folk-songs. All these prize-winners hail from Co. Kerry. Mr. Denis Fleming, prize historical essay; Tadgy O'Donoghue (Dublin) and Denis Reen, prizes for unpublished songs; John O'Leary (Cork) dancing prize; and John O'Leary (Macroom), recitation prize, hail from Co. Cork; but possibly they, too, are Kerry men.

Now it is plainly time for the other provinces of Ireland to waken up.

Mr. P. T. M'Ginley (winning a £5 prize for original story) and Cornelius Boyle, of Doochany, Co. Donegal, saved the credit of Ulster. There is going to be a Gaelic festival for Donegal alone in September, and we trust it will bring to the front a host of talent which can be drilled to encounter the overweening Munster men before next May. Mr. T. Ward, of Belfast G.L., is, as far as we know, the only Connaught prize-winner in the composition section, but we are glad to see a few Connaught teachers on the list of those gaining the Cleaver prizes. Kerry men, however, headed the list—Patrick Murphy, of Ballinakiller, Cahirciveen, holding the William O'Brien Silver Cup, and John Hickson, Lispole, and E. O'Sullivan, Castledrum, coming second and third respectively.

The festival was followed by a conference of Gaelic League branches on Wednesday, 25th, and a public meeting in the Mansion House on the same evening.

THE FEIS CEOIL IN BELFAST.

Mr. O'Neill Russell contributes a special article on this subject. The feature which interested us most was the reception of the Scotch, Welsh, and Breton delegates, whose presence proved to the good people of Belfast that the Gaelic race is still a power in the world. Much regret was felt at the absence of both Dr. Douglas Hyde and Dr. Sigerson, the most distinguished representatives of the Irish Gaelic movement. The death of Mrs. Sigerson, which occurred not much more than a month before the May festival, was the regrettable cause of Dr. Sigerson's absence from the Feis and Oireachteas, in both of which he takes an ardent and active interest. We especially regret that Dr. Sigerson was unable to attend the Belfast gathering, where his presence might have reminded the people of Ulster that their province has at least one acknowledged poet to boast of.

Gaelic Tableaux in Belfast.

On the last night of the Feis Ceoil week a unique entertainment was given under the auspices of the local Gaelic League in Belfast—namely, a series of living pictures representing scenes from the Red Branch and Fenian tales. We give to our readers the programme in Irish, and it will be seen that Queen Meave, Ferdia and Cuchullin, Finn M'Coul and his knights, and the lovers, Diarmuid and Grania, were brought upon the stage. An ambitious venture many will say, and yet the unanimous opinion was that no more lovely pictures had ever been represented in Belfast. We were fortunate in securing a Queen Meave, who was stately and proud and fair; a dark, graceful Grania, athletic, finely-made young men to personate the warriors, and for Angus Og, a tall and slender youth, who personated the supernatural guardian of the lovers perfectly.

Coming to more modern subjects, we showed the visit of Granuaile to the Court of Elizabeth. The English Queen radiant with jewels, in all the majesty of her royal robes and crinoline formed an admirable contrast to the simply clad Queen of Connacht. Then came the scene in which the Earl of Howth's son is carried off by Gallowglasses in revenge for his discourtesy. Dark Rosaleen appeared next, a personification of Erin, leaning on her harp and wreathed with roses.

Scenes from peasant life, in which figured lovely red-cloaked colleens, were given last of all, and a step-dance, to the tune of the pipes, ended the entertainment.

The following members of the Belfast Art Society helped to organise the tableaux:—Miss J. Douglas, Miss Edith M'Cann, Miss Rosamund S. Praeger, Mr. John Carey, and Mr. Robert May (who undertook the post of armourer and designer). Mrs. Arthur Hutton was the leading spirit in arranging the ancient scenes, and co-operated with Miss Alice Milligan, Miss Dinsmore, Miss Johnston, Miss Praeger, Miss Moore, and others in preparing the dresses.

Mr. M'Ferran, Mr. M'Cowan, and Mr. Carey were the final managers of the performance. The Gaelic League, at a recent committee meeting, passed a hearty resolution of thanks to all these helpers. The programme of the ancient pictures are as follow (in Irish):—

50 Gaelic tableaux in Belfast: sketches and description by Milligan of show performed in 1898 by the Belfast Gaelic League and the Belfast Arts Society.

Without your help we feel very much afraid of trying them as none of us have had much experience in tableaux. I feel sure in as far as attracting a large audience they are quite sure to be successful, everyone in Dublin seems anxious for them ... you ... have such a genius for dramatic effects that if you came we are certain of a magnificent success.[35]

Milligan and Anna Johnston joined the Daughters of Ireland and helped with the organization's drama classes. In 1901, along with the Fay brothers, they staged two shows: the first took place in April and the second as a protest during Horse Show Week in August. The performances included short plays by Milligan as well as several different 'types' of tableaux: some conveyed stories, others depicted narratives from music; pictures were enacted by the women almost like the pageants that would characterize the later Gaelic League language demonstrations. The construction of the tableaux shows exemplified the material skills of local production. Great care and attention were devoted to making the clothes, to the designs for costumes, and to sourcing the materials in Ireland. The *United Irishman* commended their work: 'We have heard nothing but praise on every side of the tableaux, and the Inghinidhe na hÉireann are deserving of all praise'.[36]

One of the most often performed tableaux in pre- and post-partition Ireland was that of 'Erin Fettered, Erin Free'. Maud Gonne described how the children's matinée in August 1901, staged by Milligan and *Inghinidhe na hÉireann*, repeated the tableau of Ireland as a woman eventually liberated:

As the curtain rose on the last tableaux of Erin Fettered and Erin Free, and Erin as a beautiful girl with broken chains falling from her and a drawn sword in her hand appeared.[37]

Milligan witnessed an identical 'living picture' during a post-partition tableaux show held in the grounds of the Loreto Convent in Omagh. She declared in her press report, that people at the back of the field did not need to hear the orator's narrative descriptions because 'every one knew what the pictures meant':

Pale, downcast, mournful, a figure in white, veiled to the knee in transparent black, wearing heavy fetters. Behind her at the back of the stage an empty throne. Every individual in the audience knows at a glance it is Eire ... Justice at length advances, the fetters are removed and fall with a clang.[38]

People knew how to interpret the images that were a part of the visual iconography of Irish Republican consciousness. These pictures re-enacted on stages by living

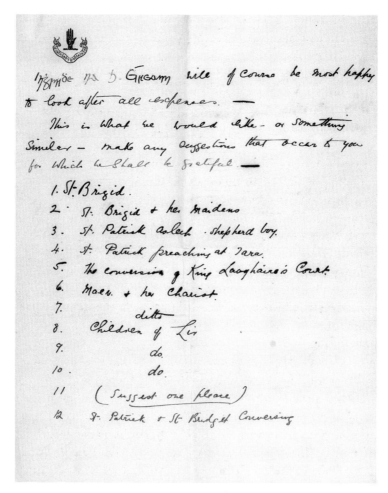

51 Maud Gonne's list of tableaux that she asked Alice Milligan to design for a
show with the Fay brothers and *Inghinidhe na hÉireann* (Daughters of Ireland)
in 1901.

people had been familiar since the late nineteenth century when they were
pubished in the Irish nationalist presses. Both the *Weekly Freeman* and *United
Ireland* carried a regular glossy pull-out colour supplement illustrating images
(usually female) of Ireland struggling against her colonial oppressor. Her ankles or
wrists were chained; sometimes she was gagged, usually depicted in a doorway
entering or pointing to a prison cell [Plate 18]. Such sketches were always
accompanied by a caption with the words 'Erin' is thinking or speaking. They are
very similar to the tableaux that Milligan staged in which the physical body was
also a symbolic representation that generated broader political and cultural

meaning. In tableaux Milligan re-activated familiar codes that were already in circulation in Irish melodrama, costume pageants and street parades, in theatre posters and in the illustrations in the nationalist press.

The *United Irishman* reported how the audience at the *Inghinidhe na hÉireann* show of April 1901 appealed for the women to re-enact the series of tableaux several times. It was in this very show that many of the later 1923 prisoners gained their first experience of performing tableaux:

> Maeve, greatest of Ireland's heroines, Grania Mhaol visiting Elizabeth and pulverising the virgin monarch, who strove to impress the splendid Irishwomen; St. Brigid, the Inghean Dubh, Red Hugh's mother; Sarah Curran, and Anne Devlin, the betrothed and faithful servant of Emmet. Ireland fettered and crouching over her unstrung harp at the base of the Celtic cross, and then Ireland Free, erect against the cross, her harp now strung at her feet, her green robe flowing round her, the cap of liberty on her head, and in her hand a shining sword. This tableau evoked a tremendous outburst of enthusiasm and shouts of 'Aris! aris!' caused its repetition again and again.[39]

Anne Devlin was a figure often portrayed through silent re-enactment on stage by Irish women at the beginning of the twentieth century. Luke Gibbons writes of Anne Devlin's unwillingness to betray Robert Emmet to the British in the face of torture as an 'act of intransigence' suggesting that 'Anne's silence is similar to her domestic or maternal persona. It is not a submissive silence, standing outside signification and, by extension, language power and representation.'[40] The pictorial stillness of Pat Murphy's 1984 film *Anne Devlin* is visually similar to the tableau versions performed by Irish women earlier in the century. It was the memory of this silence as an act of resistance that the women prisoners of 1923 re-animated when they re-staged Devlin and Emmet. Such silence under torture was protest. Silence after death was power. Just as Emmet's speech from the dock projected the republican struggle into the future, the pictures by the women hunger strikers of 1923 also projected, through silence, a future beyond the moment of their production [Plate 19]. Alice Milligan played a key part in finding and developing the form for this utopian possibility.

The radical modernism of Ireland's Cultural Revival

Milligan's dramas relied on a kind of performance practice that makes their value and meaning almost inaccessible to us now; it is as though they are written in a

52 One of only two surviving photographs of the Irish tableaux staged by the Belfast Gaelic League during the Irish Cultural Revival period. This picture depicts Anna Johnston as Princess Grania's waiting maid, from *The Gentlewoman*, London, 1898.

language that is not English and is not Irish, but something in-between. Can what was released to audiences then, be re-released to us now? Anna Johnston as the waiting maid forever pours the sleeping potion into a silver pot held by Princess Grania who was played by Edith McCann in 1898 in the Ulster Hall at the Gaelic League music festival. Queen Maeve looks out at us directly, clasping her spear and shield. This is the only image of Elsie McGowan ever seen. No records in the official archives chart her life. Resting on her shoulder in a white gown, hands clasped together, hair falling around a half secret smile is 'Miss Davidson' alias Daughter of Finbarr.

These are two of four surviving photographic images of Milligan's theatre practice. The photographs were probably not taken in context. The lighting suggests that they were restaged under the glass roof of photographic studios in Belfast and Letterkenny. Writing in 1931 of such nineteenth-century studio photographs, Walter Benjamin observed: 'Everything about these early pictures was built to last ... the very creases in people's clothes have an air of permanence'.[41] Yet, although these pictures are taken in a studio, they are meant to represent and convey 'live' performance. The theatre show is a display of stillness, yet the photograph cannot capture the 'aura' of that stillness. These pictures do not have the same unification, the same confidence in 'permanence'. They are part of a cultural movement to transform the static, to alter the un-democracy that has been permanent. These are anonymous costumed performers. They are not people photographed for themselves or because of who they are. They are photographed for the roles they perform. The women photographed in 1898 perform within a movement. The 'use' of their image is not for themselves; the 'use' of their image resides in the performance of Ireland. Writing of the French photographer Eugène Atget (1857–1927), Benjamin wrote that he had achieved 'the emancipation of the image from aura'. Atget 'looked for what was unremarkable, forgotten, cast adrift'.[42] It is perhaps in Benjamin's description of Atget that we get close to the significance of the tableaux images and the community theatre practice they played a crucial role in forming. These extraordinary pictures of the Irish tableaux in Belfast are from *The Gentlewoman*, a London magazine devoted to illustrated images of Empire – the travels of the English monarchy, the decadent pastimes of the aristocracy. The Irish tableaux in June 1898 were an amusing addition to their column about the successful music festivals of the 'Celtic fringe'. In this journal, these costumed images of 'yesteryear' from the loyalist bastion of Belfast, depicted nothing more than quaint 'gentle' women doing their bit to celebrate traditions that did not threaten Empire, but instead enhanced its cultured texture. They were performing local familiar parlour games in ambitious home-made native costume.

53 One of the four surviving photographs of Irish tableaux. This scene depicts the Queen
Maeve tableaux staged in Belfast in 1898, from *The Gentlewoman*, London, 1898.

But the potion that Johnston was pouring in 1898 was anything but a drug to induce sleep. This was not the moment at which Oisin was about to leave Ireland for the land of forgetfulness. Milligan's Ossianic trilogy, staged by the Irish Literary Theatre in 1900, explored the moment of his return. In her plays, audiences witness the moment that Oisin wakes up and touches a new Ireland that reactivates political consciousness. The audience and St Patrick watch as Oisin's re-found memories are enacted as tableaux on an inner stage; the personal is shared as the historically national. The caoine enacted at the end of the 'Brian of Banba tableaux series' demonstrated how the living in 1901 were alive to the possibilities of the undead; Queen Maeve and Elsie McGowen simultaneously look out at us in battle gear. A picture of a mythical struggle, it is also a struggle taking shape in Belfast in 1898. These pictures remain a memory of the beginning of re-memory. They depict radical cultural and language activists who were concerned with all that had been 'unremarked, forgotten, cast adrift' by the economic, social, political and cultural devaluation of Ireland under British colonial rule. These were people intent on exploring utopia. The Gaelic Legaue drama groups, with Milligan at the helm, developed a powerful theatrical genre that was able to generate a communal sense in a country (and a city) where community was sectarianized, where many women were denied votes, jobs and education, and Irish national history and language were outlawed.

The silence of the tableau was not a silence of submission. It was political. Tableaux operated through code. The women prisoners in A Wing of Kilmainham in 1923 did not need to tell the prisoners in B Wing what they were performing. The people at the back of the field in Omagh in 1938 did not need to hear an orator describe the tableaux on stage. They recognized what they were seeing; they understood the context and the iconography. What these audiences were seeing was not simply what was being performed in front of their eyes. The 'captions' to the images are implied and therefore endlessly 'open'. The 1898 photographs of tableaux are perhaps examples of what Andrew MacNamara calls, 'contra pictures' in which primitivism and modernity are fused.[43] Tableaux were deeply modern because they displayed a hyper-primitivism: they were a very self-aware part of a highly sophisticated visual culture. Their stillness and costumed reference to legend and precolonial Ireland (even in photographs) was not antiquated or anti-modern. In a period when Ireland was considered 'visually illiterate',[44] visual culture was a vital dynamic in reclaiming public space and in capturing the public imagination. The idea that modernism was something that happened abroad (in the economic markets won in places such as the 1893 Chicago World Fair) ignores the very modern technologies and culturally nuanced activism that operated at a local community level that was at the heart of the Revival.

The visual archive of photographs, the glass slides, sketches, drama reviews, musical scores and play scripts do not contain the aura or the resonant meaning of 'the community' essential to Milligan's vision for national theatre. The participatory 'live' event, the releasing of historical memory in public space, and the binding relationships of collegiality and co-operation were as much a part of Milligan's theatre practice as a printed script or a set of costumes. This is what makes Milligan's plays and tableaux so difficult to reproduce or to fully comprehend. Archival traces, such as these photographs give a glimpse of a national theatre practice that was linked with the movement to regenerate the Irish language. Community was at the heart of this project. Photographs and newspapers were critical aids in disseminating that memory. *The contest of the Druids with St Patrick at Tara* (1898) was the first recorded example of a play performed (see figure 42) in the Irish language and was a mixture of tableaux and spoken drama. As such, the show was a forerunner of the way in which Milligan's Ossianic trilogy was theatrically realized as a fusion of dramatic forms. Staged on 23 November 1898 at Letterkenny by members of the Gaelic League, the trilogy was in part performed in Irish and in part through tableaux.

Milligan helped organize cultural events for the Gaelic League in a number of Irish communities, including Liverpool, where she worked with Piaras Béaslaí. He agreed with her that drama helped to create a cultural community:

> Since the inception of the language movement more plays have been written in Irish than any other kinds of creative work … the reason … they find drama the easiest way of reaching the public … It is far easier to induce 300 people to come to a hall and witness a play in Irish than it is to induce 300 people to purchase and read a book in Irish. Even persons who do not understand a word of Irish can come to a play in that language … while those large number of English speakers who cannot read their own language can only be reached by the medium of drama.[45]

As Béaslaí suggests, the audience could follow the action and understand the Irish through interpreting the staged gestures and tableaux. The pictures illustrate the words in the same way as the personified body of Ireland often expressed meaning in the pull-out colour illustrations of the nationalist newspapers [Plate 20]. These illustrations were accompanied by text: both dialogue with each other in much the same way as graphic novels use images to communicate narrative.

John Berger wrote in *Ways of seeing* in 1972 that 'Images were first made to conjure up the appearance of something that was absent'.[46] What was absent in Ireland was an empowered public visual art that portrayed national history and

54 Photograph of tableaux staged in Cushendal, *c.*1906. This is when Roger Casement cleared an overgrown field for the stages to be built on.

Irish life. It was these images that Milligan wanted to conjure. There was a lasting structural legacy too in the monologue, the storytelling and the musical performance that often accompanied the 'living picture'. Its most striking features – the frozen moment, the suspension of action, the strangeness of breathing bodies held motionless, waiting, being heard in voices articulated by others offstage in song or storytelling – had a profound impact on Irish theatre. Theatrical stillness was key to the development of the Irish modernist aesthetic. Milligan's influential early tableaux shows were watched and admired by Yeats and by many others who went on to participate in Irish theatre. Yeats' 'Abbey style' was defined by stillness. In 1900, he argued in *Beltaine* that the aim of an Irish National Theatre was to make 'literary drama permanent in Ireland during our time, and give the Irish nation a new method of expression'.[47] He placed the emphasis of this 'new method of expression' on language. He told readers of *United Ireland* in 1903 that a national theatre must 'get rid of everything that is restless, everything that draws the attention away from the sound of the voice'.[48]

Yeats fined his Abbey actors for moving too much, for letting the books fall from their heads during rehearsal; threatened to put them in urns.

The Irish national theatre movement is famous for its reliance on language to provoke a communal consciousness.[49] But for Milligan, gesture was perhaps even more important than the spoken word. Yet a sense of communal identity was hard to achieve with people who did not share language and traditions, in a colonized country where words were censored, the experience of women suppressed, private letters blacked out, flags banned, meetings infiltrated; where sexuality was forced to operate in coded gesture; and where (as the vast archive of police records show) spoken words in public were often recorded by undercover government colonial officials. For Milligan, there was no boundary between disseminating ideas and protest on streets and performing images from Irish history and culture on official stages. Nor was there any 'official' stages for Irish drama until the Revivalists opened their own National Theatre in 1904. The tableaux produced on formal stages (such as the Gaiety, the Rotunda and the Father Mathew Hall) often resembled public demonstrations and the heavily costumed pageants orchestrated for the Gaelic League [Plates 21 and 22].

Influenced by Milligan's use of visual iconography as social protest, during the 1897 royal visit to Dublin, James Connolly and Maud Gonne used a magic lantern to project onto Dublin's city walls photographs of the famine that they had witnessed in the West of Ireland. The Land League in the 1880s similarly photographed scenes of Irish distress and evictions; they often re-staged evictions in cities and towns where they also projected photographs to rally support and raise funds. Another good example of this agitprop mode of theatre took place in front of the General Post Office on O'Connell Street, Dublin in 1905. The Gaelic League Committee, headed by Milligan, utilized 'living pictures' to protest against the Civil Service boycott of Irish language postal addresses. At this time the Irish language was under increasing official pressure to disappear. Gaelic League bank accounts were being closed down by the English government; anyone who displayed public commercial signs in Irish was arrested; and post that was written in Irish to Irish-language addresses was systematically destroyed. The *Weekly Freeman* reported how crowds gathered to watch a silent mime of this dispute when the parade reached Dublin's General Post Office. The crowd was invited to bear witness to the colonial state's discrimination:

> The platform itself represented in a concentrated form the G.P.O. with all
> its works and pomp. There is a counter – the inevitable counter. At one side
> stood an Irishman in typical Gaelic costume offering a parcel addressed in
> Irish to the affable clerk at the other side … but as the packages were

handed over to him, he, in the most deprecatory way, firmly, but surely sent them back.[50]

Tableaux operated as a link between ideas of national theatre and the cultural regeneration of the Irish language as a spoken medium. But they had other elective affinities too. Theatre, photography and the magic lanterns were the most immediately obvious of these; but cinema and art installation are by now also recognisably among them (see Plate 27).

Prisoners wrote to Milligan after 1916 saying that their moment of political consciousness came when they participated with her in forging local theatrical and cultural events. A letter from one Irish Volunteer in 1917 concluded: 'If we ever write the history of [the language movement in Castlecomer] we can tell of how you came to the rescue in the days when everyman's hand was against us'.[51] Jack Yeats' 1923 painting 'Communicating with Prisoners' depicts an act of similar solidarity in which women on the outside wave across to the women prisoners inside [Plate 23]. This image is the most resonant visualization of the historical solidarity that was being enacted in silent theatre inside the prison walls. By staging tableaux of Emmet and Devlin to their comrades in Kilmainham, the women hunger strikers of 1923 made symbols of their bodies. Discussing the hunger strike of 1981, Maud Ellmann suggests 'By hungering, the protestors transform their bodies into the "quotations" of their forebears and reinscribe the cause of Irish nationalism in the spectacle of starving flesh'.[52] The 1923 tableaux performance demonstrates how the meaning of these theatrical pictures could not be confined within the moment of their production. By embodying the past in 'living pictures' the prisoners were able simultaneously to envision a future.

Conclusion: 'The scattering of the company'

> This title scrawled on a page of one of the notebooks in the Bunting collection … Poignantly sad and touching, the song has historic memories. Bunting himself played it at one of the last social gatherings given in Belfast to Wolfe Tone before sailing for America. For me, the song suggests the scattering of another company that used to gather in Belfast, following faithfully in the track of those harp festival organisors, striving to revive Irish music and the Irish tongue …
>
> Alice Milligan, *Irish Statesman*, 16 June 1928.

Alice Milligan's commemorative obituary article for Conan Maol (John O'Shea) 'The scattering of the company' acknowledges him as a gifted teacher of Irish in Belfast before the Gaelic League was officially founded in the city. The 'company' that Milligan refers to was the language class that launched a vibrant and committed body of northern cultural activists; this was the group through which Alice Milligan first came into contact with Anna Johnston with whom she would work so closely in establishing an international journal to promote Irish culture. They held their language classes in the Ulster Museum and then in a noisy attic room above a linen warehouse on the Belfast quays. Milligan's prose reads like a homage not just for an individual but for the ideals of the United Irishmen and for the hard-working community generated a hundred years later during the Irish Cultural Revival. Her words are a lament for the lost moments of Belfast's rich cultural past, for friends who are gone and for a partitioned country in which she feels herself to be 'interned'. Later in the article, she records how in 1902 Conan Maol came by unexpectedly to keep her company in Belfast the night before their friend Anna Johnston was to be buried:

> One of the saddest, loneliest evenings of my life, I sat in the deserted home from which the parents and sister of Ethna Carbery had gone to the home in Donegal where she lay dead. Next day I was to follow … I was busy writing sad letters to break the news to many who would care. The door opened softly, without a knock. Conan came in and sat by the fireside with me, smoking and talking quietly.[1]

One of the key things that we learn from Alice Milligan's career is the importance and centrality of community. The 'historic memories' released by

Bunting's music and the 'historic memories' of the cultural activism of her own generation are connected by solidarity. Conan Maol's entrance into the empty house in Belfast where Milligan sat alone in despair at one of the 'saddest, loneliest' moments of her life is a metaphor for the broader movement that she and her comrades created together. The history of colonization that the Cultural Revivalists struggled to counter was saturated in such moments of premature loss, displacement, exile and personal pain.

Alice Milligan's writings map these recurring Irish historical narratives of familial displacement and longing in multiple literary and theatrical genres: she writes about land wars, evictions, the Famine, the 1641 massacres, the seventeenth-century plantations, emotional dispossessions, the denial of language and native cultural identity, numerous state executions, four rebellions, endless burials, the First and Second World Wars, the Irish War of Independence, the Civil War and Partition. This is no easy literature. This was no easy life to live. Forging cultural connections, which were local, national and international, was a profound intervention in a landscape defined by segregation and sectarianism. At the same time as she published her memories of Belfast's language movement, she wrote privately about the censorship of her own life in Co. Tyrone. A month before Milligan wrote her obituary article commemorating a previous era in the *Irish Statesman* in 1928, she posted a letter to William Smith O'Brien to tell him that she didn't have copies of her own work or the *Shan Van Vocht* for his archive collection. Her postscript to this letter reminds us that from 1921 to April 1953, Milligan lived in a new but not unfamiliar context of disempowerment, discrimination and severe lack of liberty that was at once personal and political. Aware that her own reputation as a republican may impact upon her brother's employment opportunities in the North (as well as on his fragile well-being as an alcoholic) Milligan warned O'Brien not to write to her on paper connected with the worker's movement for democracy:

> You will not mind my saying that it is not advisable to write to me on Transport Union paper (on envelope) I live as guest with a brother who is in Ulster government employment and not very progressive surroundings – I tucked your letter out of sight when it came, I never found it again.[2]

In the midst of her life as a dependent family carer, 'community' for Milligan could often only be reached at the level of the unconscious imagination. In 1930 when she was living 'interned … across the border',[3] she wrote to tell George Russell of a dream she had had of him and of their friend, the late Susan Mitchell. She suggests that the dream was connected to the disappointment she had

encountered the day before when her brother William drove his car in another
direction than the road she wanted to take:

> We drove part way to see you and I was disappointed when Willie turned
> the car down by Glen Lake instead … 'That's where Æ is painting', I said.
> In my dream I was walking all alone by the sea edge and met a happy party
> just like a group in your pictures chasing the waves and there was a donkey
> and … you were chatting away … when along the sea edge smiling and life
> like came Susan and walked among us and I said 'I never knew we could get
> across these sands this way' – so much lovely colour was in the picture –
> cloudy mountains, placid dreamy sea – I never once dreamed of her before
> – it was like a compensation for my disappointment of 12 July.[4]

The death of her brother and nephew only released Milligan into further intensive
work as a full-time carer. In 1940 she wrote to Máire Nic Shiubhlaigh: 'I am
awfully tied since my brother's death – his wife an invalid with loss of memory &
liable to have another stroke. I can get help but no one to stay at night. I can rarely
be a night away.'[5]

   She could not get to Belfast or cross the border to Dublin in order to broadcast
her own work; indeed, she couldn't even receive the Free State radio at 'home':

> It is only in past years I was free politically – even yet I wouldn't be free only
> my sister in law is too ill to interfere. It used to be I couldn't bring the press
> into the house – and even yet we don't get Athlone on the wireless … you
> asked me about writing … I can't undertake to do anything.[6]

Milligan's version of not doing anything included writing radio shows about the
theatre movement, drafting poems about many figures such as the Yeats sisters,
editing early play scripts, translating Hyde's poems into English, publishing weekly
poems and articles in nationalist newspapers, raising subscriptions for Joseph
Campbell's New York *Irish Review*, fundraising for Indian famine relief while
campaigning in every way possible against Partition. Milligan had fought in the
anti-colonial movement; she spent the last three decades of her life fighting in the
anti-Partition movement. She was a critical founder of both. The ongoing struggle
she endured after 1921 does not mean that her cultural and political life's work
had been a failure. In 1940 she wrote: 'I am at present absorbed politically in the
North where the fight goes on.'[7]

   After Milligan's own death in April 1953, the Department of External Affairs
circulated a document to its employees (possibly written by a young Conor Cruise
O'Brien) that read:

> Her magazine [the *Shan Van Vocht*] reflected her personality; for in its pages literature and politics were mingled without incongruity ... the radius of her friendship was an index of her quality. W.B. Yeats, Standish O'Grady, Arthur Griffith, John O'Leary – these are only a handful of the names which add up to a roll call of modern Irish history.[8]

The 'radius of her friendship' is indeed a 'who's who' of almost a century in Irish literary and political history. But this astonishing checklist also reveals to us the textured networks of connection that Milligan generated throughout her life-time. Milligan transgressed all formal social boundaries and she saw no difference between politics and culture or between literature and activism. She sought out cultural ways to negotiate religion and identity. She campaigned for political prisoners through the state as well as through poetry; she developed links between theatre and language teaching; between local community and national protest. She is the one figure who connects the multiple alignments and individuals that made up the Irish Cultural Revival.

By reassessing Milligan's life we can chart the imaginative connections and collaborations that changed Irish cultural history and which ironically left few officially recognized traces. Alice Milligan's early cultural work in Antrim with Roger Casement, for instance, provides a critical Irish anti-colonial background to his international human rights work. Milligan's persistent campaigning to save Casement's life in 1916 forms a significant part of her own human rights work. Their friendship was deeply embedded within a shared history of local activism; of fundraising for Irish language classes; the development of diplomas and prizes; work that was undertaken at the most local level in the early years of the twentieth century across the north. In July 1916, Milligan revealed to Clement Shorter how she found herself selling books in Liverpool late one Sunday afternoon: 'In order to raise my fare to Dublin'.[9] She was returning at what she hoped would be a liminal moment when further loss of life might be avoided. She speculated in the wake of the Battle of the Somme that the Ulster unionists could use their favour with the British government to support Casement: 'I think I will return to Ireland to find if there is a softening feeling in Ulster which might be worked to get them, the Carsonites, to ask for a reprieve.'[10] Milligan hoped that the bond formed abroad between Irish soldiers fighting at the Somme would engender a new understanding of each other at home: 'For just three or four weeks Protestants and Catholics particularly in County Tyrone joined together.'[11] Her letters of supplication to the British home office in London convey her belief that the tragedy of war experienced by Irish men and women abroad would allay further strife at home:

I have reason to believe that the good sense of the rank and file has returned to them since they have seen the horrors of war abroad, they will not so lightly speak of civil war – but the formation of the Ulster Volunteer army, instead of a united Irish army, was a threat to Irish liberty which could not be ignored. Roger Casement and others answered that threat in the only possible way. If he hangs without the Ulstermen saying a word on his behalf, it will read very badly in history.[12]

After visiting Milligan in 1929, the poet Pádraic Colum observed that community was at the heart of what motivated Milligan to write: 'she has only written out of some affection for some comrade or out of some mood of exaltation that she wanted some comrades to share in; never for fame and certainly never for money.'[13] Not writing for money or personal fame was a characteristic of Milligan's generation; she and her associates most often worked in an alternative economy in which their skills were exchanged. The Irish language is a good example of how such a gift exchange operated. Thomas Concannon translated Milligan's work into Irish. In a letter dated February 1900 he discusses his translation of one of her stories while asking her to respond to a collection of Irish language fiction that he posts to her. An extract from this letter gives us a glimpse of the generosity of time that the Revivalists gave to each other in the promotion of 'the cause' for which they felt they were collectively working:

> Manuscript reached me yesterday. The language is most simple and easy translated. I have one page done already. Send on a second instalment, I will have it ready by Sunday evening I think. How long will the story be? There is no trouble at all in getting it published … I would like to do something for the *Independent* for it is doing good work for the cause and the conduct of the Irish department, is a most gracious young person and an enthusiast in the cause … You know Miss Butler don't you … Send on the rest of Brian's story anyhow I.O. and I will turn it out as quickly as I possibly can. Any short articles or stories you may have from time to time that you think would go well into Irish well – send them along …[14]

Concannon's friendly response to translation is the antithesis of the negative extremism that Milligan encountered from some Gaelic League members who argued that Irish identity could only be expressed in the Irish language. Milligan could obviously read Irish and must have studied it for the best part of her life. Yet while she was at the frontline of the language movement she worked hard to keep the cultural movement open. The nuanced space in which she operated made the Irish language available to people who were not nationalists or republicans; to

55 This sketch of Roger Casement was made by Milligan in the court room during his trial in 1916. The picture was confiscated by a guard who when returning it to her after the trial said: 'You note I allowed you to finish it before I took it away.' This story was told to the author by Sheila MacAleer who heard it from Milligan in the 1930s.

those who did not define themselves as Irish or consider Ireland their shared 'common land'.[15] She made a vital point that 'the language movement' was not 'identical with nationality'.[16] She articulated what Thomas MacDonagh would later define as 'the Irish mode' when she made a case for the intrinsic historical and contemporary value of the English language as spoken in Ireland. In some rough lecture notes Milligan makes clear her position with reference to three of Ireland's most significant revolutionary thinkers:

> In this English tongue … the hopes the aspirations … have been given … the strongest patriotism. Wolfe Tone's diary – the dying words of Robert Emmet – the jail journal of Mitchel – the Lyrics of Thomas Davis – a man's soul is more than our words – a nation's life is not bound up in its distinction of language … a study of its history – which is its past to nurture an ideal which is its future …[17]

We most often think about the Irish Revival as a movement in parts: the literary renaissance, the establishment of the Irish National Theatre, the co-operative societies and the language revival. Milligan viewed the Gaelic League as the one organization that connected every part of the Revival and made them cohere as a movement. Milligan envisaged the language movement as a revolutionary weapon, not just as an eventual outcome of that revolution. She defined 'the Gaelic Revival' movement as 'the very soul of democracy and patriotism'.[18] It was in their daily lives that Milligan and her generation experienced the 'democracy' of a republic. In the last decade of the nineteenth century they took control of the postal systems, the transport networks, and the printing presses to completely re-imagine the lives mapped out for them as subjects of empire. They established co-operatives in the face of colonial economic embargoes; they created an international movement to save a language that was on the brink of extinction after years of political neglect and legal repression. By producing an Irish national literature and by opening the Irish National Theatre they proclaimed culture as a priority of their new society. They engendered a political power into this new Irish culture that made it utterly transformative.

Their greatest achievement was probably the networks of solidarity that they forged with each other in a colonial landscape that advocated exile, poverty and isolation. It was Milligan's belief that by acting collectively the Irish could achieve a cultural identity: 'in the teeth of English opposition' and 'without English aid'.[19] She told an audience of Irish emigrants in London in 1900 that the cultural movement was about finding lost voices and listening closely to what those voices had said in the language that they had spoken. By searching out the suppressed and the forgotten and the marginalized in 'our colonial history' and while living under the rule of 'an alien government' together they would find themselves and create a new sense of 'home':

> The Gaelic Revival teaches us to listen to these voices – it brings you to your native hill sides – it teaches of honour and love and comradeship among you – here in the cosmopolitan capital – the Irish – you no longer become lost in this vast Babylon.[20]

Milligan was eager to unite the central body of the Gaelic League executive to the needs of local communities. These communities were very often not on the island of Ireland: she sought out Irish emigrants and worked to help them form their own Gaelic League branches. In 1905 she wrote to Liverpool-Irish playwright and Gaelic League activist Piaras Béaslaí to offer her assistance in supporting the Irish cultural movement in Liverpool:

What is the state of the case in Liverpool branches? Are either of them in need of funds for rent, teaching, prize funds for any deserving object? … Let me know … I would like to be a *help*, if there is need for help in your work … I could give you help and suggestions for dramatic entertainments … as my great forte is the costuming of historical plays – tableaux …[21]

Her local activism meant that she worked hard to discover what Irish language and cultural associations required in their earliest days. She translated her findings back to the centre at meetings in Dublin and to a national and international audience through newspaper articles.

In further describing the work that she could contribute to the Liverpool Irish movement, Milligan demonstrates that she was one of the pioneers at the very beginning of the League's travelling teacher programmes. Her career gives us a unique insight into the micro-economics of the cultural movement that she was very much a part of constructing and road-testing. In a second letter to Béaslaí she informed him about the challenge she had set herself in raising funds for the Central Executive in Dublin, while simultaneously responding to the complex needs of the local branches. Her letters provide the missing economic and experimental individual dimension of the cultural movement. Milligan's career shows us an alternative version of the Cultural Revival narrative before it was 'set down hard and fast':

I could give a lecture in a small hall for a Gaelic League branch [in Liverpool]. I bring a lantern, slides and screen and am responsible financially if such a thing should occur as a loss but hitherto everything has worked well. The system and business arrangements of the lecture scheme have not been set down hard and fast yet … I am more or less experimenting. Last month I lectured entirely for the benefit of the Central funds taking all proceeds outside expenses. But I only visited towns where I depended on the general public, or where the branches had no need of money but were willing to work for the movement generally – But to continue this system would make me a mere money raiser for the League and would preclude me from visiting country districts where a struggle is being made to keep up a native district teacher – So I have tried to arrange in Ireland for a series of meetings, by which such hard working branches will benefit. That is after defraying expense & and small fee to the Central funds – the organisers of the meeting make proceeds for their local needs.[22]

After Milligan published her first United Irish play in 1898 and after she staged the first Irish language play in Letterkenny, Douglas Hyde wrote to congratulate her. In doing so he acknowledged Milligan's commitment to the local dimension of the cultural movement: 'I see you have now turned playwright! You really can put your hand to anything. I thought it very good. You see clearly as I too have always seen, that the League's work is nearly useless till it gets into the Irish districts. On the whole you are going well.'[23] Hyde may have been the key founder of the Gaelic League, but Alice Milligan did much to create the cultural conditions that would give the language a resonant bedrock within Irish communities. She also devoted much of her life's work to publicizing the philosophy of Gaelic League and to fundraising for its success. She had an especially profound impact in the north where she helped open teaching colleges, set up language classes, and initiate Irish cultural events. For Milligan, the search for an Irish national theatre was the same as the development of an Irish language movement. In connecting her ideas for national theatre with the League's branch system, Milligan devised a way to project Irish culture out from the centres of Dublin and Belfast and into the future. Milligan worked to stage plays through the silence of gesture (as with the tableaux), in English, with music, through bi-lingual scripts and storytelling, and in Irish. She included audiences in the production of plays and in the understanding of the productions they witnessed.

Milligan's career is a portal to the earliest days of the Irish national theatre movement. Between 1897 and 1901 there were few Irish plays or scenes of Irish drama (and tableaux) written by Irish writers that were ready for performance. Milligan was ready with plays, scripts, costumes, scenes of tableaux and ideas for staging at the very moment that the concept of an Irish national theatre came collectively into being. Her early theatre work was the touch-paper for an emerging generation of theatre practitioners. At a time when Ireland had no national drama, Milligan opened up the archive of early Irish literature to argue that bardic recitals were a foundational example of Irish drama. 'English is a great literature … we have something as unique as the tale of Troy … in drama and in lyric and in song … a priceless inheritance the voice of our country'.[24] Milligan aimed to facilitate drama in Irish communities everywhere. She did not value one language above another nor did she view that a native literature resided in one region of Ireland. Instead, she promoted the production of scenes of daily life, of contemporary political protest, of the visual enactment of drama from songs that were familiar and known. She made everything available through newspapers; gave over copyright to the Gaelic League; wrote everything to exist in both languages. It is little wonder that her contemporaries considered her to be 'the most successful producer of plays before the Abbey got its triumphant way'.[25]

Yet the influential success of Milligan's theatre work lay most often in what Milligan stimulated and encouraged in other people's creative practice. There are numerous small examples to illustrate this: George Russell was inspired to write his play *Deirdre* after watching Milligan's tableaux of that Irish legend in 1901 [Plate 24]. Pádraic Colum records how he began to write plays after seeing Milligan's early dramas. Yeats wrote that he wanted to hear his own drama spoken in Dublin accents after Milligan and the Fay brothers cast her plays with Irish rather than English actors. These early plays provided vital early performance opportunities for the performers who would become the great Abbey actors. In fact, Milligan performed on stage with Sarah Algood in 1901. Because she aligned herself with Irish feminist groups, her plays gave many young women their first break in theatre: Máire Nic Shiubhlaigh had joined the Gaelic League in 1898 and the Daughters of Ireland in 1900. Milligan immediately cast her as Deirdre in her tableaux production staged in Dublin; Russell went onto cast her as the lead in his play of the same name after witnessing this show. Molly Algood would later play Deirdre in Synge's posthumous *Deirdre of the sorrows* in 1910.

Milligan worked with the Fay brothers in productions of her plays and tableaux and worked with George Moore and Yeats on the second season of the Irish Literary Theatre. She was a great supporter of the Ulster Literary Theatre, the Abbey and the achievements of Yeats, Gregory and Synge. But her conception of Irish national theatre was localized, decentred and did not reside in a building or an in-house of professional players and playwrights. Milligan rejected the institutional organization of national theatre in both Dublin and Belfast in order to facilitate an engagement with Irish drama within local districts and Irish communities at home and abroad. Such commitment to local audiences was vital to Milligan's theatre practice: she published plays and costume designs in newspapers to make them democratically available at a reasonable price, in multiple copies, and quickly enough to be staged by small groups that lacked resources.

The shows that so impressed Douglas Hyde, W.B. Yeats and George Russell had all developed out of Milligan's Gaelic League work in the north. It was after seeing Milligan's work in Belfast that Maud Gonne wrote: 'you are so clever and have such a genius for dramatic effects'.[26] It is no coincidence that Milligan was still editing and revising her script of *Oisín in Tír na nÓg* in Omagh in 1940 for Máire Nic Shiubhlaigh to produce on radio. This was a play first staged in Belfast in 1899 when it embodied the people and the ideas of the Revival; this was a play that when performed again in Belfast in 1917 by the Morrow brothers (former members of the Belfast Arts Club and active members of the Ulster Literary Theatre) released ideas about national memory and the dangers of both remembering and forgetting. Milligan's career reveals to us for the first time the prominence of a visual culture in a theatre movement that has so far been heralded for its textual literary achievements. Some of the visual cultural practice that influenced Milligan came out of the arts schools in Belfast and the technologies of the prominent unionist cultural organizations that she was part of in the 1880s.

Milligan's theatre productions in Belfast gave centre stage to the work of artists such as the sculptor and children's illustrator Rosamund Praeger; painters such as Robert May and John Carey; watercolourist Grace Douglas who had studied art in Paris and Italy. Milligan incorporated into the Revival photography and magic lantern shows; she had gained experience of both as a member of the Belfast Antiquarian Society and the Belfast Naturalist Field Club. Milligan's cultural practices thus open up a set of forgotten associations that existed between late nineteenth-century northern unionism and the arts in Ireland. There are obvious reasons why this and other archives are hard to trace. The history of magic lanterns in Ireland is difficult to retrieve: glass slides smash and magic lanterns were quickly replaced by the technologies that promoted the moving image. But their disappearance from the archives does not lessen their impact on the formation of an independence movement in Ireland: for Milligan, visual projections were a central means of teaching, of protest, and of theatre.

The success of Milligan's cultural practice resided in its radical modernism: in the nuanced way in which she fashioned ideas of community out of what was at once familiar and new. People could relate to what they saw on stage because they created what they performed themselves. Similarly, Irish readers could immediately recognize and connect with Milligan's literary publications and journalism: she expressed histories, legends, stories and ideas that were already resting in the national consciousness like sediment. This was something that the founder of the Gaelic Athletic Association, Michael Cusack, communicated to Milligan in 1897: 'I recognized the expression of my own dreams … when I read the *Shan Van Vocht*.'[27] The Belfast journal that Milligan co-founded with Anna Johnston was another of those conceptual moments that would have a power beyond measure not least on global Irish networks in places as far apart as Buenos Aires, South Africa and Scotland. As the *Irish Book Lover* pointed out in 1953: 'This paper had an immense influence on the early republican movement … the poetic publications of these two enthusiastic women were an inspiration when the Irish Ireland movement was probably at its nadir.'[28] Milligan's cultural work had most impact at the start of events that kept changing as rapidly as she kept moving: the traces of her initial work were quickly incorporated into what would become, in Connolly's words, 'the cornerstones' of the nation.[29]

By 1896 Milligan firmly believed in 'separatism from imperialism'. Yet the political neutrality and the anti-sectarian policy of the Gaelic League were critical to her ideas of cultural practice and political protest:

THIS BOOK, PUBLISHED AT THE REQUEST OF
SOME EXILES IN THE ARGENTINE REPUBLIC,
WHO CHERISH IRELAND'S HOPE, IS DEDICATED
TO

DR. GEORGE SIGERSON,

AS ONE TO WHOM THEY, WITH ME, WOULD
DESIRE TO YIELD A MEASURE OF THE HOMAGE
DUE TO HIS FAME AS A POET AND INTERPRETER
OF OUR NATIVE GAELIC BARDS; BUT ABOVE
ALL, IN RECOGNITION OF HIS STEADFAST
FRIENDSHIP TO CHARLES KICKHAM AND JOHN
O'LEARY

"beannaċt le caṫaiḃ na ḃ-ḟiann"

56 Dedication page of Milligan's 1908 collection of poems *Hero Lays*, edited by Æ;
the collection was financed by the Irish community in Argentina who had
subscribed to the *Shan Van Vocht* in the 1890s.

The Gaelic League's neutrality ... it says to the Republicans and
Parliamentarians alike – Speak Irish – it opens its classes and attracts to its
ranks and admits to its council men of every political persuasion ... it is our
duty to be heart and soul with the Gaelic League helping this to be done –
and when we have learned Irish – we can say things that it is not the duty of
the Gaelic League to say and which it is not necessary to say at Gaelic
League meetings. At the Gaelic League it is good to mix and mingle with
people of another way of thought ... all these influences are awake and at
work in Ireland at the present moment.[30]

It was no easy achievement to 'mix and mingle with people of another way of
thought'. This was especially true of the cultural work Milligan undertook
throughout her life with family members who held differing political views to her
own. Milligan faced endless (often very public) recriminations from unionists and
nationalists. The north was at the heart of much of this conflict. From the very
outset, Milligan was aware that the north presented a particular set of challenges
that were equally rooted in both the sectarian colonial plantations and the

revolutionary United Irish movement. The north was always the unofficial centre to Milligan's work: she not only attempted to make the north a key part of the Irish Revival, but she worked hard to devise forms of cultural production that were inclusive of religious, regional and political difference.

From her first publications Milligan began to explore the kinds of difficulties any united independence movement would face if the north was not included. In her 1890 novel *A Royal Democrat* a southern Irish MP standing in Belfast is asked: 'Are the Northerns as black as they are painted?' His answer illustrates the complex multiplicity of identity politics in late nineteenth-century Ireland: 'Without believing any nonsense about there being two nations in Ireland, I would say that there are a goodly number in Belfast and County Down who have nothing Irish about them.'[31] Milligan attended many political pro and anti-Home Rule meetings in the late 1880s. She uses her fiction to place misinformation and public prejudice into a realm of national debate. When asked by a character in the novel to describe Belfast's Ulster Presbyterians, Kildare reflects:

> There are many of them who are shrewd, and enlightened – worth winning over, in fact, for their principles are democratic enough, and I think their opposition to us is carried on principally on religious grounds. They truly hate Catholics, most of them; and you have noticed, I'm sure, that the Ulster Unionist leaders, where they are not of the landlord party who encourage religious strife for their own ends, are, and have been in the past, Low Church clergymen or Presbyterian ministers.[32]

As this extract shows, even in her early twenties Alice Milligan displayed an articulate awareness of contemporary politics. She spent her life trying to achieve a space in which culture and politics could initiate dialogue. The *Irish Times* wrote after her death that she had succeeded in this aim: 'Alice Milligan showed that an honourable synthesis was possible. Her political idealism and literary achievement were interlocking expressions of a forthright and withal sensitive personality. She attained a harmony of ideas which in no way conflicted with one another.'[33] She entered the Revival movement with an astute sense of her own political journey: she knew that as a northern Protestant Irish Republican woman who was a writer, a cultural practitioner and a political activist, she embodied everything that was troubling in Ireland's history and everything that would disturb its future.

Milligan's ideas of Irish culture were communitarian and deeply political. Hers was a committed art that was feminist and modernist to its core. The reasons why Milligan has been written out of Ireland's cultural history are a key part in developing our understanding of her story. All her life Milligan aligned herself with what her friend Molly Killeen referred to as 'the remnant who stayed outside'.[34] Their histories, their literature and politics simply did not enter into the canonical frameworks of an Irish culture that could be institutionalized, celebrated, taught, performed, exhibited, published or republished. Irish women, in particular, were very conscious of being written out of the events and organizations they helped create. Jenny Wyse Power wrote to tell Milligan about the self-congratulatory stance taken by their male counterparts in the theatre movement. The new history of the theatre movement already being promoted in 1902 by Yeats did not include the profound influence of the women who had inspired, written, performed and funded so much early Irish drama:

> I didn't go until the last performance but on the whole they were really good. Mr Russell and Mr Yeats each made speeches praising the Fays for having founded the National Theatre – and never once referred to the Society [Daughters of Ireland] that had financed the whole affair.[35]

In the pages of the *Shamrock* in 1919 Susan Mitchell argued for the inscription of the critical part played by women in Irish history:

> The story of the men who loved Ireland has often been told, and I, with other Irish women, rejoice to do them honour, but I am a little jealous that of Irishwomen the hero tale has not been told, for they too love their country and work for it, and it is time their candle was taken out of its bushel and set upon a candlestick to give light to the dwellers in this our house.[36]

She argued that Milligan was a dynamic force in shaping new political and cultural conceptions of the Irish nation. Milligan, with all her strange idiosyncrasies and 'Ulster grit', had acted when 'the men were listless and without hope', and in a 'dark disheartened day' had taken 'up the torch of the fallen runners and carried it bravely forward'.[37] Conceiving of Irish anti-colonial history as a series of continuities through which each generation inherits the baton from its predecessor, Mitchell described Milligan as the latest runner in a political marathon inaugurated by the Fenians in the very year that she was born:

> To this end the torch was handed on by the runners through the centuries, and when one fell another took his place, and I think that Alice Milligan is the link that binds the nationality we know to-day to the Fenian movement whose spirit informs all of her work.[38]

Susan Mitchell tried to write Irish women such as Alice Milligan back into the story of Ireland in 1919 [Plates 25 to 28]. Her words reveal how conscious Irish women were during the Irish War of Independence of their own increasing lack of independence. The human rights of Irish women, Mitchell argued, were being further erased in Irish social, political and cultural life. One of the key methods of erasing human rights is to erase people from history. After 1921, Milligan had an intense awareness that she was being censored, interned, silenced. She was a woman whose life was committed to the achievement of a democratic independent United Ireland: she was the unmarried dependent who lived under Partition as a full-time carer for family members and within an undemocratically elected state that opposed her political world view and did not acknowledge her cultural or literally activism.

Milligan spent most of her life crossing cultural and political boundaries. As a woman active in political life, and as a northern Protestant committed to the republican cause, she complicates traditional historical cartographies. Milligan's story is not an easy one to tell or to understand. So many women are defined in society by their sexuality, their marital status and their relationships with men. Similarly confusing for contemporary society is the political makeup of her family and Milligan's cultural collaborations with them. That her family grave was desecrated by both loyalists and republicans proves that the complexity of her familial politics (unionists, members of the British army, OBE winners) was not easy to accept in a climate that demanded clear-cut religious and political affiliations.

In retrieving Milligan's story from a scattered archive we can see how she was concerned with constructing a cultural movement from another scattered unofficial archive. By assessing her cultural work for the first time we can re-evaluate what we as a society value and remember. When Alice Milligan died in April 1953 she died in poverty in a cottage kept by two sisters who were not related to her. She had nothing. She left nothing. There were no daughters, grand-daughters or sons. There was no house that had stored all of her effects and publications. Letters that she received after Partition were hidden, censored or lost. Who would collect her papers? Where would they be catalogued and stored? In Northern Ireland? In the Republic? Some friends did send in letters and documents to a Brother Allen of O'Connell Schools in Dublin who hoped to write a biography about her in 1954. Many of these papers came from the very boxes that Milligan had left in Dublin when she fled with her British army brother to the north during the Civil War. Some of Ernest Milligan's daughters had kept letters and a diary that has now been deposited with the National Library of Ireland. Most of Milligan's conversation and ideas reside in the vast collections of letters that she wrote and that her comrades in the Revival received and kept. Letters, like newspapers, are the key to understanding the Irish Cultural Revival. The storing of letters and the gifting to national archives demonstrates an astute confidence that what belonged to them (what was created by them) formed a key part of Ireland's national history.

But the vast bulk of Milligan's story can be found in the Irish newspapers. Culture, for Alice Milligan, was the daily news. Newspapers were like letters. They were personal and directly addressed the communities she wanted to reach and to hear from. They were cheap, local, national and international. Newspapers connected a broad readership through Ireland's excellent transport links: along with the six daily postal deliveries, newspapers were the engine that fired the Irish Cultural Revival. They gave Milligan, like so many of her contemporaries, a voice and an audience. Milligan published her poems, short stories, plays, essays, association minutes, Gaelic League reports, travelogues, memoirs, letters, journalism, reviews and opinions in the unindexed pages of over sixty Irish newspapers from the 1880s through to the late 1940s. Even Yeats in his later years still published his poetry in the pages of the Irish newspapers. For those who helped shape the Irish Cultural Revival, newspapers remained a direct and public way to place culture at the centre of daily politics and protest. The story of the Irish Women's Association; the responses to her controversial first novel; the fascinating story of Belfast's cultural history; Milligan's epic travels as a Gaelic League worker; the 1898 centenary, the drama movement and her work in founding an anti-Partition movement in Omagh – indeed, so much of the information in this book came out of public archives.

In July 1916 Alice Milligan wrote to acknowledge the death of Jenny Wyse Power's daughter and in doing so she remembered an earlier time when the daughter had performed Irish tableaux:

> What a loss to Ireland, of one who was so learned in the most essential things of Gaelic Culture, and so young. Many will sorrow for you and with you. I remember her as Finola, protecting her little brothers, and in the Transfiguration scene, looking heavenward – in what grave sad scenes many of our actors have figured in this year of mourning.[39]

So many of the friends Milligan had worked with in the Cultural Revival died in 1916. It was an ominous and tragic and confusing year of bloodshed, executions, deportations and imprisonment. Milligan described to Sinéad de Valera that she felt something had come to pass that had 'been foreseen and foretold'.[40] This was an anxiety that Yeats also felt when he contemplated whether 'that play of mine sent out certain men the English shot'. People who died in the aftermath of 1916 became fixed in Milligan's memory, often in the theatrical pictorial roles she had witnessed and directed so many years before. Yeats' poem 'The circus animal's desertion' captures what the collective performance of tableaux meant during the Irish Cultural Revival period and what the recollection of the tableaux came to mean in the years that followed Partition: 'Character isolated by a deed / To engross the present and dominate memory.'[41] The Easter Rising engendered a new static dimension to these early tableaux shows, as though the body of a nation still awaiting speech had been stilled and silenced in the waiting. There are so many scenes of tableaux in Irish literature and drama: Gabriel's gaze in Joyce's *The Dead* fixed upon his wife Gretta as she remembers another love from another time in another place that he cannot access apart from in his own imagination. And perhaps it is at the level of the imagination that Milligan's ideas reside. Her cultural and political activism communicated to an unknown future that depended on nothing less than a radical act of hope:

> Freedom is as yet to all appearances a far off thing; yet must we who desire it work for it as ardently and as joyously as if we had good hope that our own eyes should behold it.[42]

Notes

Introduction

1 A. Roy, *Listening to grasshoppers* (2009), p. x.

2 Sheila Turner Johnston argued in 1994 that Milligan's activities and literature should be relegated safely to the past: 'Alice's style and language are that of the late 19th century and early 20th century. So are her politics. If you superimpose upon her any prejudgments formed by the events in late 20th century Ireland you do her a great disservice. She is not here now to give her opinions, so let us leave her in her own day or leave her alone.' *The harper of the only God* (1993), p. 4.

3 'In memoriam Francis Ledwidge' in S. Heaney, *Opened ground* (1998), pp 176–7.

4 *Shamrock*, 1 Mar. 1919.

5 Ibid.

6 *Irish Review* Apr.–Sept. 1914.

7 *Irish Statesman*, 2 Jan. 1926.

8 W.B. Yeats, *Autobiographies* (1955), p. 449.

9 In 1941 Irish Taoiseach Éamon de Valera awarded Milligan an honorary doctorate on behalf of the National University of Ireland.

10 The exhibition was opened in November 2010 by Fiona Shaw and ran until March 2011. Video and photographic documentation along with a curator's tour of the exhibition can be seen on YouTube. I am working with the National Library of Ireland to create an online version of the exhibition that will include all the media coverage, exhibits, photographic and video documentation as well as all digital content that appeared in the exhibition. It is hoped the exhibition will also travel to Northern Ireland and the US.

11 G. Russell, *Letters of Æ*, ed. A. Denson (1961), p. 50.

12 D. Kiberd, *Inventing Ireland* (1995), p. 3.

Chapter One: Alice Milligan: a life

1 *Irish Homestead*, 28 Feb. 1920.

2 *Irish Review*, Apr.–Sept. 1914.

3 Ernest Milligan Papers in the private possession of Alice Milligan's great nephew Michael Stone.

4 J.W. Henderson, *Methodist College Belfast, 1868–1938*, 2 vols (1939), I. p. 122.

5 At the age of eighty-four she told one journalist that at 'Methodee' she 'became an Intermediate Exhibitioner. With the prize money she won she went to Donegal to study Irish.' Interview with Kevin McGrath, *Sunday Press*, Sept.–Oct. 1946.

6 Ceannt and O'Brennan Papers, NLI MS 41,492 /1–5.

7 *King's College department for ladies: calendar*, syllabus of lectures 1887–8, pp 353–6.

8 The fees for attendance were a guinea a term and 5s. per lecture. Milligan appears in the King's College for Women examination class lists for Christmas 1886, Easter Term 1887 and Midsummer Term 1887.

9 Ceannt and O'Brennan Papers, NLI MS 41,492 /1–5.

10 *Glimpses of Erin* (1888), p. 264.

11 *A Royal Democrat* (1890), p. 43.

12 Ceannt and O'Brennan Papers, NLI MS 41,492 /1–5.

13 *An Claidheamh Soluis*, 1 Oct. 1904.

14 *Sunday Press*, Sept.–Oct. 1946.

15 Ceannt and O'Brennan Papers, NLI MS 41,492 /1–5.

16 Ibid. The scholars included: 'Sir John Gilbert whose works on the period of

Owen Roe's Wars I was then studying … Prof Ingram of TCD author of *Who fears to speak of '98*. I made friends with Fr Denis Murphy S.J. who was writing the life of *Red Hugh O'Donnell*.' In later years these texts would provide the background for many of her historical poems and plays.

17 Alice Milligan Diary, NLI MS 47,782.
18 J.H. & M.E. Cousins, *We two together* (1950), p. 11.
19 Alice Milligan Diary, NLI MS 47,782.
20 Ibid.
21 Ibid.
22 Ibid.
23 Ibid.
24 Ibid.
25 Ceannt and O'Brennan Papers, NLI MS 41,492 /1–5.
26 *Irish Statesman*, 16 June 1928.
27 NLI Acc. 5835 Folder 1, p. 4.
28 *United Irishman*, 9 Jan. 1904.
29 Ceannt and O'Brennan Papers, NLI MS 41,492 /1–5.
30 Ibid.
31 Alice Milligan Diary, NLI MS 47,782.
32 Ceannt and O'Brennan Papers, NLI MS 41,492 /1–5.
33 Newspaper cutting in Ceannt and O'Brennan Papers, NLI MS 41,492 /1–5.
34 *Northern Patriot*, 23 Nov. 1895.
35 A. Milligan Papers, Allen Library. Dated 14 Dec. 1901.
36 Breansan S. Mac Aodha, 'Was this a social revolution?' in S. O'Tuama, *The Gaelic League idea* (1993), p. 22.
37 Eoin MacNeill Papers, NLI MS 10, 882.
38 Unidentified newspaper cutting in E. Milligan Papers, with Michael Stone.
39 L. MacManus, *White light and flame* (1929), p. 1.
40 *An Claidheamh Soluis*, 24 June 1905.
41 A. Milligan Papers, Allen Library.
42 Ibid.
43 *New Ireland*, 27 Apr. 1918.
44 E. Coxhead, *Daughters of Erin* (1979), p. 55.
45 *Catholic Bulletin*, Oct. 1916.
46 *An Claidheamh Soluis*, 2 Sept. 1905.

47 *Northern Whig*, 3 Oct. 1907.
48 Ibid.
49 Æ (ed.), *New Songs* (1904), p. 2.
50 P. Colum, *Cross roads in Ireland* (1930), p. 90.
51 Russell, *Letters of Æ*, p. 109.
52 *Ulster Herald*, 17 Sept. 1966.
53 F.J. Bigger Papers, Belfast Public Library, MS J297. Milligan annotated the poem to the effect that it was published in her school magazine *EOS* and later republished in *Glimpses of Erin*. Milligan dates the poem July 1888.
54 *Irish Independent*, 28 Sept. 1912.
55 *Northern Whig*, 12 Nov. 1909.
56 Ibid.
57 *Evening Telegraph*, 22 Feb. 1910.
58 'With the Gaels of Tyrone: Ancient Patrimony of the O'Neills – Miss Milligan Takes Down Songs and Music From the Lips of Old Residents', 25 June 1910, article in F.J. Bigger Papers, Belfast Public Library.
59 C. Milligan Fox, *Annals of the Irish harpers* (1911), p. x.
60 J. Dunne & P.J. Lennox (eds), *The glories of Ireland* (1914), p. v.
61 A. Milligan, 'Irish heroines' in Dunne & Lennox (eds) *The glories of Ireland*, p. 162
62 Ibid., pp 168–9.
63 *Irish Review*, Apr.–Sept. 1914.
64 A. Milligan Papers, NLI MS 5048.
65 D.J. O'Donoghue Papers, UCD MS LA15/1150.
66 A. Milligan Papers, Allen Library.
67 F.J. Bigger Papers, Belfast Public Library.
68 Ernest Milligan to Henry Mangan, 30 Oct. 1953. A. Milligan Papers, Allen Library.
69 Máire Nic Shiublaigh Papers, NLI, MS 27, 631 (i).
70 *Derry Journal*, 4 Apr. 1953.
71 Seumas O'Sullivan Collection, TCD MS 4646/3825.
72 F.J. Bigger Papers, Belfast Public Library.
73 Ibid.
74 Bulmer Hobson Papers, NLI MS 13,158–13,175.

75 *Sunday News*, 11 Sept. 1966.
76 A. Milligan Papers, Allen Library.
77 Seumas O'Sullivan Collection, TCD MS 4646/ 3826.
78 Ibid.
79 Sinéad de Valera Papers, NLI MS 18, 311.
80 Ibid.
81 Ibid.
82 Seumas O'Sullivan Collection, TCD MS 4646/ 3826.
83 Bulmer Hobson Papers, NLI MS 13,158–13,175.
84 Ibid.
85 Joseph McGarrity Papers, NLI MS 17, 539.
86 Seumas O'Sullivan Collection, TCD MS 4646/3826.
87 *Ulster Herald*, 7 July 1939.
88 E. Young, *Flowering dusk* (1945), pp 57–8.
89 Charles Milligan to Henry Mangan, 30 Apr. 1953. A. Milligan Papers, Allen Library.
90 *New Ireland*, 23 Nov. 1918.
91 *Irish News*, 28 Apr. 1909.
92 Joseph McGarrity Papers, MS 17, 539.
93 Hand-written version of the poem by Milligan in the Ceannt and O'Brennan Papers, NLI MS 41,492 /1–5.
94 Erskine Childers Papers, TCD MS 7847–51/806.
95 A. Milligan Papers, Allen Library.
96 F.J. Bigger Papers, Belfast Public Library.
97 Bulmer Hobson Papers MS 13,158–13,175.
98 Ibid.
99 Ibid.
 1 Ibid.
 2 A copy of this booklet can be found in Ceannt and O'Brennan Papers, NLI MS 41,492 /1–5.
 3 A. Milligan, *Stories of the Celtic nations* (1927).
 4 Colum, *Cross roads in Ireland*, pp 90–1.
 5 Ernest Milligan to Henry Mangan, 22 July 1953. A. Milligan Papers, Allen library.
 6 Ceannt and O'Brennan Papers, NLI MS 41,492 /1–5.
 7 Ibid.
 8 Ibid.
 9 Joseph McGarrity Papers, NLI MS 17,539.
10 Ceannt and O'Brennan Papers, NLI MS 41,492 /1–5.
11 Ibid.
12 Ibid.
13 Charles Milligan wrote reflection on his life in booklets such as *My Bangor* from the 1890s, p. 197.
14 Ceannt and O'Brennan Papers, NLI MS 41,492 /1–5.
15 *Irish Press*, 30 June 1937.
16 Ibid.
17 Ceannt and O'Brennan Papers, NLI MS 41,492 /1–5.
18 Joseph McGarrity Papers, NLI MS 17,539.
19 Ceannt and O'Brennan Papers, NLI MS 41,492 /1–5.
20 Ibid.
21 Máire Nic Shiublaigh Papers, NLI MS 27, 631 (i).
22 Ceannt and O'Brennan Papers, NLI MS 41,492 /1–5.
23 Ibid.
24 Ibid.
25 Ibid.
26 Ibid.
27 Ibid.
28 Seumas O'Sullivan Papers, TCD MS 4630–49/1264, 1266/3824–8.
29 Ceannt and O'Brennan Papers, NLI MS 41,492 /1–5.
30 Ibid.
31 Ibid.
32 Ibid.
33 Ibid.
34 Ibid.
35 Ibid.
36 Ibid.
37 Ibid.
38 Ibid.
39 Ibid.
40 Ibid.
41 Ibid.
42 Ceannt and O'Brennan Papers, NLI MS 41,492 /1–5.
43 Ibid.

44   Ibid.
45   Ibid.
46   Ibid.
47   Ibid.
48   *Irish Press*, 22 Apr. 1936.
49   Alice Milligan Diary, NLI MS 47,782.
50   Ceannt and O'Brennan Papers, NLI MS 41,492 /1–5.
51   Seumas O'Sullivan Papers, TCD MS 4630–49/1264, 1266/3824–8.
52   Ceannt and O'Brennan Papers, NLI MS 41,492 /1–5.
53   Ibid.
54   Ceannt and O'Brennan Papers, NLI MS 41,492 /1–5.
55   A. Milligan, 'Historical pageant at Omagh field', *Derry Journal*, 12 May 1938.
56   Máire Nic Shiublaigh Papers, NLI MS 27, 631 (i).
57   Ceannt and O'Brennan Papers, NLI MS 41,492 /1–5.
58   Ibid.
59   For a report on Milligan's speech at grave of Thomas Davis see *Derry Journal*, 24 Sept. 1937. Milligan's speech at the opening of the Tyrone feis was reported in the *Ulster Herald*, 7 July 1939. Milligan's lecture for the '98 commemorations in Wexford was recorded in *The People* (Wexford), 2 July 1938.
60   Charles Milligan to Henry Mangan, 28 Oct. 1953. A. Milligan Papers, Allen Library.
61   Private interview with the author, 21 Sept. 2006.
62   Connolly's play was published for the first time in a special issue of the international postcolonial journal *Interventions* co-edited by the author: 'Under which flag? Revisiting James Connolly', *Interventions*, 10:1 (2008), 26–47.
63   From 'At the Castle June 26', Ceannt and O'Brennan Papers, NLI MS 41,492 /1–5.
64   Joseph Campbell Papers, TCD MS 10,202.
65   Joseph McGarrity Papers, NLI MS 17,539.
66   Ceannt and O'Brennan Papers, NLI MS 41,492 /1–5.
67   Ibid.
68   Ibid.
69   *Irish Press*, 3 Aug. 1933.
70   Ceannt and O'Brennan Papers, NLI MS 41,492 /1–5.
71   Newspaper cutting in Ceannt and O'Brennan Papers, NLI MS 41,492 /1–5.
72   Joseph McGarrity Papers, NLI MS 17,539.
73   Joseph Campbell Papers, TCD MS 10,202.
74   Ibid.
75   Ceannt and O'Brennan Papers, NLI MS 41,492 /1–5.
76   Ibid.
77   Ibid.
78   Ibid.
79   Ibid.
80   Walter Benjamin, 'On the concept of history' in Hannah Arendt (ed.), *Illuminations*, p. 255.
81   *Derry Journal*, 5 Apr. 1938.
82   Ceannt and O'Brennan Papers, NLI MS 41,492 /1–5.
83   Ibid.
84   Ceannt and O'Brennan Papers, NLI MS 41,492 /1–5.
85   Ibid.
86   Ibid.
87   Ceannt and O'Brennan Papers, NLI MS 41,492 /1–5.
88   P. Pearse, *A hermitage* (1915), p. 192.
89   Ceannt and O'Brennan Papers, NLI MS 41,492 /1–5.
90   I am grateful to Gerry Adams for writing to me to share this information.
91   These two verses are taken from a five-page manuscript of his unpublished poem, 'Alice Milligan: Mountfield, Tyrone' given to me by Benedict Kiely in 1997.
92   A. Milligan Papers, Allen Library.
93   Ceannt and O'Brennan Papers, NLI MS 41,492 /1–5.
94   Newspaper cutting in Ceannt and O'Brennan Papers, NLI MS 41,492 /1–5.
95   Ibid.
96   Ibid.

97 Ceannt and O'Brennan Papers, NLI
    MS 41,492 /1–5.
98 *Ulster Herald*, 3 Oct. 1942.
99 The author of this study has completed
    a bibliography detailing all of Milligan's
    public output from 1880s to 1940s.
    This will be made available on the web
    in 2012.
1   Ceannt and O'Brennan Papers, NLI
    MS 41,492 /1–5.
2   Alice Milligan Diary, NLI MS 47,782.
3   *Irish Times*, 20 Apr. 1953.
4   From Mrs O'Brolcain (Molly Killeen)
    to E. Milligan, 1 July 1953, A. Milligan
    Papers, Allen Library.
5   A. Milligan Papers, Allen Library.
6   Letters from Charles and Ernest
    Milligan to Brother Allen, Alice
    Milligan Papers, Allen Library.
7   Alice Milligan Papers, Allen Library.

Chapter Two: Revival

1   A. O'Day, *Parnell and the first Home
    Rule episode, 1884–1887* (1986), p. ix.
2   W.E. Gladstone, *Aspects of the Irish
    question* (1892), pp 13–14.
3   Ibid., pp 13–14.
4   Ibid., p. 47.
5   Quoted in O'Day, *Parnell and the first
    Home Rule episode, 1884–1887*, p. 197.
6   Irish National League, *Tracts on the
    Irish question* (1886), p. 5.
7   Ibid., p. 7.
8   Irish Loyal and Patriotic Union, *Irish
    public opinion on Home Rule* (1886),
    pp 5–6.
9   Ibid., p. 6.
10 A. Webb (ed.), *The opinions of some
    Protestants regarding their Irish Catholic
    fellow-countrymen* (1886), p. 20.
11 Ibid.
12 Declan Kiberd explains: 'Undoubtedly
    England's only European colony differed
    from imperial territories in Africa, most
    obviously as a result of Ireland's centuries
    of enforced intimacy with England …
    While Europe's race for empire in Africa
    occurred in the latter half of the nineteenth
    century, England had occupied Ireland
    for more than 700 years. Thus at the time

of Ireland's de-colonization, the imperial
culture had penetrated far more deeply
than in Africa or Asia.' D. Kiberd 'White
skins, black masks?: Celticism and
negritude', *Eire-Ireland*, 31 (1996), 162.
13 *Glimpses of Erin*, p. 12.
14 Ibid., p. 183.
15 Gladstone, *Aspects of the Irish question*,
    p. 47.
16 Ibid.
17 S. Lysaght, 'Contrasting natures: the
    issue of names' in John Wilson Foster
    (ed.), *Nature in Ireland: a scientific and
    cultural history* (1997), p. 447.
18 C. Hutchinson, 'Bird study in Ireland'
    in Foster (ed.), *Nature in Ireland*,
    p. 267.
19 Alice Milligan Diary, NLI MS 47,782.
20 An earlier father–daughter analogy in
    Irish literary history might be Maria
    Edgeworth and her father, author and
    inventor Richard Lovell Edgeworth.
21 *Glimpses of Erin*, p. 21.
22 MacManus, *White light and flame*, p. 5.
23 *Glimpses of Erin*, p. 43.
24 *Address by Gavin Duffy for the London
    Irish Literary Society, 1892* (1896), p. 26.
25 *Glimpses of Erin*, p. 271.
26 Ibid., p. 210.
27 Quoted in D. Kiberd, *Irish classics*
    (2000), p. 129. Kiberd argues that 'Her
    project was to defend the Anglo-Irish
    aristocracy against the charge of being
    muscular, horse riding dullards and to
    remind colonial administrators in
    Dublin and London of the dignity and
    beauty of the literature of the ancient
    Gael.' Ibid., p. 619.
28 *Glimpses of Erin*, p. 207.
29 Ibid., p. 187.
30 Ibid., p. 188.
31 Ibid., p. 187.
32 Ibid.
33 Ibid., p. 137.
34 Ibid., p. 184.
35 Ibid., pp 187–8.
36 Quote from Alice Milligan's 'Ode to
    political tourists', F.J. Bigger Papers,
    Milligan Scrapbook, Belfast Public
    Library.
37 *Glimpses of Erin*, p. 233.

38 Ibid., p. 274.
39 Ibid., p. 275.
40 F.J. Bigger Papers, MS J297. Milligan
    annotated the poem to the effect that it
    was published in her school magazine
    EOS and later republished in *Glimpses
    of Erin*.
41 *Glimpses of Erin*, p. 276.
42 This is similar to the complex
    doubleness within the narrative
    structure of Maria Edgeworth's novel,
    Castle Rackrent.
43 *Glimpses of Erin*, p. 202.
44 Ibid., p. 199.
45 Ibid., p. 165.
46 Ibid., p. 174.
47 Ibid., p. 13.
48 Ibid., p. 207.
49 Ibid., pp 207–8.
50 Ibid., p. 19.
51 Ibid., p. 196.
52 'The history of the ballad singer',
    A. Milligan Papers, Allen Library.
53 *New York Times*, 2 Aug. 1883.
54 *A Royal Democrat*, p. 167.
55 Luke Gibbons discussed in detail the
    cultural references in Joyce's *Ulysses* to
    Irish secret societies at the UCD Joyce
    Centre Annual Conference, April 2009.
56 Joyce, *Ulysses*, p. 441.
57 *Glimpses of Erin*, p. 264.
58 Ibid., p. 203.
59 Ibid., p. 196.
60 *Glimpses of Erin*, p. 19.
61 Ibid., p. 259.
62 *Glimpses of Erin*, p. 230.
63 Ibid., p. 211.
64 *A Royal Democrat*, p. 43.
65 Ibid., p. 48.
66 Ibid., p. 32.
67 Ibid., p. 38.
68 Ibid., p. 43.
69 *Glimpses of Erin*, p. 177.
70 *A Royal Democrat*, pp 15–16.
71 Ibid., pp 16–17.
72 Ibid., pp 19–20.
73 *Irish News*, 5 Mar. 1890.
74 *United Ireland*, 22 Mar. 1890.
75 *A Royal Democrat*, p. 160.
76 Ibid., p. 276.
77 Ibid., p. 53.

78 Ibid., p. 53.
79 Ibid., p. 163.
80 Ibid., p. 224.
81 Ibid., p. 17.
82 F.C. Mather, *Chartism* (1972), p. 21.
83 Ibid., p. 22.
84 Feargus O'Connor, letter to the
    Northern Star, 15 May 1841.
85 A member of the Irish Universal
    Suffrage Association, *Chartism and
    Repeal* (1842), p. 16.
86 Rachel O'Higgins, 'The Irish influence
    in the Chartist movement', *Past and
    Present*, 61:20 (1961), 85.
87 Quoted by O'Higgins, ibid., 86.
88 Quoted by O'Higgins, ibid., 85.
89 Report of select committee to enquire
    into the state of Ireland since 1835, HL
    1939 (486) xi. Quoted in O'Higgins,
    ibid., 85.
90 Quoted in Mather, *Chartism*, p. 23.
91 *A Royal Democrat*, p. 71.
92 O'Higgins, 'The Irish influence in the
    Chartist movement', p. 84.
93 *A Royal Democrat*, p. 124.
94 Ibid., p. 53.
95 Ibid., p. 53.
96 Ibid., p. 159.
97 Ibid., p. 164.
98 Ibid., p. 216.
99 Ibid., p. 216.
1   Ibid., p. 214.
2   Ibid., p. 266.
3   Ibid., p. 197.
4   Ibid., p. 275.
5   Ibid., p. 47.
6   Lady Morgan, *O'Donnell. A national
    tale* (1815), p. vii.
7   *A Royal Democrat*, p. 229.
8   Ibid., p. 19.
9   Ibid., p. 18.
10 Letter from MacSwiney to Milligan,
    March 1905. A. Milligan Papers, Allen
    Library.
11 *A Royal Democrat*, p. 13.
12 *Glimpses of Erin*, p. 187.
13 *A Royal Democrat*, p. 287.
14 Ibid., p. 288.
15 Ibid., p. 215.
16 A vision which articulates Broadbent's
    plan for Ireland in Act One of Shaw's

play *John Bull's Other Island*: 'There are great possibilities for Ireland. Home Rule will work wonders under English guidance.'

17 *A Royal Democrat*, p. 21.

18 Ibid., p. 57.

19 Ibid., p. 163.

20 Ibid., p. 29.

21 *Leader*, 17 July 1909.

22 *Selected plays of Lady Gregory* ed. Mary Fitzgerald (1983), p. 157.

23 *Evening Telegraph* quoted by Henry Mangan, *Poems by Alice Milligan* (1954), pp xv–xvi.

24 Statistic from Elizabeth Butler Cullingford lecture, Notre Dame Irish Seminar, O'Connell House, 19 June 2009.

25 D. Grimstead, 'Melodrama as echo of the historically voiceless', in T. Hareven (ed.), *Anonymous Americans* (1971), p. 80.

26 I discuss this film in more detail in my article 'A contested life: James Connolly in the twenty-first century' in C. Morris & S. Thompson (eds), *Interventions*, 10:1 (2008), 102–15.

27 A. Milligan, *The daughter of Donagh* (1920), dedication to Richard Barry O'Brien.

28 Private correspondence with the author.

29 S.R. Gardiner, *Cromwell's place in history* (1897), p. 57.

30 L. Pilkington, 'Imagining a minority: Protestants and Irish cultural politics' *Graph: Irish Cultural Review*, 3:2 (1998), 13–17. The essay is revised and expanded in 2002 'Drumcree and the Celtic Tiger: the cultural legacy of Anti-Catholicism in Ireland' in P. Kirby, L. Gibbons & M. Cronin (eds), *Reinventing Ireland* (2002), pp 124–42.

31 Letter from Milligan to the *United Irishman*, 9 Jan. 1904.

32 The play version of the novel, *The daughter of Donagh* was published in the *United Irishman* throughout December 1903: Act I, 3 Dec.; Act II, 12 Dec.; Act III, 19 Dec.; Act IV, 26 Dec. 1903. The following short stories

by Milligan are all set in 1654 and include the names of the characters featured in *The Cromwellians*: *The lady of one hand* (*Irish Emerald*, 14 Jan. 1899); *Young Mitchil of the pipes: a tale of the Cromwellian settlement* (*Irish Emerald*, 21 Jan. 1899); *The wolf-hunt of Lug-na-Fulla* (*Irish Emerald*, 8 Apr. 1899).

33 I located and identified this nine page hand-written extract in papers held in the Allen Library, O'Connell Schools, Dublin.

34 *The Cromwellians*, Alice Milligan Papers, Allen Library, MS p. 189.

35 Ibid.

36 M. Poster, *Sartre's Marxism* (1979), p. 21.

37 *United Irishman*, 9 Jan. 1904.

38 S. MacManus (ed.), *We sang for Ireland* (1951), p. 1.

39 *Leader* (San Francisco), Jan. 1905.

40 *Ulster Examiner*, 7 Sept. 1940.

41 S. Deane, 'Cannon fodder: literary mythologies of Ireland' in J. Lundy & A. Mac Poilin (eds), *Styles of belonging* (1991), pp 27–8.

42 *Leader*, 17 July 1909.

43 *Irish Weekly Independent*, 5 Jan. 1895.

44 *Irish Weekly Independent*, 5 Jan. 1895.

45 B. Mhic Shéain, 'Glimpses of Erin Alice Milligan: poet, Protestant, patriot', *Fortnight*, April 1994, p. 3.

46 A. Milligan Papers, Allen Library.

47 Colum, *Cross roads in Ireland*, pp 91–3.

48 MacManus, *We sang for Ireland*, p. 109.

49 E. Milligan Papers, in Michael Stone collection.

50 P. Henry, *An Irish portrait* (1931), pp 6–8.

51 Ceannt and O'Brennan Papers, NLI MS 41,492 /1–5.

52 Lily MacManus, *White light and flame*, p.5.

53 Alice Milligan Diary, NLI MS 47,782.

54 Ibid.

55 Ibid.

56 Ibid.

57 Healy repeatedly claimed through his newspaper, the *Weekly National Press* that Parnell had redirected party funds

raised in 1889 to fund his own personal campaign in 1891. For further details of the string of allegations levelled against Parnell see F. Callanan, *The Parnell split, 1890–91* (1992), pp 121–34.

58 'If I had seen his face I would know whether to trust him – I want McCarthy to win just now – but I am not of them. (O'Connor, Davitt Vesey Knox & a few were honest – but the Leinster Hall dissenters!!)', Alice Milligan Diary, NLI MS 47,782.

59 Ibid.

60 Ibid.

61 The National Library opened in the exact month *A Royal Democrat* was being reviewed in the nationalist presses. A copy of the novel was eventually deposited at the library just as Ireland was partitioned in 1922.

62 Alice Milligan Diary, NLI MS 47,782.

63 Ibid.

64 Ibid.

65 Ibid.

66 A. Milligan, 'Recollections of the Shelley Society', Ceannt and O'Brennan Papers, NLI MS 41,492 /1–5.

67 Alice Milligan Diary, NLI MS 47,782.

68 Ibid.

69 'The north is up!' *Irish Weekly Independent*, 21 Dec. 1895.

70 'Nationalism & the Gaelic League', Alice Milligan Papers, Allen Library.

71 Alice Milligan Diary, NLI MS 47,782.

72 J. Kelly, 'Parnell in Irish Literature' in D.G. Boyce & A. O'Day (eds), *Parnell in perspective* (1991), p. 245. For a detailed assessment of the literary impact of the split in the Irish Parliamentary Party and Parnell's death see Richard Fallis, *The Irish Renaissance* (1978), pp 57–9; 'The Death of Parnell', in F. Callanan, *The Parnell Split, 1890–91*, pp 160–86.

73 Alice Milligan Diary, NLI MS 47,782.

74 *Irish Weekly Independent*, 6 July 1895.

75 *The Irish Review*, Apr.–Sept. 1914.

76 *Shan Van Vocht*, Aug. 1896.

77 *Shan Van Vocht*, 7 Aug. 1896.

78 J.P. Satre, *Existentialism and humanism* (1997 reprint), p. 47.

79 *A Royal Democrat*, p. 48.

Chapter Three: Identity

1 *Fainne an Lae*, 5 Mar. 1898.

2 'The scattering of the company', *Irish Stateman*, 16 June 1928.

3 Ibid.

4 Gaelic League member P.T. M'Ginley writing in the *Derry Standard*, 5 Apr. 1899.

5 *Shan Van Vocht*, August 1896.

6 W.P. Ryan, *The work of the Gaelic League* (1902), p. iv.

7 Alice Milligan Papers, Allen Library.

8 T.J. Campbell, 'Fifty years of Ulster: the Irish Revival', *Irish Weekly and Ulster Examiner*, 8 February 1941 (2).

9 Gordon McCoy, 'From cause to quango?: The Peace Process and the transformation of the Irish language movement' in John M. Kirk & Donall P. Ó Baóill (eds), *Linguistic politics* (2001), p. 206.

10 *Shan Van Vocht*, 5 July 1897, p. 114.

11 Letter to *An Claidheamh Soluis* in 1899, quoted in R. Kearney, *Postnationalist Ireland* (1997), p. 114.

12 Ryan, *The work of the Gaelic League*, p. iv.

13 Eoin MacNeill Papers, NLI MS 10,874.

14 Ibid.

15 Ibid.

16 J. Hannay, 'Is the Gaelic League political?: Lecture delivered under the auspices of the Branch of the Five Provinces', 23 Jan. 1906, NLI, L0 P77.

17 D. Hyde, *The Gaelic League and politics* (1914), p. 5.

18 'Nationalism & the Gaelic League', A. Milligan Papers, Allen Library, p. 3.

19 Ibid.

20 Ibid.

21 Newspaper cutting on the inside cover of Ernest Milligan's edition of his sister's *Collected poems*, E. Milligan Papers in Michael Stone Collection.

22 'Nationalism & the Gaelic League', A. Milligan Papers, Allen Library, pp 2–3.

23 *Shan Van Vocht*, 7 Feb. 1896.
24 Gaelic League, *Our line of advance: a pamphlet for workers* (1917), p. 2.
25 *An Claidheamh Soluis*. 2 Sept. 1905.
26 R. Kirkland, *Cathal O'Byrne and the northern revival in Ireland, 1890–1960* (2006), p. 108.
27 S. Brooks, *The new Ireland* (1907), p. 33.
28 *Shan Van Vocht*, Oct. 1897.
29 *Shan Van Vocht*, Aug. 1897.
30 *Shan Van Vocht*, 4 Oct. 1897.
31 Joseph Devlin was the organization's fourth secretary and among its presidents were the MPs William Redmond, Thomas Sexton and Michael McCartan. Members were well placed in the presses which gave the society extensive publicity across Ireland. The first secretary of the Society, John McGrath, worked on the *Daily News*, J.P. Gaynor was a columnist for the *Freeman's Journal*, John McGrath was literary editor of *United Ireland* and the third secretary, T.J. Hanna, worked on Belfast's nationalist paper the *Irish News*.
32 Diary entry 18 Apr. 1918 in Anne Olivier Bell (ed.), *Virginia Woolf selected diaries* (2008), p. 41.
33 M. Gonne, *A servant of the queen* (1974), p. 291.
34 *Irish News*, 8 Mar. 1895.
35 Ibid.
36 *Northern Whig*, 14 Nov. 1894.
37 Ibid., 6 Nov. 1894.
38 Ibid., 14 Nov. 1894.
39 Ibid., 5 Nov. 1894.
40 *Northern Whig*, 22 Nov. 1894.
41 Ibid.
42 *Shan Van Vocht*, 7 June 1897.
43 *Irish Weekly Independent*, 4 Nov. 1893.
44 *Irish News*, 8 Mar. 1895.
45 Ibid.
46 Ibid., 11 Mar. 1895.
47 Ibid., 8 Mar. 1895.
48 Ibid.
49 Ibid., 13 Feb. 1895.
50 A letter from Dublin Castle was returned to Alice Milligan dated 1 Mar. 1895: 'I have acknowledged the receipt of your letter of the – instant, forwarding copy of Resolutions passed at the meeting of the council of the Irish Women's Association held on 1st and 4th instant, in the case of John Twiss, a prisoner under sentence of death in Cork male prison. And to state that the same will be submitted to His Excellency, the Lord Lieutenant, without delay'. (A. Milligan Papers, Allen Library). The next petition on behalf of a prisoner that Milligan sent was to the British Home Office was on behalf of Roger Casement in 1916.
51 E. Mason & R. Ellmann (eds), *The critical writings of James Joyce* (1959), p. 198.
52 P. O'Leary, *My story*, trans. Cyril O'Ceirin, (1974), p. 148.
53 Roger Dixon, '"By appointment to emperors": Marcus Ward and Company of Belfast' in J. Gray & W. McCann (eds), *An uncommon bookman* (1996), p. 40.
54 *United Ireland*, 7 Sept. 1895.
55 A. Morgan, *Labour and partition* (1991), p. 200.
56 Further information about Hobson and Milligan can be found in Marnie Hay's *Bulmer Hobson and the nationalist movement in twentieth-century Ireland*, (2009).
57 *Northern Patriot*, 15 Oct. 1895.
58 Ibid.
59 Ibid., 23 Nov. 1895.
60 Ibid., 15 Oct. 1895.
61 The IWA's home reading scheme was strongly influenced by the Home Reading Union organized by the London Irish Literary Society.
62 *Northern Patriot*, 15 Oct. 1895.
63 Ibid.
64 *United Ireland*, 15 Feb. 1896. See pp 178–9 for a discussion on Speranza.
65 *Irish News*, 8 Mar. 1895.
66 *Northern Patriot*, 15 Oct. 1895.
67 *Northern Patriot*, Dec. 1895.
68 Ibid., Oct. 1895.
69 A. Milligan Papers, Allen Library.
70 *Northern Patriot*, 25 Jan. 1896.
71 *Irish Weekly Independent*, 18 Jan. 1896.

72 J.S. Crone Papers, Belfast Public
    Library, MS 16–30 CR10 No. 30.
    Dated 17 Feb. 1896.
73 'Grand old lady of Irish letters: Alice
    Milligan at 84' by Kevin McGrath.
    Newspaper cutting in the inside cover
    of Ernest Milligan's copy of his sister's
    Poems, Michael Stone Archive.
74 *United Ireland*, 1 Feb. 1896.
75 Ibid.
76 Ibid.
77 Owen McGee, 'Fred Allan (1861–1937):
    Republican, Methodist, Dubliner',
    Dublin Historical Record, 56:2 (Autumn
    2003), 210.
78 *United Ireland*, 1 Feb. 1896.
79 *Northern Patriot*, 15 Oct. 1895.
80 Ibid., 23 Nov. 1895.
81 *United Ireland*, 1 Feb. 1896.
82 *United Ireland*, 15 Feb. 1896.
83 *United Ireland*, 1 Feb. 1896.
84 *Northern Patriot*, July 1896.
85 Ibid., June 1896.
86 Ibid., July 1896.
87 Ibid.
88 Anna Johnston letters, F.J. Bigger
    Papers, Belfast Public Library.
89 *Northern Patriot*, Apr. 1896.
90 Ibid., July 1896.
91 Ibid., Feb. 1896.
92 For further discussion on this see Ann
    Douglas, *The feminisation of American
    culture* (1977), pp 44–80.
93 'Literature and Politics', *United Ireland*,
    16 Dec. 1893.
94 *Irish Weekly Independent*, 21 Sept. 1895.
95 *Shan Van Vocht*, 7 Feb. 1896.
96 Ibid.
97 W.P. Ryan, *The Irish Literary Revival*,
    (1894), p. iv. Ryan continued the
    debate about the revival in an exchange
    of letters with 'J.M'G' published in
    United Ireland, Apr. 1894.
98 'Notes for Gaelic Athletes', *Shan Van
    Vocht*, 7 Feb. 1896.
99 Notre Dame Irish Seminar Lectures on
    Joyce, July 2009.
1   *Shan Van Vocht*, 7 Mar. 1898.
2   A. Milligan Papers, Allen Library.
3   *Shan Van Vocht*, 7 Mar. 1898.

4   Ibid.
5   'Our paper and its supporters', *Shan
    Van Vocht*, Mar. 1896.
6   *Irish Weekly Independent*, 18 Jan. 1896.
7   Founder of the Gaelic League Douglas
    Hyde (1860–1949), poet Alice Furlong
    (1860–1946), president of the Celtic
    Literary Society William Rooney
    (1873–1901), poet Nora Hopper
    (1871–1906), essayist and poet Lionel
    Johnston (1867–1902), Irish politician
    F. Hugh O'Donnell (1846–1916),
    Francis A. Fahy (1854–1935) founder of
    the Southwark Irish Literary movement,
    poets Patrick Joseph McCall (1861–
    1919) and Thomas Ekenhead Mayne
    (1867–99), medical doctor and poet
    George Sigerson (1836–1925), poet
    William Butler Yeats (1866–1939),
    Fenian John O'Leary (1830–1907), and
    the author and historian Standish
    O'Grady (1846–1928).
8   Letter to F.J. Bigger from artist, designer,
    illuminator, herald painter, J. Vinycomb,
    3 Feb. 1904. F.J. Bigger Papers, Belfast
    Public Library.
9   F.J. Bigger Papers, Belfast Public Library.
10 Ibid.
11 Ibid.
12 Ibid.
13 *Shan Van Vocht*, Mar. 1896.
14 Ibid., Aug. 1896.
15 Letter to Anna Johnston from J. Brolly
    (255 Cumbernauld Road, Denvistown,
    Glasgow), 24 Feb. 1898. A. Milligan
    Papers, Allen Library.
16 *Irish Republic*, 6 Sept. 1896 (copy held
    in Crime Special Branch Papers, Public
    Records Office, Dublin: 3/317
    11078/S–12954/S Carton 11).
17 E. Boland, *Object lessons* (1995),
    pp 142–3.
18 Ibid., pp 134–5.
19 Article by 'Btransna' of the Celtic
    Literary Society, Dublin, *Shan Van
    Vocht*, 2 Feb. 1896.
20 *Shan Van Vocht*, 4 Sept. 1896.
21 M. Nic Shiubhlaigh, 'Women pioneers',
    Wolfe Tone Annual (1945), 21–3.
22 *Shan Van Vocht*, 6 Mar. 1896.

23 A. Milligan Papers, Allen Library.
24 'Can Irish republicans be politicians?' *Shan Van Vocht*, 6 Nov. 1896.
25 *Shan Van Vocht*, 7 Feb. 1896.
26 'Socialism and Nationalism', *Shan Van Vocht*, Jan. 1897.
27 Ibid.
28 *Shan Van Vocht*, 7 Feb. 1896.
29 P. Colum, *Arthur Griffith* (1951), p. 46.
30 S. MacManus (ed.), *The four winds of Eirinn* (1927), pp xi–xii.
31 I am grateful to John Horgan for this observation.

Chapter Four: Memory and commemoration: 1798 in 1898

1 J. Connolly, *Labour in Irish history* (1910; 1956 reprint), p. 59.
2 *Irish News*, 1 Jan. 1898.
3 *Shan Van Vocht*, 3 Jan. 1898.
4 Alice Milligan Diary, NLI MS 47,782.
5 Seamus MacManus Papers, NLI Acc. 4271 Item No. 6, dated 25 July 1951.
6 Alice Milligan Diary, NLI MS 47,782.
7 *Irish News*, Feb. 1895. Pender's lecture was later published as a series in the *Shan Van Vocht* starting on 5 July 1897.
8 *Irish News*, 7 June 1895.
9 Ibid.
10 Ibid., 7 Sept. 1895.
11 Ibid.
12 *Glimpses of Erin*, p. 177.
13 Ibid., pp 180–1: lines 25–8.
14 W.H. Maxwell, *History of the Irish rebellion in 1798* (1845), pp 152–5.
15 S.W. Myers & D.E. McKnight (eds), *Sir Richard Musgrave's memoirs of the Irish Rebellion of 1798* with a foreword by David Dickson (1995), p. 419.
16 See for instance, G. Taylor, *A history of the rise, progress, cruelties, and suppression of the Rebellion in the County of Wexford in the year 1798* (1864), p. 115.
17 Quoted in P. Wauchope, *Patrick Sarsfield and the Williamite war* (1992), p. 247.
18 *Irish Weekly Independent*, 21 Dec. 1895.
19 *Irish News*, 7 June 1895.
20 *Irish Weekly Independent*, 21 Dec. 1895.

21 M. Elliot, *Partners in revolution* (1982), p. 3.
22 *Glimpses of Erin*, p. 177.
23 *Irish News*, 11 Mar. 1895.
24 J. Kelly (ed.), *Thomas Davis* (1998), p. 108.
25 *Irish News*, 11 Mar. 1895.
26 *Irish Weekly Independent*, 21 Dec. 1895.
27 *Irish News*, 7 June 1895.
28 Ibid.
29 Cousins, *We two together*, p. 11.
30 *Belfast Evening Telegraph*, 23 May 1898.
31 Ibid.
32 Ibid., 2 June 1898.
33 *Irish Weekly Independent*, 21 Dec. 1895.
34 Ibid., 26 June 1895.
35 *Shan Van Vocht*, 15 Jan. 1896.
36 Ibid., 6 Dec. 1897.
37 Ibid., 7 Aug. 1896.
38 Ibid.
39 *Irish Weekly Independent*, 20 Aug. 1898.
40 'The '98 movement', *Irish Weekly Independent*, 20 Aug. 1898. A copy of the voting sheet survives in NLI Henry Dixon Papers, Acc. 4529.
41 PROD CSB: Ref. 15611/S MF CO 904/68, p. 9.
42 PROD: Microfilm CO 904 Reel 68, p. 295.
43 F.J. Bigger Papers, Belfast Public Library, MI5 Folder 1.
44 *Shan Van Vocht*, 2 Aug. 1897.
45 Ibid.
46 Ibid., 4 Apr. 1898.
47 *Irish News*, 5 Mar. 1898.
48 *Shan Van Vocht*, 6 June 1898.
49 Ibid., 1 Aug. 1898. The foundation stone was eventually incorporated into the 1997 monuments erected at Croppies Acre.
50 Ibid., 5 Sept. 1898.
51 A. Milligan, *The life of Wolfe Tone* (1898), p. 5.
52 *Shan Van Vocht*, 7 Mar. 1898.
53 *Daily Nation*, 16 Aug. 1898.
54 PROD: CBS 3/716 16628/S–18107/5 Carton 14.
55 *Irish Weekly Independent*, 21 Dec. 1895.
56 *Shan Van Vocht*, 6 Sept. 1897.

57 T.J. O'Keefe, 'The efforts to celebrate the United Irishmen', *Éire-Ireland*, 23 (1988), 56.

58 *Irish News*, 8 Jan. 1898.

59 Ibid., 15 Jan. 1898.

60 *Times*, 18 Mar. 1898.

61 Ibid.

62 *Shan Van Vocht*, 12 Mar. 1897.

63 Ibid., 4 Sept. 1897.

64 F.J. Bigger Papers, Belfast Public Library, MI5 Folder 1.

65 Quoted in O'Keefe, 'The efforts to celebrate the United Irishmen', 63.

66 *Irish News*, 7 Sept. 1897.

67 *Shan Van Vocht*, 6 Sept. 1897.

68 Ibid., 6 Sept. 1897.

69 Ibid.

70 Ibid., 3 Jan. 1898.

71 PROD CSB: Ref.15611/S MF CO 904/68, p. 145.

72 *Shan Van Vocht*, Jan. 1898.

73 Ibid., 4 Apr. 1898.

74 *Shan Van Vocht*, May 1898.

75 *Irish Weekly Independent*, 20 Aug. 1898.

76 D. Keogh & N. Furlong (eds), *The women of 1798* (1998), p. 7.

77 *Shan Van Vocht*, 6 Apr. 1897.

78 Ibid.

79 Ibid., Sept. 1897.

80 For further insight into Alice Milligan's involvement with the secret societies see L. Ó Broin, *Revolutionary underground* (1976), pp 78–81.

81 PROD: CSB 15611/S MF CO 904/68, p. 9.

82 Sinéad de Valera Papers, NLI MS 18, 311.

83 Ceannt and O'Brennan Papers, NLI MS 41,492 /1-5.

84 *Irish Press*, 27 Feb. 1937.

85 H. Concannon, *Women of Ninety-Eight* (1919), p. xiv.

86 *Shan Van Vocht*, 6 Apr. 1897.

87 *Northern Patriot*, 15 Oct. 1895.

88 See C.L. Innes, *Woman and nation in Irish literature and society, 1880–1935* (1993), pp. 142–3.

89 *Shan Van Vocht*, 3 Jan. 1898.

90 Ibid., 1 Aug. 1898.

91 Ibid.

92 PROD: CO 904 Reel 68, p. 295.

93 Feb. 1898 PROD: CSB CO 904/68, p. 10.

94 *Shan Van Vocht*, Sept. 1897.

95 Ibid., 7 Aug. 1896.

96 Ibid., 6 Dec. 1897.

97 E. Showalter, *The female malady* (1987), pp 145–6.

98 M. Warner, *From the beast to the blonde* (1994), p. xxi.

99 *Irish Weekly Independent*, 6 Apr. 1895.

1 F.J. Bigger Papers, Belfast Public Library A 86, p. 46.

2 *Irish Weekly Independent*, 21 Dec. 1895.

3 *Shan Van Vocht*, May 1896.

4 Ibid., 5 July 1897.

5 Ibid., 6 Sept. 1897.

6 Concannon, *Women of Ninety-Eight*, p. 323.

7 PROD: CBS CO 904 Reel 68, p. 430.

8 'Socialism and Nationalism', *Shan Van Vocht*, Jan. 1897.

9 Quote from 'A rebel's wooing', *Shan Van Vocht*, 7 Aug. 1896.

10 The manuscript of the last act of *The French are on the sea* is in A. Milligan Papers, Allen Library. Milligan signed it under the pseudonym 'An t-Sean Bean Bhocht'. She recalled her conversation with Yeats in the *United Irishman*, 9 Jan. 1904. Jenny Wyse Power encouraged Milligan to take advantage of the £100 prize money advertised by Whitbread in the *Weekly Freeman* in 1902. (NLI Alice Milligan Papers, MS 5048 Item 48, dated: 7 Apr. 1902).

11 Two of Milligan's '98 short stories which are set in 1798 – 'A rebel's wooing' and 'The little green slippers' – conclude with similar emigration boat scenes.

Chapter Five: Drama

1 *Irish Statesman*, 2 Jan. 1926.

2 *Shamrock*, 22 Feb. 1919.

3 'Gaelic League and nationalism', manuscript of lecture by Milligan, A. Milligan Papers, Allen Library.

4 S. O'Sullivan, *The rose and the bottle* (1946), p. 118.

5 S. Watt, *Joyce, O'Casey and the popular theatre* (1991), p. 45.

6   E. Boyd, *Contemporary drama of Ireland* (1916) p. 289.
7   *Shamrock*, 22 Feb. 1919.
8   'Staging and costume in Irish drama: some practical hints', *Ireland's Own*, Mar. 1904.
9   *Irish Weekly Freeman*, 15 Mar. 1902.
10   Ibid.
11   Ibid.
12   T.P. Gill Papers, NLI MS 13, 480 (9).
13   J. Holloway, 'Irish plays' in Stephen J.M. Brown (ed.), *A guide to books on Ireland* (1912), p. 253.
14   *Sinn Féin*, 19 June 1909.
15   Quoted in John P. Harrington (ed.), *Modern Irish drama* (1991), p. 379.
16   *Sinn Féin*, 4 Feb. 1907.
17   Ibid., 26 June 1909.
18   Ibid.
19   Ibid.
20   A. Milligan Papers, Allen Library. Dated 14 Dec. 1901.
21   A. Milligan Papers, Allen Library.
22   *Ireland's Own*, 30 Mar. 1904.
23   *Sinn Féin*, 26 June 1909.
24   *Irish Weekly Freeman*, 7 June 1913.
25   *Irish Statesman*, 2 Jan. 1926.
26   'Irish women poets: number three Alice Milligan', radio transcript by Lennox Robinson (1939), RTÉ, MS 2269.
27   Letter regarding translation in A. Milligan Papers, Allen Library. The play was published in the *Irish Weekly Freeman*, 15 Mar. 1902. All quotes from the play are from this source.
28   Yeats, *Autobiographies*, p. 449.
29   Frank Fay Papers, NLI MS 10, 953 pp 1–2.
30   *United Irishman*, 22 Oct. 1904.
31   A version of O'Grady's *Red Hugh* was performed in the woods of Sheestown, Co. Kilkenny on 15 August 1902 and was published as *Red Hugh's captivity: a masque* in O'Grady's own journal, *All Ireland Review*, 29 Mar. 1902.
32   U. Ellis-Fermor, *The Irish dramatic movement* (1939), p. 40.
33   Ella Young, *Flowering dusk*, pp 57–8.
34   *United Irishman*, 4 June 1904.
35   Holloway, 'Irish plays', p. 253.

36   *United Irishman*, 4 June 1904.
37   Ibid.
38   D. Hyde, *A literary history of Ireland* (1899), p. 511.
39   *Daily Express*, 16 Sept. 1899.
40   D. Kiberd, *The Irish writer and the world* (2005), p. 71.
41   *Daily Express*, 16 Sept. 1899, p. 3.
42   E. Mason & R. Ellmann (eds.), *The critical writings of James Joyce* (1959), p. 70.
43   T.P. Gill Papers, NLI MS 13, 480 (9) Item 1.
44   Ibid.
45   *United Irishman*, Apr. 1904.
46   'The lamentation of Oisín after the Fenians', *Transactions of the Ossianic Society*, 3 (1855), 231–93. 'Lay of Oisín on the Land of Youth; as he related it to Saint Patrick', ibid., 4 (1856), 234–88. 'The dialogue of Oisín and Patrick', ibid., 3 (1856), 3–64.
47   *All Ireland Review*, 18 Aug. 1900.
48   *Daily Express*, 23 Sept. 1899.
49   Dedication in A. Milligan, *The last feast of the Fianna* (1900).
50   *United Irishman*, 24 Feb. 1900.
51   Ibid.
52   Ibid., 3 Mar. 1900.
53   Ibid., 24 Feb. 1900.
54   A. de Blácam, 'Oisín has come back again', *Sceala Eireann*, 14 June 1944, 'Torna' Papers, U115. 94. 7(8), University College Cork Library, Spead Collections.
55   G. Mac E., 'Poetic play in Irish', 21 June 1944, CUSC 'Torna' Papers, U115. 94. 2. 2–6, University College Cork Library, Spead Collections.
56   'Cultural nationalism, 1880–1930' in Seamus Deane (ed.), *Field Day anthology of Irish writing*, vol. II (1991), p. 516.
57   *United Irishman*, 11 May 1899.
58   Ibid., 13 May 1899.
59   *Daily Express*, 1 Apr. 1901.
60   *An Claidheamh Soluis*, 10 Feb. 1900.
61   *Freeman's Journal*, 20 Feb. 1900.
62   R. Kearney, *Postnationalist Ireland* (1997), p. 114.
63   Ibid.

64   *Lady Gregory's diaries, 1892–1902*, p. 227.
65   Ibid.
66   E. Milligan Papers, in possession of Mr Williams (grand nephew of A. Milligan) Durham.
67   *Freeman's Journal*, 20 Feb. 1900.
68   *Leader*, 18 May 1901.
69   J. Flannery, *Yeats and the idea of a theatre* (1976), p. 160.
70   *Daily Express*, 21 Jan. 1899.
71   *Derry Standard*, 5 Apr. 1899.
72   Eoin MacNeill Papers, NL MS 10,882, dated 28 Dec. 1898.
73   Ibid.
74   *Daily Express*, 21 Jan. 1899.
75   *An Claidheamh Soluis*, 10 Nov. 1900.
76   *Irish News*, 28 Mar. 1917.
77   Ibid.
78   Note attached to the 1944 bi-lingual publication of *Oisín in Tír na nÓg*, National Library of Ireland, book reference: Ir 89162 (8 m 26).
79   *The daughter of Donagh*, published in four acts in the *United Irishman* (5, 12, 19, 26 Dec. 1903). Republished in book form by Martin & Lester, Dublin 1920. The quotations referenced in this chapter are from the 1903 publication.

Chapter Six: Republican tableaux and the Revival

1   I discuss Milligan's work with magic lanterns, *tableaux vivant*, the 1893 World Fair and the Gaelic League in more detail in my essay, 'Alice Milligan: Republican tableaux and the Revival' in Seamus Deane & Ciaron Deane (eds), *The Field Day Review* 6 (2010), 132–65.
2   University College, Dublin: Visual Cultures Postdoctoral fellowships document, 2006.
3   *United Irishman*, 13 Apr. 1901.
4   Diaries of Joseph Holloway, NLI MS 179 /1799; Apr. 1901; Microfilm: P 8517 Reel 4, 103.
5   *Songs of Old Ireland: A collection of fifty Irish melodies unknown in England* (London, 1882), p. 1.

6   *United Irishman*, 13 Apr. 1901.
7   Ibid.
8   *Cork Examiner*, 20 May 1905.
9   *United Irishman*, 13 Apr. 1901.
10   Thomas Davis, 'Hints from Irish historical painting' reprinted from the *Nation* (July 1843) in *Thomas Davis: essays and poems with a centenary memoir, 1845–1945* (Dublin, 1945).
11   *Shan Van Vocht*, 4 Sept. 1898.
12   *United Irishman*, 7 July 1901.
13   *Irish Weekly Independent*, 6 Dec. 1894.
14   *Shan Van Vocht*, 6 June 1898.
15   *Derry Journal*, 12 Sept. 1898.
16   *United Irishman*, 7 July 1900.
17   *United Irishman*, 13 Apr. 1901.
18   *An Claidheamh Soluis*, 10 Feb. 1900.
19   *Leader* (San Francisco), 10 Jan. 1905.
20   *An Claidheamh Soluis*, 15 Apr. 1905.
21   Ibid., 31 Mar. 1906.
22   *An Claidheamh Soluis*, 6 Oct. 1906.
23   Mary Hutton Papers, NLI MS 8611 (13).
24   *Shan Van Vocht*, 2 Sept. 1898.
25   *Irish News*, 17 March 1902.
26   Timothy G. McMahon, *Grand opportunity: the Gaelic Revival and Irish society, 1893–1910* (Syracuse, 2008), p. 210.
27   *Derry Journal*, 27 May 1938.
28   Máire Nic Shiubhlaigh, *The splendid years: recollections as told to Edward Kenny* (Dublin, 1955), pp 2–3.
29   P. Colum, 'The early days of the Irish theatre' *Dublin Magazine*, 4 (1949), 11–17.
30   S. Clarke, *Feis na nGleann: a history of the Festival of the Glens* (Holywood, 1990), p. 18.
31   Kirsten Gram Holstrom, *Monodrama, attitudes, tableaux vivants: studies on some trends of theatrical fashion 1770–1815* (Stockholm, 1967), p. 229.
32   A. Milligan Papers, Allen Library.
33   Ibid.
34   *Shan Van Vocht*, 4 Oct. 1897.
35   A. Milligan Papers, NLI MS 5048 (36).
36   *United Irishman*, 3 Apr. 1901.
37   Ibid., 7 Sept. 1901.
38   *Derry Journal*, 27 May 1938.
39   *United Irishman*, 13 Apr. 1901.

40 Luke Gibbons, 'The politics of silence: Anne Devlin, women and Irish cinema' in *Transformations in Irish Culture* (Cork, 1996), p. 114.

41 'Little history of photography' in *Selected writings* 2: *1927–1934* (London, 1999), p. 514.

42 Ibid., p. 518.

43 Andrew MacNamara, 'Early photographs in Ireland'; talk delivered at Roundtable 'Modernism, visual culture and Ireland', National Library of Ireland, 25 Sept. 2009.

44 Ibid.

45 Piaras Béaslaí Papers, NLI MS 33, 952 (15).

46 John Berger, *Ways of seeing* (London, 1972), p. 3.

47 *Beltaine*, 5 (1900).

48 *United Ireland*, 4 Apr. 1903.

49 Bernadette Sweeney, *Performing the body in Irish theatre* (London, 2008), pp 194–5.

50 *Weekly Freeman*, 18 Mar. 1905.

51 A. Milligan Papers, Allen Library.

52 Maud Ellmann, *The hunger artists: starving, writing & imprisonment* (London, 1993), p. 14.

Conclusion: 'The scattering of the company'

1 *Irish Statesman*, 16 June 1928.

2 William O'Brien Papers, NLI ACC 13969, 30 May 1928.

3 A. Milligan, 'In memoriam Æ', *Dublin Magazine*, 10:4 (July 1935), 2–3.

4 Arnold Marsh Papers, TCD MS 8, 400/118–9.

5 Nic Shiubhlaigh Papers, NLI. Accession no. 5835.

6 Ibid.

7 Ibid.

8 *Ireland: Weekly Bulletin of the Department of External Affairs*, 183 (20 Apr. 1953), Stanford University Library Manuscripts James Healy Papers (M0273).

9 Clement Shorter Papers, Leeds University, dated July 1916.

10 Ibid.

11 Home office, PRO HO 144/1637/311643/65, 24 July 1916.

12 Ibid.

13 Colum, *Cross roads in Ireland*, p. 90.

14 A. Milligan Papers, Allen Library.

15 'Nationalism and the Gaelic League', A. Milligan Papers, Allen Library.

16 Ibid.

17 Ibid.

18 Ibid.

19 Ibid.

20 Ibid.

21 Piaras Béaslaí Papers, NLI MS 33, 951 (12).

22 Ibid.

23 A. Milligan Papers, Allen Library.

24 'Nationalism and the Gaelic League', A. Milligan Papers, Allen Library.

25 Susan Mitchell, *Shamrock*, 22 Feb. 1919.

26 A. Milligan Papers, Allen Library.

27 Ibid.

28 *Irish Book Lover*, Apr. 1953.

29 Connolly, *Labour in Irish history*, p. 59.

30 'Nationalism and the Gaelic League', A. Milligan Papers, Allen Library.

31 *A Royal Democrat*, p. 140.

32 Ibid., pp 149–50.

33 *Irish Times*, 20 Apr. 1953.

34 Letter from Molly Killeen, A. Milligan Papers, Allen Library.

35 A. Milligan Papers, Allen Library, 1902.

36 *Shamrock*, 22 Feb. 1919.

37 Ibid., 1 Mar. 1919.

38 Ibid.

39 A. Milligan Papers, Allen library.

40 Sínead de Valera Papers, NLI MS 18, 311.

41 I am grateful to Declan Kiberd for this astute observation and reference point.

42 Alice Milligan, *Shan Van Vocht*, 7 Feb. 1896.

Bibliography

PRIMARY SOURCES

Works by Alice Milligan grouped according to genre (novels, plays, short stories, biography and poetry).

Travel

Alice & Seaton Milligan, *Glimpses of Erin* (Belfast, 1888).

Novels

A Royal Democrat (London, 1890).

The Cromwellians. Unpublished novel (1891–3) surviving pages held in Alice Milligan Papers, Allen Library.

Plays

The green upon the cape (*Shan Van Vocht*, Apr. 1898).

The French are on the sea. Unpublished and incomplete manuscript held in Alice Milligan Papers, Allen Library.

The last feast of the Fianna (*Daily Express*, 23 Sept. 1899); (London, 1900).

Oisín in Tír na nÓg (*Daily Express*, 7 Oct. 1899); (*Sinn Féin*, 23 Jan. 1909).

Oisín and Pádraic (*Daily Express*, 4 Nov. 1899); (*Sinn Féin*, 20 Feb. 1909).

The harp that once. Performed August 1901 by *Inghinidhe na hÉireann* and Fay brothers in Antient Concert Rooms, Dublin. Unpublished. First appeared as a short story in the *Shan Van Vocht*.

The deliverance of Red Hugh O'Donnell (*Irish Weekly Freeman*, 15 Mar. 1902).

The daughter of Donagh (*United Irishman*, 5, 12, 19, 26 Dec. 1903); (Dublin, 1920).

Brian of Banba (*United Irishman*, 30 Apr. 1904).

The last of the Desmonds (*United Irishman*, 4 June 1904).

The earl of Essex. Unpublished manuscript, National Library of Ireland.

Short Stories

Stories of the Celtic nations (Dublin, 1927).

'The dark rose of Rathmullan' (*Northern Patriot*, 15 Oct. 1895).

'A boy from Barnesmore' (*Shan Van Vocht*, 15 Jan. 1896).

'A captain's daughter' (*Shan Van Vocht*, 7 Feb.; 6 Mar.; 3 Apr. 1896).

'A rebel's wooing' (*Shan Van Vocht*, 7 Aug. 1896).

'"The harp that once –!" A story of Connaught after Humbert' (*Shan Van Vocht*, 7 Mar. 1898).

'Murdher in Irish' (*Cornhill Magazine*, June 1898).

'The lady of one hand' (*Irish Emerald*, 14 Jan. 1899).

'Young Michil of the pipes: a tale of the Cromwellian settlement' (*Irish Emerald*, 21 Jan. 1899).

'The wolf-hunt of Lug-na-Fulla' (*Irish Emerald*, 8 Apr. 1899).

'The outlaws bride' (*Irish Emerald*, 15 Apr. 1899).

'Knights errant; or, The Enniskillen conclave: a tale of a masonic banquet and its consequences' (*Irish Emerald*, 17 Mar. 1900).

'Kirsteen of the dancing' (*Irish Weekly Independent*, 16 Mar. 1901). Republished as 'Kirsteen of the dancing: a true story of the highland clearances' (*Ulster Guardian*, 26 Oct. 1907).

'Kate from California' (*Irish Weekly Independent*, 12 Dec. 1903).

'The insurance dowry' (*Irish Weekly Independent*, 14 Mar. 1903).

'Dun Angus in Aran' (*Irish Homestead*, 25 July 1903).

'Kate of Glencara: a study from life' (*Irish Homestead*, 3 Oct. 1903).

'St Columbcille's prophecy, or Among the roses at Rathmullan' (*Derry Post*, 29 Dec. 1906).

'What's bred in the bone: the young idea. An Ulster tragedy' (*Ulster Guardian*, 12 Oct. 1907).

Biography

The life of Wolfe Tone (Belfast, 1898).

Alice & Charlotte Milligan Fox, *Annals of the Irish harpers* (1911).

Poetry

Between 1891 and 1894 Milligan contributed poetry regularly in *United Ireland* and the *Irish Weekly Independent*. Her poetry also appeared in the *Northern Patriot*, *Shan Van Vocht*, the *Irish Homestead*, the *Irish Peasant*, *Sinn Féin*, *New Ireland*, and the *United Irishman*. Some poems appeared in *Glimpses of Erin* (1888) and were republished in the American paper, the *Irish Press* and the *Boston Pilot* through 1889.

Collections of Milligan's poetry include:

Æ (ed.), *New songs: a lyric selection* (London, 1904).

Milligan, A., *Hero Lays* (Dublin, 1908).

Milligan, A., *Poems of Alice Milligan* (Dublin, 1944).

MacManus, S. (ed.), *We sang for Ireland: poems by Ethna Carbery, Seamus MacManus, Alice Milligan* (Dublin, 1951).

Mangan, H. (ed.), *Poems by Alice Milligan* (Dublin, 1954).

Turner Johnston, S. (ed.), *The harper of the only God: a selection of poems by Alice Milligan* (Omagh, 1993).

Alice Milligan Papers, Allen Library: manuscript collection of Alice Milligan's Papers gathered by E. Milligan and W.P. Allen. Held in Allen Library, O'Connell School, Dublin.

Diary: Alice Milligan Diary, NLI MS 47,782.

E. Milligan Papers, Scotland: Mr and Mrs Michael Stone, owners of a private collection. Mr Stone's mother was the niece of Alice Milligan. Ernest Milligan was Mr Stone's grandfather. When I looked at these archives in the 1990s the family were based at 'Askival' House in Fort Augustus, Scotland. Mr Stone's mother was the niece of Alice Milligan. Ernest Milligan was Mr Stone's grandfather.

E. Milligan Papers, Durham: Mr and Mrs Williams, owners of a private collection of Ernest Milligan's Papers, Witten Gilbert, Durham. Mr Williams' mother was the niece of Alice Milligan. Ernest Milligan was Mr Williams' grandfather.

F.J. Bigger Papers: Francis Joseph Bigger Papers, Central Lending Library, Belfast.

MANUSCRIPT SOURCES RELATING TO ALICE MILLIGAN

A. Milligan Papers, Allen Library: manuscript collection of Alice Milligan's Papers gathered by E. Milligan and W.P. Allen. Held in Allen Library, O'Connell School, Dublin.

Alice Milligan Private Diary, 1891–3: National Library of Ireland.

E. Milligan Papers, Scotland: Mr and Mrs Stone, 'Askival', Fort Augustus, Scotland.

E. Milligan Papers, Durham: Mr and Mrs Williams, Ash Tee Cottage, 8 Front Street, Witten Gilbert, Durham.

F.J. Bigger Papers: Francis Joseph Bigger Papers, Central Lending Library, Belfast.

Letters to Alice Milligan: NLI, MS 5048.

Bulmer Hobson Papers: NLI, MS 13,158–13,179.

Ceannt and O'Brennan Papers, NLI MS 41,492 /1–5.

Mary Hutton Papers: NLI, MS 8611.

Eoin MacNeill Papers: NLI, MS 10,882.

F.R. Higgins Papers: NLI, MS 10,864 (8).

Seamus O'Sullivan Papers: TCD, MS 4630–49/1264/1266/3, 824–8.

Arnold Marsh Papers: TCD, MS 8,400/118–9.

Joseph Campbell Papers: TCD, MS 163/217.

Clement Shorter Papers, Leeds University.

Piaras Béaslaí Papers, NLI MS 33, 951.

A. de Blácam, 'Oisín has come back again', *Sceala Eireann*, 14 June 1944, CUSC 'Torna' Papers, University Library, Cork U115. 94. 7(8).

William O'Brien Papers, NLI ACC 13969.

T.P. Gill Papers, NLI MS 13, 480.

Diaries of Joseph Holloway, NLI MF. P8517.

Frank Fay Papers, NLI MS 10, 953.

John Smith Crone Papers, Belfast Public Library.

Máire Nic Shiublaigh Papers, NLI, MS 27, 631.

Joseph McGarrity Papers, NLI, MS 17, 539.

Erskine Childers Papers, MS 7847–51/806.

PUBLISHED SOURCES: CONTEMPORARY MATERIAL

Bigger, F.J., 'Rural libraries in Antrim', *Irish Book Lover*, 13 (1921), 47–52.

Bourgeois, M., *J.M. Synge & the Irish theatre* (London, 1913).

Boyd, E., *Ireland's Literary Renaissance* (Dublin, 1916).

— *The contemporary drama of Ireland* (Dublin, 1918).

Brooks, Sydney, *The new Ireland* (Dublin, 1907).

Brown, S.J. (ed.), *A guide to books on Ireland* (New York, 1912; Lemma, 1970).

Bryce, J. (ed.), *Handbook of Home Rule being articles on the Irish question* (London, 1887).

Cambell, T.J., *Fifty years of Ulster, 1890–1840* (Belfast, 1941).

Cassidy, J., *The women of the Gael* (Dublin, 1924).

Colum, P., *Cross roads in Ireland* (New York, 1930).

— 'Early days of the Irish theatre', *Dublin Magazine*, 4 (1949), 11–17.

— *Arthur Griffith* (Dublin, 1951).

Concannon, H., *Women of Ninety-Eight* (Dublin, 1919).

Corkery, D., *The hidden Ireland: a study of Gaelic Munster in the eighteenth century* (Dublin, 1924).

— *Synge and Anglo-Irish literature* (London, 1931).

Cousins, J. & M. Cousins, *We two together* (Madras, 1950).

Davitt, M., *The fall of feudalism in Ireland or The story of the Land League revolution*, (London, 1904).

De Blácam, A., *A study of New Ireland's social and political aims* (Dublin, 1918).

— *The black North: an account of the Six Counties of unrecovered Ireland: their people, their treasures, and their history* (Dublin, 1938).

— *Gaelic literature surveyed* (Dublin, 1929).

— 'Oisín has come back again', *Sceala Eireann*, 14 June 1944.

Donovan, A., *The Irish rebellion of 1898: a chapter in future history* (Dublin, 1893).

Duffy, G., *The ballad poetry of Ireland* (Dublin, 1845).

— *Thomas Davis: the memoirs of an Irish patriot, 1840–1846* (London, 1890).

— *What Irishmen may do for Irish literature* (London, 1893).

— *Address for the London Irish Literary Society* (London, 1892).

Dunne, J., & P.J. Lennox (eds), *The glories of Ireland* (Washington DC, 1914).

Fitzpatrick, T., *The king of Claddagh: a story of the Cromwellian occupation of Galway* (London, 1899).

Gardiner, S.R., *Cromwell's place in history* (London, 1897).

Gladstone, W.E., *Aspects of the Irish question: a series of reflections since 1886* (London, 1892).

Gonne, M., *A servant of the Queen: reminiscences* (London, 1974).

Gordon, J., & I. Gordon, *'We Twa': reminiscences of Lord and Lady Aberdeen* (London, 1925).

Graves, A.P., & C. Villiers Stanford, *Songs of old Ireland: a collection of fifty Irish melodies unknown in England* (London, 1882).

Gregory, A., *Gods and fighting men* (London, 1905).

— *Selected plays of Lady Gregory*, ed. Mary Fitzgerald (Washington, 1983).

Gwynn, S., *Today and tomorrow in Ireland: essays on Irish subjects* (Dublin, 1903).

— (ed.), *Charlotte Grace O'Brien: selections from her writings and correspondence* (Dublin, 1909).

Heaney, Seamus, *Opened ground: selected poems 1966–1996* (New York, 1998).

Hewitt, J., 'The bloody Bray', *Threshold*, 3 (1957), 15–32.

Hinkson, P., *Seventy years young: memories of Elizabeth Countess of Fingall* (London, 1937).

Hobson, B., *Ireland yesterday and tomorrow* (Tralee, 1930/1968).

Hyde, D., *On the necessity for de-anglicising Ireland* (London, 1893).

— *Literary history of Ireland from earliest times to the present day* (Dublin, 1899).

— *The Gaelic League and politics* (Dublin, 1914).

Lowry, M., *The story of Belfast and its surroundings* (London, 1913).

Lynd, R., 'More or less about Irish literature', *Irish Book Lover*, 13 (1922), 157–62.

McHenry, M., *The Ulster Literary Theatre in Ireland* (Philadelphia, 1931).

MacManus, L., *Nessa* (Dublin, 1902).

— *White light and flame: memories of the Irish Literary Revival and the Anglo-Irish War* (Dublin, 1929).

— 'A Cromwellian', *All Ireland Review*, 13 Dec. 1902.

MacManus, S. (ed.), *The four winds of Eirinn* (Dublin, 1927).

Marks, M., *Thorough: a novel* (London, 1894).

Maxwell, W.H., *History of the Irish rebellion in 1798; with memoirs of the Union and Emmet's insurrection in 1803* (London, 1845).

Mayne, R., 'The Ulster Literary Theatre', *Dublin Magazine*, 31 (1955), 15–21.

Milligan, A., 'In memoriam AE', *Dublin Magazine*, 10:4 (July 1935).

Molloy, J.L., *Songs of Ireland: including the most favourite of Moore's Irish melodies* (London, 1873).

Moore, T., *Poetical works* (London, 1880).

Moran, P., *Historical sketch of the persecution suffered by the Catholics of Ireland under the rule of Cromwell* (Dublin, 1865).

Nic Shiubhlaigh, M., 'Women pioneers', *Wolfe Tone Annual* (1945), 21–3.

— *The splendid years: recollections as told to Edward Kenny* (Dublin, 1955).

O'Connor, T.P., *Herself-Ireland* (London, 1917).

O'Donoghue, D.J., *The poets of Ireland: a biographical dictionary* (London, 1892).

O'Grady, S., *History of Ireland, I: the heroic period* (Dublin, 1878).

— *History of Ireland II: Cuchulain and his contemporaries* (Dublin, 1880).

— *The crisis in Ireland* (Dublin, 1882).

— *Selected essays and passages* (Dublin, 1917).

O'Sullivan, S., *The rose and the bottle* (Dublin, 1946).

Pearse, Patrick, *A hermitage*, (Dublin, 1915).

Pender, M., *The green cockade: a tale of Ulster in Ninety-Eight* (Dublin, 1898; London, 1898).

Pentland, M., *A bonnie fechter: the life of Ishbel Marjoribanks marchioness of Aberdeen and Temair, 1857–1939* (London, 1952).

Plunkett, H., *Ireland in the new century* (London, 1904).

— *The United Irishwomen* (Dublin, 1911).

Ralph, J., *Harper's Chicago and the World Fair* (New York, 1893).

Robertson, A.I., *Women's need of representation: a lecture upon the necessity of giving women the parliamentary franchise* (Dublin, 1873).

Russell, George, *Letters of Æ*, ed. Alan Denson (London, 1961).

Ryan, D., *The sword of light: from the Four Masters to Douglas Hyde, 1636–1938* (London, 1939).

Ryan, W.P., *The Irish Literary Revival: its history, pioneers and possibilities* (London, 1894).

— *The work of the Gaelic League: points for Irish people in Great Britain: how to start and conduct branches* (London, 1902).

Sadler, A., *The confederate Chieftains: a tale of the Irish Rebellion of 1641* (London, 1888).

Shaw, G.B., *John Bull's Other Island and other plays* (London, 1970).

Stopford Green, A., *Loyalty and disloyalty: what it means in Ireland* (Dublin, 1919).

Taylor, G., *A history of the rise, progress, cruelties, and suppression of the Rebellion in the County of Wexford in the year 1798* (Belleville, 1864).

Todd, J. *Wars of the Gaedhill and the Gaill* (London, 1867).

Young, Ella, *Flowering dusk: things remembered accurately and inaccurately* (New York, 1945).

Young, R., *Ulster in '98: episodes and anecdotes* (Belfast, 1893).

Yeats, W.B., *Explorations* (London, 1962).

— *Autobiographies* (London, 1953).

— *The variorum edition of the plays of W.B. Yeats* (London, 1966).

PAMPHLETS

Gaelic League, *Our line of advance: a pamphlet for workers* (Dublin, 1917).

Heinrick, H., *What is Home Rule?* (Liverpool, 1886).

Irish National League, *Tracts on the Irish question: I. Ulster* (Dublin, 1886).

— *The election of 1885* (Dublin, 1886).

The Irish Loyal and Patriotic Union, *Irish public opinion on Home Rule* (Dublin, 1886).

Webb, A. (ed.), *The opinions of some Protestants regarding their Irish Catholic fellow-countrymen* (Dublin, 1886).

SECONDARY PUBLISHED WORKS

Allison, J. (ed.), *Yeats's political identities: selected essays* (Ann Arbor, MI, 1996).

Anderson, B., *Imagined communities reflections on the origin and spread of nationalism*, (London, revised edition 1991).

Barnard, T., 'Crisis of Irish identity among Irish Protestants, 1641–1685', *Past and Present*, 127 (1990), 39–83.

Baron, C., '"Tales of sound and fury" reconsidered: melodrama as a system of punctuation', *Spectator* (US) 13 (1993), 46–59.

Beckett, J.C., *Belfast: the making of the city* (Belfast, 1983).

Bell, A.O. (ed.), *Virginia Woolf selected diaries* (London, 2008).

Bell, S.H., *The theatre in Ulster* (London, 1972).

Benjamin, Walter, *Illuminations* (New York, 1968).

Berger, John et al., *Ways of seeing* (London, 1972).

Boehmer, E., *Colonial and postcolonial literature: migrant metaphors* (London, 1995).

Boland, E., *Object Lessons: the life of the woman and the poet of our time* (Manchester, 1995).

Booth, M., *Victorian spectacular theatre, 1850–1910* (London, 1991).

— *Theatre in the Victorian age* (Cambridge, 1991).

Boucicault, D., *The colleen bawn: or, The brides of Garryowen* in D. Krause (ed.), *The Dolmen Boucicault* (Dublin, 1984).

Boyce, D.G., *The Irish question and British politics* (London, 1996).

Boyce, D.G., & A. O'Day (eds), *Parnell in perspective* (London, 1991).

Bradley, A., & M. Gialanella Valiulis (eds), *Gender and sexuality in modern Ireland* (Amherst, MA, 1997).

Brady, C. (ed.), *Interpreting Irish history: the debate on historical revisionism, 1938–1994* (Dublin, 1994).

Bratton, J., J. Cook & C. Gledhill (eds), *Melodrama: stage, picture, screen* (London, 1994).

Brennan, Maeve, *The Visitor* (Washington, 2000).

Brewster, B., & L. Jacobs, *Theatre to cinema* (London, 1997).

Brown, M., *The politics of Irish literature from Thomas Davis to W.B. Yeats* (London, 1972).

Brown, T., *Northern voices: poets from Ulster* (Dublin: Gill & Macmillan, 1975).

— *The whole Protestant community: the making of a historical myth* (Derry, 1985).

Burke, A., 'Reading a woman's death: colonial text and oral tradition in nineteenth-century Ireland', *Feminist Studies*, 3 (1995), 553–86.

Byrne, O., *The stage in Ulster* (Belfast, 1997).

Callanan, F., *The Parnell split, 1890–91* (Cork, 1992).

Campbell, F., *The dissenting voice: Protestant democracy in Ulster from Plantation to Partition* (Belfast, 1991).

Chapman, M., '"Living pictures": women and *tableaux vivants* in nineteenth-century American fiction and culture', *Wide Angle*, 18 (1996), 23–52.

Chatterjee, P., *The nation and its fragments: colonial and postcolonial histories* (Princeton, NJ, 1993).

Chevasse, M., *Terence MacSwiney* (Dublin, 1961).

Christie, I., *The last machine: early cinema and the birth of the modern world* (London, 1994).

Clare, J., *'Art made tongue-tied by authority'. Elizabethan and Jacobean dramatic censorship* (Manchester, 1990).

Clarke, S., *Feis na nGleann: a history of the Festival of the Glens* (Holywood, Co. Down, 1990).

Collins, P. (ed.), *Nationalism and unionism: conflict in Ireland, 1885–1921* (Belfast, 1994).

Connolly, J., *Labour in Irish history* (Dublin, 1910; 1956 reprint).

Connolly, S. (ed.), *The Oxford companion to Irish literature* (Oxford, 1996).

Conrad, K., 'Occupied country: the negotiation of lesbianism in Irish feminist narrative', *Eire-Ireland*, 21 (1996), 123–8.

Corcoran, N., *After Yeats and Joyce: reading modern Irish literature* (Oxford, 1997).

Coulter, C., *The hidden tradition: feminism, women and nationalism in Ireland* (Cork, 1993).

Coxhead, E., *Daughters of Erin: five women of the Irish Renaissance* (Dublin, 1979).

Cronin, M., *Translating Ireland: translation, languages and cultures* (Cork, 1996).

Crossman, V., 'The *Shan Van Vocht*: women, republicanism, and the commemoration of the 1798 Rebellion', *Eighteenth Century Life*, 22 (Nov. 1998), 128–39.

Cullen M., & M. Luddy (eds), *Women, power and consciousness in 19th Century Ireland* (Dublin, 1995).

Cullingford, E.B., *Yeats, Ireland and fascism* (Cambridge, 1981).

Davis, T., *Actresses as working women: their social identity in Victorian culture* (London, 1991).

Deane, S., *Heroic styles: the tradition of an idea* (Derry, 1984).

— *Celtic Revivals: essays in modern Irish literature, 1880–1980* (London, 1985).

— 'Parnell: the lost leader', in D. MacCartney (ed.), *Parnell: the politics of power* (Dublin, 1991), pp. 183–91.

— (ed.), *Field Day anthology of Irish writing* (3 vols, Derry, 1991).

— *Strange Country: modernity and nationhood in Irish writing since 1790*, (Oxford, 1998).

Douglas, A., *The feminisation of American culture* (London, 1977)

Eagleton, T., *Heathcliff and the Great Hunger* (London, 1995).

— *Crazy John and the Bishop and other essays on Irish culture* (Cork, 1998).

Edelstein, T.J. (ed.), *Imagining an Irish past: the Celtic Revival, 1840–1940* (Chicago, 1992).

Elliot, M., *Partners in revolution: the United Irishmen and France* (New Haven, CT, 1982).

Ellis-Fermor, U., *The Irish dramatic movement* (London, 1939).

Ellmann, Maud, *The hunger artists: starving, writing & imprisonment* (London, 1993).

Elsaesser, T. (ed.), *Early cinema: space, frame, narrative* (London, 1990).

Evans, E.E., *Ulster: the common ground* (Dublin, 1971/84).

Fallis, R., *The Irish Renaissance: an introduction to Anglo-Irish literature* (Dublin, 1978).

Fitzpatrick, D., *The Irish in Britain, 1815–1939* (London, 1989).

Flannery, J., *Yeats and the idea of a theatre: the early Abbey Theatre in theory and practice* (New Haven, CT, 1976).

Fleischmann, R., *Catholic nationalism in the Irish Revival: a study of Canon Sheehan, 1852–1913* (London, 1997).

Ford, A., 'The origins of Irish dissent', in K. Herlihy (ed.), *The religion of Irish dissent 1650–1800* (Dublin, 1996), pp 9–30.

Foster, J.W., *Fictions of the Irish Literary Revival: a changeling art* (New York, 1987).

— *Colonial consequences: essays in Irish literature and culture* (Dublin, 1991).

— (ed.), *Nature in Ireland: a scientific and cultural history* (Dublin, 1997).

Foster, R.F., *Modern Ireland, 1600–1972* (London, 1988).

— *Paddy & Mr Punch: connections in Irish and English history* (London, 1993).

— *W.B. Yeats: a life. I: the apprentice mage, 1865–1914* (Oxford, 1997).

Frazier, A., *Behind the scenes. Yeats, Horniman, and the struggle for the Abbey Theatre* (London, 1990).

Friel, Brian, *Selected plays* (London, 1984).

Gibbons, L., K. Rockett & J. Hill (eds), *Cinema and Ireland* (London, 1987).

— *Transformations in Irish culture* (Cork, 1996).

— 'Constructing the canon: versions of the national identity', in S. Deane, A. Carpenter, & J. Williams (eds), *Field Day anthology of Irish writing* (Derry, 1991), vol. 2, pp 950–1223.

— '"A shadowy narrator": history, art and romantic nationalism in Ireland, 1750–1850', in C. Brady (ed.), *Ideology and the historians* (Dublin, 1991), pp 99–127.

— 'From Ossian to O'Carolan' in F. Stafford & H.Gaskill (eds), *From Gaelic to Romantic: Ossianic translations* (Amsterdam, 1998), pp 226–51.

Gilbert, J., *Perfect cities: Chicago's utopias of 1893* (Chicago, 1991).

Glandon, V., 'The *Irish Press* & revolutionary Irish nationalism, 1900–1922', *Eire-Ireland*, 16 (1981) 21–33.

Gledhill, C. (ed.), *Home is where the heart is: studies in melodrama and the women's film* (London, 1987).

Goldring, M., *Pleasant the scholar's life: Irish intellectuals and the construction of the state* (London, 1994).

Gram Holstrom, K., *Monodrama, attitudes, tableaux vivants: studies on some trends of theatrical fashion, 1770–1815* (Stockholm, 1967).

Gray, J., & W. McCann (eds), *An uncommon bookman: essays in memory of J.R.R. Adams* (Belfast, 1996).

Greenacre, D., *Magic lanterns* (Buckinghamshire, 1999).

Grimstead, D., *Melodrama unveiled: American theatre and culture, 1800–1850* (London, 1968).

— 'Melodrama as echo of the historically voiceless', in T. Havern (ed.), *Anonymous Americans: explorations in nineteenth century social history* (Engelwood Cliffs, NT, 1971), pp 80–98.

Hay, Marnie, *Bulmer Hobson and the nationalist movement in twentieth-century Ireland* (Manchester, 2009).

Hanna Bell, S., *The theatre of Ulster* (Dublin, 1972).

Harrington, J.P. (ed.), *Modern Irish drama* (London, 1991).

Harp, R., 'The *Shan Van Vocht* (Belfast, 1896–1899) and Irish nationalism', *Éire-Ireland*, 24 (1989), 42–9.

Hartnoll, P., *The theatre: a concise history* (London, 1997).

Henderson, J.W., *Methodist College Belfast, 1868–1938* (2 vols, Belfast, 1939).

Henry, P., *An Irish portrait: the autobiography of Paul Henry* (London, 1931).

Herr, C., *For the land they loved: Irish political melodramas, 1890–1925* (New York, 1991).

Hogan, R., R. Burnham & D. Poteet, *The rise of the realists, 1910–15* (Dublin, 1979).

Hogan, R., & R. Burnham, *The art of the amateur, 1916–20* (Dublin, 1984).

Hogan, R., & J. Kilroy, *The Irish Literary Theatre, 1899–1901* (Dublin, 1975).

— *Lost plays of the Irish renaissance* (London, 1970).

Holmes, J., & D. Urquart (eds), *Coming into the light: the work, politics and religion of women in Ulster, 1840–1940* (Belfast, 1996).

Howarth, H., *The Irish writers 1880–1940: literature under Parnell's star* (London, 1958).

Howes, M., *Yeats's nations: gender, class and Irishness* (Cambridge, 1996).

Hunt, L., *Politics, culture and class in the French Revolution* (London, 1984).

Hutchinson, J., *The dynamics of cultural nationalism: the Gaelic Revival and the creation of the Irish nation state* (London, 1987).

Ingram, A., & D. Patai (eds), *Rediscovering forgotten radicals: British women writers, 1889–1939* (Chapel Hill, NC, 1993).

Innes, C.L., *Women and nation in Irish literature and society, 1880–1935* (Athens, GA, 1993).

Irish Universal Suffrage Association, 'A member of', *Chartism and repeal: an address to the repealers of Ireland* (Dublin, 1842).

Jacobs, L., 'The woman's picture and poetics of melodrama', *Camera Obscura*, 31 (1993), 120–47.

Jeffares, A.N., *Anglo-Irish literature* (Dublin, 1982).

Jorden, D.E., *Land & popular politics in Ireland: County Mayo from the Plantation to the Land War* (Cambridge, 1994).

Katz Clarke, B., *The emergence of the Irish peasant play at the Abbey Theatre* (Ann Arbor, MI, 1982).

Kearney, R., *Myth and motherland* (Derry, 1984).

— *Transitions: narratives in modern Irish culture* (Manchester, 1988).

— *Postnationalist Ireland: politics, culture, philosophy* (London, 1997).

Kelleher, M., & J. Murphy (eds), *Gender perspectives in nineteenth-century Ireland: public and private spheres* (Dublin, 1997).

Kelly, J. (ed.), *Thomas Davis: literary and historical essays, 1846* (Poole, 1998).

Kelly, J., & E. Domville (eds), *The collected letters of W.B. Yeats, vol. I: 1865–1895* (Oxford, 1986).

Kelly, J., W. Gould & D. Toomey, *The collected letters of W.B. Yeats, vol. II: 1896–1900* (Oxford, 1994).

Kelly, J., & R. Schuchard, *The collected letters of W.B. Yeats, vol. III: 1901–1904* (Oxford, 1994).

— 'The fall of Parnell and the rise of Irish literature: an investigation', *Anglo-Irish Studies*, 2 (1976), 1–23.

— 'Parnell in Irish literature' in D.G. Boyce and A. O'Day (eds), *Parnell in perspective* (London, 1991), pp. 242–83.

Keogh, D., & N. Furlong (eds), *The women of 1798* (Dublin, 1998).

Kiberd, D., *Synge and the Irish language* (London, 1979).

— *Anglo-Irish attitudes* (Derry, 1984).

— *Inventing Ireland* (London, 1995).

— 'White skins, black masks?: Celticism and negritude', *Eire-Ireland*, 31 (1996), 162–75.

— *Irish classics* (London, 2000).

— *The Irish writer and the world* (Cambridge, 2005).

Kilroy, P., *Protestant dissent and controversy in Ireland, 1660-1714* (Cork, 1994).

Kirby, Peadar, Luke Gibbons & Michael Cronin (eds), *Reinventing Ireland: culture and the Celtic Tiger* (London, 2002).

Kirk, John M., & Donall P. Ó Baóill (eds), *Linguistic politics: language policies for Northern Ireland, the Republic of Ireland, and Scotland* (Belfast, 2001).

Kirkland, Richard, *Cathal O'Byrne and the northern revival in Ireland, 1890–1960* (Liverpool, 2006).

Kirshenblatt-Gimblett, B., *Desire culture: tourism, museums, and heritage* (London, 1998).

Kohfeldt, M.L., *Lady Gregory: the woman behind the Irish renaissance* (London, 1985).

Krause, D. (ed.), *The Dolmen Boucicault* (Dublin, 1964).

Leach, William R., *The Wonderful Wizard of Oz by L. Frank Baum* (California, 1991).

Leerssen, J., *Remembrance and imagination: patterns in the historical and literary representation of Ireland in the nineteenth century* (Cork, 1996).

Liesenfeld, V., *The stage and the licensing act* (London, 1981).

Litton, H. (ed.), *Revolutionary woman: Kathleen Clarke, an autobiography, 1878–1972* (Dublin, 1991).

Loeber, M., & R. Loeber, 'Do historical novels inspire Irish historical studies?', *Bulletin of Early Modern Ireland Committee*, 1 (1994), 34–50.

Lloyd, D., *Nationalism and minor literature: James Clarence Mangan and the emergence of Irish cultural nationalism* (London, 1987).

— *Anomalous states: Irish writing and the post-colonial moment* (Dublin, 1993).

— 'Discussion outside history: Irish new histories and the "subalterity effect"', *Subaltern Studies*, 10 (1997), 261–80.

Loughlin, J., *Gladstone, Home Rule and the Ulster question, 1882–93* (London, 1986).

Luddy, M., & C. Murphy (eds), *Women surviving* (Dublin, 1989).

— 'An agenda for women's history, 1800–1900: Part II', *Irish Historical Studies*, 28 (1992), 19–37.

Lundy, J., & A. Mac Póilin (eds), *Styles of belonging: the cultural identities of Ulster* (Belfast, 1991).

McBride, I., *The Siege of Derry in Ulster Protestant mythology* (Dublin, 1997).

McBride White, A., & A. Jeffares (eds), *The Gonne–Yeats letters, 1893–1938* (London, 1992).

MacCarthy M., & J. Morrow (eds), *The Munster plantation in 1641: English migration to Southern Ireland, 1583–1641* (Oxford, 1986).

McClintock, H.F., *Handbook on the traditional old Irish dress* (Dundalk, 1958).

McCullough, J., 'Edward Kilanyi and American *Tableaux Vivants*', *Theatre Survey: the American Journal of Theatre*, 16 (1975), 25–41.

— *Living pictures on the New York stage* (Ann Arbor, MI, 1981).

McCormack, W.J., *From Burke to Beckett: ascendancy, tradition and betrayal in literary history* (Cork, 1994).

McDiarmaid, L. (ed.), *Lady Gregory: selected writings* (London, 1995).

McDowell, R.B., *Alice Stopford Greene: a passionate historian* (Dublin, 1967).

McGee, Owen, 'Fred Allan (1861–1937): Republican, Methodist, Dubliner', *Dublin Historical Record*, 56:2 (Autumn 2003), 205–16.

Mac Liammoir, M., *Theatre in Ireland* (Dublin, 1964).

MacMahon, Timothy, *Grand opportunity: the Gaelic Revival and Irish society, 1893–1910* (New York, 2008).

Marcus, P.L., *Yeats and the beginning of the Irish renaissance* (London, 1970).

Martin, Joann & Carolyn Nordstrom (eds), *Paths to domination, resistance, and terror* (London, 1992).

Mason, E., & R. Ellmann (eds), *The critical writings of James Joyce* (London, 1959).

Mather, F.C., *Chartism* (London, 1972).

Matthew, C. (ed.), *The Gladstone diaries, vol. XII, 1887–1891* (Oxford, 1994).

Mathews, P.J., *Revival: the Abbey Theatre, Sinn Féin, the Gaelic League and the co-operative movement*, vol. 12, Field Day Critical Conditions Series (Cork, 2003).

Maume, P., 'Parnell and the I.R.B. oath', *Irish Historical Studies*, 24 (1995), 363–70.

Merritt, R., 'Melodrama: postmortem for a phantom genre', *Wide-Angle*, 5 (1983), 24–31.

Metcher, P., 'Mary Ann McCracken: a critical Ulsterwoman within the context of her times', *Etudes Irlandaises*, 14 (1989), 143–58.

Mhic Sheain, B., 'Glimpses of Erin Alice Milligan: poet, protestant, patriot', supplement to *Fortnight*, Apr. 1994.

Millis, S., *Discourses of difference: an analysis of women's writing and colonialism* (London, 1993).

Misteil, P. (ed.), *The Irish language and the unionist tradition* (Belfast, 1994).

Moody. T.W., 'The *Times* versus Parnell and Co., 1887–90', *Historical Studies*, 6 (1965), 147–69.

Morgan, A., *Labour and Partition: the Belfast working class, 1905–23* (London, 1991).

Morgan, Lady, *O'Donnell. A national tale* (London, 1815).

Morris, C., & T. Spurgeon (eds), *Interventions: Under which flag? Revisiting James Connolly*, 10:1 (2008).

Morris, C., 'Becoming Irish? The paradoxes of identity', in *Irish University Review, Special Issue: The Irish Literary Revival*, ed. Margaret Kelleher (Spring/Summer 2003), 79–98.

— 'From the margins: Alice Milligan and the Irish Cultural Revival, 1888–1905' (PhD thesis, University of Aberdeen, 1999).

— 'In the enemy's camp: Alice Milligan and *fin de siècle* Belfast', in N. Allen and A. Kelly (eds), *The cities of Belfast* (Dublin, 2003), pp 62–73.

— 'Alice Milligan: Republican tableaux and the Revival' in Seamus Deane & Ciaron Deane (eds), *The Field Day Review*, 6 (2010), 132–65.

— *Alice Milligan and the Irish Cultural Revival*, booklet to accompany National Library of Ireland exhibition (Dublin, 2010).

Myers, S.W., & D.E. McKnight, *Richard Musgrave's memoirs of the Irish rebellion of 1798* (Indiana, 1995).

Nairn, T., *Faces of nationalism: Janus revisited* (London, 1997).

Neale, S., *Cinema and technology: image, sound, colour* (London, 1985).

Nelson, J.M., 'From Rory and Paddy to Boucicault's Myles, Shaun and Conn: the stage Irishman on the London stage, 1830–1860', *Éire-Ireland* 13 (1978), 79–105.

Ó Broin, Leon, *Revolutionary underground: the story of the Irish Republican Brotherhood, 1858–1924* (London, 1976).

O'Ceirin, K. & C. O'Ceirin, *Women of Ireland: a biographical dictionary* (Galway, 1996).

O'Cleirigh, N., 'Lady Aberdeen and the Irish connection', *Dublin Historical Record*, 34 (1985), 28–32.

O'Connor, U., *Celtic dawn: a portrait of the Irish Literary Revival* (Dublin, 1984; 1999).

O'Day, A., *Gladstone, Home Rule and the Ulster question, 1882–93* (London, 1986).

— *Parnell and the first Home Rule episode, 1884–87* (Dublin, 1986).

O Doibhlin, D., *Womenfolk of the Glens of Antrim and the Irish language* (Derry, 1996).

O'Farrell, P. (ed.), *The '98 reader: an anthology of song, prose and poetry* (Dublin, 1998).

O'Hehir, K., 'Alice Milligan: the Celtic Twilight's forgotten star' (MA Thesis, University of North Dakota, 1991).

O'Higgins, Rachel, 'The Irish influence in the Chartist movement', *Past and Present*, 20 (1961), 83–96.

Ojo-Ade, F., 'Contemporary South African theatre & the complexities of commitment', *New Trends and Generation in African Literature*, 20 (1990), 120–34.

O'Keefe, T.J., 'The efforts to celebrate the United Irishmen: the '98 centennial', *Éire-Ireland*, 23 (1988), 51–73.

— 'The art and politics of the Parnell Monument', *Éire-Ireland*, 14 (1984), 6–25.

O'Leary, P., *My story*, trans. Cyril O'Ceirin (Cork, 1974).

O'Leary, P., *The prose literature of the Gaelic Revival, 1881–1921: ideology and innovation* (Pennsylvania, 1994).

O'Malley, C., *A poet's theatre* (Dublin, 1988).

O'Neill, M., *From Parnell to De Valera: a biography of Jenny Wyse Power, 1858–1941* (Dublin, 1991).

O Riordain, M., *The Gaelic mind and the collapse of the Gaelic world* (Cork, 1990).

O'Tuama, Sean, *The Gaelic League idea* (Cork, 1972; 1993).

Owens, G., 'Nationalist monuments in Ireland, *c.*1870–1914: symbolism and ritual', in R. Gillespie & B. Kennedy (eds), *Ireland: art into history* (Dublin, 1994), pp 103–235.

Pethica, J. (ed.), *Lady Gregory's diaries, 1892–1902* (London, 1996).

Pilkington, Lionel, 'Imagining a minority: Protestants and Irish cultural politics,' *Graph: Irish Cultural Review*, 3:2 (1998), 13–17.

— *Theatre and the state in twentieth-century Ireland: cultivating the people* (London, 2001).

Plunkett, H., *Ireland in the new century* (London, 1904).

Poster, Mark, *Sartre's Marxism* (London, 1979).

Pratt, M.L., *Imperial eyes: travel writing and transculturation* (London, 1992).

Pyle, H., *Red-headed rebel. Susan Mitchell: poet and mystic of the Irish Cultural Revival* (Dublin, 1998).

Racine, C., 'Alice Milligan and Irish nationalism', *Harvard Library Bulletin*, 3 (1992), 47–52.

Regan, S., 'W.B. Yeats and Irish cultural politics in the 1890s' in S. Ledger & S. McCracken (eds), *Cultural politics at the fin de siecle* (Cambridge, 1995), pp 66–84.

Richards, S., & D. Cairn, *Writing Ireland: colonialism, nationalism and culture* (Manchester, 1988).

Rivera, D., *My art, my life: an autobiography* (London, 1960; 1991).

Robbins, B., 'Telescopic philanthropy: professionalism and responsibility in *Bleak House*' in H.I. Bhabha (ed.), *Nation and narration* (London, 1990), pp 213–30.

Roddie, R., 'John Wesley's political sensibilities in Ireland, 1747–89' in K. Herlihy (ed.), *The religion of Irish dissent, 1650–1800* (Dublin, 1996), pp 93–104.

Roy, Arundhati, *Listening to grasshoppers: field notes on democracy* (London, 2009).

Rupp, L.J., *Worlds of women: the making of an international women's movement* (Princeton, NJ, 1997).

Rushdie, Salman, *The Wizard of Oz* (London, 1992).

Rydell, R.W., *All the world's a fair: visions of empire at American international expositions, 1876–1916* (London, 1984).

Said, E., *Orientalism* (London, 1978).

— *Edward Said – two films: Out of place/The last interview* (Icarus Films).

Shohat, E., & R. Stam, *Unthinking Eurocentrism: multiculturalism and the media* (London, 1994).

Showalter, E., *The female malady: women, madness, and English culture, 1830–1980* (London, 1987).

Sihra, M. (ed.), *Women in Irish drama: a century of authorship and representation*, (London, 2007).

Smith Clark, W., *The Irish stage in the country towns, 1720–1800* (Oxford, 1965).

Stewart, A.T.Q., *The summer soldiers: the 1798 Rebellion in Antrim and Down* (Belfast, 1995).

Sweeney, B., *Performing the body in Irish theatre* (London, 2008).

Thomas, N., *Colonialism's culture: anthropology, travel, and government* (Oxford, 1994).

Turner Johnston, S. (ed.), *Alice: a life* (Omagh, 1994).

Thuente, M.H., *W.B. Yeats and Irish folklore* (Dublin, 1980).

Vardic, N.A., *Stage to screen: theatrical method from Garrick to Griffith* (Cambridge MA, 1949).

Viswanathan, G., *Outside the fold: conversion, modernity and belief* (Princeton, NJ, 1998).

Ward, M., *Unmanageable revolutionaries: women and Irish nationalism* (London, 1995).

— *Maud Gonne: Ireland's Joan of Arc* (London, 1990).

— *In their own voice: women and Irish nationalism* (Dublin, 1995).

— 'Conflicting interests: the British and Irish suffrage movements', *Feminist Review*, 50 (1995), 127–47.

— *Hannah Sheehy-Skeffington* (Cork, 1997).

Warner, M., *From the beast to the blonde: on fairytales and their tellers* (London, 1994).

Watson, G.J, *Irish identity and the Literary Revival: Synge, Yeats, Joyce and O'Casey* (London, 1979).

Watt, S., *Joyce, O'Casey and the Irish popular theater* (New York, 1991).

Wauchope, P., *Patrick Sarsfield and the Williamite war* (Dublin, 1992).

Welch, R., *The Oxford companion to Irish literature* (Oxford, 1996).

— (ed.), *Wexford: history and society* (Dublin, 1987).

Westerkamp, M.J., *The triumph of laity: Scots-Irish piety and the great awakening, 1625–1760* (Oxford, 1988).

Young, R., *Travellers in Africa: British travelogues, 1850–1900* (Manchester, 1994).

— *Colonial desire: hybridity in theory, culture and race* (New York, 1995).

Index

Compiled by Julitta Clancy. Page references in italics denote illustrations.

Abbey Theatre, 18, 26, 63, 79, 120, 152, 180, 221, 228, 237, 287
  'Abbey style' of acting, 37, 275–6
  Antigone production, AM's poem on, *57, 58, 59*
  Milligan's influences, 37
Aberdeen, Lady, 31, 88, 168, 209
Act of Union 1800, 94–5, 104, 192, 206
Algood, Molly, 287
Algood, Sarah, 287
All Ireland Review, 240
Allan, Fred, 166, 167, 168, 207
Allen, Brother, 292
American Catholic University, 45
American Irish Historical Society, 210
Amnesty Association, 34, 164, 166, 167, 182
Amnesty International, 15, 75
Amnesty movement, 166, 208, 217
An Claidheamh Soluis (The Sword of Light), 76, 242, 247, 259
Angel Records, 82
Anglo-Irish, 116, 118, 120, 123, 137, 211
Anglo-Irish Treaty 1921, 57, 80, 81, 82, 119
Annals of the Irish harpers (Milligan Fox), 45
Anne Devlin (film), 269
anti-colonial struggle, 20, 34, 170, 172, 223, 280, 281, 291; *see also* nationalism; republicans
  1798 centenary commemorations, 185, 188–9, 196–7, 260
  banners, 260
  'Erin', 267–9
  Milligan's writings, 55, 56, 68, 71, 123, 234, 291–2

Protestant contribution, 134, 147, 191–5
anti-feminism, 216
Anti-Partition League, 57, 69, 78
anti-Partition movement, 20, 62, 68, 71, 75, 151, 280, 293
Antient Concert Rooms, Dublin, 233, 258
Antigone (E. Young), 59
Antrim, battle of, 189, 195, 214
Antrim, county, 41, 45, 59, 71, 77–8, 80, 100, 260
archival sources, 19–20, 22, 221, 245, 253, 274, 288, 292, 293
Ards District Lodge, 198–9
Argentina, 42
Armour, Revd J.B., 33
Armour, Jenny, 33
Arnold, Matthew, 30
Ashe, Thomas, 58
Aspects of the Irish question (Gladstone), 85
Atget, Eugène, 271
Austria-Hungary, 113

Balfour, A.J., 169
Ballinahinch, Co. Down, 216
Banba (journal), 60
Bangor, Co. Down, 48
Bank Buildings, Belfast, 24, *28, 29*
Barbados, 120
Bates, Sir Dawson, 73
Bath (England), 45, 49
BBC, 69
Bean na h-Eireann, 209
Béaslaí, Piaras, 274, 284, 285
Beckett, Samuel, 37

Belfast, 20, 61, 78, 85, 87, 92, 99, 127, 133,
　　140, *141*, 144, 145, 146, 147, 148,
　　152, 153, 154, 156, 169, 173, 183,
　　189, 193, 207–8, 262, 271, 273, 287
　　1798 centenary commemorations, 36,
　　　　198–200, 200–1, 204
　　anti-Partition meetings, 68
　　Bigger's house in, 174
　　bigotry and sectarianism, 67
　　city library, 132
　　cultural movement, 44, 140–2
　　Ferguson Centenary, 44–5
　　general elections, 29–30, 58
　　Irish language movement; *see* Belfast
　　　　Gaelic League; Irish language
　　McCracken Society offices, 164
　　Milligan and, 16, 20, 29, 31–2, 42,
　　　　44–5, 59, 132, 136–7, 139, 168;
　　　　family and education, 24–6, 28,
　　　　29, 78, 128–9; theatre
　　　　productions, 58, 287–8
　　newspapers and journals; *see Irish News*;
　　　　Northern Patriot; *Northern Whig*;
　　　　Shan Van Vocht
　　unionist community, 29, 134–5, 136–7,
　　　　153
　　women's movement, 141–2, 156; *see*
　　　　also Irish Women's Association
Belfast Amnesty Association, 164, 167
Belfast Antiquarian Society, 288
Belfast Arts Club, 287
Belfast Arts Society, 262
Belfast Centenary Committee, 198
Belfast College of Art, 36
Belfast Evacuation Scheme, 65
Belfast Evening Telegraph, 193–4
Belfast Gaelic League, 58, 148, 226, 245,
　　246, 262, 265, *266*, 271, 274
Belfast Museum, 143, 247
Belfast Naturalist Field Club, 26, 32, 87,
　　99, 128, 143, 182, 256, 288
　　Glimpses of Erin, and, 87–8

Belfast Peace Agreement, 16, 145
Belfast Pipe Band, 262
Beltaine, 184, 275
Benedict, Pope, 53
Benjamin, Walter, 73, 271
Berger, John, *Ways of seeing*, 274
'Big House' fiction, 118, 120
Big House tradition, 123
Bigger, Francis Joseph, 32, 40, 45, 48, 49,
　　50, 59–60, 77, 112, 143, 149, 159,
　　164, 168, 174, 197, 203, 214, 262
　　Shan Van Vocht, relationship with, 174
Blasket Islands, 113
Bleak House (Dickens), 86
Board of Assistance, 65
Boland, Eavan, 178
Boland, Harry, 59
book sales, 49–50, 54
Bowen, Elizabeth, 118
Bowens' Court (Bowen), 118
Boyd, Eleanor, 77, 80
Boyd, Ernest, 223
Boyd, J.W., 174–6
Boyd, Sinclair, 143
Boyne, Battle of the, 94
Bracken, J.K., 138
Brecht, Bertolt, 222
Brian Boru, 264
Britannia, 100, 101, 102
British Army, 50, 62, 70, 128
British Labour Party, 45
British Liberal Home Rule Federation,
　　154–5, 158
British Parliament, 150
Brittania, 100–2
Brolly, J., 176
Brooke, Charlotte, 91
Brooks, Sydney, 149
Brown, Terence, 241
Browning, Robert, 30
Brugha, Cathal, 59
Bundoran, Co. Donegal, 97

Bunting, Edward, 128, 278, 279
Burke, Edmund, 182
Burns, Charlotte (AM's mother), 24
Byrne, Alfie, 75
Byrne, Myles, 72, 73, 74

Campbell, Joseph, 72, 280
Carbery, Ethna; *see* Johnston, Anna
Carew, Sir George, 235
Carey, James, 96–9
Carey, John, 58, 288
Carleton, William, 91
Carlyle, Thomas, 95
Caroline, Queen, 108
Carsonites, 53
Casement, Roger, 15, 18, 40, *41,* 45, 69,
    149, 218, 275
  Gaelic League, and, 41, 260, 262, 281
  Milligan's relation to, 41, 51, 53–4,
    174, 281, 282
  Protestantism, and, 40
  sketch of, 132, *283*
  trial and execution, 39–40, 51, 53–4,
    55, 60, 62, 70, 207
Catholic Association, 204
Catholic Church, 40, 127
  Gaelic League's mixed classes,
    opposition to, 149, 228
Catholic Emancipation, 104, 192, 193
Catholics, 118, 124, 125
Cavanagh, Michael, 71
Cave Hill, Belfast, 180, 185, *186,* 187,
    188, 260, 276
Ceannt, Áine, 31, 62, 66, 71, 72, 73, 74,
    75, 76, 78, 127–8, 208
Ceannt, Éamonn, 66, 73–4, 75
Celtic Union Congress (Edinburgh,
    1907), 41–2
centenary commemorations for 1798, 20,
    34, 36, 71, 72, 184, 185, 187,
    196–220
  '98 Clubs, 198, 200–1

'98 Executive, 196–8, 201, 202–3,
    205, 207
  Centenary Committee, 152, 202
  commemorative art, 260
  loyalist opposition, 198–200
  Milligan's agenda, 198
  Scotland '98 Committees, 176
  Shan Van Vocht, role played by, 182
  tensions and internal conflict, 197,
    200–5, 217, 231
  Wexford commemorations, 69
  women and, 206–20
Central Branch Gaelic League, 229
Charles I, King, 116
Chartists, 107–8
Chicago World Fair (1893), 273
Childers, Erskine, 59
Childers, Mrs Erskine, 59
Church of Ireland, 147
Civil War, 50, 56, 58, 59, 80, 118, 119,
    151, 158, 292
Clarke, John, 162, 164, 165, 167, 168
Clarke, Kathleen, 75
Clarke, Tom, 75
class system, 91–2
Cloughaneely, Co. Donegal, 40, 148
Coffey, Denis, 79
Colbert, Con, 75
Collins, Michael, 59
Colum, Pádraic, 61, 72–3, 127, 183, 262,
    282, 287
community drama, 221, *222,* 224, 228–9
community remembrancing, 16
Concannon, Helena, 79, 215
Concannon, Thomas, 71, 259, 282
Congress of Celtic Union (Edinburgh,
    1907), 41–2
Connacht, 120
Connolly, James, 18, 34, 45, 69, 75, 150,
    170, 180, 181, 185, 211, 217, 218,
    276
  Irish Republic, concept of, 181

Connolly, Joseph, 62
Connolly, Sean, 69
Constitution of Ireland (1937), 72, 73
Cook's Travel, 100, 209
Cork, 39, 92
Cork National Players, 223
Cork National Theatre Society, 235
Cormac Mac Airt, 103
Cousins, James, 29, 127, 193, 244
Coxhead, Elizabeth, 40
Crime Special Branch, 205, 207
Cromwell, Oliver, 95, 116, 118, 119, 120
Cromwellian plantations, 115–16, 120
Cromwellian settlement, 104, 119
The Cromwellians (Alice Milligan), 26, 31,
    84, 117, 118–20, 120–1, *122*, 123,
    216, 249
Crone, John Smyth, 164
Croppies Acre (Dublin), 200
Cross roads in Ireland (Colum), 61
Cuchulainn (legendary figure), 58
Cultural Revival; *see* Irish Cultural Revival
Cumann na mBan, 252
Cumann na nGaedael, 234
Curran, May, 229
Cusack, Michael, 288
Cushendal, Co. Antrim, 262, 275

Daily Express, 226, 227, 237, 242, 246
Daly, Ned, 75
Daughters of Ireland; *see Inghinidhe na
    hÉireann*
Davis, Thomas, 30, 69, 78, 146, 147, 153,
    178, 191, 192, 193, 256, 260, 283
Davitt, Michael, 30, 105, 106, 115, 130, 134
de Blácam, Aodh, 241
de Valera, Éamon, 18, 62, 69, 78, 79, 81, 82
    Anti-Partition League, 69
    escape from Lincoln Prison, 55, 156
    Milligan's political loyalty to, 56–7
de Valera, Sinéad (Ní Fhlannagáin), 51,
    53, 55, 56, 60, 207, 293

De Vere, Aubrey, 89
The Dead (Joyce), 294
Deane, Seamus, 124
Decca Records, 82
Declaration of Human Rights 1948, 145
Deirdre of the sorrows (Synge), 287
Department of External Affairs, 280–1
Derry, 27, 31, 32, 62, 112, 148, 198, 262,
    285
Derry Gaelic League, 245
Derry Journal, 49, 60, 70, 257, 261
Derry Standard, 246
Dervorgilla (Gregory), 117
Desmond, Joan, 234–5
Devlin, Anne, 178, 252, 269, 277
Devlin, Joseph, 167, 201, 204
Dickens, Charles, 86
Dickson, David, 190
Dickson, Edith, 179, 182
Digges, Dudley, 233
Dillon, John, 105, 201
Dixon, Henry, 181, 196, 207, 208
Dobbin, Henry, 208
Dobbs, Margaret, 149; *The doctor and Mrs
    Macauley*, 248
Donegal, county, 62, 63, 64, 67, 97, 100,
    137, 143, 145, 256–7, 260
Donegal Gaelic League, 274
Donegal Independent, 116
Donegal plantation papers, 116
Douglas, Grace, 288
Doyle, Angela, 252
drama, 79, 111, 218, 220, 221–3
    bi-lingual productions, 146
    community drama, 221, *222*, 224, 228–9
    costumes, 224–6, 229
    Irish theatres, 223; *see also* Abbey
        Theatre
    library scheme, 229–30
    Milligan's plays and tableaux; *see*
        Ossianic trilogy; plays; *tableaux
        vivants*

national theatre movement; *see* Irish
National Theatre; Irish national
theatre movement
newspapers, published in, 226–7
Ossianic dialogues, 237
Drogheda, Co. Louth, 119
Dublin, 27–9, 31, 32, 49, 50, 54, 59, 61,
65, 66, 68, 72, 78, 85, 103, 123, 130,
134, 173, 262
1798 centenary commemorations
(1898), *199,* 200, *201,* 260
Civil War, 59
Irish language classes, 143
newspapers, 161
Oireachtas (1899), 246
Parnell's funeral procession, *135*
royal visit (1897), 276
theatre, 223; *see also* Abbey Theatre;
Irish National Theatre
Dublin Castle, 70, 75, 99, 156, 197, 200,
207
Dublin Corporation, 200
Dublin Gaelic League, 244
Dublin Irish Literary Society, 161
Dublin Municipal Council, 200
Dublin Penny Journal, 91
Duffy, Gavan, 90, 159
Dundalk, Co. Louth, 36–7

Easter Rising 1916, 24, 39, 40, 48, 54, 55,
59, 67, 69, 73, 151, 181, 218, 293–4
Declaration, 151
women in, 74, 151
Edinburgh, 41
Edmund Burke Debating Society, 182
Educational Company of Ireland, 60
Edward VII, King, 113
Elliot, Marianne, 191–2
Ellis-Fermor, Una, 234
Ellmann, Maud, 277
emigrant Irish communities, 259, 284–5
emigration, 91

Emmet, Robert, 72, 78, 147, 159, 193,
198, 252, 269, 277, 283
English democratic puritanism, 121
English language, 283
English people, 95, 106
tourists in Ireland, 92–4, 99, 100, 138
English policy in Ireland, 104, 112–16
Enniscorthy, Co. Wexford, 72
Enniskillen, Co. Fermanagh, 54
Eos (Methodist College magazine), 25
Erin, 100–2, 111
European Republicanism, 188
Evening Telegraph, 117
Exhibition Hall, Belfast, 265

The Faerie Queene (Spenser), 26
Farrelly, Agnes, 149
Father Mathew Hall, Dublin, 276
Fay, Frank, 233–4, 241, 242
Fay brothers, 36, 233, 239, 267, 268, 287,
291
Feis Ceoil, *261,* 261–2
feminism, 149–50; *see also* Irish Women's
Association (IWA); women
Fenians, 17, 31, 33, 42, 106, 108, 125–6,
158, 159, 179, 207, 291; *see also*
Amnesty Association
anniversary celebrations, 165–6
Ferdia (legendary figure), 58, 59
Ferguson, Samuel, 89, 128
centenary commemorations, 44–5
Fermanagh, county, 143
Festival of the Glens (1904), 148–9
Fianna Fáil, 152
Fine Gael, 80
First World War, 44, 45, 59, 62, 75, 112,
281–2
FitzGerald, Lord Edward, 109, 159
flags, 69–70
Flanagen, Brendan, 69
Flanagen, Pat, 70
Flannery, James, 244

Flight of the Earls (1607), 93
Foley, Dermot, 143
Foster, Arnold, 30
Four Irish songs (Milligan sisters), *46, 47, 254*
Foynes Gaelic League, 264
freedom, 15–16, 49, 106–7, 185, 192, 294
Freeman's Journal, 242, 244
French revolution, 178, 216
Friel, Brian, *Translations,* 116
Furlong, Alice, 179
Furlong, Nicholas, 206
futurism, 111–13

The Gael, 60
Gaelic Athletic Association (GAA), 138, 173, 288
Gaelic Journal, 181
Gaelic League, 19, 27, 28, 34, 36, 48, 51, 55, 71, 79, 90, 142, 145, 146, 147, 155, 173, 182, 185, 206, 223, 226, 227, 229, 236, 242, 244, 255, 259, 264, 265
    cultural festivals, 69
    fundraising, 259–60
    GPO tableau (1905), 276–7
    Milligan's involvement in, 37–42, 54, 123–4, 144–7, 228; criticisms of Milligan, 137, 143; local activism, 284–6; magic lantern shows, 37, 38, 79, 88, 184, 230, 256–60; plays and *tableaux,* 37, 58, 79, 90, 148, 184, 221, 230, 246–7, 252, 260–1, 265–8, 271, 273, 274, 276–7, 286–7
    mixed classes, Church opposition to, 149, 228
    negative extremism, 282
    non-sectarianism, 146
    northern origins and Belfast contributors, 141, 143; *see also* Belfast Gaelic League

opposition to, 39, 262
political neutrality, 137, 147, 288–9
Protestants in, 39–40
Tableaux Committee, 260
Ulster Delegates, 41
women and, 149, 151
Gaelic Ulster, 61, 73
Gaiety Theatre (Dublin), 276
Gardener, J.R., 26
Gardiner, S.R., 119
General Post Office, Dublin, 276
The Gentlewoman, 270, 271, 272
Gibbons, Luke, 98–9, 170, 269
Gilbert, Sir John, 120
Gilbert and Sullivan, 135
Gill, T.P., 226
Gill & Co. publishers, 81–2
Gladstone, William Ewart, 85, 87, 94, 113
Glendon, Fr, 233
Glens of Antrim, 260
Glimpses of Erin (Seaton and Alice Milligan), 26, 27, 84, 85–102, 103, 104, 106, 111, 113, 114, 119, 121, 128, 129, 130, 157, 158, 190, 192
    Belfast Naturalist Field Club, origins in, 87–8
    contents, 88–9
    duality at centre of, 94–6
    economic deprivation, interpretation of, 91–2
    English tourists, views on, 92–4, 99, 100
    Erin and Brittania, 100–2, *101*
    historical and political context, 85–6
    historical writings, 91, 104–5
    poetry, 88, 89–90
    secrecy, consciousness about, 96–7
    women in, 100–2
The glories of Ireland (Dunne and Lennox, eds), 45–8
Goldsmith, Oliver, 65, 89
Gomez, Alice, 135

Gonne, Maud, 18, 36, 40, 75, 83, 151–2, 152–3, 159, 168, 179, 182, 188, 206, 207, 223, 265, 268, 276, 287
Gortmore, Co. Tyrone, 112
Graves, A.P., 156, 255
Gray, Betsy, 215–16
Gray, William, 143
Greenaway, Kate, 157
Gregory, Augusta, 36, 103, 117, 213, 221, 223, 227–8, 242, 243–4, 287
Griffith, Arthur, 36, 79, 113, 184, 242, 258, 281
Grimstead, David, 118
Gwynn, Stephen, 40

Hales, professor, 26
Hannay, James Owen, 147
Harrington, T., 202
Heaney, Seamus, 16–17
Henry, Paul, 127
historic memories, 69, 215, 278, 279
historical archives, 116
Hobson, Bulmer, 50, 53, 60, 149, 154, 158, 184
Hobson, Mary, 154, 155–6, 158
Holloway, Joseph, 45, 227, 235–6, 238, 239, 254–5
Holstrom, Kirsten Gram, 264
Home Rule, 26, 85–6, 87, 94, 99, 102, 112, 116, 117, 123, 131
Home Rule Bill, 1912, 44
Hope, James, 195, 215
Hopper, Nora, 34, 182
Horgan, John, 184
Horniman, Annie, 26
House of Commons, 202
Houston, Seán, 75
Hull, Eleanor, 45
human rights, 145, 281, 292
Hussey, Michael, 143
Hutchinson, Clive, 87
Hutton, Margaret, 48, 149, 260, 265

Hyde, Douglas, 45, 59, 71, 146–7, 182, 203, 223, 241, 255–6, 280, 285–6, 287
de-Anglicization of Ireland, call for, 170
founding of Gaelic League, 148
A literary history of Ireland, 237

identity politics, 20–1, 40, 119–20, 124–5, 140, 231, 245, 279, 290; *see also* Irish identity; nationalism; unionists
Indian famine relief movement, 78
Inghinidhe na hÉireann (Daughters of Ireland), 36, 56, 151, 153, 184, 223, 233, 252, 254, 260, 265, 267–9, 287, 291
Inventing Ireland (Kiberd), 20–1
Invincibles, the, 97
Ireland's Own, 224
Irish-Americans, 110, 176, 209
Irish Book Lover, 49, 164, 288
The Irish Bookshop (Dublin), 49, 54
Irish Citizen Army, 69
Irish Cultural Revival, 16, 18–19, 20–1, 30–1, 33, 36, 56, 120, 139, 140, 252; *see also* Irish language; Irish national theatre movement
accomplishments and impact of, 21, 172
Belfast, in, 140–2
commemoration, and, 216; *see also* centenary commemorations for 1798
Connolly's views, 217
multi-dimensional movement, 17, 170, 284
newspapers and journals, 184
radical modernism, 269–77
railway network, use of, 100
women, role of, 151, 152
Irish Folk Song Society, 53, 97, 259
Irish Free State, 24, 50, 68, 72, 140, 145
Irish Freedom, 76
Irish Homestead, 129, 184

Irish identity, 18, 20–1, 44, 84, 86, 87,
    100, 117–18, 124–5, 143, 153, 231,
    284
    colonial stereotypes, 40, 43–4, 100,
        124, 138
    language, and, 143, 146–8, 234–6,
        241–2, 282–3
    religion, and, 39–40, 43, 124, 137–8,
        146, 211, 242–3, 281, 290
    visual culture and, 256, 262
Irish Independent, 44, 132, 241; *see also*
    Irish Weekly Independent
Irish Industries Association, 31, 32, 51,
    154, 168
Irish Industries Committee, 88
Irish language, 27, 28, 31, 37–8, 39, 45,
    127, 140, 172, 233, 235–6, 242, 282;
    see also Gaelic League
    Belfast's language movement, 31–2, 78,
        137, 140, 141, 142–3, 148, 149,
        157, 278, 279
    Catholicism, association with, 146–7
    court cases, difficulties encountered in,
        157
    drama, 241–2, 274
    Irish identity, and, 143, 146–8, 234–6,
        241–2, 282–3
    Irish speakers, numbers of, 172
    Milligan and, 31–2, 142–9; *see also*
        Gaelic League
    papers and journals, 184
    revolutionary weapon, as, 284
    unionist attitudes to, 145
Irish Language Society, 155
Irish Language Week (Dublin), 260–1
Irish Literary Reading Circle, 182
Irish Literary Revival, 133, 134
Irish Literary Society, 34, 137, 226
Irish Literary Theatre, 18, 36, 82, 90, 223,
    227–8, 233, 239, 241, 242, 243, 273,
    287
Irish Loyal and Patriotic Union, 85

Irish music, 37, 45, 46, 47, 61, 128, 129,
    143, 154, 155, 156, 172, 216, 246,
    247, 255, 259, 262, 275, 278–9
Irish National Aid and Volunteer
    Dependant's Fund, 54
Irish National Dramatic Society, 233
Irish National Federation League, 202,
    203
Irish National Foresters, 176
Irish National League, 85
Irish National Literary Society, 71
Irish National Party, 29, 98
Irish National Theatre, 20, 222, 223, 228,
    275, 276, 284; *see also* Abbey Theatre
Irish national theatre movement, 36, 37,
    82, 221–2
    anti-colonialist agenda, 223
    component groups, 223
    language, reliance on, 276
    Milligan's involvement in, 36–7, 223–
        30, 286–7, 286–8
    women, role of, 291
Irish National Theatre Society, 223
Irish News, 105, 146, 153, 156, 181, 189,
    193, 201, 203, 248
Irish parliament, 192
Irish Parliamentary Party (IPP), 85, 103,
    104–5, 105–6, 112, 123, 131, 150,
    167, 197, 201, 202, 203–4, 205, 217
Irish peace process (1990s), 146
Irish Players Society, 223
Irish Preservation Society, 27, 28
Irish Press, 62, 67, 70, 74, 208
Irish public opinion on Home Rule (1886),
    85
Irish question, 85
Irish Republic, 178, 181
Irish Republican Army (IRA), 50, 59, 73,
    81
Irish Republican Brotherhood (IRB), 33,
    62, 164, 166, 196, 207, 208, 217
Irish Review, 17, 72, 280

Irish self-determination, 102, 130

Irish Socialist Republican Party, 45, 150, 181

Irish songs, 45, *46, 47*

Irish Statesman, 230, 278, 279

Irish Times, 65, 74, 80, 101, 290

Irish Volunteers, 17, 51, 169, 277

Irish Volunteers Dependants' Fund, 58

Irish Weekly Freeman, 32, 224, 226, 230, 233, 244, 268

Irish Weekly Independent, 32, 132, 133, 164, 166, 168, 196, 207, 214

    Milligan's column, 126, 136, 161

Irish Women's Association (IWA), 32, 33, 34, 140, 149–51, 152, 153–8, 154, 155, 156, 157, 161–2, 179, 182, 189, 192, 216, 293

    Home Reading Circles, 158, 159

    inclusivity policy, 153

    role and objective of, 153, 155

    unionist opposition, 154–5, 162

Irish Women's Centenary Union, 150–1, 206–7, 208, 209–10

Irwin, Thomas Caulfield, 91

Johnson, L., 135

Johnston, Anna ('Ethna Carbery'), *23,* 32, 33, 48, 63, 80, 106, 133, 143, 149, 152, 158, 167, 172, 183, 188, 197, 203, 207, 215, 257, 265, 267, *270,* 271, 273

    Boyd, relationship with, 174–5, 174–6

    death of, 48, 278

    journals, co-editing of; *see Northern Patriot; Shan Van Vocht*

    reaction to discovery of her real name, 164–5

    withdrawal from McCracken Society, 165

Johnston, Lionel, 180

Johnston, Maggie, 63–4

Johnston, Robert, 33, 164, 207–8

Journal of Irish Folk Song, 45

Joyce, James, 98–9, 157, 239, 294

Joyce, Myles, 156, 157

Kearney, Richard, 242–3

Keating, Geoffrey, 91

Keenan, Michael, 108

Kelly, John, 134

Keogh, Dáire, 206

Kiberd, Declan, 20–1, 237–8, 252

Kickham Society, 182

Kiely, Benedict, 19, 76–7

Kildare Club, 244

Killeen, Molly, 81, 82, 291

Kilmainham Jail (Dublin), 73, 76

    women prisoners, 252, 273, 277

King's College, London, 25–6, 28, 85, 119

Kirkland, Richard, 148

Knox, John, 61

Knox, Kathleen, 179

Ladies' Land League, 207

Land League, 105, 106, 109, 115, 207, 276

land question, 91, 92

Lavery, minister, 198–9

Lawless, Emily, 42, 159

Leader, The (San Francisco), 116, 123–4, 125

Leamy, Edward, 31

Ledwidge, Francis, 16

Letterkenny, Co. Donegal, 240, 246, 256, 274

Liberals, 93, 94, 154

The life of Wolfe Tone (Alice Milligan), 200, 209–10, *210, 211*

Limerick, battle of, 191

Lincoln Prison, 156

Linen Hall Library (Belfast), 45, 169

Listening to grasshoppers: field notes on democracy (Arundhati Roy), 15

A literary history of Ireland (Hyde), 237

Liverpool, 27, 29, 281, 284–5

Loach, Ken, 118, 119
local activism, 284–6
London, 133, 173, 259, 284
London Irish Folk Song Society, 97, 259
London Irish Literary Society, 80, 161
Lough Swilly, 93
Loyalists, 125
loyalists, 120
Lysaght, Sean, 87
Lyttle, Revd, 189

MacAleer, Sheila, 81, 283
McBride, John, 75, 176
McBride, Sean, 15, 18, 75, 82
McCabe, Mr, 203–4
McCann, Edith, 265, 271
McCarthy, Justin, 131
MacCathmhaiol, Seaghan, 46, 254
McCoy, Gordon, 145
McCracken, Henry Joy, 159, 195, 214, 215; *see also* McCracken Literary Society
McCracken, Mary, 178
McCracken Literary Society, 32–3, 34, 140, 155, 158, 159, 161, 164–9, 189, 197, 216–17; *see also Northern Patriot*
  advert of *Christmas story, 160*
  commemorative gatherings, 159
  internal tensions, 152, 162–7; Milligan and Johnston's departure, 162, 164, 167, 178
  library and reading room, 159–61
  political affiliations, 159
  unionist opposition, 162
MacDermot, Sean, 75, 76
MacDonagh, Thomas, 17, 18, 22, 39, 48, 75, 77, 137, 260
McGarrity, Joseph, 53, 59, 61, 63, 70, 71–2
MacGinley, Patrick, 143
McGowan, Elsie, 271, 273
MacKillip's Ladies Collegiate School, Derry, 27

MacManus, Lily, 130
MacManus, Seamus, 34, 40, 51, 80, 123, 127, 182, 183
MacNamara, Andrew, 273
MacNeill, Ada, 40, 55, 149, 260, 262
MacNeill, Eoin, 144, 146–7, 148, 246
MacNiece, Louis, 127
McSweeny, Mr, 28, 29
MacSwiney, Terence, 39, 40, 113
Madden, Dr, 159, 215
magic lantern shows, 17, 34, 37, 38, 79, 88, *139,* 172, 230, 256–60, 288
  1798 centenary commemorations, 187, *201,* 216
  magic lantern, *258*
  Parnell's funeral procession (1891), *135*
Mallin, Michael, 75
Mangan, Henry, 82, 227–8
Mangan, James Clarence, 156
Marcus Ward publishing company, 157
Markievicz, Constance, 40, 74, 151, 209
Martin, Mrs John, 210
Martin & Lester press (Dublin), 60
Martyn, Edward, 223, 227, 242, 244
Maxwell, Kate, 209–10
May, Robert, 288
Methodist College Belfast, 24–5, *25,* 28
Methodists, 24, 85–6, 95, 166, 183
Mhic Sheain, Brighid, 127
Miligan, Ernest, 48
Milligan, Alice, *23, 81*
  biographical overview, 22–4; *1866– 1915,* 23–48; *1916–30,* 49–61; *1930–53,* 61–83
  drama, involvement in; *see* drama; Irish national theatre movement; plays; *tableaux vivants*
  education, 24–6, 32, 119; self re- education programme, 22, 28–9, 30, 32
  family; *see* Milligan family

family carer, as, 49, 50, 61–4, 65
Irish language, and; *see* Gaelic League;
    Irish language
journals, co-editing of; *see Northern*
    Patriot; *Shan Van Vocht*
nationalism, 29–34
radio, use of; *see* radio broadcasts
women's movement, and; *see* Irish
    Women's Association; women
writings, 26–7, 30; *see also The*
    Cromwellians; Glimpses of Erin;
    plays; poems; *A Royal Democrat*
Milligan, Charles, 50, 57, 62, 69, 82
Milligan, Edith; *see* Wheeler, Edith
Milligan, Edward, 61, 62
Milligan, Ernest, 24, 45, 50, 61, 66, 80,
    81, 82
Milligan, Eveleen, 156
Milligan, Maud, 61, 62, 63, 65, 66, 77
Milligan, Seaton, 24, 28, 38, 45, 63, 85,
    87, 88, 91, 99, 114, 123, 128, 157,
    166; *see also Glimpses of Erin*
    library of, 49
Milligan, William, 45, 50, 53, 59, 60, 61,
    64, 65, 280
Milligan family, 24, 26, 43–4, 49, 50, 60,
    61–2, 124, 127, 128–30
    archives, 19, 292–3
    political complexities, 292
    self-education, 128–9
Milligan Fox, Charlotte, 27, 45, 48, 49,
    53, 97, 132, 179, 244, 259
Milton, John, 120
Mitchel, John, 150, 159, 193, 209, 210,
    283
Mitchell, Susan, 17, 22, 139, 223, 224,
    279, 280, 291, 292
Moneyreagh, 32, 33, 153
Moore, George, 242, 243–4, 287
Moore, Thomas, 89, 262
Morgan, Austen, 158
Morgan, Lady, 111

Morrow, Frank, 247–8
Morrow, Fred, 58
Morrow brothers, 287
Mountcharles, Co. Donegal, 257
Mountfield, 65, 66, 71, 77, 82
Mulcahy, Richard, 80, 81, 82
Murphy, Cillian, 118
Murphy, Fr John, 190
Murphy, Fr Michael, 190
Murphy, Pat, 269
Musgrave, Richard, *Memoirs,* 190

Napoleon, 126
The Nation, 168–9, 192
National Bank, 39
National Federation and National League
    (NFNL), 201–3
national identity; *see* Irish identity
national language; *see* Irish language
National Library of Ireland (Dublin), 18,
    28, 31, 43, 80, 130, 132, *136,* 169,
    230, 292
National Literary societies, 173, 182
National Literary Theatre, 79
national theatre movement; *see* Irish
    national theatre movement
national unity, 39, 133
National University of Ireland, 79
National Workingmen's Club, 164
nationalism, 29–30, 31–2, 105, 121; *see*
    also northern nationalists
    language, and, 147; *see also* Irish
        language
    literature, 159
    newspapers, 32–4, 226
    'political tourists', 92–4, 100
    Protestant nationalists, 39–40, 48,
        192–3
    tensions within, 162, 164–5, 197,
        200–5, 217
New Ireland, 54, 55
The new Ireland (Brooks), 149

New Irish Library, 182
New York, 72, 82, 86, 176
New York Times, 98
newspapers and journals, 111, 112, 293
    Cultural Revival, associated with, 184
    nationalist, 32–4, 132, 226
    plays published in, 226–7, 234, 240,
        249
    unionist, 154
Nic Shiubhlaigh, Máire, 49, 63, 68, 262,
    280, 287
    praise for Milligan and Johnston, 180–1
Northern Anti-Partition Council, 57
Northern Council for Unity, 69
Northern Ireland, 24, 50, 67, 73, 115,
    137, 140, 141, 164, 190, 292
    historical cultural legacy, 140
    Irish language, treatment of, 144, 145
    Peace Agreement (1998), 16, 145
northern nationalists, 76, 162, 164–5
Northern Patriot, 32–4, 140, 152, 158,
    161, 168, 169, 197, 208–9, 217
    first issue, *163*
    Milligan and Johnston' departure from,
        162–7
    Shan Van Vocht, contrasted with, 173,
        178
    subscription rates, *165*
northern Protestants; *see* Ulster
    Protestants; unionists
Northern Whig, 154–5
novels (by Alice Milligan); *see The*
    Cromwellians; *A Royal Democrat*
Nutt, Alfred, 227

O'Brennan, Kitty, 66, 74, 78
O'Brennan, Lily, 63, 66, 68, 70, 72, 73,
    75, 80
O'Brien, Charlotte Grace, 86
O'Brien, Conor Cruise, 280
O'Brien, M.J., 176
O'Brien, William, 105, 201, 203

O'Brien, William Smith, 108, 279
O'Byrne, Cathal, 64
O'Connell, Daniel, 134
O'Connell Schools, Dublin, 292
O'Connor, Feargus, 107, 109
O'Curry, Eugene, 91
O'Daly, Mr, 76
O'Doherty, Sir Cahir, 106
Ó Donnchadha, Tadhg ('Tórna'), 172, 241
O'Donnell, Patrick, 97, 98
O'Donnell, Red Hugh, 55–6, 156, 159,
    234, 257
O'Donoghue, D.J., 48
O'Donovan, James, 159
O'Donovan, John, 66, 89, 91, 143
O'Donovan Rossa, Jeremiah, 77
O'Faoláin, Sean, 74
O'Grady, Standish, 226, 234, 281
O'Growney, Fr Eugene, 241
O'Hanrahan, Mr, 75–6
O'Higgins, Rachel, 108
O'Keefe, Thomas, 202
O'Keefe, Timothy, 202, 203
O'Leary, John, 77, 150, 159, 200, 206,
    207, *243,* 244, 281
O'Leary, Fr Peter, 146, 147
O'Mahony, John, 132
O'Neill, Eamonn, 229
O'Neill, Hugh, 257
O'Neill, Owen Roe, 82, 159
O'Neill Russell, 175
O'Shea, Katherine, 131
O'Shea, Patrick John ('Conan Maol'),
    143, 278–9
Ó Siochrú, Micheál, 119
O'Sullivan, Estella, 64
O'Sullivan, Seamus, 64
Office of Public Works (Belfast), 59
Omagh, Co. Tyrone, 19, 24, 64, 70, 71,
    72, 74, 80, 128, 267, 273, 287, 293
Omagh Court House, 69
Orange Order, 94, 125, 193, 198–200, 216

Ormond Players, 233
Ossianic tales, 90, 237
Ossianic trilogy (Alice Milligan), 58, 90,
    227, 231, 237–45, 273, 274
  chronology, 247
  conception of, 246–7, 248–9
  Irish language translations, 241–2
  The last feast of the Fianna, 79, 82, 226,
    227, 238, *238*, 239, 241, *243*,
    243–5, 246, 249, 264
  Oisín and Pádraic, 238
  Oisín in Tír na nÓg, 238, 287
  tableaux, 246–8
Our Irish theatre (Gregory), 227–8

Parnell, Charles Stewart, 18, 29, 30, 31,
    67, 84, 98, 104–5, 106, 109, 130–6,
    180, 193
  death and funeral, 112, 121, 132, 133,
    134–5, *135*
  sketch of, *131*
Parnell split (1890), 85, 130
Parnellites, 130, 132, 136
  newspapers, 132
Partition, 50, 54, 58, 67, 69, 71, 85, 278,
    280, 292; *see also* anti-Partition
    movement
*Partners in revolution: the United Irishmen
    and France* (Elliot), 191–2
Patrick, Saint, 90
Pattern, Winifred, 179
Pearse, Patrick, 38, 39, 75, 76, 77, 146,
    147, 242
Pearse, Willie, 75
PEN, 74, 78
Pender, Moira, 154, 155, 174, 179, 189
Pender, M.T., 156
Pender, Nora, 156
People's Rights Society, 182
Phoenix Park murders, 97
photographic images, 88, 253, 256, 258,
    270, 271, 272, 273, 274, 276, 288

Pilkington, Lionel, 120
plays (by Alice Milligan), 36–8, 79, 230–
    51, 285–6; *see also* Ossianic trilogy;
    tableaux vivants
  Brian of Banba, 231, 240
  The daughter of Donagh, 58, 120–1,
    227, 231, 233, 249, 251
  The deliverance of Red Hugh O'Donnell,
    55–6, 224, 226, 231, 233, 234,
    235
  The earl from Ireland, 230, 231
  The French are on the sea, *218*, 218–20,
    219, 230, 231
  The green upon the cape, 230, 231–3,
    234
  The harp that once, 230, 231
  Irish language, and, 146, 241–2, 274
  The last of the Desmonds, 231, 234–6
  newspapers, published in, 226–7, 234,
    249
  radical modernism, 269–77, 288
  The wearing of the green, 224
Plunkett, Joseph Mary, 75
poems (by Alice Milligan), 31, 32–3, 42–
    3, 53, 60, 71, 80–2, 88, 89, 123, 190
  'A ballad of Roger Casement', 70
  'Antigone at the Abbey Theatre', *57*,
    58, 59
  'At the Castle', 70
  'Brian of Banba', 31, 76
  Hero Lays, 42, 60, *289*
  historical ballads, 132–3
  in 1916–22 period, 54–6, 57–9, 70,
    75–6
  'Ode for 6 October', 133
  'Ode to political tourists', 43–4, 93–4
  'The ash tree of Uisneach', 70
  'The lament of Niamh', 90
  'Till Ferdia came', 58, 59
  'Under which flag?', 69
  'When I was a little girl', 42–3, 125–7,
    128

Poems and ballads (Rooney), 260
political tourists, 92–4, 100
Portadown, 32
Portadown, Co. Armagh, 153
poses plastiques, 247, 254, 262; see also *tableaux vivants*
Poster, Mark, 121
Postnationalist Ireland (Kearney), 242–3
Power, Mrs, 229
Praeger, Rosamund, 58, 149, 265, 288
Prendergast, John Patrick, 91, 120
Presbyterians, 193
Protestants, 31, 104, 116, 118, 120, 123, 124, 125, 134, 137, 155, 193, 194; *see also* Anglo-Irish; Ulster Protestants; unionists
    alienation, 194
    colonial legacy, 84, 121, 137
    Home Rule, and, 85–6
    identity, 39–40
    Irish language, and, 39–40, 58
    loyalism, 120
    massacre of 1641, 95
    Milligan's Protestant heritage, 123, 124
    nationalists/republicans, 39–40, 48, 147, 191–5
    United Irishmen, 33, 34, 187, 188, 191
psychical beliefs, 51–4, 60

Queen's College, Belfast, 28
Queen's University, Belfast, 78

radical modernism, 269–77, 288
radio broadcasts, 28, 31, 64, 69, 78, 127–8, 280, 287
railways, 99–100
    rebellion of 1798, 33, 39, 72, 104, 107, 159, 174, 194
        centenary commemorations; *see* centenary commemorations for 1798
        Milligan's plays, 231, 251

sectarian interpretations, 190, 193
    women, role of, 206
Red Hugh O'Donnell (O'Grady), 234
Redmond, John, 112
religious identity; *see* Irish identity
Reliques of Irish poetry (1789), 91
repeal of the Union, 192
Republic of Ireland Act 1948, 112
republican flag, 69–70
republican ideal, 216, 220
republicans, 61, 96–7, 124; *see also* Easter Rising 1916; Irish Republican Brotherhood; United Irishmen
    anti-Treaty, 56–7, 119
    prisoners, 54–6, 57–8; women in Kilmainham Jail, 252, 273, 277
    Protestant, 193, 194, 195
Ribbonmen, 108, 109
Robinson, Lennox, 230
Roche, Fr Philip, 190
Rolleston, T.W., 31, 48, 51, 147, 181, 226, 239
Rooney, William, 182, 260, 262
Rossetti, Gabriel, 26
Rotunda (Dublin), 276
Rowan, Hill Wilson, 108
Roy, Arundhati, 15
Royal Antiquarian Society, 26, 256
A Royal Democrat (Alice Milligan), 26–7, 84, 102–16, 121, 123, 128, 130, 131–2, 133, 134, 135, 136, 138, 157, 290
    English policy in Ireland, 112–16
    futurism, 111–13
    newspapers in, 112
Royal Irish Academy, 26, 28–9, 88, 143
Ruskin, John, 100, 156
Russell, George (Æ), 17, 18, 19, 42–3, 51, 53, 60, 127, 221, 234, 244, 279, 287, 289, 291
    Deirdre, 286–7
Ryan, Mark, 62, 207
Ryan, William Patrick, 144, 170

St Anne's Cathedral, Belfast, 248
St Colum's Minor Hall, Derry, 246
St George's Church, Belfast, 248
St Malachi's Priory, Dundalk, 233
Salisbury, Lord, 85
San Francisco *Leader*, 123–4, 125
Sands, Bobby, 76
Sarsfield, Patrick, 191
Sartre, John Paul, 138
Savage, John, 89
Scotland, 176
Second World War, 68
sectarianism, 44, 118, 119, 145, 155, 189,
    196, 200, 279, 289–90
  Irish language, and, 146–7
  rebellion of 1798, interpretations of,
    189–90, 193
1798 Centennial; *see* centenary
  commemorations for 1798
Sexton, Thomas, 30
Shamrock, 224, 291
Shamrock Library Series, 182
Shan Van Vocht, 34–6, *35*, 42, 71, 80, 106,
    138, 140, 144, 145, 162, 169–84, 196,
    197, 200, 203, 204–5, 206–7, 209,
    216, 217, 257, 260, 279, 281
  adverts, *177*
  advisory board, 34
  bi-lingual anti-sectarian dialogue, 170
  centenary commemorations for 1798,
    and, 182, 194–6, 210–14, 215
  contributors, 173–4, 179, 180, 181,
    182
  cultural events, reporting of, 182
  derivation of name of, 178–9
  dissolution of (1899), 184
  educational aims, 181–2
  founding of, 158, 168, 169
  influence of, 288
  international subscriptions, 176
  language movement, coverage of, 181
  launch (1896), 33–4

  Milligan's writings in, 182–3
  national journal, as, 173
  nationalism of Tone, 183
  Northern Patriot, contrasted with, 169,
    173, 178
  plays published in, 226, 231, *232*
  production of paper, 174–5, 183–4
  women's writings, 178–9
'Shan Van Vocht' (song), 179
Shaw, George Bernard, 26
Sheehy, Mary, 236
Sheehy, Revd Nicholas, 236
Sheehy-Skeffington, Hannah, 152, 236
Shelley Society, 26, 133
Shorter, Clement, 281
Sigerson, Dora, 133
Sigerson, Dr George, 71, 289
Sinn Féin, 58, 62, 113
Sinn Féin (newspaper), 88, 226, 227
Sligo, county, 100
Somme, battle of the, 281
Songs of Old Ireland (Graves), 255
Sons of the Sea Kings (Alice and William
  Milligan), 45
South African Amnesty Association, 176
Spanish Armada, 93
Spenser, Edmund, 26
'Speranza' (poet), 178–9
Spring Rice, Mary, 149, 264
Stephen's Green, Dublin, 200
Stokes, George, 91
Stokes, Margaret, 91
Stopford Green, Alice, 55, 149
Stories of the Celtic nations (Alice
  Milligan), 60
Stormont Government, 67
Sullivan, Sean, 79
Swan, Louise, 154
Synge, 242
Synge, John Millington, 27, 87, 103, 221,
  231, 237–8, 287

tableaux vivants, 18, 19, 36–8, 55, 58–9, 76, 79, 83, 111, 129–30, 137, 145–6, 157, 172, 174, 218, 230, 244–5, 246–51, 286, 294; see also *poses plastiques*
  'Erin fettered; Erin free', 68
  Irish language revival, 260–2, 276–7
  Milligan's conception, 262
  Ossianic trilogy, 246–9, 273
  photographic images, *270, 271, 272, 275*
  political silence, 273
  radical modernism, 269–77
  republican tableaux, 252–64
  script, *263*
  sketches, *248, 253, 266*
  women and nation, 264–9
Tandy, Napper, 78
Taylor, George, 190
Teeling, Bartholomew, 159
Tennyson, Alfred Lord, 30
The Irish Literary Revival: its history, pioneers and possibilities (Ryan), 170
theatre; see drama; Irish National Theatre; plays
Times (London), 202
Todd, James, 240
Tone, Theobald Wolfe, 39, 93, 147, 159, 174, 183, 185, 187, 188, 191, 198, 204, 209, 231, 243, 260, 283
  statue (Dublin), 187–8, 200, 205–6, 218, 276
Tories, 30, 94
Tory Party, 85
tourists, 92–4, 99, 100, 138
Transactions of the Ossianic Society, 240
Translations (Friel), 116
Trinity College Dublin, 91
Twiss, John, 156–7
Tycur, Co. Tyrone, 80
Tynan, Katharine, 132, 133
Tyrone, county, 45, 59, 61, 80, 129, 279–80, 281; see also Omagh

Irish speaking in, 143
Milligan's childhood in, 117–18, 127–8

Ua Laoghaire, Peadar (Peter O'Leary), 157
Uladh, 184
Ulster ('the north'), 39, 68, 128, 289–90; see also Belfast; Northern Ireland
  colonial isolation, 140, 162
  Gaelic League, 40–1
  historical landscapes, 120
  political differences, 43–4, 140–1, 289–90; see also northern nationalists; Ulster Protestants; unionists
Ulster Anti-Partition Council, 69
Ulster Centenary Committee, 202
Ulster Covenant (1912), 44, 53
Ulster Examiner, 124
Ulster Hall, Belfast, 248, 271
Ulster Herald, 43, 54
Ulster Journal of Archaeology, 91
Ulster Literary Theatre, 58, 158, 184, 247, 287
Ulster Literary Theatre Society, 223
Ulster Male Choir, 248
Ulster Museum, 278
Ulster Orchestra, 248
Ulster Plantation, 104
Ulster Presbyterians, 61, 290
Ulster Protestants, 85, 124, 127, 137, 189; see also unionists
  siege mentality, 125–6
  United Irishmen, in, 33, 34, 187, 188
Ulster Union of the Gaelic League, 148
Ulster Volunteers, 282
Ulster Women's Unionist Council, 62
Ultach, 145
Ulysses (Joyce), 98–9
unionists, 26, 29, 39, 42–3, 48, 50, 53, 85, 87, 105, 116, 125, 126, 128, 136–7, 140, 154, 166, 180, 193–4,

198, 216, 281, 289, 290, 292; *see also Northern Whig*
constructive unionism, 123, 130
Covenant (1912), 44
cultural organisations, 288
Irish language, attitudes to, 145, 146
Milligan's renunciation of, 137
'political tourists', 92–4, 100
Unitarian Church School (Belfast), 156
United Ireland (journal), 31, 32, 33, 105, 132, 133, 184, 268, 275
United Irishman, 36, 121, 159, 226, 227, 234, 236, 240, 241, 249, 254–7, 267, 269
United Irishmen, 17, 33, 48, 72, 78, 107, 109, 147, 156, 178, 183, 185, 187, 195, 215, 216, 220, 231, 260
1798 centenary commemorations; *see* centenary commemorations for 1798
ideals of: in Milligan's work, 188–96, 278; political unity, 189; religious unity, 191
Protestants, 33, 34, 187, 188, 191
sectarianism in, 189–90
United Irishmen '98 Centennial Association, 202
United States, 176

Vinycomb, John, 157, 174

War of Independence, 17, 50, 151, 158, 292
Ward, John, 157
Ward, T., 143
Warner, Marina, 213
Wars of the Gaedhill and the Gaill, 240
Watt, Stephen, 223
We sang for Ireland (Milligan, Johnston and MacManus), 80, 127
Webb, Alfred, 86
Weekly Freeman; see Irish Weekly Freeman

'West Britainism', 84
West Cork, 39
Westminister parliament, 150
Wexford, county, 72, 119, 190
rebellion of 1798, 190; commemorations, 69, 71
Wheeler, Edith (nee Milligan), 27, 45, 46, 53, 62
Wheeler, Mr, 214
Whitbread, J.W., 220
Whitman, Walt, 30
Why we should encourage Irish industries (pamphlet, 1893), 154–5
Wilson, Florence, 58
The wind that shakes the Barley (film), 118–19
women, 149–50; *see also* Irish Women's Association
'98 centenary commemorations, and, 206–20
1916 Rising, in, 74
discrimination against, 152
erasing from history, 291, 292
Glimpses of Erin, depicted in, 100–2
in Irish history, 47–8
Irish language movement, 149
national movement, and, 152–3
national theatre movement, role in, 291
nationalism, and, 210–11
prisoners in Kilmainham, 252, 273, 277
rebellion of 1798, role in, 206
tableaux vivants as cultural platform for, 264–9
Women of Ninety-Eight (Concannon), 215
Women's Guild (London), 151
Woolf, Virginia, 151
Wordsworth, William, 30
Workers' Republic, 211
Workingman's Institute (Belfast), 128
Wright, Charles, 91
Wyse Power, Jenny, 291, 293

Yeats, Jack, 277
Yeats, William Butler, 17, 18, 19, 26, 31,
    36, 69, 74, 75, 90, 103, 124, 130,
    131, 133, 134, 168, 188, 206, 218,
    220, 221, 233–4, 239, 240, 242, 243,
    275–6, 281, 287, 291, 293–4
    Autobiographies, 17, 37
    Cathleen Ní Houlihan, 178
    'Easter 1916', 74

national theatre, and, 223, 227, 228
    The wanderings of Oisín, 90
Young, Ella, 56, 59, 234
Young, R.M., 159
Young, Robert, 214
Young Ireland League, 182
Young Ireland movement, 108, 147, 159,
    196
Young Ireland Society, 150, 167–8